John Oliver Killens

John Oliver Killens

A Life of Black Literary Activism

KEITH GILYARD

THE UNIVERSITY OF GEORGIA PRESS
ATHENS AND LONDON

439211890

© 2010 by the University of Georgia Press

Athens, Georgia 30602

www.ugapress.org

Set in Minion Pro by Graphic Composition, Inc., Bogart, Georgia

Printed digitally in the United States of America

Library of Congress Cataloging-in-Publication Data

Gilyard, Keith, 1952–

John Oliver Killens : a life of Black literary activism / Keith Gilyard.

   p. cm.

Includes bibliographical references and index.

ISBN-13: 978-0-8203-3513-1 (alk. paper)

ISBN-10: 0-8203-3513-4 (alk. paper)

1. Killens, John Oliver, 1916–1987.

2. Killens, John Oliver, 1916–1987—Political activity.

3. African American authors—Biography.

4. African Americans—Intellectual life—20th century. I. Title.

PS3561.I37Z66 2010

813'.54—dc22

[B]   2009039080

British Library Cataloging-in-Publication Data available

IN MEMORY OF
LEON FREDERICK JACKSON
(1951–2008)

IN HOPES HE IS FINE AND STILL LOOKING OUT FOR ME

Contents

Acknowledgments

In this context, endings are fun. I thank all who spirited me to this point. The initial impetus came from the late Lorenzo Thomas, an outstanding poet and critic who inspired me for many years. After reading *Liberation Memories*, my book about John Oliver Killens's rhetoric and poetics, Lorenzo exhorted, "You can't stop there. You have to write the biography." And so, after overcoming my initial resistance, I agreed. I hope Lorenzo would have approved the final version.

This book would not have taken shape without tremendous assistance from the truly wonderful Killens family. I feel privileged to have spent numerous hours at 1392 Union Street, to have met and conversed with Grace Killens, Jon Charles Killens, Barbara Killens-Rivera, Louis Reyes Rivera, and other members of the family—from Abiba, Barra, and Kutisa on down—and to have sat in John Oliver Killens's study, pulled up to his desk, fingered his typewriter, and pored over the books in his personal library. Inevitably, I felt project fatigue here and there, but Ms. Grace and Barbara and Louis would just push me forward. Maybe John did, too, there in his study.

Novelist Arthur Flowers, a dedicated cultural son of Killens, provided encouragement from Day One. "Be measured with this," he advised, worried that I would become too compulsive early on and flame out. A voice as insistent as Lorenzo's belonged to Alan Wald, a truly outstanding scholar and perhaps the most perceptive reader of Killens's fiction, who has been exceedingly generous with overall assistance, including providing feedback on the entire manuscript. If he had any information about Killens, he made sure I saw it and went far beyond normal collegiality when he presented me, an avid collector, with a copy of the May 1952 issue of the *California Quarterly*, in which Killens's first published story appeared.

John's younger brother, Richard Leo Killens, graciously received me in his home in Washington, D.C., where his granddaughter, Geri Avery, joined us and was quite instructive. I also had productive phone conversations with Charliemae Peterson, Killens's sister, and her son, David Peterson.

I heartily thank my first research assistant on this project, my daughter, Amina Gilyard. She accompanied me to Macon, Georgia, in the summer of 2002 to jump-start this venture. Sixteen years old at the time, she spent days with me in the library and about town collecting data, researching leads, and conducting interviews. Fortunately, she proved to be better than I am at writing and organizing notes.

I thank all the folks I met in Macon on that crucial trip for their assistance: Lafayette Bonner and Valeria Williams, high school classmates of Killens; Thomas Bonner; Robert Williams; Robert L. Scott Jr.; the Reverend Mark Pierson; Chester Fontenot; and Tina McElroy Ansa. Perhaps most important during those days was Muriel McDowell Jackson, a most inspirational genealogy librarian and archivist at Washington Memorial Library. I conversed with Robert Williams, Tina McElroy Ansa, and Muriel McDowell Jackson on subsequent trips to Macon and am especially grateful for Tina's invitation to participate in Macon's November 2006 Georgia Literary Festival and for the enthusiastic and sustained help offered by Muriel and other library staff.

I similarly thank the staffs of the Moorland-Spingarn Library at Howard University; the Schomburg Center for Research in Black Culture at New York Public Library, most notably Alison Kwame; the Howard Gotlieb Archival Research Center at Mugar Memorial Library at Boston University, particularly Sean Noel; the Rockefeller Archive Center at Rockefeller University in Sleepy Hollow, New York; and the Amistad Research Center at Tulane University in New Orleans, especially Christopher Harter. I also thank Beth M. Howse, special collections librarian at Fisk University in Nashville. Most of the archival work, however, was done at the Manuscript, Archives, and Rare Book Library on the top floor of the Robert Woodruff Library at Emory University in Atlanta. The great Randall Burkett deserves kudos for overseeing, as curator of African American collections, the acquisition of the largest collection of John Oliver Killens papers. Moreover, David Faulds, Susan Potts McDonald, Naomi Nelson, Kathy Shoemaker, and other library staff members were extraordinarily accommodating whenever I showed up, usually unannounced, to work on Collection 957. Lita Hooper, Lawrence Jackson, Regine Jackson, Mark Sanders, Michael Simanga, and Kevin Young were also important in my Atlanta conversations.

For helping me to tease out some of the facts and importance of Killens's career, along with other research matters, I thank Malika Adero, Abdul Alkalimat, Mignon Holland Anderson, Bettina Aptheker, Blake Bailey, Adam Banks, William H. Banks Jr., Phillip Bonosky, Leo Branton Jr., Titus Brown, Dorothy Burnham, Steve Cannon, John Carter, Federico Cheever, Clinton Crawford, Laraine Fergenson, Rene Gadling, Nikki Giovanni, Maryemma Graham, Carole Gregory, Nathan Hare, James Hill, Gerald Horne, Esther Cooper Jackson, Lawrence Jackson (again), Bennett Johnson, Joseph Kaye, Charles King, Woodie King Jr., Norman Loftis, Janet Lyon, Haki Madhubuti, Louise Meriwether, E. Ethelbert Miller, Kathryn Mitchell, Mark Morrisson, Elizabeth Nunez, Jose Pineiro, Sterling Plumpp, Ishmael Reed, Paul Robeson Jr., Sonia Sanchez, Gus Savage, Bill Sayles, Geneva Smitherman, Sterling Stuckey, Askia M. Toure, Halima Toure, Jerry W. Ward Jr., Mary Helen Washington, Haskell Wexler, Sarah Wright, Fred Yette, and Samuel Yette.

Having flexibility with regard to research leaves and teaching arrangements was a vital element in the process of producing this book. For support along those lines, I gladly acknowledge Susan Welch, dean of the College of Liberal Arts at the Pennsylvania State University, along with English Department heads Robert Caserio and Robin Schulze and my colleagues at the Center for Democratic Deliberation, Cheryl Glenn and Michael Hogan. I also thank Susan Griffin and the English Department at the University of Louisville for hosting me as the Thomas R. Watson Visiting Distinguished Professor of Rhetoric and Composition during the fall of 2007. I made considerable revisions to the manuscript during that stint.

For the numerous hours of tedious work they put in, I remain forever grateful to my research assistants in the English Department at Penn State, Kevin A. Browne (who almost earned coauthor credit), Matthew Newcomb, Ersula J. Ore, Sarah Rude, and Stephen Schneider. Considerable thanks also go to Damon Cagnolatti and Mike Riden, who were always willing to assist with technological matters.

James L. W. West III, my department mate and a distinguished biographer, volunteered to read the manuscript; his comments were critical to its final form. Bernard W. Bell offered abundant in-house guidance as well—and a bottle of champagne upon my completion of the book. I am fortunate to have had my version of what we at Penn State call the Bell Experience. And I offer my sincerest gratitude to an anonymous reviewer who generously read two drafts and tried to steer me past the challenges of the genre. The shortcomings, of course, are mine.

I thank Wayne State University Press, which published my earlier book on Killens. I especially acknowledge Kristina Stonehill and the ever-helpful Kathryn Wildfong for taking the time to field inquiries about permissions.

Of course, I thank the superb staff at the University of Georgia Press, particularly editor-in-chief Nancy Grayson, Jon Davies, John Joerschke, John McLeod, and Beth Snead, along with my thoroughly professional copy editor, and Ellen D. Goldlust-Gingrich.

As always, I appreciate the love and support of my family, both near and extended. On this occasion, I think particularly of Ethel Harris, who touched us in the flesh until the age of ninety-nine.

John Oliver Killens

Introduction

Any emerging novelist would be thrilled to receive the critical reception that John Oliver Killens did for *Youngblood* when the book appeared in the spring of 1954. Although a few southern reviewers predictably balked at the damning portrait of white supremacy, and his hometown newspaper, the *Macon Telegraph*, ignored the book, positive and effusive praise prevailed nationally. Taylor Glenn, a transplanted Maconite who wrote for the *Bridgeport (Connecticut) Sunday Post*, announced, "The story of Crossroads and its people, the genteel, the middle class, the peckerwoods, and the Negroes, is the most exciting adventure, the most pulsating excursion, I've had in all the novels I've read this year." No reviewer understood the story's social and political geography more than Glenn, who spent much of his article describing Macon before endorsing Killens's portrayal of their native city: "Whether he calls it Crossroads, or I call it Macon, on one side of whose tracks he was born, I on the other, is unimportant—I can vouch for its veracity, its authenticity." Glenn then concluded, "*Youngblood* is more real than Dreiser's *American Tragedy*, of which I was immediately reminded, more searching of Negro-white relations than Lillian Smith's *Strange Fruit*, far, far more faithful to its setting, more detailed in its delineation, more powerful in its presentation than *Invisible Man*."[1]

Explicitly or implicitly, Ralph Ellison's novel frequently would be a basis of comparison. John Henrik Clarke surely had *Invisible Man* in mind when he labeled Killens's novel a story of "healthy Negroes" and the best black novel to date.[2] In a *New York Times* review, Granville Hicks suggested that both Ellison's "invisible men" conception and Richard Wright's outsider metaphor were legitimate ways to examine the race problem, freeing African American authors from "rigid poses of indignation" and allowing them to be more artistically resourceful. Yet Hicks conceded that protest novels possessed considerable value and believed that "so long as they are as sincere and credible as John Killens' *Youngblood*, we can be grateful for them."[3] Killens understood the compliment paid by Hicks but eschewed the social-protest label, preferring instead to call his book a "Novel of Affirmation" that "asserts the human dignity of all people everywhere."[4] Killens also preferred realism in his quest to dramatize black life, explaining that "romanticism would tend to cover it up, sentimentalize it. Naturalism takes the lid off and lets the light and air in, but realism does the real probing that is required."[5]

Trying to fix *Youngblood*'s place in recent African American fiction, *People's World* reviewer Al Richmond hailed the book as a "literary milestone," declaring, "For the first time the Negro American, who looms as an ever more imposing figure in the political and social conflicts of our time, assumes full stature in a contemporary novel." He further credited Killens with composing a "work of great optimism" that expresses a "deep faith in his people" and breaks with the "pattern set by Richard Wright's *Native Son* and since followed to its sadder extremes by Wright and other Negro American novelists." Richmond would have applauded almost any departure from what he termed the "Wright–Chester Himes trend," but he considered *Youngblood* "a novel of such scope, such vitality, and such genuine artistry" that he exclaimed, "Hallelujah!"[6]

Henry Winslow began his review in *Crisis* by addressing the perception among critics, most notably Irving Howe, that William Faulkner's depictions of southern life, particularly of African Americans, had been rendered with unsurpassed skill. *Youngblood*, asserted Winslow, "should be a revelation to both Faulkner and Howe, for here is a graphic portrait *of* people, not merely *about* them." Although, like many readers, Winslow found the novel prolix, "more film than focus," he concluded, with Faulkner still in mind, "When a born storyteller has a clear understanding balanced between human nature and human society, the net effect makes for new light in August."[7] Ann Petry, already a literary star in her own right, judged the book "a fine novel, vivid, readable."[8]

Propelled by such a strongly favorable critical response, Killens enjoyed one of the most impressive cultural careers of the twentieth century. His friends, colleagues, collaborators, and students included Paul Robeson, Langston Hughes, Alphaeus Hunton, James Baldwin, Lorraine Hansberry, Harry Belafonte, Ossie Davis, Ruby Dee, Martin Luther King Jr., Shirley Graham Du Bois, John Howard Lawson, Robert Ryan, Alvah Bessie, Herbert Biberman, Haskell Wexler, Maya Angelou, Malcolm X, Nikki Giovanni, James Farmer, Burt Lancaster, Jackie Robinson, Haki Madhubuti (Don L. Lee), Bebe Moore Campbell, Terry McMillan, and Tina McElroy Ansa. Killens indeed is a key link in progressive cultural and political developments between the Harlem Renaissance and Old Left activism to the Black Arts movement and a variety of civil rights and New Left strategies. Ironically, though, his run as a writer with mainstream publishers in the adult market lasted barely fifteen years, and he is now relatively unknown and hardly appreciated. One explanation of Killens's cultural fate is that his radical politics ultimately overdetermined his literary efforts and thus compromised his acceptability within an increasingly conservative corporate publishing climate, an assessment that contains some truth. Nonetheless, Killens left behind reams of exemplary prose, testimony that he was a vernacular genius, a master of folktales and humor, comparable to Wright and Zora Neale Hurston. No comprehensive study of the African American novel—indeed, the American novel—can ignore his contribution to the genre.

Taken as whole, Killens's fiction corpus is analogous to the drama of August Wilson. Just as Wilson created a cycle of ten plays, each designed to illustrate one of the decades of the twentieth century, most of Killens's major works are connected to particular eras and sets of concerns in American history. *Great Gittin' Up Morning* explores the antebellum period through the eyes of a fictionalized Denmark Vesey and his partners in an 1822 slave rebellion in South Carolina. The story is geared primarily toward younger readers, but it has gravity comparable to *Black Thunder*, Arna Bontemps's excellent 1936 novel about the Gabriel Prosser insurrection. *Great Black Russian*, Killens's posthumously published novel about Alexander Pushkin, who was a contemporary of Vesey on the world scene, also participates in this project. Although not about American or African American history per se, the novel celebrates achievement by those of African descent. *Slaves*, a novelization, was inspired by Harriet Beecher Stowe's *Uncle Tom's Cabin*. The adolescent novel *A Man Ain't Nothin' but a Man* examines interracial workers' dynamics during the post-Emancipation era. *Youngblood* portrays the struggle on Jim Crow terrain toward black self-determination and workers' solidarity over the first third of the twentieth century. *And Then We Heard the Thunder* is easily the best fictional treatment of the African American military experience during World War II. *'Sippi* dramatically chronicles developments from the onset of the modern civil rights movement to the dawn of the Black Power era. *The Cotillion* depicts cultural politics in the post–Malcolm X yet pre-1970 period. An unpublished manuscript, "The Minister Primarily," satirically comments on the 1970s. But no matter the period covered, Killens's work reflects a quest for freedom. This is its outstanding ideological—and sometimes structural—trait.

This quest for freedom is also the lasting significance of his life. Political and social struggle was the primary source of his art, a fact that sometimes paradoxically pulled him away from practicing his literary craft. In a 1984 interview, he explained why he embraced the roles of both writer and activist: "The writer should involve himself or herself wherever his or her people are struggling so that he or she can understand the meaning of struggle and interpret the struggle in his or her work."[9] To give a cultural voicing to freedom, therefore, Killens had to discipline himself to embrace lengthy stretches of solitude, an endeavor that strained against his activist desires and gregarious personality. Yet the fact that he often emerged from self-imposed exile—to organize, to teach, to negotiate, to interpret, to host—makes him a doubly compelling figure. How well did he pull off the artist-activist juggling act?

In some ways, Killens's career can be characterized as a series of spectacular almosts. Enamored with the silver screen, as many novelists are for reasons of financial compensation and audience size, he tried desperately to become the first African American to author a major Hollywood movie. He was credited as such for the 1959 *Odds against Tomorrow*, but the screenplay actually was created by the blacklisted Abraham Polonsky. Killens's *And Then We Heard the Thunder* was a solid contender to win the Pulitzer Prize for fiction, an honor that had not yet gone to an African American. But rather than forge that sort of history, the committee awarded no prize in fiction in 1964. A decade later, with a few aesthetic concessions on his part, *The Cotillion* would have been adapted for Broadway. However, there was no chance the author would compromise. Success and status, though surely sought after and welcome, were never his bottom line—he twice turned down professorships at Harvard University.

In the final analysis, the near misses or near hits were not solely personal failures but also were social transactions constrained in part by a cultural politics anathema to Killens's sense of freedom. The promise of 1954 was both fulfilled and denied. Killens's fate as a writer and central cultural figure is best understood in the context of the environments from which he sprang and the turbulent times in which he lived and worked and as an aspect of the incredibly full, rich, and somewhat overburdened life he led.

CHAPTER ONE

A White Man's Republic, 1915–1928

Another boy? She sat robustly pregnant, past the eighth month and round enough of belly, carrying high enough to deliver another son, or so the old folks would say. Her oldest son, Charles Jr., born February 4, 1914, paused restlessly at her knee, poised to burst in a matter of days into a new calendar year and then, a few weeks later, into the "Terrible Twos." She hoped the toddler would continue to strive and be okay, Lord willing, though his earthly father did not put much stock in divine grace. For Charles Sr., the key lay in his proper molding of the child. Of course, he would concede, luck was also needed to avoid danger.

The year 1915 dripped away. The Age of Washington had just ended, sealed by the Wizard of Tuskegee's death on November 14. Roads to African American progress no longer would be shaped by favors that Booker T. bestowed or withheld.

The expectant nineteen-year-old, a schoolteacher by trade, was in league with the National Association for the Advancement of Colored People, an outfit more aggressive than Washington ever had been in pursuing civil and political rights for African Americans. The organization was on the verge of exponential growth, with legions of former Washington supporters planning to join. After all, as she and her husband already figured, true dignity, despite whatever patronage mill existed, could not be achieved through accommodation to segregation.

That same year, an outsider presumed to have a superior perspective. Maurice Evans, a South African born in England, published his self-described impartial study of race, *Black and White in the Southern States*, which was based on his 1914 tour through the American Southland. Already a confirmed segregationist, he drew what were for him two new conclusions. One, the physical brutality accompanying Jim Crow indeed was unfortunate. Two, the Negro, however, really was inferior. This latter view would be vigorously contested in the pages of the *Journal of Negro History,* the official publication of Carter G. Woodson's Association for the Study of Negro Life and History, formed the preceding September.[1]

While the dialogue unfolded, D. W. Griffith cast the Ku Klux Klan as heroic. *Birth of a Nation*, a movie Washington had denounced, made its Atlanta debut in December 1915 to wildly cheering white audiences. Virginia native Woodrow Wilson, the first person of southern birth elected president since the Civil War, avidly supported the film: "It is like writing history with lightning. And my only regret is that it is all so terribly true."[2]

Up in New York City, exhibitors at the Hippodrome were preparing a show, *March of the States*, in which characters portrayed as lynching victims represented Georgia.[3] Chagrined Georgians who attended the show could not deny the telling relevance of the display.

Just a bit south of New York, Paul Robeson was flourishing in his freshman year at Rutgers College, overcoming racial obstacles in the classroom and on the football field. In the spring of 1915, Robeson had won a four-year academic scholarship in a highly competitive process. It was a decisive moment in his life. "Equality might be denied," he wrote, "but I *knew* I was not inferior."[4]

Five days after Washington's death, Joe Hill faced the firing squad in Utah. The poet laureate of the Industrial Workers of the World, more popularly known as the Wobblies, had been convicted of murder on specious evidence, a conviction motivated, many felt, by his labor activities. Before his execution, he urged his supporters to organize rather than mourn.[5]

John Oliver Killens entered the world in Macon, Georgia, on January 14, 1916, the son of Charles Myles Killens and Willie Lee Coleman Killens, both of whom had been born in the Macon area in the 1890s. John soon acquired the nickname Little Brother, shortened to simply Brother after the family's third and final son, Richard Leo Killens, arrived on April 1, 1918. John received his middle name in honor of his maternal grandfather, William Oliver Coleman, who grew up in Macon and graduated from Lewis High School in the 1880s. Coleman, a school official, married Carrie Walker, a woman John Killens recalled as having had "great strength and courage" who hailed from Eatonton, Georgia, a small town about fifty miles north-east of Macon.[6] The Coleman-Walker union produced four children—Willie Lee, Louise, Katherine, and William Jr. William Oliver Coleman died in 1912.

The Killens line of the family also had established roots in Macon by the 1880s. John's paternal grandparents, Richard Killens and Mariah Hill, were wed in the city on July 12, 1887. However, Richard Killens had to flee town after an altercation during which he apparently menaced a white adversary with a gun. Under an assumed name, he eventually resettled in Europe. Mariah continued to reside in Macon, and in 1910, she married Anderson Gilbert. Like Carrie Coleman, Mariah Gilbert left a strong and favorable impression on her grandson.

Charles Myles Killens and Willie Lee Coleman met as children and married in Macon on September 18, 1913. The groom, commonly known as Myles, was six days shy of his twentieth birthday. Willie Lee, born March 17, 1896, was seventeen. The newlyweds resided in the Gilbert home at 156 Virgin Street, the base from which they negotiated the pitfalls and opportunities of adult life in the segregated South.

Macon, a railway and waterway hub spread out along the banks of the Ocmulgee River, functioned as a prominent antebellum city in what some historians refer to as the Lower South Industrial Complex.[7] Located in Bibb County, Macon sat virtually at the geographical center both of Georgia and the Confederacy. This location offered the city some protection from Union forces during the Civil War, and its infrastructure remained relatively undamaged. After taking Atlanta, eighty miles away, General William Tecumseh Sherman bypassed Macon on his famous March to the Sea, and the city's postwar economic recovery therefore proceeded rapidly. In the collective white mind, recovery meant returning earnestly to the business, as advocated by *Daily Telegraph* editor Joseph Clisby, of building a "white man's Republic."[8]

Seven thousand African Americans lived in Macon at the close of the war. As nominally free men and women, large numbers of them became the exploited servants, sharecroppers, and mill hands indispensable to white businessmen. As late as the 1920s, some African American workers at the Willingham Cotton Mill were paid only pennies per hour. And much of those wages returned directly to the Willinghams, who had built a series of shanties they rented to their workers. Occupants dubbed this area Willingham Quarters.

The Progressive Era, the first two decades of the twentieth century, a period often associated in the public imagination with momentous moral uplift, political reform, and economic progress, had little positive impact on the lives of African Americans in the South. Scholars have even suggested that the era represented the "nadir of Afro-American history."[9] If so, conditions in Georgia comprised a major reason. No less keen an observer than W. E. B. Du Bois asserted that Georgia was the state that best exemplified the "Negro problem."[10] In 1903, Du Bois noted in *The Souls of Black Folk* that Georgia was the only state whose African American population surpassed one million, and he surmised that the number resulted from the particular zeal with which slaveholders had amassed Africans in service to King Cotton. Indeed, life in Georgia had grown far removed from the "model society" supposedly envisioned by the Trustees for Establishing the Colony of Georgia in America when they requested a charter from the Crown.[11] Located at the same latitude as Jerusalem, as several proponents of colonization pointed out, Georgia was to be a place, according to the trustees, where large landholdings and slavery would be prohibited. But West Dougherty, a locale not far from Macon, ultimately became, in Du Bois's words, "perhaps the richest slave kingdom that the modern world ever knew."[12]

Georgia's Progressive Era quasi-slave economy was buttressed by social and legal mechanisms of white supremacy. For example, the state had no compulsory education law until 1916; only Mississippi waited longer to enact such legislation. Georgia delayed so long primarily because whites strongly desired to withhold formal education from African Americans. In 1919, Georgia became the first state to reject the Nineteenth Amendment, a move inspired not so much by opposition to women's suffrage in general as by the specific effort to keep the right to vote from African American women. Following the eventual ratification of the amendment, Georgia governor-elect Thomas M. Hardwick vowed to uphold the law by promoting the "enfranchisement of all white women in accordance with the Anthony amendment and the disfranchisement of all black women on the same plan that the negro men are now disfranchised in Georgia."[13]

The ultimate mechanism of control was racist violence. Georgia perennially led the nation in officially recorded lynchings, including sixteen in 1916.[14] In 1922, when John Killens turned six, a bout of Saturday evening inebriation turned into a highly publicized display of mob justice. Shortly after six o'clock on a summer evening, John "Cocky" Glover, an African American known in the area as a petty criminal, entered Hatfield's poolroom on Broadway, in the heart of Macon's black business district, and began menacing patrons with a .25-caliber handgun. When police arrived, Glover opened fire. In the ensuing exchange, he killed deputy sheriff Walter Byrd and wounded patrons Sam Brooks and George Marshall, both of whom died several days later. Glover escaped the scene, and police immediately began to shut down businesses in the area, forcing African Americans, including guests at the Douglass Hotel, into the streets. Random arrests were made, several people were beaten, and mail delivery was impeded. Whites spread fear throughout black Macon, conducting house-to-house searches and sometimes shooting at African Americans in the streets. Whites also used the occasion to threaten Macon's most prominent African American, Charles Henry Douglass, who received a police escort and had his home guarded through the night.

Finally cornered early Tuesday morning aboard a northbound train that stopped in Griffin, Georgia, Glover wounded another law enforcement officer before being subdued and turned over to Bibb County police for the trip back to Macon. A mob of four hundred people made sure he never made it alive, seizing Glover from authorities just north of the city, hanging and shooting him, and leaving his body in a ditch across the Monroe County line, near Forsyth. The lynch mob subsequently recovered the corpse and dumped it on Macon's Broadway, where a crowd pummeled the body under a blazing summer sun. Glover's body was then dragged to the lobby of the Douglass Theatre, where members of the mob prepared to incinerate it. After initially being overwhelmed, police officers claimed the body intact and took it to the police barracks at City Hall. Glover eventually was buried in Forsyth.

Glover likely would have been hanged for his crimes after a trial, but the viciousness of the mob disturbed some white citizens, who found the spectacle "sickening" and felt that the military should have been used to reestablish order.[15] For Killens, the Glover incident, sometimes referred to as Macon's Orgy, remained so memorable that two decades later he began his first completed novel manuscript with a version of the event.[16]

The episode proved life changing for another notable African American. Elijah Poole, who had been employed for several years at the Cherokee Brick Company and the Southern Railroad Company, observed Glover's body being dragged through the streets. The experience was the proverbial final straw for Poole in the South. Later to become prominent as Elijah Muhammad, he took his wife, toddler son, and infant daughter to Detroit in the spring of 1923. He said he had seen enough white brutality in Georgia to last him twenty-six thousand years.[17] Poole's flight was typical.

Tens of thousands of African Americans fled Georgia's racist violence and economic hardship, including fifty thousand in 1916 alone.[18] By the waning hours of the Progressive Era, African Americans who remained in the South found the color line (to use Du Bois's term) transformed into the "color wall, thick, high, almost impenetrable."[19]

Despite such barriers, blacks registered some political, economic, educational, and cultural advances. The establishment in the 1870s of Pleasant Hill, one of the nation's oldest African American townships, resulted from such vision and energy. Situated on approximately 430 acres adjacent to the Macon corporation line, Pleasant Hill became home to many of the servants who worked in the colonial mansions along nearby College Avenue. These servants usually lived in simple "shotgun houses" or "wood-framed vernacular structures" owned by white landlords.[20] But by the early twentieth century, Pleasant Hill had also become a "thriving neighborhood of small businesses, doctors, dentists, educators, mail carriers, grocers, draymen, and many other self-employed citizens."[21] Most of these black professionals constructed and owned more substantial homes, including two-story Victorian cottages that constituted more modest versions of the homes on College Avenue. Educator, historian, and Pleasant Hill resident Robert Williams, whose family connection to the neighborhood dated back to 1879, explained, "In the late 1800s and early 1900s, it was where blacks tried to be property owners and voters. People there attempted to take part in city life as much as they could in those days."[22]

Williams's account of civic participation was not entirely accurate. Pleasant Hill did not join Macon until the early 1900s, and some community residents opposed the move. The advantages of annexation included city services and lower insurance rates. However, the residents of Pleasant Hill would be subjected to Macon city taxes. The debate swung decidedly in favor of annexation after a late-night fire originated in William Nixon's Pleasant Hill home on July 13, 1903. Nixon's house and four others were destroyed as a nervous crowd of two thousand took to the streets, some dragging their household goods with them. Others soaked their carpets and blankets with water to minimize the chance that they would be ignited. As the fire raged, residents muttered that four of the houses could have been saved had Pleasant Hill been a part of the city: a city fire company equipped with engine and hose stood at the corporation line, watching the destruction but unable to intervene legally beyond the city of Macon without explicit orders. Pleasant Hill residents agreed to annexation shortly thereafter.

Williams's statement about early African American civic activity in Pleasant Hill nonetheless contains more than a sliver of truth. In 1870, Jefferson Franklin Long, the neighborhood's most prominent resident, became the first African American from Georgia to win election to the U.S. Congress. Long, who was born a slave in 1836 and who was a tailor by trade, was the first African American to address Congress as a speaker and maintained a business in Pleasant Hill until his death in 1901. Into this community, now on the National Register of Historic Places, John Oliver Killens was born.

His parents exemplified Pleasant Hill's spirit and industry. Willie Lee Coleman Killens, who graduated from high school in 1911 at the age of fifteen, taught for several years at the East Macon School before beginning a career at the local office of the Atlanta Life Insurance Company, a business founded in 1905 by Alonzo Franklin Herndon. By 1915, Atlanta Life was one of the nation's four leading black insurance companies, along with Standard Life, North Carolina Mutual, and National Benefit Life.

Myles Killens lacked a high school diploma but was nonetheless bright, read voraciously, and possessed good management skills. He worked as a key assistant and bookkeeper for Charles Henry Douglass, regarded as Macon's wealthiest African American. Born in 1870, Douglass had started as an enterprising child, selling wood and vegetables, chopping cotton, and renting and repairing bicycles. He later worked as the director of the Georgia Loan and Savings Company and organized the Florida Blossom Minstrels and Comedy Company, which made him familiar with the minstrel circuit and the network of theaters in which African Americans habitually performed. In 1911, he founded the Douglass Theatre, which became Macon's premier entertainment facility open to African Americans and which has subsequently hosted such legends as Bessie Smith, Ma Rainey, Cab Calloway, and Duke Ellington. Douglass extended his holdings to include a hotel, grill, and poolroom. In short, in the words of longtime Maconite Thomas Bonner, "He owned everything."[23] Indeed, Douglass possessed about thirty pieces of property in and around Macon. As early as 1915, he reported an annual income of approximately $40,000, a sum equivalent to nearly $850,000 in current dollars.[24]

John Oliver Killens's memories of his early days thus cohered around his knowledge of and experience with black fear caused by white oppression as well as incidents of African American valor, achievement, and community spirit in the face of such hardship. One night when Killens was about ten years old, he was walking near his home when two white men pulled along-

side him in a car and inquired about the sexual services of a "colored gal."
Killens yelled, "Go get your dear old mother like you been doing!" before
retreating hastily, in tears. He later wished he had been older and more aggressive in response, but he also knew that being a child had afforded him
some protection. Although Killens possessed fond as well as painful memories of his childhood, he was never sanguine about the prospects of living
in Macon, referring to it as the place where he "had lived as a boy but could
never grow up to be a man."[25]

A subsequent preadolescent incident left an even greater psychic scar.
On the way to and from classes at the segregated Pleasant Hill School, a dilapidated structure without running water and sufficient heat, Killens and
several of his schoolmates passed the mansions of wealthy whites, often
crossing paths with white children going to and from their own school,
which had much better facilities. One day, a white student asked a friend
of Killens, "Hey nigger, what you learn in school today?" The boy replied,
"I learned your mother was a whore." As the black boys laughed, the white
boy became enraged and struck Killens's friend in the face, touching off a
melee during which punches were thrown, rocks hurled, and sticks wielded.
No one was seriously injured, the battle ended indecisively, and Killens and
his schoolmates continued home, proud of their scrapes, bruises, and hard-
won dignity.[26]

The next morning, a squadron of police officers converged on Pleasant
Hill School and dragged several African American children from the building. Not all of them had participated in the fight, and some who had been
involved, including Killens, were overlooked. The children were taken to
the courthouse, and their mothers were summoned and afforded a choice:
they could beat their sons in front of the authorities, or they could watch
their sons, none of whom was older than age twelve, be carted off to the reformatory. All of the mothers whipped their sons. Killens later described
the incident as epitomizing Jim Crow's goal of "grind[ing] down black men
bit by bit and turn[ing] them into eunuchs."[27] The cruelest aspect, he believed, was the manipulation of African American mothers.

While African American life in Macon was undeniably defined to a large
degree by racist whites, African Americans were not restricted solely to re-
active postures. Blacks formed churches, societies, associations, and clubs
that promoted a sense of worldly and spiritual health and a sense of cultural
continuity. Killens saw a variety of black workers who, away from white
control, assumed dignified positions as deacons, elders, and club presidents.

He did not see life as totally bleak or overdetermined by oppression, and he remembered much happiness in a childhood spent amid pine trees, honeysuckle, and magnolia. He had a sense of belonging to a community that believed in African American potential and was dedicated to the wholesome development of its children: "Everybody cared, everybody believed in you and your capacity as a human being, and you belonged to everybody, so everybody was determined that you do your very best."[28]

All things considered, an aspiring African American writer in Macon could hardly have hoped for a better start, as the Killens family was one of educators, storytellers, lovers of the written word, and social commentators. The Killens clan exemplified family affection, strength, accomplishment, political vision, and debate. Although Willie Lee Killens taught school only briefly, her sister, Louise Coleman Ketch, pursued a long career in education. In addition, Willie Lee Killens served as the president of the Paul Laurence Dunbar Literary Club at Steward Chapel African Methodist Episcopal Church, a group that met regularly to discuss works by African American authors.[29] John Killens immensely enjoyed Dunbar's poems, such as "The Party" and "An Ante-Bellum Sermon." Dunbar's "When Malindy Sings" reminded Killens of his mother, who was an accomplished soprano often requested at funerals and other ceremonies.[30] Robert Williams sometimes sat with his aunt, Fannie Mae Lockhart Jenkins, who served as the organist at Steward Chapel, while she played, and he remembered "Miss Willie" singing brilliantly in the choir.[31]

The entire Coleman family was involved with Steward Chapel, one of Macon's most important African American churches. Founded in 1865, it was the city's first church built by and for African Americans. It may also be the first and only church in the city that African Americans burned to the ground: opposing factions clashed in the church, and a suspicious 1869 fire destroyed the original building. The congregation continued to meet at the old Temperance Hall at New and Pine Streets and at City Hall before establishing a headquarters in a local armory and ultimately building a new permanent home on Forsyth Street, where the church still resides.

Steward Chapel traditionally has stood at the forefront of the struggle for social equality in Macon. The church prides itself on having been involved in contentious issues while other organizations yielded to pressure and remained on the sidelines. It was often the site of education conventions and labor meetings, some of which Killens remembered. In the 1950s, Steward Chapel hosted speakers such as Benjamin E. Mays, Mary McLeod

Bethune, and Martin Luther King Jr., who delivered his only major address in Macon, "There Is No East and No West," there on September 19, 1957, before more than six hundred people despite heavy rain.[32]

John Killens enjoyed the camaraderie and certainly the rhetorical performances at church gatherings, though he grew somewhat skeptical of religious doctrine. To the extent that he valued it, it represented a story of African American progress and freedom. In his fiction, he portrayed the church as a site of resistance, but he also decried what he saw as perverse uses of the Gospel, particularly as it became entwined with African American submissiveness. He lamented the "whitewashing" that caused some members of his community to stay within their socially prescribed roles and accept menial jobs and segregation: "We believed that rich white folks were good white folks, and poor white trash were bad white folks, which strangely enough contradicted Our Lord and Savior, Jesus Christ."[33]

John's father encouraged and even prompted his son's skepticism. Although Myles and Willie Lee separated, somewhat amicably, when John was seven years old, Myles retained a strong and vital hand in his son's upbringing. Physically, John was brown-skinned and handsome and bore a strong facial resemblance to his fair-skinned mother. But he was his father's child, eager to please, and he consequently became one of Myles's favorite educational experiments. The elder Killens consciously tried to inculcate in his son unshakable racial pride, a keen understanding of the politics of Jim Crow, a relentless love of learning, and an abiding passion for justice. The boy's nascent personality traits—sensitivity, gregariousness despite being soft-spoken, and competitiveness—apparently merged with Myles's social engineering and John's youthful visions of grandeur to motivate him to enter the racial public sphere with exceptional zest. He was growing into a quiet though tenacious welterweight with a heavyweight ego and commendable work ethic, ingredients that would enable him to become a champion of some sort.

Myles Killens became a fan of Langston Hughes because of the poet's irreverence and willingness to question authority, including that of religion. Killens called his son's attention to Hughes's work and instructed the boy to appreciate the writer's boldness. As he did for many others, Hughes became John Killens's first real-life literary hero.[34] And Myles, too, remained a hero as well as a model of intellectual curiosity and persistence for his son. Decades later, he graduated from a Chicago high school as the valedictorian of his class, matching the achievement of his oldest son, Charles.

Other strong influences on John's developing imagination included Mark Frazier, a cousin on his mother's side, and John's maternal uncle, William Oliver "Son" Coleman Jr., whom Killens admiringly termed "excellent and outrageous liars."[35] Born in 1903, Son Coleman, an especially memorable figure around Pleasant Hill, was slightly built and extremely light-skinned and bore a remarkable resemblance to his mother, Carrie Coleman. An elevator operator and an electrician, he spent hours patrolling the neighborhood and telling stories. All of Pleasant Hill's children loved Son Coleman.[36]

Killens also held fond memories of several of his paternal relatives with whom he and his brother, Richard, spent a summer in Glenwood, Georgia. His father's cousin, known simply as Cousin Nancy, was married to Cousin Joe, who worked the turpentine mills. Although his relatives lived in a two-room cabin with paneless windows along with walls covered with newspaper and pages from store catalogs, Killens described them as "Black and beautiful and unbelievably generous people." In addition, he remembered "Big Meeting," an annual August revival that drew folks from all over central Georgia. They arrived in wagons, on horseback, in dilapidated trucks and cars, on foot—"a great big Black and beautiful git-together."[37]

But no cultural or literary role model surpassed John Killens's paternal great-grandmother, Georgia Killens, born in 1856, and she ranked highly in emotional importance as well. Neither the favored firstborn nor the baby of the family, John reveled in the attention he received as Granny's favorite. Or perhaps he chose her first while they sat near the fireplace, she mellifluously spinning tales, he listening intently, consummate storyteller and ideal audience.[38]

Granny constantly fired his youthful imagination with tales of antebellum and Reconstruction life that expressed truths from a black perspective. For him, she was the first to put the lie to myths about the docility of slaves or the indolence of black freemen, characteristically remarking, "Aaah Lord, Honey, the half ain't never been told!"[39] Decades later, a portion of this phrase became the title of a lengthy autobiographical essay by her great-grandson. During Killens's preschool years, Granny, a rangy, dark-complexioned woman, often took her great-grandson on long evening walks outside their Virgin Street home. At times, they would get lost, and a search party would be sent after them. Killens did not mind, however; he was a sucker for Granny's stories as well as an admirer of her nobility, pride, and sense of justice. He incorporated his favorite Granny story into his first novel, *Youngblood*.[40]

When she was a child on an antebellum plantation, an overseer spied on the slaves at night by hiding beneath the cabin where they gathered to sing and to plot. Granny framed this aspect of the story by singing the spiritual "Steal Away to Jesus" and explaining that Jesus was both sacred and secular and was found not only in heaven but also north of the Mason-Dixon Line. The slaves too had spies and knew not only about the interloping overseer but also about his favored spot under the cabin. One night, the gathered slaves turned over a wash pot of boiling water where they knew the overseer was lying just as they sang "Pharaoh's army got drownded." According to Granny, "When that water hit that cracker through those planks in the floor, he let out such a whoop and holler and came out from under there and took off across the field like eighty going North. We laughed until we cried." That overseer caused no further trouble. Granny then sucked her teeth, contemptuous of the notion that all slaves were brainwashed and passive, commenting, "Humph! Talking about 'All the darkies am a-weeping.' We wept all right, honey bunch. We wept for joy and shouted halleluyah when Ol' Masser got the cold cold ground that was coming to him."[41]

Georgia Killens died in 1922, when John was six. The boy already felt obliged and challenged to emulate her work as a storyteller. By the age of ten, he was emerging as an excellent student and insatiable reader. Somewhat bashful, he spent hours absorbed in the Rover Boys, Tom Swift, and stories by Horatio Alger Jr. and O. Henry. John took his books to bed, sometimes with a flashlight, squeezing in late-night reading beyond the vigilance of his mother. At least one other precocious child in Macon did the same. A little girl originally from Brooklyn, New York, who was a year younger than Killens, attended Hazel Street School. Like John, Lena Horne was being escorted on walks through African American communities and downtown along Broadway and Cherry Street.

Despite his early attraction to storytelling and books, John Killens did not follow a straight line from such interest to the active pursuit of story writing. He had no real conception and no practical model of what the writing life involved. Not surprisingly, his first focused thoughts about a career centered on the medical profession. Becoming a doctor had all the proper requirements to stroke the ego of an ambitious and motivated Pleasant Hill child: he could serve his people while achieving middle-class and even elite status for himself. One night, however, while chopping wood, he cut his left big toe to the bone, and he decided that if such bloody cases were part of a doctor's routine, he would pass.[42]

At Pleasant Hill School, his love of language deepened, especially under the tutelage of his most influential teacher there, Lillie Hill Taylor, a classic example of the dedicated African American teacher who despite her su-perficial malevolence really cared enormously about her students and had no doubt that they could succeed. Taylor had taught young John's mother, father, and older brother and was a legend in the Killens household. John sought to avoid her and enroll in another seventh-grade class, but after his efforts failed and he appeared in her classroom on the first day of school, Taylor challenged him and advised, "There won't be any trouble between us unless you start it. But I tell you in front, I intend to get it from you, if you got it." She apparently extracted plenty and instilled much. Killens eventu-ally listed Taylor, along with his parents and great-grandmother, as one of the four people most responsible for his early literary achievements.[43]

For eighth grade, Killens transferred to Ballard Normal School, a private institution in Pleasant Hill that offered African American students' only opportunity to receive an accredited high school education in Macon. His older brother, Charles, was already a Ballard student, slated to enter the tenth grade. Members of the Killens family and the broader community dreamed that John would travel a road straight through Ballard to a college degree, respect, and prosperity.

CHAPTER TWO

Avoiding the River, 1928–1936

Ballard Normal School ranked as one of the most important educational institutions in Georgia for African Americans.[1] An outgrowth of the Lincoln Schools founded in Macon by the Western Freedmen's Aid Commission and the Freedmen's Bureau in 1865, Ballard served as the educational springboard for generations of African American students and became the principal source of trained African American teachers for central Georgia. The accomplishments of its alumni, beginning with early graduates such as Lucy Craft Laney and William Scarborough, were probably unmatched by those of graduates of any African American high school in the South. Laney, a member of Atlanta University's first graduating class in 1873, went on to become active in the women's club movement and the National Association for the Advancement of Colored People (NAACP). A brilliant and pioneering educator, she founded and presided over Augusta's highly regarded Hainey Institute, a school Chester Himes attended. Scarborough also received a degree from Atlanta University and became a distinguished educator, an author, president of the Afro-American League, and the first African American member of the Modern Language Association. He eventually assumed the presidency of Wilberforce University.

Ballard's stellar record was grounded in the unusual nature of the school's development and the valiant struggle to keep it functioning. African Americans in Macon, like those in many

southern communities following the Civil War, evinced tremendous enthusiasm about the chance to develop schools. Never has there been, in fact,
greater sacrifice on behalf of educational efforts in the history of the United
States than that demonstrated by African Americans in the South.[2] They
would not—nor could they logically—wait on state government to take the
lead. Mandated state support for secondary education did not exist in Georgia until the second decade of the twentieth century. Even then, state support at any educational level fit the mold of separate and unequal. Therefore, African Americans undertook whatever initiatives were possible, and
education enthusiasts in Macon received a particular break. Soon after their
establishment, control of the Lincoln Schools shifted to the American Missionary Association (AMA). Based in New York, the organization had been
incorporated in 1846, partly in protest against other missionary societies
that failed to agitate strongly enough for black political rights. Growing out
of a committee that had been active in the *Amistad* case, the AMA pursued
with great fervor the objective of educating the newly emancipated population. Over the next few decades, it founded more than five hundred schools
attended mostly by African Americans. Universities that trace their roots to
AMA activity include Howard, Hampton, Dillard, Fisk, and Atlanta.

For much of Ballard's operation, its students had the unusual advantage
of a highly trained, racially mixed faculty even while living in Jim Crow
Macon. Social equality was not merely an ideal for a progressive civics class
but was exemplified by Ballard's teachers. Although the school taught industrial arts, which helped it to attract adequate funding, the curriculum
also stressed teacher training and college preparation. Ballard officials refused to align themselves strongly with the educational philosophies of
Booker T. Washington and Samuel Armstrong or the practices at Tuskegee
and Hampton, where industrial education prevailed.

The AMA's involvement generated controversy. Despite the organization's
radical doctrine of brotherhood, the arrangement was somewhat paternalistic, and although the AMA pushed for African American empowerment
and claimed to be nonsectarian, it became clear, as the organization ambi-
tiously built chapels wherever it went, that one of the group's major mo-
tives was gaining converts to the Congregational Church. But the message
from the African American community, which consisted largely of Bap-
tists, Methodists, and Presbyterians, remained unequivocal. In exchange
for their children's tuition, they wanted academic excellence, not Congre-
gationalism.

In addition to the religious divide, which in most instances was handled without rancor, Ballard faced other early threats to success. White locals vehemently opposed both an integrated faculty and a liberal arts curriculum for African Americans, leading to several incidents of what was probably arson. Although the danger the local white community posed to white Ballard teachers, who were from New England and several western states, diminished, most white Maconites always considered those teachers pariahs.

Other problems ranged from ongoing financial struggles, which were related to the general poverty of local African Americans, to eventual competition from other educational initiatives and even to burglary and disease. A smallpox outbreak in Macon killed approximately five hundred African Americans shortly after the war. Despite these setbacks, Lewis High (the school's original name, chosen in honor of General John R. Lewis, who directed the Georgia operations of the Freedmen's Bureau) opened in March 1868.

Surviving along with the AMA's initiative was William Oliver Coleman, who graduated from the school in the mid-1880s. In 1888, the institution, with Lewis's blessing, was renamed Ballard Normal School after receiving grants from New York philanthropist John Ballard and members of his family. Two of Coleman's daughters, Willie Lee and Louise, graduated from Ballard. Willie Lee entered in 1906 and graduated third in 1911. Two years later, Louise finished second in her class.

In 1926, after having given birth to three boys, Willie Lee Coleman Killens participated when Ballard hosted the annual meeting of the Georgia Conference of Accredited High Schools and Colleges. A modern facility had been built on Forest Avenue, equipped with a contemporary science laboratory, auditorium, and library, and Ballard was increasingly recognized as one of Georgia's premier schools for African Americans. The library was particularly important because access to an adequate library had become a necessity for students who harbored ambitions to attend college, and city regulations barred African Americans from using the public library. Assuming that family finances remained even remotely decent (no sure thing given that the Great Depression was in the offing), Willie Lee Killens intended that her sons would attend Ballard. Tuition and fees would just have to be found. John Killens enrolled in August 1928, following his older brother, who had enrolled in 1926.

Charles Killens set the bar high. In 1931, he graduated as valedictorian of his class, with the highest recorded average in school annals.[3] He served as president of the senior class and of the Hi-Y Club, an arm of the YMCA through which all male students performed community service projects. (Girls participated in the Tri-Y.) Charles Killens later described Ballard as representing the "greatest thing that ever happened for Blacks who were fortunate enough to come under its influence."[4]

Many Ballard graduates from the 1920s and 1930s had similarly fond memories of their experiences. Dorothy Cooper Bonner, who graduated along with John Killens in 1933, remembered that teachers and the principal visited students' homes on Saturdays and that Ballard helped her to gain an appreciation for the cultural dimensions of life. Morgan Brown, another Killens classmate, felt that the curriculum, with its inclusion of courses in Latin, English literature, ancient history, and chemistry, compared favorably with those of such prep schools as Andover, Phillips Exeter, and Groton and performed a parallel function. John Killens noted the "sense of history as an Afro-American" that Ballard provided.[5] The students sang "Lift Ev'ry Voice and Sing," also known as the Negro national anthem, in the auditorium, learned about Frederick Douglass and Harriet Tubman in history class, and celebrated Negro History Week. An African American performer visited the school every year to deliver dramatic readings from the works of writers such as Paul Laurence Dunbar and Langston Hughes. John Killens was not quite as studious as his brother, but he performed very well. Classmate Lafayette Bonner remembered him as "a brilliant fellow."[6]

At Ballard, Martha Logan, who taught grammar and English composition, further encouraged Killens's formal explorations in language. Logan had compared notes with Lillie Taylor, Killens's earlier teacher, and facilitated his development as much as she could. On several occasions, she left him in charge of English hour. He began writing a novel but stopped after about thirty pages. A few months later, he began a second project, only to give up in "profound frustration" after about forty pages.[7] He apparently did not realize that such efforts were noteworthy for a thirteen-year-old. In the ninth grade, he received an unintended morale boost. His teacher, Helen Beeman, who had come down to Macon from St. Albans, Vermont, assigned a paper on description. Killens labored for two days to get the words just right, wanting to impress the woman, on whom he had a crush. Beeman read his paper aloud to the class, and he sat listening proudly until she announced that his paper constituted exactly what she did not want: she did not want students to copy from a book. Killens failed to convince her that he had done otherwise, but he apparently faced no punishment for the matter. The romance was over, however, and the aspiring writer was hurt. More important, the incident represented an acknowledgment of his promise: he reasoned that his work must have been good.

Despite the positive spin he placed on Beeman's feedback, Killens made no further ambitious attempts at fiction while at Ballard. In fact, a close friend and schoolmate, Pierce "Pebbie" Brunson, became the more successful young writer. Both boys wrote brief items for the school newspaper, the *Ballardite*. Killens's last article, "The Armistice," appeared in the November 1933 issue, several months after his graduation. He wrote youthfully and optimistically, "On November 11th, we celebrate the great birthday of a new world with peace. As we celebrate this great significant day let us think of those who made the supreme sacrifice and try to preserve forever World Wide Peace."[8] Brunson, however, went on to compose a series of sports articles for the *Macon Telegraph*, a practice he continued while in college and in the years beyond.

Ballard operated under the leadership of Raymond Goodwin von Tobel. A native of Connecticut and a graduate of Brown University, the principal stayed in regular contact with fellow New Englander W. E. B. Du Bois, who was on the faculty of Atlanta University. Von Tobel exemplified the sort of person that Du Bois had in mind when he described the AMA's involvement in schools in the South as "a gift of New England to the freed Negro: not alms, but a friend; not cash, but character."[9]

Von Tobel began teaching at Ballard in 1908, serving as an instructor for several subjects, including math and history. One of his first students was Willie Lee Coleman. Although relatively inexperienced, the twenty-seven-year-old teacher was appointed principal in 1911. After two years, the AMA transferred him to North Dakota to run a mission school for Sioux Indians. In 1914, he returned to Ballard, remaining the school's principal until he died in 1935 at the age of fifty-one as the result of injuries suffered in an automobile accident. Von Tobel was largely responsible for shaping Ballard into an exemplary modern school "through the 'boom' of the 1920s and the 'bust' of the Depression and early 1930s."[10] A skillful diplomat, he kept peace with both Macon's black and white communities.

Despite von Tobel's obvious importance and his occasional presence in the Killens home, the faculty member at Ballard who exerted the most influence on John was assistant principal Lewis Hendrix Mounts, a white man who continually impressed on Killens the need for social service. Killens already felt this way, at least to some degree, because of his father's influence, but Mounts felt that the idea could never be emphasized enough, intoning, "Whatever you become in life, your profession should always be available to be in the service of your people." Killens later recalled, "How many times did I hear that saintly, truly Christian white man repeat those words? Doctor, lawyer, teacher, businessman 'in the service of your people.'"[11]

Mounts, who joined the Ballard faculty in 1914, hailed from Iowa and had earned baccalaureate, master's, and doctoral degrees in sociology and economics at the University of Iowa. He also had been ordained a Congregational minister and headed the First Congregational Church of Macon. At Ballard he taught sociology, economics, history, Latin, and religion in addition to organizing and advising the Hi-Y Club. Killens attended many of the club's weekly meetings at Mounts's cottage, which was across the road from the Ballard campus and the site of premeeting comradeship. He and some of his classmates also went on hikes with Mounts, a nature lover. In addition, Killens performed community service in Macon under Mounts's supervision and accompanied Mounts and other members of the club to Hi-Y conventions elsewhere in Georgia, usually riding in the teacher's Model T Ford. Mounts enabled Ballard students to attain prominent positions in the state council.

Mounts achieved legendary status in Pleasant Hill, where a housing development bears his name. According to Lafayette Bonner, Mounts was "strictly for the Negro."[12] In Killens's words, "Professor Mounts was so closely identified with the Black community that when he was seen downtown conversing with whites, on the rare occasions someone would speak with him, at least one Black person reacted, 'Humph! Mr. Mounts standing there talking to them white folks like he think he's white, or something. He must be letting down the race.'"[13] Valeria Williams, a classmate of Killens, declared that Mounts "made you think you could do anything."[14] Charles Killens termed Mounts "a most unforgettable human being . . . a minor deity."[15]

John Killens was clearly in the mood for Mounts's progressive rhetoric. The spirit of service, along with concrete perceptions of the economic and political climate, led Killens to the goal of becoming a labor attorney. During his years at Ballard, the nation plunged into the Great Depression. More than one thousand banks collapsed, waves of other businesses failed, and unprecedented levels of unemployment resulted. The economic disaster drastically affected Ballard. After a countywide crop failure in

1929, the Fourth National Bank, a local institution important to African Americans, collapsed, and enrollment at the school consequently declined from between 350 and 400 to 215. The AMA reduced teachers' salaries by 10 percent and considered closing the school, a dramatic step the organization took with several other educational institutions. However, members of Macon's African American community stepped up their support. The Reverend M. A. Fountain, pastor of Steward Chapel, spearheaded a crucial fund-raising drive. Ballard also made its first ever appeal to the general public for funds using the somewhat disingenuous argument that despite the white community's unease with the AMA's social liberalism, the school was socializing black students in accordance with the prevailing values of the white South. On February 7, 1933, during Killens's senior year at Ballard, von Tobel told the *Macon Telegraph*, "Whatever question there may have been in the mind of anyone about the desirability of a white faculty has been answered by the excellent work that faculty has done in helping to adjust the Negro students to the white viewpoint."[16]

The depression era saw an intensification of union activity both in Georgia and nationwide, as those workers fortunate enough to be employed were subjected to declining wages and horrendous job conditions. Macon's local labor movement also received a boost from the U.S. Congress's 1932 passage of a measure, sponsored by Nebraska senator George Norris and representative and future New York City mayor Fiorello LaGuardia, that banned antiunion contracts and curtailed judicial power to ban strikes and picketing.

Steward Chapel hosted several organizing meetings involving Macon's African American community, and amid these developments, John Killens continued to drift leftward, partly influenced by Mounts's theories regarding sociology and economics, though Killens's main political vision remained that of the classic "race man" variety. Labor law would not only enable him to serve his community but also provide him with fame and material comfort: "Marry a pretty bourgeois girl, raise some handsome bourgeois children, live a fairly comfortable middle-class life and render a service to my people."[17] Maybe, at long last, he would even squeeze in the writing of a novel.

But that would be in the relatively distant future. Although he was rather thin and never surpassed five feet, nine inches in height, Killens possessed above-average athletic ability and exuberantly pursued sports: playground football, volleyball, track and field, baseball, and basketball. During one baseball game, he was drilled in the head by a throw as he was sliding into second base. He had more luck with basketball, his accurate shot the strength of his game.

The adolescent Killens also began to overcome his boyhood shyness. Girls took to him, but for a long time he remained too awkward to do much about it. One girl dropped a note on his desk at the start of the ninth grade, informing him, "You have wonderful eyes but you're hard to win." His aloofness was sometimes mistaken for arrogance. However, by the eleventh grade, his tongue became "a teensy bit untied, and lubricated."[18] As his interest in girls rose, his grades dipped slightly, though he maintained an excellent record overall.

While Killens's social prospects improved, his parents' marriage disintegrated. Despite his fervent wish that his parents reconcile, they divorced, and in 1930, Myles Killens married Emma Mae Savage. In 1934, the union produced a daughter, Charliemae Killens, whom John described as adorable.[19]

Despite the breakup of his marriage to Willie Lee, Myles continued to exert strong influence on John. During the summer of 1932, when the boy was sixteen, Myles enlisted his aid at the Douglass Hotel Grill, located at 363 Broadway in downtown Macon. Late one night, two white men entered the establishment and demanded to be served. One of the men, who was drunk, became verbally abusive. The elder Killens refused to cave in and calmly but firmly directed the men around the corner to Cherry Street, which was the main stretch for white-owned businesses. According to John Killens, the man protested, "I don't want to go around on no Cherry Street. I want my ham and eggs right here. And I want them in a hurry." When his friend tried to pull him away, he further blustered, "Hell naw! This nigger tryna get smart with me. . . . We gon settle this right now!" When Myles asked him not to use such language in his place of business, the man responded, "Your place of business? Your place of business? A nigger ain't got no place of business." The friend told Myles, "Don't pay him no mind, boy. He just had too much to drink," but Myles pulled a pistol from underneath the counter and retorted, "You'd better tell your buddy he'd better not get so drunk that he can't smell my whiskey." The drunken man then seemed to sober up and went out the door "mumbling threats and curses."[20] Proud of his father and the example he set, John Killens nonetheless understood well the danger. Regardless of the circumstances that led a black man in Macon to lose control, it was relatively easy to end up like Cocky Glover. Killens again pondered the price of African American manhood in the South and how long he could forestall having to make a major payment.

At around the same time, he worked as a bellhop at the Dempsey Hotel, where he would spend more time in close contact with white men and, more significantly, white women. While he always exercised caution in his general dealings with white men, maintaining a sense of where to draw the borders of defiance, virtually no room existed for a misstep involving white womanhood. Killens recalled that a typical scenario involved him being summoned to a room where a white woman might be scantily clad or even unclad, usually paying him no mind. Although he would try to ignore her as much as he could, her male companion might well ask the boy what he was staring at. Killens knew that the answer "Nothing" would be considered an insult. Moreover, the man might assert that Killens was indeed eye-balling the woman and then bait him further by asking if he were calling the man a liar. Killens would then be trapped: saying "No" would be an admission that he had been paying attention to the woman; responding "Yes" would be an act of unacceptable insolence. The only way out was to muster as much deference as possible and hope a little semantic soft-shoe would do the trick: "No, sir. You are mistaken, sir." Killens later wrote, "There were two or three incidents like that per week, with variations, but somehow you got through the summer with your manhood and your sanity intact."[21]

The potential for disaster that Killens perceived was real. Just a year earlier in the adjacent state of Alabama, as he was fully aware, nine African American youths, one of them only thirteen years old, were falsely accused of raping two white women. All of the defendants were convicted, and eight were sentenced to death. Although the Scottsboro Case generated widespread and spirited protest along with a heroic legal campaign by the International Labor Defense that ultimately reversed several of the convictions and rescinded the death penalty for the rest of the men, all of the Scottsboro Nine served at least six years in prison, and some remained incarcerated for as long as nineteen years. On May 9, 1933, near the end of John Killens's senior year in high school, the *Macon Telegraph* covered a march in Washington that was intended to gain President Franklin D. Roosevelt's intervention in the case. The paper branded Scottsboro supporter James Ford a "Negro Communist," a charge thoroughly in keeping with its general policy of running negative stories about African Americans and the labor move-ment and doing its best to tie both to the growing communist "menace."[22]

John Killens compiled a high school average of 91, third best in his class, but faced the prospect of failing to graduate as a consequence of some inci-dent of misbehavior. He never explained the episode, and his schoolmates never addressed the matter directly. Lafayette Bonner vaguely recalled that condoms had been circulated, while Valeria Williams remembered a group of boys who had engaged in some devilment, but she did not associate Kil-lens with that group.[23] Whatever the reason, school officials reached a com-promise with Killens, allowing him to receive his diploma but barring him from most graduation festivities. He appeared in a school play, *The Story of Ballard*, on the night of May 5, 1933. Some members of his family did not know of his punishment, so he dressed for the prom and other official par-ties and left home just to kill time with his own private celebration or, more precisely, meditation. The most meaningful personal fact of Killens's final weeks at Ballard was that he had secured no college seat for the following academic year. He wanted to attend Atlanta's Morris Brown College, a fa-vorite destination for Ballard graduates, including his brother, Charles, who had completed two years there and was working toward a baccalaureate. But according to Richard Killens, a mix-up involving African Methodist Epis-copal church finances prevented John Killens from receiving a scholarship that would have enabled him to attend Morris Brown.[24] Although Charles returned to Morris Brown for his junior year and many members of John's graduating class—despite possessing academic averages lower than his—would leave Macon for further education, he had to remain and would not be enrolled in school. Mercer University, one of the region's premier insti-tutions of higher education, lay within walking distance of Killens's house, but the all-white school did not admit African Americans for another three decades.

Killens began his first summer after high school just as President Roosevelt, who had been inaugurated on March 4, concluded his first hundred days in office, tirelessly pushing his New Deal initiatives and winning passage of the National Industrial Recovery Act. Roosevelt's plans included govern-ment spending to stimulate the economy, establishing a minimum wage, and, of particular interest to Killens, provisions for collective bargaining.

Killens bided his time by doing odd jobs, including additional work at the Dempsey Hotel. His endeavors earned him little money, but the work at the hotel paid extra benefits in the long run because the experience gathered there heavily informed the latter portions of his first published novel, *Youngblood*.[25] He also learned by surveying Macon's overall labor scene; in particular, he studied closely how racism undermined union solidarity.

Like the rest of the country, residents of Macon suffered mightily during the Great Depression. The cotton textile industry, centered in Georgia, Alabama, and the Carolinas, had been weakened before 1929, when the boll weevil attacked the cotton crop. The added strain of a national depression led to the loss of numerous farms in Bibb County, with African Americans hit at a rate five times greater than whites.[26] The resultant scarcity of food, along with a high unemployment rate, which peaked at 25 percent nationally in 1933, led to long lines at soup kitchens in the city. Beleaguered Maconites thus stood among the twelve million people on soup lines throughout the nation.

The economic crisis intensified Macon's Jim Crow policies. As the number of job opportunities shrank, whites began to take employment in menial positions that had previously been considered appropriate for blacks. Some whites resented having to accept "nigger jobs," like Killens's position at the hotel, but accepted them for lack of better opportunities.[27] Whatever industrial foothold African Americans had gained was perpetually tenuous. Owners sometimes employed them as a marginal or contingent labor force to pressure whites into accepting low wages and deplorable work conditions and thereby maximize profits. Given Macon's virulent racism, most black workers felt no personal allegiance to white workers, who frowned on interracial labor activism even though it promised to improve working conditions for everyone. After studying the overall situation in Macon, Jesse O. Thomas, an official with the National Urban League, called the city one of the most backward in the entire South.[28] Nonetheless, enough workers, mostly in the cotton mills and garment plants that lay at the heart of Macon's industry, began to challenge the low-wage economy to make the contest between labor and capital a running story in the local press. More than fifty feature stories about labor issues appeared in the *Macon Telegraph* during the year following Killens's graduation from Ballard.

In September, twenty-five thousand people marched in a Macon parade that was part of the Blue Eagle Drive, launched by the National Recovery Administration (NRA), which essentially called on employers to pay a minimum wage of forty cents per hour for a thirty-five-hour week. Consumers were urged to shop only at businesses that displayed the Blue Eagle logo. But progress for laborers remained slow. By the following summer, after months of increased organizing and numerous walkout threats, a number of mills were shut down by strikes not only in Macon but throughout the South.[29] At Macon's Bibb Manufacturing Company, violence broke out between striking groups and company loyalists on several occasions, with white workers physically attacking African American strikebreakers.[30] Union organizers were arrested, and on one occasion, strikers overpowered the police.[31] As rallies in support of the strike drew thousands, the National Guard was mobilized; even the city's eighty-five firemen were sworn in for special police duty in areas around mills, which by then had been described as war zones. Indeed, bullets and tear gas were used to subdue strikers at Payne Mill.[32]

To resume his formal studies, Killens enrolled at Edward Waters College in the fall of 1934. A tiny African Methodist Episcopal school in Jacksonville, Florida, just over the state line and only a few hours by road or rail from his hometown, Edward Waters represented another outpost among the Reconstruction initiatives in education for African Americans. Founded in 1866 as the Brown Theological Institute, the school was renamed Edward Waters College in 1892 to honor the church's third bishop. Destroyed by fire in 1901 along with most of Jacksonville, the school was barely surviving in the hard economy of the 1930s.[33] When Killens arrived to pursue the two-year, preprofessional course of study, he found that Edward Waters did not represent much of an academic step up from Ballard.

In social and political terms, Killens perceived Jacksonville as less racially charged than Macon, more an expression of a rather uneventful stay or of faulty recall than a perceptive assessment of the city's politics. Florida had the country's highest per capita lynching rate.[34] Although Ku Klux Klan activity had waned statewide since 1920, when the Florida KKK was considered the "most formidable paramilitary force in the United States," Jacksonville remained a hotbed of Klan activity.[35]

On campus, Killens took yearlong courses in English composition, French, chemistry, algebra, and ancient history. He barely managed a C average for the fall semester, though his grades improved slightly in the spring.[36] He moved more markedly away from his boyhood shyness and became too socially active, if not yet in a strongly political sense, to excel academically.

Killens arrived at Edward Waters with two friends from Macon, Charles Sheftall and Charles Walker. He and Sheftall, a football player, roomed together, and their room served as a social hub. Dormitory mate Thomas Jenkins remembered Killens as an "easy-going, friendly and easy-to-get-along-with guy."[37] Most people would have agreed with this assessment of him as amiable and soft-spoken, though he could become a firebrand under certain circumstances. Killens and Sheftall often addressed each other as "Ole Lady": Jenkins recalled them saying, "Hi there ole lady, come here ole lady and what you yapping about etc. ole lady."[38] Killens later incorporated such dormitory talk in *Youngblood*: "Richie had angrily challenged his first roommate about calling him Old Lady all the time, and his roommate had told him to pay it no mind. 'It doesn't mean a thing. Roommates always call each other Old Lady. That's because they're supposed to look out for each other—take care of each other. That's what old ladies are for, isn't it? The trouble with you freshmen you're too damn sensitive.'"[39] Killens's circle of friends at Edward Waters also included Jennifer Lee Hampton, a woman from Ocala, Florida, who later worked as a missionary in Borneo and who was profiled, along with her husband, in the same June 1958 issue of *Ebony* magazine that contains commentary about Killens.[40] And Killens may have profiled Hampton. The parents in *Youngblood* name their daughter Jenny Lee.

Killens's most notable personal development at Edward Waters may have been a crisis in faith. Myles Killens's skepticism about religion and John Killens's later assertions about not being a religious person may have been bridged by a late-adolescent period of intense questioning of his embrace of Christianity. How, for example, could the teachings and practices of the African Methodist Episcopal Church help foster an understanding of Jim Crow and the sojourn of Africans in the New World as well as the challenge of evolutionary biology? Killens later portrayed his quandary in autobiographical fiction:

> I can still remember how my first four months of college, I got on my knees in prayer to the Almighty God every night. The next few months I said my prayers in bed. Then there came a period when sometimes I said my prayers and on other occasions I forgot them. I became dubious but never disclaimed my God for fear that he might actually exist. Finally, I came to the

point where I became a firm non-believer and did not care who knew it. I
felt better for it. Now there was no confusion. I considered myself a confirmed atheist. Many of my college companions had chosen the ministry as
a profession because as they shamelessly expressed it, "It is a nice and easy
racket." I groped diligently and sincerely for the truth in this religion business and emerged an atheist.[41]

To illustrate his comfort with his convictions and point to some of the
complexities involved, Killens told a joke about a drought-stricken town
in which all the residents had chosen a particular Sunday to attend church
and pray to God for an abundance of rain. A little boy arrived with a large
umbrella. An elderly deacon wondered incredulously whether the young
lad expected rain. The boy, a true believer, instantly rejoined, "Certainly sir.
Isn't that what we're going to pray for this morning?"[42]

After another summer in Macon, Killens did not return to Edward
Waters for a second year when the road opened to Morris Brown, from
which his brother, Charles, had recently graduated with a degree in business
administration, and where Pierce Brunson, too, would soon be enrolled.

Roosevelt's relief efforts were having a salutary effect on some Americans,
and the labor front had quieted down. However, controversial Georgia governor Eugene Talmadge, who hailed from the Macon area, vehemently opposed the New Deal, declaring it worse than communism.[43] The New Deal
promised to ameliorate the economic misery of many African Americans,
and to the extent that it achieved this goal, it undermined the low-wage
economy that served the interests of the white plantation owners and mill
bosses—precisely the people to whom Talmadge was most committed. Talmadge did not oppose the idea of federal largesse flowing into Georgia, but
he sought to control those funds for his political benefit and continually
locked horns with the federal government over NRA policies and actions.
Talmadge, for example, never supported equal wages for black workers.[44]
Invoking visions of a second Reconstruction, Talmadge, a political ally of
white supremacist author Thomas Dixon, played to the fears of Bibb County's whites. He took less than 24 percent of the county's gubernatorial vote
in 1932 but increased that figure to 37 percent in the 1934 election.[45]

Killens had long imagined that he would have to leave Macon when he
reached adulthood. He certainly did not envision spending much of his
time in Talmadge's Georgia. Following the lead of his brother, Charles, he
decided to try to take advantage of the New Deal and the expanding op-

portunities in the federal workplace. Although slated to be in college in the coming fall, he took a civil service examination offered in Macon during the summer of 1935.

Morris Brown was the only college in Georgia founded by African Americans. The institution faced significant fiscal problems but nevertheless was a vibrant and viable four-year college within a relatively thriving university complex. Its major challenge, aside from raising funds, was coordinating its efforts and activities to take full advantage of its proximity to Spelman, Morehouse, and Clark Colleges and Atlanta University. The General Education Board, the philanthropic entity founded by John D. Rockefeller, partly sponsored Morris Brown and lauded its "splendid accomplishments."[46]

Killens advanced further down the path toward becoming a labor and civil rights attorney and thus a member of the "reform elite."[47] He joined a new wave of students who, largely under the influence of Du Bois, whose monumental *Black Reconstruction in America* was published the same year that Killens enrolled at Morris Brown, exhibited class consciousness along with their acute sense of racial discrimination. Macon had shown Killens enough of the pitfalls of racism and capitalism; Du Bois provided the most cogent and exciting analysis.[48]

During November of his first semester in "New Deal Atlanta," Killens saw the potential for mass-based movement when the African American community boycotted an A&P grocery store on the west side of town, not far from campus.[49] A white clerk had beaten an unemployed African American father of three for allegedly stealing a pound of sugar. Despite intimidation tactics by police and the Ku Klux Klan, the boycott proved effective. The clerk was dismissed, and the store eventually closed.[50]

Killens attended a series of Sunday afternoon discussion groups at Morris Brown and its neighboring historically black colleges.[51] On occasion, a few white students would show up from Emory University or Georgia Tech. The group usually touched on the issue of race relations, and on one occasion, a white student triumphantly declared that he had the answer to the racial problem in the United States: "The way to get rid of the nigrah problem is to collect all the nigrahs together and take them to the river and dump them in." After another forum, a visiting white professor told Killens and several other African American students they were likeable fellows, totally unlike the lower-class African Americans over on Decatur Street who the professor thought made life difficult for everyone else.[52]

On less serious occasions, Killens participated freely in parties and other social activities. He pledged Omega Psi Phi, a black fraternity whose membership included Langston Hughes and Arna Bontemps, and survived the considerable hazing process. One winter night he was roused from sleep at about two o'clock and asked to walk one of the fraternity brothers to his home several miles away. As a pledge, Killens was expected to grant the request. The fraternity member consoled Killens as they walked, describing the warm beds and bountiful, home-cooked breakfast that awaited them. But when they finally arrived at the house, the brother went in and locked the door behind him, leaving Killens to walk alone back to campus along a route through a white section of Atlanta where his mere presence at that hour would likely be construed as guilt. Although Killens safely reached campus a little before five o'clock in the morning, he turned away from Omega Psi Phi, "gave my Big Brother my lamp (the pledge pin) and told him where to shove it."[53] He would never again think very highly of or see much logic in the antics of black Greeks.

By the beginning of 1936, Killens was back in Macon, and so was Governor Talmadge. Talmadge and his allies organized a Grass Roots Convention at the Macon Auditorium with the goal of defeating Roosevelt's reelection bid. Walter White, the NAACP's executive secretary, telegrammed Talmadge and the conference's cosponsor, wealthy Texas lumberman John Kirby, to tell them to put black civil rights on the convention agenda because Georgia was violating the Fourteenth and Fifteenth Amendments almost daily. As the crowd of three thousand delegates assembled, they saw a Confederate flag displayed as a backdrop and found in every seat an issue of *Georgia Women's World*, a magazine published by the Atlanta-based National Women's Association of the White Race. Some observers suspected that Talmadge secretly funded the magazine, which, among other complaints, lambasted Eleanor Roosevelt for her relatively progressive position on race relations.[54]

Much to Talmadge's delight, the U.S. Supreme Court had declared Roosevelt's National Recovery Act unconstitutional the preceding year, but Congress countered quickly with the National Labor Relations Act of 1935, known as the Wagner Act after one of its leading proponents, Robert Wagner, a member of the U.S. House who also served as chair of the NRA and who, like LaGuardia, was a future mayor of New York City.

By the spring of 1936, Charles Killens, after a period of selling insurance for Atlanta Life, embarked on a career at the Government Printing Office in Washington, D.C. Younger brother John soon followed him to Washington, but to a job more in line with his interests. The National Labor Relations Board had been established to administer the provisions of the National Labor Relations Act, including such matters as supervising union elections and investigating charges of unfair labor practices. Although taking a full-time job would interfere with John Killens's pursuit of a college education, at least in the short term, the opportunity to become a steadily employed civil servant proved impossible to ignore. On April 27, 1936, twenty-year-old Killens became the board's first African American employee, a messenger who received an annual salary of about one thousand dollars.[55]

CHAPTER THREE

Mr. Killens, 1936–1942

Macon residents accorded significant stature to the Killens brothers, imagining them—and anyone who held a government position in Washington—to be working "in the White House" helping Franklin Roosevelt run the country.[1] Friends also associated the Killenses with a citified flamboyance expected to be on display during visits home. John Killens became a bit of a clotheshorse; his trousers and suits were usually full cut, even baggy, in the style of the day. He usually appeared in public clean-shaven, kept his rapidly thinning hair trimmed short, and was fond of hats. He generally sought an understated elegance. Neither he nor Charles would miss a party or hesitate to host one. But they were not in the White House.

The National Labor Relations Board (NLRB) stood on Vermont Avenue, about a mile from 1600 Pennsylvania Avenue, and John Killens had enough trouble just getting through his first day on the job. Because he had been a lifelong resident of the Deep South, the racial codes of the federal workplace initially puzzled him.[2] He was expected to exchange handshakes with whites and treat them as though they were all like Lewis Hendrix Mounts back at Ballard. In addition, in a move surprising to him, coworkers addressed him as "Mr. Killens." Killens recalled that he spent much of his first day trying to locate the "colored" water fountains and restrooms. By four in the afternoon, he decided to "go for broke" and worry later about the consequences.[3] There were none, but Killens nevertheless found the episode humiliating because of the history of segregation it evoked. With retrospective clarity, he stated that he should have realized that no separate facilities would have been constructed solely for him. In any event, he enjoyed simply being regarded as a man.[4]

Although Killens found the office environment favorable, his job was immediately imperiled because of continual legal action by corporations against the agency. The NLRB did not attain secure status until the U.S. Supreme Court upheld the Wagner Act in 1937. Killens would keep his government job. On May 20, 1937, he was promoted to File Clerk, Grade CAF-1, at $1,260 per annum.[5]

Even after the Supreme Court guaranteed the NLRB's continued existence, the board continually engendered the wrath of conservative enemies because it served as a key check on corporate capital. In the late 1930s, a committee headed by Virginia congressman Howard Smith produced an eight-thousand-page, thirty-volume attack on the NLRB, accusing it of partiality in the handling of labor disputes and calling for substantial amendments to the board's charge. The Smith Committee also charged that the board was riddled with communists.[6] However, the committee focused on David Saposs, a noncommunist who headed the economics section, and ignored the actual communist presence in the agency.[7] Although they never became dominant, at least two Communist Party cells operated at the NLRB—a high-level one that involved board secretary Nathan Witt, economist Edwin Smith, and attorneys Allan Rosenberg, Martin Kurasch, and Joseph Robison, and a lower-level one organized by another lawyer, Herbert Fuchs.[8] This tiered structure enabled communist-front organizations fairly easily to circulate petitions and solicit money among NLRB employees.

One leader of the lower-level cell, David Rien, befriended Killens and encouraged him to become active in the NLRB's internal union politics, invaluable practical experience for a budding unionist. Rien eventually persuaded Killens to make a bid for the union's vice presidency, though Killens did not win. The extent of Killens's involvement with the Communist Party during his tenure at the board remains unclear.[9] He unquestionably had contact with numerous party members and frequently espoused standard communist doctrine, and he seemed to be a joiner by nature. But whether in Washington he was a left-liberal sympathizer mainly concerned with racial justice, a fellow traveler, or a card-carrying party member, he quickly understood the extra political caution required of federal employees.

Killens had landed in what arguably constituted the intellectual and activist center of African America. Ideas and activities of all types swirled at a frantic pace, particularly in the U Street District, which formed the heart of black life in Washington, and on the nearby campus of Howard University, the "capstone of Negro education."[10] Prominent faculty at Howard included Alain Locke, Sterling Brown, Eugene Clay Holmes, Abram Harris, Ralph Bunche, Charles Houston, William Hastie, and Doxey Wilkerson.

Community protests had been launched to combat racist discrimination and to advocate educational, health, housing, and economic advances. One of the more notable efforts was led by the youthful New Negro Alliance, headed by John Aubrey Davis. The group was founded in August 1933 during protests against the firing of three African American employees, two of whom were Howard University students, by the white-owned Hamburger Grill on U Street. Black picketers caused such a decrease in business that the owner rehired the three workers two days after firing them. Emboldened by this success and drawing increasing support from various segments of the African American community, the New Negro Alliance conducted "Don't Buy from Where You Can't Work" campaigns in Washington throughout the 1930s, including a lengthy effort against Peoples Drug Stores that began in June 1938.[11]

Killens obviously had the group and its activities in mind when he wrote the section of *Youngblood* in which Richard Wendell Myles is a student at Howard and becomes involved in protests: "The Better Jobs for Colored Committee had a campaign going against a chain drugstore company to get them to hire Negro pharmacists and clerks in Negro sections of the city." When Richard joins the demonstration on U Street, he meets Henrietta Saunders, who will become his girlfriend: "She carried a big sign that read, 'DON'T BUY WHERE YOU CAN'T WORK,' and he carried one that said— 'THE POLICY OF THIS STORE IS ANTI-NEGRO—PASS IT BY.'"[12]

Impossible to avoid in activist circles was the tall, dignified, and distinguished Alphaeus Hunton. A tireless perfectionist, he participated in numerous prolabor and antiracist activities. Originally from Georgia, like Killens, Hunton was taken north as a toddler after the 1906 Atlanta race riots. He grew up mostly in New York City, although he spent a couple of years in Germany and Switzerland while his mother, Addie Waite Hunton, studied at Kaiser Wilhelm University in Strasburg. By the time of his appointment to the faculty of Howard in 1926, where he later shared an office with Sterling Brown, Hunton had earned a master's degree from Harvard University. While at Howard, he also earned a doctorate from New York University. Although Hunton taught a variety of English courses and administered the first-year English program, he specialized in Victorian literature, having written a doctoral thesis on "Tennyson and the Victorian Political Milieu" in which he offered a Marxist interpretation of the poet's shortcomings and claimed that in all respects he "spoke for the politically dominant class in Victorian England." Hunton's literary convictions had been influenced by his dissertation director, Edwin Berry Burgum, a leading Marxist and editorial board member of the Marxist scholarly journal *Science and Society*.[13]

Hunton had joined the recently formed National Negro Congress and held the posts of vice president and chair of the labor committee for the organization's Washington Council. He also cofounded the Howard Teachers' Union, known also as the American Federation of Teachers, Local 440, in 1936. Hunton always served in an administrative capacity with the group, which extended its political activities far beyond what its name suggested and frequently was active in the city's African American community. Members included Sterling Brown, Abram Harris, Ralph Bunche, and Doxey Wilkerson.

Killens supported the Washington branch of the National Negro Congress, although he claimed not to have been an official member. Following Hunton's lead, Killens attended meetings about such issues as police brutality and contributed to various fund-raising drives. He, like many of the city's other African American activists, both neophyte and mature, sought a praxis that merged insights of an ever-present and deeply felt racial consciousness with a class analysis that construed contemporary racism as one of the ravages of capitalism. In line with this collective pursuit were numerous debates about the analytic merits of race versus class. Prominent black communist Harry Haywood's Black Belt Thesis, supporting the right of African American sovereignty in the South, a platform adopted by the Communist Party, was a much-discussed item.[14] So was W. E. B. Du Bois's bitter rejection of the Communist Party (a group he would later join) accompanied by some of the most accommodationist statements of his career, though his assertions about self-reliance and securing "a place for ourselves" were not incompatible with Haywood's ideas.[15] Du Bois's actions aside, the Communist Party, with its platform of racial equality and record of championing African American causes, reached its heyday in the African American community during this period. As activist Len De Caux reflected, "I don't recall the communists pulling their punches on any aspect of black rights."[16] Nationally, the party increased its African American membership from fewer than two hundred in 1928 to more than five thousand by 1939. Ossie Davis, a contemporary and friend of Killens who was also both a native of Georgia and a Howard University student during the 1930s, succinctly expressed the intellectual and emotional conundrum, particularly concerning communism and nationalism, faced by his generation of emerging activists: "Though layered, my loyalty was never split; always at the bottom, even if I did have to constantly shuffle my tactics, was black itself. I was 'red' only when I thought it a smarter way of being 'black.'"[17]

Killens fell under the direct influence of a second Howard University faculty member, controversial sociologist E. Franklin Frazier, whom Killens understood to be a maverick, almost completely irreverent. Born into a working-class environment in Baltimore in 1894, Frazier received a scholarship to attend Howard University in 1912. As a student activist and fierce opponent of racist discrimination, he outspokenly refused to participate in a segregated inaugural parade for Woodrow Wilson. After a series of short-term teaching jobs and a period of graduate study, he joined the faculty of Morehouse College in 1922 and directed the Atlanta School of Social Work. He lacked the personality to perform the obeisance whites expected and required of African Americans in Dixie, and he thus encountered extraordinary difficulty in 1927 when he published a satiric essay, "The Pathology of Race Prejudice," which defined racism as a form of insanity. Alain Locke, one of his former professors, found the piece too abrasive, even for a New Negro, and declined to publish it in his landmark anthology. The liberal publication *Forum* ultimately printed the essay, and amid the ensuing fervor, which included a lynching threat by the Ku Klux Klan, Frazier hastily retreated from Atlanta. He attended the University of Chicago, where he worked with prominent sociologist Robert Park to complete his doctorate.

In August 1933, Frazier was among a group of intellectuals invited by Du Bois and National Association for the Advancement of Colored People (NAACP) president Joel Spingarn to attend the Second Amenia Conference convened at Spingarn's Troutbeck estate in New York.[18] At that event, designed to assess and chart African American political direction, it became clear that Frazier operated outside both mainstream liberalism and the NAACP's middle-class "race men" focus. He saw hope in a pluralistic workers' movement. In the latter portions of his 1939 study, *The Negro Family in the United States*, Frazier envisioned an African American industrial proletariat that would adopt a workers' perspective and cast its fortunes with the overall working class.[19] Frazier grew especially critical of his friend and supporter Du Bois, who Frazier felt had strayed too far ideologically from being a "Socialist of the Path." Given Du Bois's elitism, Frazier found his notions about black separatism to be whimsical and romantic. "Nothing could be more unendurable for him," Frazier wrote, "than to live within a Black Ghetto or within a black nation—unless perhaps he were king, and then probably he would attempt to unite the whites and blacks through marriage of the royal families."[20]

Frazier earned a big reputation for operating with directness and flair. He was already an "academic star," "activist," and "gladiator" when he arrived at Howard in 1934 to head the sociology department.[21] On campus, "Forceful Frazier" exhorted students and other leaders to address crises in the African American community.[22] Killens appreciated Frazier's "radical audacity." Mindful of Frazier's criticism of the flawed but nonetheless great Du Bois, Killens remarked, "No cow was too sacred for E. Franklin Frazier."[23]

In the fall of 1937, Killens had his academic records forwarded to Howard. He transferred units in algebra, chemistry, economics, English, French, geometry, history, Latin, and physics. The following semester, he enrolled in Sociology 198: The Negro in America, which was taught by Frazier. Killens thus received concentrated doses of Frazier's arguments against racial theories and against the pathological explanations concerning the plight of African Americans in the work of turn-of-the-century scholars such as Frederick Hoffman and Joseph Tillinghast and in the writings of the more contemporary Jerome Dowd and Edward Reuter.[24] Most consistently and importantly, Frazier argued that African Americans' travails were best explained in terms of the structural conditions of enslavement and its aftermath, which included an economy organized along capitalist and white supremacist lines. In other words, Frazier saw the generative sociological question as involving the "impact of racism on family life, the interconnection between economic inequality and personal problems, and the difficulty of preserving human relationships in a society based on exploitation and inequality."[25]

As at least a potential member of Frazier's "brown middle class," Killens paid particular attention as his instructor predicted that the African American middle class, to be comprised increasingly of white-collar employees, would eventually become less snobbish and would think of itself as other intellectual workers did—that is, as unprivileged relative to the truly wealthy.[26] As a budding Marxist, Killens would also particularly have noted Frazier's assumption that members of the black industrial proletariat were becoming more conscious of themselves in class terms and would not remain under the intellectual influence of the African American middle class.[27] Overall, Killens grasped enough of Frazier's ideas to earn a B.

Campus learning never comprised more than a fraction of the curriculum that Killens fashioned for himself. He also looked to contemporary expressive culture, for example, including sports. Like many other observers, he read the psychology of African Americans through the pugilistic victories of Joe Louis, whom Killens described as "strong wine for our much-abused egos. Every fight he ever fought, we were in the ring with him. *Our* Joe, not your Old Black Joe. And every triumph he experienced, we experienced. . . . He was, to black folk, the Magnificent Vicarious Experience."[28] Killens trekked to Yankee Stadium on June 22, 1938, when Louis knocked out Max Schmeling, a victim of both U.S. and Nazi propaganda. Killens saw African American men, many of them strangers to one another, embracing and weeping for joy. In Washington, African Americans overturned streetcars and buses. Killens recalled an incident that occurred in a tiny town in Alabama when the black population gathered in a dance hall to listen to the radio broadcast of a different Louis bout. When the referee counted out yet another Louis knockout victim, all of those in the crowd jumped up at once as the count reached ten, creating enough force to collapse the dance floor. That several people suffered injuries hardly dampened the celebration. Killens remarked, "Some of the Black Bourgeoisie were embarrassed by the violence the Brown Bomber perpetrated against the King's English, but to most Negroes the important thing was the violence Joe was perpetrating against Whitey, Mister Charlie."[29]

Killens did not return to Howard in the fall of 1938, instead furthering his informal education by seeing more of the country.[30] A man who worked with Charles Killens had purchased a new Buick and was headed to Los Angeles to attend the American Legion's annual convention. Killens eagerly tagged along. He had no interest in the convention (and was not even eligible to be a legion member), but he could not pass up the adventure.

Taking a circuitous route, the men stopped in Chicago and in St. Louis, where a piece of their luggage that had been tied to the back of the spare tire was stolen while they dined in a restaurant. They proceeded to Council Bluffs, Iowa, then to Tulsa, Oklahoma, where Killens engaged people in lively talk about the Great Tulsa Race Riot of May 31–June 1, 1921. More than thirty-five blocks of the African American community had been burned to the ground, and at least twenty-six blacks and ten whites were killed. Some African Americans fled to the hills and to surrounding towns. The National Guard was eventually deployed to restore order—and Jim Crow. Killens stayed at the "only colored hotel" in the city. Nevertheless, "No matter, Jim Crow, race riot, or whatever, nothing could dampen my spirit this particular evening. I was almost halfway across AMERICA."[31]

Passing through the west, Killens saw a vast factory with a sign at the entrance announcing, "THIS IS YOUR PLANT; EVERY WORKER A CAPITALIST." "But what would happen," Killens wondered aloud, "if a worker took that slogan seriously, took some equipment out of the front gate?" He was accused of being "a spoilsport, a wet blanket, always looking on the dark side of everything." But, he asked later, "Being of a dark complexion, how could I do otherwise?"[32]

The travelers spent a couple of days at Wyoming's Yellowstone National Park, with its "Old Faithful Geyser, and bears that walked around amongst people, and hordes of bison, a place where nature seemed to have beautifully run amok." In Salt Lake City, they stayed in "another colored hotel" before crossing over into Arizona to visit the Grand Canyon and then moving north into Nevada. They spent a night trying to sleep in the car in the Mojave Desert, but Killens was disturbed by the howling of animals that were "too close for comfort for me and my imagination." The next day, shortly after noon, the travelers reached Los Angeles.[33]

There, Killens took in the sights with a friend from Morris Brown. They visited the home of actress Louise Beavers, who had starred in 1934's *Imitation of Life*, the first major Hollywood film to focus on a black woman. Although Killens was highly critical of the film, he respected Beavers's performance and was convinced that she and actress Hattie McDaniel (who won an Oscar for her performance in *Gone with the Wind*) played their roles with "tongue planted firmly in cheek."[34] Killens went on a bus tour through Beverly Hills and, always the sports fan, attended a UCLA football game at the Los Angeles Coliseum. One of the players he saw was Kenny Washington, who in 1946 became one of the first African Americans to play in the National Football League. Killens did not get to see Number 13 at his best on the night of September 23. Washington fumbled three times early in the game but rebounded to help the Bruins vanquish visiting Iowa, 27–3.

Although Killens was traveling through the West rather than the Deep South of his childhood, he did not miss the importance of the segregated hotels and the masking required of talents such as Beavers as well as the fact that many universities would not have welcomed Washington. Like Frederick Douglass, Killens felt that the United States was fundamentally a southern country.[35]

Paul Robeson was an internationally renowned African American singer, actor, scholar, and activist who attracted intense media scrutiny when in May 1939, after a decade abroad, he announced, "Having helped on many fronts, I feel that it is now time for me to return to the place of my origin."[36] He settled in New York City the following October.

Jeopardizing his career, Robeson, a personal friend of Frazier, never wavered from espousing a strong message against capitalism, racism, fascism, and colonialism. He eventually believed that scientific socialism represented a higher stage of human evolution and that the Soviet Union, where he had spent considerable time, most realized the socialist ideal as a nation. He defended Soviet domestic and international actions, including the Nazi-Soviet nonaggression pact signed in August 1939. Robeson's logic seemed somewhat solid when Hitler invaded Russia on June 22, 1941, and an Anglo-Soviet alignment followed. Actually, Robeson's major political troubles did not commence until he pushed his pro-Soviet line into the Cold War era.

Robeson ultimately had tremendous influence on Killens, who later wrote, "Paul Robeson happened to me and the course of my life was charted. He was for me Black manhood and Black personhood incorporated. He was my Patron Saint."[37] The twenty-three-year-old Killens was particularly inspired by Robeson's commitment to workers and his legal background. Although Killens had completed only a few semesters of college by 1939, he still intended to obtain a law degree and to do so within the relatively near future. He found the means in the Robert H. Terrell Law School, a night school located in Washington, D.C. The school did not require students to hold undergraduate degrees but only mandated two years of college and a demonstrated potential to handle the course of study. Killens's combined work at Edward Waters, Morris Brown, and Howard gave him enough credits for admission, and he enrolled in October 1939.

Terrell Law School was founded in 1931 after Howard University discontinued its evening law program. In response, law professor George A. Parker proposed to several of his colleagues the establishment of an evening school that would make possible a legal education for African Americans whose obligations prevented daytime study. The school was named in honor of the first African American to serve as a justice of the peace and on the Municipal Court of the District of Columbia. Terrell was also the husband of Mary Church Terrell and had thus been the patriarch of one of Washington's most prominent and influential African American families. The faculty consisted exclusively of professors who had extensive teaching and practical experience and were members of the bar in the District of Columbia and several states. The instructional method blended the textbook approach and the case method, and instructors encouraged students to take advantage of the opportunities afforded by proximity to the Library of Congress and the federal government. Students who could scrape together the hundred-dollar-a-semester tuition and could persevere through four years of classes four nights a week could pursue their dreams of a legal career.

Killens earned mostly Bs in his first-year classes, which included contracts, criminal law, personal property, torts, and legal ethics. A week past his twenty-fourth birthday, Killens completed with competence his first semester of law.

As at other educational institutions, he also maintained his involvement in extracurricular activities. He helped to launch the student publication, *The Barrister*, which debuted in the fall of 1940, and eventually became a reporter and the elected *Barrister* representative of his class. Usually a mimeographed seven- or eight-page booklet with a construction paper cover, the publication featured famous quotes about litigation, including words from Abraham Lincoln that Killens would later take to heart: "Resolve to be honest at all events, and if in your judgment you cannot be an honest lawyer, resolve to be honest without being a lawyer."[38] The publication also printed quizzes, jokes, and student news, both serious and light. In November 1940, the paper reported, for example, that "John K." had hosted a party for some members of the second-year class and had "put his hand in a hat and pulled out a 'cutie' named Miss Washington." Later that night, a drunken Otis Sprow confused his date with the host's, at which point "John, being a bit more on the sober side, took his little chick up, up (?) some place out of circulation—after which time the lights went out or yours truly went out."[39]

Killens, who lived with his brother, Charles, during this time, apparently hosted a number of parties and hangout sessions. Percy Faison, who worked at the NLRB, recalled visiting the Killens home, especially the bar in the basement, and remembered that he, John Killens, Virgil Daniels, Fred Dreher, and Vernon Green listened all night to election results. Killens often traveled to New York to watch boxing matches, and one of his favorite fighters was Henry Armstrong, who, like Killens, was a whirlwind, always punching. The future novelist, who "bet on everything," made a bundle by picking Armstrong in several key fights. In celebration, Killens would sometimes light cigarettes with a dollar bill.[40]

To the extent that Killens turned his attention beyond his job, life at law school, and his circle of friends, he found nearly everyone preoccupied with the conflict in Europe. Given his attraction to Robeson and the National Negro Congress, Killens most likely adopted, at least initially, the perspective of noninvolvement, viewing the war as an armed struggle among imperialist rivals. This was the dominant message advanced by the leadership of the National Negro Congress when the organization convened in Washington in April 1940. More than five hundred delegates were encouraged to focus on the domestic fight for African American rights.

This message was also expounded by the American Youth Congress (AYC), which Killens joined during this time. Founded in 1934, the AYC organized around such pressing issues as jobs, education, and peace. Although tainted with the label of radicalism, the AYC originally had a rather broad political base and worked in collaboration with such notables as Eleanor Roosevelt, who defended the group and coached some of its members for their appearance before the House Un-American Activities Committee in 1938. Roosevelt believed that the group, like the nation, expressed a range of political opinion from left to right. Eventually, however, a breech erupted between the AYC and Roosevelt because of her support for the war as well as her proposal for forced labor and support of the Burke-Wadsworth Conscription Bill. She stopped running political interference for the AYC and no longer publicly associated with the group.[41]

On February 7–9, 1941, the AYC held a "Town Meeting of Youth" in the nation's capital. More than five thousand people attended, though the absence of government support was palpable: chair Jack McMichael noted that "the only representatives of the Administration this year are the members of the FBI here in disguise." Nonetheless, McMichael was glad the FBI was present and told the agents, "Hope you enjoy your visit and carry back to your masters the convictions we would like to have shared with them directly."[42]

McMichael spoke inside a boxing ring at Joe Turner's Arena, an ironic setting because one of the AYC's staunchest critics was former heavyweight champion Gene Tunney. After attending an AYC conference at Lake Geneva, Wisconsin, Tunney lambasted the organization as a "tentacle of Communism." "It is Red," Tunney wrote, "and will stay unalterably Red." In contrast to the hope that Paul Robeson saw in Soviet Russia, on Tunney's 1931 trip to the country, he saw only the commissars and their friends doing relatively well. Connecting the Soviet Union with the AYC, Tunney argued, "This nation of noble fathers and noble sons, who have always sympathized with the underdog and admired the noble deed, must feel pretty sad that a wretched claque of Communist applauders can call themselves Americans."[43] Tunney had organized a countergroup, the National Foundation for American Youth, which went to Washington at the time of the AYC convention to garner support. Tunney's group delivered a basket of fruit to the White House for President Roosevelt, a gesture meant to indicate opposition to the AYC's "gimme" attitude.[44] Tunney concluded that the AYC was "un-American, unpatriotic, subversive and seditious, and it must go."[45]

But McMichael, a twenty-three-year-old divinity student, never spoke at the conference about the virtues of communism.[46] The conference opened with the playing of "God Bless America" and the singing of the national anthem. The arena was decorated with American flags and red, white, and blue bunting. McMichael then spoke about jobs, civil liberties, education, health, and peace. He noted politicians' diminishing interest in the New Deal, the spread of racism and anti-Semitism, and the rising militarism among government leaders. McMichael criticized the fact that although four million American youth remained unemployed, the American Youth Act and the Federal Aid to Education Bill were stalled in Congress, a body, he reasoned, that was "too busy with 'defense' to defend *us*."[47] The Wagner Health Bill and the Wagner-Steagall Housing Act were similarly stalled. McMichael also spoke against Jim Crow accommodations in Washington, D.C., which had hampered the AYC's convention efforts.

McMichael also stirred the crowd with antiwar remarks. A firm proponent of neutrality, he warned against the dangers of aligning with and supporting British imperialism: "Since when is it in the interests of the common people of America to enter into an alliance with the British Empire?" Then, echoing a slogan that was gaining in popularity, McMichael proclaimed, to thunderous applause, "The Yanks are not coming."[48]

Following the events at the arena, thousands of protesters, Killens among them, marched three miles from conference headquarters at the John Wesley Church to the Washington Monument to hear an address by New York congressman Vito Marcantonio, a member of the American Labor Party, who characterized the war as a pact between "two gangs of imperialistic bandits"—the Axis Powers headquartered in Rome, Berlin, and Tokyo on one hand and the Wall Street–Downing Street cabal on the other.[49]

While Killens embraced the AYC's overall goals, he had a particular interest in an affiliate group, the Southern Negro Youth Congress, which had been organized in February 1937 by African American tobacco workers in Richmond, Virginia, who were protesting poor wages and work conditions. After failing to receive assistance from the American Federation of Labor, C. Columbus Alston, Frances Grandison, and James Edward Jackson, who became a close friend of Killens, helped the workers organize a union, affiliated with the Congress of Industrial Organizations, that subsequently struck Richmond's Export Leaf and Tobacco Company and helped to improve conditions industrywide. By 1939, the Southern Negro Youth Congress was headquartered in Birmingham, Alabama. Jackson remained active and was joined in leadership by his wife, Esther Cooper; Louis Burnham; Augusta Jackson; and her husband, Edward Strong.

At the Washington conference, Esther Cooper gave an address, "Free the Negro People," in which she argued that the Roosevelt war program was having a disastrous effect on civil liberties in the South, which had seen a new wave of lynchings, police murders, and vigilante atrocities. Dorothy Greenwood, a thirteen-year-old girl in Montgomery, Alabama, had been shot by police who broke into her home; officials then refused to investigate the matter. Eighteen-year-old Nora Wilson, a sharecropper from Wetumpka, Alabama, had been imprisoned without trial for allegedly slapping her boss. In Memphis, Tennessee, political machine leaders had organized beatings of labor organizers, and the U.S. Department of Justice had refused to intervene.[50]

Cooper also explained that seventy-eight years after the Emancipation Proclamation, slavery still existed under the guise of the sharecropping system. She noted further that only 130 of 62,000 pilots serving in the national defense program were African Americans, as were only 3 of 180,000 people being trained as technicians. President Roosevelt and what Cooper called his "Poll-Tax Congressmen" supported aid to the British Empire but did not support the right to vote for African Americans. "Youth of America," she exhorted, "don't be taken in by the appeasers or the Uncle Toms who give lip service to democracy but are in full accord with the war program." She urged African American and white youth to unite in the effort to instantiate genuine democracy and truly liberate the South.[51]

Killens certainly endorsed Cooper's position and continued to support the Southern Negro Youth Congress's activities; in addition, this linkage ul-

timately benefited Killens's literary career. His association with the group—
and particularly with James Jackson and Edward Strong—enabled Killens
to meet Richard Wright when Killens was dispatched to the airport to pick
up the author and escort him to a speaking engagement in Washington. Although in awe, Killens found Wright a "pleasant-faced man and a genial literary giant with a robust zest for life and laughter." Killens was immediately
inspired to read *Uncle Tom's Children* and *Native Son*. He always preferred
the former, especially the short story "Bright and Morning Star."[52]

Killens joined the battle against racism, segregation, and economic exploitation on yet another front as well. The National Council of Law Students, an organization that arose out of a December 1940 meeting at Howard University, established a Committee on Equal Opportunities in Legal
Education. The group consisted of students from several schools, including Harvard, Howard, and Terrell. Thurgood Marshall, then special counsel for the NAACP, and John P. Davis of the National Negro Congress
served as mentors. The committee sent letters to the departments of education in seventeen states with law schools for white students only, asking
whether provisions existed for state aid for African Americans to study in
other states. The committee also sought to establish an adequate bar review
course for African Americans, particularly in Washington, D.C. It viewed
the absence of such a course as a major reason for the low passage rate by
African Americans on the District of Columbia Bar.

In the October 1941 issue of *The Barrister*, Killens, who had recently been
elected one of the magazine's two representatives from the third-year class,
urged fellow students to become or remain active in the Terrell Law Students Guild, an affiliate of the National Council of Law Students. He argued
that the council could not "effectuate its program without the fullest cooperation of its affiliate chapters" and called on "all progressive law students
of Terrell" to help in an active campaign.[53] True to his labor roots and interests, he also contributed the issue's lead article, "An Unfair Labor Practice
under the Wagner Act," reprinting section 8 of the National Labor Relations
Act, which prohibits interference with unions and the right to collective
bargaining through appropriate representatives.[54]

Into his third year of law school, Killens had passed more than twenty
courses, mostly with a mix of Bs and Cs. He performed fairly strongly during the fall 1941 semester, earning Bs in evidence, corporations, labor law,
and constitutional law to go with a C in practice court. John O. Killens,
counsel for the plaintiff, filed a brief on behalf of Lester Hamilton in the case

of *Lester Hamilton v. Bessie Wheat and Albert Wells.* Hamilton had borrowed fifty dollars from Wheat and provided a watch worth one hundred dollars as collateral. Wheat subsequently sold the watch to Wells, who had knowledge of the prior transaction, for seventy-five dollars. When Hamilton demanded his watch and did not get it, he filed with the court. In his eight-page brief, Killens worked through the required steps—theory of the plaintiff's case, facts to be proved, statement of law and authority, and instructions—to conclude that Hamilton "be given judgment as against both or either of the defendants without a set off of the amount of the loan by either."[55]

However, Killens's most important legal matter that year occurred in the world beyond school. By attending an AYC conference the previous July in New York City and allegedly contributing three dollars, he drew the attention of the Federal Bureau of Investigation (FBI). The AYC had been designated a subversive organization, and Killens, as a federal employee, was investigated under the Hatch Act. At the beginning of October, the bureau's New York office informed special agent S. A. McKee in Washington that Killens had executed a delegate card at the convention. On August 2, 1939, the Act to Prevent Pernicious Political Activities, popularly known as the Hatch Act after its principal sponsor, New Mexico senator Carl Hatch, went into effect. The measure circumscribed the political activities of federal employees and required them to sign affidavits stating compliance. After determining that Killens worked for the NLRB, McKee wrote to J. Edgar Hoover's office advising that an appropriate investigation would be made unless instructions were issued to the contrary. Hoover's office subsequently ordered McKee to "fully develop complete information concerning the subject's connections with any 'subversive' organizations including his present activities and relationship thereto."[56]

During the ensuing months, the FBI interviewed fourteen people from the NLRB and Killens's neighborhood and received a variety of conflicting reports about him. Agents learned that Killens had lived for a spell at 3120 Thirteenth Street, N.W., a few blocks from the law school, with James Harris, said to be a member of the Communist Party from 1933 to 1939 and one of the officers in the National Negro Congress. One informant contended that at least one Communist Party meeting had been held at that address in 1940. Others noted Killens's affiliation with the communist faction, particularly Rien, at the NLRB. Still others affirmed his loyalty and dismissed the idea that he was a member of the Communist Party or other so-called un-American organizations. Some pointed to Killens's service as a neighborhood air raid warden as a sign of his patriotism and suggested that he seemed "very interested in the Allies winning the present world conflict." One person expressed surprise about being interviewed concerning Killens's loyalty, offering that he knew Killens to be entirely American. Another noted that Killens had voiced vigorous opposition to the publication of the Dies List (a roster compiled by a U.S. House committee headed by Martin Dies of Texas that named "several hundred thousand individuals" who held "subversive ideas" and could be subjected to such tactics as being "killed by exposure") but that the only other political criticisms he had heard Killens make were related to injustices concerning African Americans.[57]

While the FBI investigation into Killens's personal life unfolded, the United States entered World War II. Killens embraced the position promulgated by the National Negro Congress in its pamphlet, *Negro People Will Defend America*, which he carried around for several days. The document included the text of a resolution adopted at an emergency meeting of the group's national executive board on December 9, 1941, two days after the Japanese attack on Pearl Harbor. The pamphlet argued that "the fate of America is the fate of the Negro people."[58] Making the fight against fascism and Hitlerism the number one imperative and deeming America's cause just in the face of grave circumstances, the National Negro Congress encouraged African Americans to enlist in the military "by tens of thousands" and exhorted farmers and workers who would not serve in the military to increase production of the goods indispensable to the successful prosecution of a war campaign. However, the organization also explicitly connected African American participation in the war effort with equal opportunities in the labor force, expressing confidence that no one in government—or any loyal white American, for that matter—would deny African Americans the chance to contribute fully to the national defense by working in war industries. The National Negro Congress also explicitly debunked the notion, which enjoyed some currency in the black community, that the Japanese were somehow the vanguard force and liberators of the darker races, pointing to Japanese imperialism in China and elsewhere. Along with urging everyone to join with China, the Soviet Union, and Great Britain to destroy fascism in Japan, Germany, Italy, and wherever else it might crop up, the organization expressed solidarity with the rank-and-file Japanese, whom the group's leaders felt were exploited and had been forced into war.

On February 26, 1942, the FBI interviewed Killens at its Washington field office. Agent R. F. Ryan asked the standard questions about loyalty and government overthrow before focusing on Killens's connections to the AYC, the

National Negro Congress, and the Washington Committee for Democratic Action. Killens confirmed his past membership in the Washington Committee for Democratic Action, a small group in which he had been involved with Hunton and Frazier, and his current enrollment in the AYC but denied ever having had official status in the National Negro Congress. The final exchange between Ryan and Killens, though, was curious:

> Q. At this time you may have the opportunity of making any statement of your own which you think is pertinent to this inquiry if you so desire.
>
> A. I would like to state at the time of joining the Washington Committee for Democratic Action I did not think it was affiliated with any party or had any affiliations that advocated the overthrow of our Government or disloyalty to our Government. The same is true of the National Negro Congress and the American Youth Congress.
>
> Q. All right, thank you very much.[59]

"The same is true" perhaps represents a moment of imprecise phrasing, but it could also be an admission of membership in the National Negro Congress. Similarly, "at the time of joining" could suggest that party affiliations had at some point become apparent to Killens. Ryan did not press those points, however. Nor did the FBI mention the connection to Harris or any relationship to the Southern Negro Youth Congress.

Killens undoubtedly consulted with fellow activists before the interview. To be summoned to the Washington field office was a quotidian experience in activist circles; a body of lore about handling the visits existed. Killens probably consulted with Frazier, who was subpoenaed the same month and was also queried about the AYC, the National Negro Congress, and the Washington Committee for Democratic Action. On February 16, during his interrogation, Frazier denied being a member of those organizations. He also denied being a member of a fourth activist group, American People's Mobilization.[60]

In March, Hoover wrote to Henry A. Millis, chair of the NLRB, requesting his "official comment as to the ultimate disposition of this case either by exoneration, dismissal or other administrative action." Millis carefully analyzed documents pertinent to the case, including the U.S. Constitution, the Hatch Act, and statutes of the Civil Service Commission, before deciding, "While some significance might be attached to this combination of activities, it appears from the report that Killens is a negro and a member of the National Association for the Advancement of Colored People." Millis continued, "All of the organizations which he joined or whose meetings he attended stress negro rights and oppose racial discrimination. It therefore appears that his explanation of his activities was entirely plausible. Moreover, there is nothing in the report which indicates that Killens himself has any subversive tendencies or beliefs." Millis concluded, "Since this report has not disclosed evidence which would support a prima facie case for dismissal proceedings, the Board is constrained to deem the report tantamount to exoneration."[61] In fact, shortly after the close of the investigation, Killens was promoted to assistant chief property and supply clerk, grade CAF-4, with an annual salary of $1,800.[62]

Being cleared and promoted, though important, seemed a slight gesture given that military service loomed. Killens found the Army Air Corps the most appealing option, and he submitted an application to the Aviation Cadet Examining Board at Bolling Field in Washington. He solicited letters of recommendation from two coworkers at the NLRB, A. B. Hunt and Herbert R. Glazer. On May 16, Hunt described Killens as an "industrious, able and honest employee" and a "loyal and patriotic citizen."[63] Two days later, Glazer weighed in: "He is an outstanding employee in all respects and we place complete confidence in his ability and efficiency."[64] However, Killens's application was nevertheless rejected. What lay ahead was soldiering on land and sea, and it would begin almost as soon as he finished his third year of law classes in June.

The last pressing issue at that point was what to do about Grace Ward Jones. Grace, once described by writer Sarah Wright as "pretty and [not] even bother[ing] to act like it," was an intellectually curious Brooklyn native who already had one great love story in her life.[65] Her father, Thomas Sylvester Jones, a schoolteacher, had courted her mother, Mabel Ward, in their native Barbados. However, when they announced their intention to marry, Mabel's father, Aubrey Ward, objected and sent her to Atlantic City, New Jersey, to stay with her brother, Edrick. After her brother proved disinclined to look after her, she moved in with friends in the Bronx. Thomas left Barbados and found Mabel, whom Killens later described as a "gentle regal woman," in New York. The couple married and produced five children, the fourth of whom was Grace. The elder Jones studied podiatry in New York and eventually opened a practice.[66]

As a Brooklyn College student, Grace Jones attended one of the nation's leading centers of student leftist activism: throughout the 1930s, students waged significant campaigns in support of labor, opposing war, and favoring the college's policies of charging no tuition and low fees. If not a member herself, she certainly knew members of organizations prominent on campus, such as the American Student Union, the AYC, the Young Communist League, and the Young People's Socialist League.[67] After becoming impatient with college life, Grace left school and, through contacts on the left, landed an office job in New York. When her company sent her to Washington, she spent the bulk of her salary on trips back to her hometown. But she remained in the nation's capital long enough to meet John at a party thrown by his brother, Charles—and was largely unimpressed. She recalled, "We danced and I forgot about him."[68] Grace already had a suitor, and she wanted to keep her romantic options open. John resolved to close them. After all, first impression aside, she had left her phone number.[69]

As the summer of 1942 arrived, the twenty-six-year-old Killens, one year from graduation at Terrell, received his induction notice. McMichael and the American Youth Congress activists were wrong. The Yanks were on the way. On July 3, Killens was inducted into the U.S. Army.[70]

CHAPTER FOUR

Chasing the Double Victory, 1942–1945

More than one million African American soldiers served in World War II. Many of them expressed optimism that their loyalty in combating the fascism and imperialism of the Axis powers would signal the demise of institutional racism in the United States. But neither the geopolitical picture nor the domestic outlook would ever be so simple. African American involvement in the titanic global conflict, while indisputably a catalyst for certain changes in national social, economic, and political arrangements, could not be leveraged into an immediate and wholesale revision of the American racial order. That the American military itself was a Jim Crow stronghold spoke volumes about the country's racial situation, even as President Franklin Roosevelt pontificated about the Four Freedoms: freedom of speech and expression, freedom of worship, freedom from want, and freedom from fear.

Those with an ear to the African American community early in 1942 heard a spin somewhat different from that of the president. Numerous blacks articulated pro-Roosevelt, prowar sentiments but firmly connected them to a black empowerment agenda. A working slogan, first popularized by the *Pittsburgh Courier*, was "Double V"—victory over fascism abroad and victory over racism at home. The catchphrase represented a variation of the standard "V for victory" motto and sentiment being adopted by the general populace. The semiotics involved and the agitation for justice by the black press in general drew the wrath of powerful adversaries. A considerable struggle involved the black press, the FBI, the Justice Department, the War Department, and the Post Office. Several African American newspapers were banned from army posts, and officials pursued charges of sedition. The black press, however, hardly bore the blame for the country's internal contradictions. Black-white civilian unity during the war years would be called into question by hundreds of racial conflicts in more than fifty American cities.

In June 1942, attorney general Francis Biddle met with *Chicago Defender* publisher John Sengstacke, who indicated that the black press would be glad to cooperate with the war effort if it received access to government officials instead of being denied interviews, as was the usual practice. The meeting eased tensions, but the black press remained under government surveillance. FBI director J. Edgar Hoover, for example, tried to obtain Espionage Act indictments against the black press until 1945. The Justice Department refused to cooperate, however, and would not allow the Post Office to revoke African American papers' second-class mailing permits.[1]

"Double V" became such a popular rallying cry that African American women translated the words into a hairstyle. John Killens subsequently used the slogan—and the black press's status as an alternative media outlet—to drive the plot of his 1962 war novel, *And Then We Heard the Thunder*, in which protagonist Solly Saunders argues, "We're American citizens and the country is at war and they need us, and when we get back we won't let them forget that we fought like everybody else." However, Saunders and several of his army buddies also write to the *People's Herald*, "Some of us feel that we do not need to go four or five thousand miles away to do battle with the enemies of Democracy. They are present with us here and now and spitting in our faces."[2] The letter embarrasses their superiors, who hurriedly train Saunders and his friends for overseas deployment.

Killens's embrace of Double V was more equivocal than that of his main character. Although he ultimately supported the war, he thoroughly understood and somewhat shared an antiwar perspective also common in the black community, another viewpoint that would convincingly inform *And Then We Heard the Thunder*, where Joseph "Bookworm" Taylor asserts, "Any time Hitler wants to make a landing here, I'll damn sure be his guide. I'll point out all the high spots and hold the friggin' candle."[3]

Bookworm pays a steep price for exhibiting what others perceive as a lack of patriotism, as did numerous real-life African Americans. In 1943, noted writer Roi Ottley reported that Charles Steptoe, a twenty-four-year-old African American, was sentenced to ten days in a workhouse for refusing to stand while the national anthem was being played in a Harlem theater. In addition, according to Ottley, an African American truck driver was charged with treason after telling an African American soldier, "You're a crazy nigger in that uniform—you're only fighting for white trash. This is a white man's government and war and it's no damn good."[4]

Killens, too, was in uniform and was on his way to New Jersey's Fort Dix, where three soldiers had recently been killed and five wounded in a fifteen-minute gun battle between black and white troops.[5] Such incidents, especially because of his proximity to them, loosened the creative talents that had lain submerged since Killens's adolescence. In addition, the outside activities that usually hampered his focus on writing—law school, civil rights work, left-wing organizations—were no longer options. At some point in his military stint, Killens began to sketch seriously his war experiences, a ritual that became increasingly important to him as the war unfolded. Demonstrating his seriousness, Killens began to mail copies of his stories to himself to ensure copyright protection.

The clash at Fort Dix epitomized the prevalent racial strife in the military, especially when white southern officers commanded African American troops. An African American soldier and a white military policeman were killed in a standoff at Fort Bragg, North Carolina. After the shooting, black companies and officers at the post who were not involved were forced to stand all night with their hands above their heads while armed military policeman patrolled the camp.[6] After a tour of military bases in England, Walter White, executive secretary of the National Association for the Advancement of Colored People, reported, "I was puzzled at the frequency, despondency and bitterness of the use of the phrase 'the enemy.' I soon learned that Negro soldiers referred not to Nazis across the channel but to their white fellow-Americans." A particularly disillusioned and angry soldier asked White, "What are we fighting for over here? Are we sent to [Europe] to fight the Nazis—or our white soldiers?"[7] Judge William Hastie, a distinguished African American legal activist who spent an embattled term as a civilian aide to Secretary of War Henry L. Stimson, observed, "The traditional mores of the South have been widely accepted by the Army as the basis of policy and practice affecting the Negro soldier."[8] Hastie resigned in 1943 over the military's recalcitrant racism. He opposed the thinking of General George C. Marshall, Stimson's chief of staff, that the military should not attempt to solve racial problems on a grand scale. An attempt to abrogate the edict "not to shake a nigger's hand" in effect at Camp Upton on Long Island apparently represented too large an undertaking.[9]

Despite the racial tensions there, Fort Dix had benefits for Killens: its proximity to New York enabled him to visit Grace Jones frequently and win her favor. However, he failed to ask her domineering father for his daughter's hand, reasoning, "I wasn't marrying him."[10] The two wed on June 19, 1943, John in full uniform and Grace a week shy of her twenty-fourth birthday. The Killens clan got along well with the Jones family: although Grace had felt some trepidation concerning how the West Indians and the African Americans would interact, "when John's father met my father, it was like they had known each other for years."[11] Killens was shipped to the West Coast later in the year, en route to a tour in the South Pacific. Grace remained at home, carrying the newlyweds' child.

The years 1942 and 1943 were particularly explosive, as military race riots erupted across the United States as well as in England and the South Pacific. The racial event that most captured Killens's imagination was a series of riots in Brisbane, Australia, on March 11–20, 1942.[12] In these clashes, which erupted primarily between black soldiers of the 394th Quartermaster Battalion and white soldiers of the 208th Coast Artillery, U.S. soldiers gunned each other down in the streets. These events directly infused the concluding section of *And Then We Heard the Thunder*. Despite the fictionalized nature of Killens's record (and the fact that he did not witness the riots firsthand), his account is the only published description. News reportage was censored. Trial records have been unavailable. The episode became, as journalist Ted Poston remarked, "one of the best kept secrets of the war."[13] The only official acknowledgment of the riots is a summary report issued the following April 12.[14] Yet references to the incident appear in memos to and from the Office of Strategic Services (the precursor to the Central Intelligence Agency) and in letters from General Douglas MacArthur to Marshall.[15]

MacArthur made his ignominious retreat from the Philippines and landed in Australia on March 21, immediately after the riots. He responded to the racial tension he encountered by developing a plan to utilize African American troops only in sparsely populated areas; however, the need for African American labor meant that his strategy was unworkable. In addition, at the end of March, MacArthur backed the Australian government's request that no additional African American troops be sent to the country and that those already deployed there be shipped to sites such as India and

New Caledonia.[16] The general was correct in his assessment that the racial conflict among GIs in Brisbane resulted from the disproportionately large number of black troops stationed in the city long term. According to one scholar, the Brisbane riots represented tragic highlights in a lengthy psycho-sexual, racial, and practically inevitable drama.[17] Australian troops resented white American soldiers' access to Anglo-Australian women, and these Australian troops sought to preserve their sexual status. As a second scholar has noted, the resentment expressed by Australian troops, especially those returning from combat duty, led to barroom brawls with Americans that made "John Wayne fights look like high school picnics."[18] The Australians eventually lost the battle for dominance and were hardly gracious losers. But they could muster only so much deeply rooted hostility given the U.S. military's important role in protecting Australia. In the uneasy truce, however, Australians felt no need to help white Americans enforce U.S.-style discrimination against African American GIs, whom Australians subsumed under the category "American." The Aussies might even have taken some glee in undermining American racist norms. If so, the joy was conflicted. After all, in their everyday dealings, most Australians were confirmed white supremacists. Eventually, the need to hold the racial line against socializing between black males and white females and against possible miscegenation trumped whatever grudge whites held on the basis of national origins. The Australians, too, erected barriers to social inclusion.

African American soldiers, therefore, had virtually no outlet for their increasing frustration, which was exacerbated by the nature of their assignments. Because of the racial reasoning prevalent in America and in the military, the majority of the African American troops were relegated to noncombat but nonetheless crucial jobs such as fumigation, laundry, road construction, and transportation.[19] The military's racial policies ensured that a large and growing contingent of African American soldiers in Australia would be immobile and restricted to menial tasks. If African Americans had been represented proportionately among the troops who shuttled between Australia and the battlefront, fewer encounters would have occurred between black and white troops in noncombat situations, and black soldiers would have had fewer opportunities to interact with Australian civilians. The scenario was tailor-made for a major race riot.

Because Killens arrived in Brisbane after the riots, he missed on a few details. The George Washington Carver Serviceman's Club mentioned in his novel, for example, was not built until after the riots. This detail also points to the broader fictional time frame of the novel, in which dates remain unspecified because Killens knew that the preriot chronology he constructed was historically inaccurate. A prolonged buildup that involved amphibious training stateside, invasions of Japanese-controlled islands in the Philippines, and months of convalescence in Brisbane for soldiers wounded on the front did not match the fact that the United States had entered the war only three months before the Brisbane disturbances. Conversely, Killens's fascination with the riots, his contact with people in Brisbane, and his tours of the city resulted in a narrative that, on the whole, exhibits fidelity to the events and to the landscape. For example, Killens has Sergeant Hank Williams proclaim, "We're all Americans," before being gunned down by a white American soldier, in keeping with reports that an African American sergeant was killed during the Brisbane riots.[20] In his novel, he faithfully depicts the resentment felt by black GIs who had full access to Brisbane but no escape from debasing treatment by white soldiers.

An Anglo-Australian woman, Celia Blake, escorts Solly Saunders about town—"to the rainbow-colored countryside, to the jungle-clad mountains, to the coral-colored beaches, to the National Art Gallery, to the museum, to the beautiful University campus, scenic and sprawling, to the movies, to Mt Bootha-tha Park, to the pastel-colored bay, to the Bainbridge docks." Once familiar with the terrain, Solly ventures out on his own: "He rode the trams, he rode the trains, he rode the buses. To the beaches, to the parks, to the outskirts of town, to the business district, to the quays." But his wanderings bring him a bitter lesson concerning his status and ultimately the emotion that would eventually lead to black revolt. He encounters Yankee military police, reminiscent of cops in Georgia, who block him from entering clubs even as he hears white American soldiers inside. Solly argues in vain, growing so angry that he thinks his head might "pop wide open."[21]

Although he spent numerous and productive hours as a self-styled correspondent and novelist in training, Killens's official duty in the Pacific theater was to serve as a member of the segregated 813th Amphibian Truck Company, whose primary mission consisted of transporting cargo from offshore ships to dumps or transfer points by using multiterrain vehicles known as ducks. After training on the California coast, the 813th arrived in the South Pacific at the end of 1943.[22] By then, Japanese forces were mainly on the defensive because the Allies had regained control of much of the territory that Japan had taken the previous year when it pressed its advantage in the region after the Pearl Harbor attack. The pivotal Battle of Midway, which turned the tide in favor of the United States, was waged on June 4, 1942, while Killens was winding up the semester at Terrell Law School.[23]

For ending the war, MacArthur, commander-in chief of the southwest Pacific, favored what was known as the South Pacific strategy, which involved a series of land assaults beginning in Australia and extending northwest to New Guinea, the Philippines, and then Japan.[24] The plan reflected the traditional U.S. Army view that the enemy had to be conquered in land battles, and the strategy was not totally devoid of merit. In addition, with an eye toward postwar diplomacy, MacArthur argued that it would be unwise to allow the Philippine people to think that their tribulations at the hands of the Japanese had not been a priority of the highest order.[25] Ultimately, though, MacArthur's plan was driven more by ego and ambition than military and diplomatic judgment. Long considered America's best frontline general, he had committed several tactical blunders as he suffered a humiliating defeat in the Philippines, barely managing to escape. MacArthur was determined to make good on his famous promise, "I shall return," and Roosevelt consented to let the general try, although it would bring formidable Japanese land forces back into the fray. And John Oliver Killens and the men of the 813th Amphibian Truck Company had little choice but to tag along.

As Killens and the 813th followed the fighting, he learned of the birth of his son, Jon Charles, on March 4, 1944. Killens needed no extra motivation to try to return home safely, but his anxiety certainly escalated. Killens would not see his son for almost two years, and he could only fret about how and what the boy was doing and offer only indirect protection. And how would he eventually bond with little Chuck?

On October 1, 1944, the 813th, led by Lieutenant John Constantino, was attached to the U.S. Sixth Army, commanded by General Walter Krueger, who was asked to play a major role in the recapture of New Guinea and the Philippines. The first target in the Philippines would be the southern island of Leyte, which would serve as a springboard to Luzon, the largest, northernmost, and most important of the islands, where lay the prized city of Manila, location of the only urban battle of the Pacific War.

On October 18, the ss *Frank J. Cuhel* pulled anchor at Humboldt Bay in Hollandia, New Guinea, and joined a tremendous convoy—MacArthur's invasion force included an armada of 430 transports, while Krueger's Sixth Army consisted of 174,000 troops. Although the historical significance of this troop movement—it surpassed the Normandy landing in scope—would have been unknown to Killens at the time he participated in it and perhaps even when he completed *And Then We Heard the Thunder*, the voyage to Leyte is the source for what he described in the novel as the "Big Invasion":

> Nine days later they steamed out of Calhoun Bay on an LST and made off to another point where they would join a task force made up mostly of Land- ing Ship Tanks. Their Ducks were on board with them. Two days later they joined the rest of the convoy and put boldly and nervously out to sea. It was the biggest task force Solly ever dreamed of. As far as you could see in all directions were LSTs bobbing up and down on the vast Pacific with the curi- ous rhythm of a prize fighter like hammering Henry Armstrong. Bobbing and weaving—weaving and bobbing. The LST was sturdy and seaworthy, they said, but she had no keel and her bottom was flat and shapeless, and when the waves were foamy she gave you many anxious moments. . . .
>
> He didn't know how many ships were in the task force. He estimated about a hundred and seventy-five LSTs, a complement of destroyers and mine sweepers and battleships and troopships and a couple of giant aircraft carriers, destroyer escorts, torpedo boats, and God and General Buford Jack only knew what others or how many others. Like the captain said, this is why your mama's baby boy was born.[26]

On October 20, while the *Cuhel* was still steaming along the 1,240-mile route from Hollandia to Leyte, MacArthur landed, wading through the water as cameras caught every practiced move. "Rally to me!" he exhorted the Philippine people.[27] As the infantry moved north across the island, American, Australian, and Japanese ships prepared to do battle offshore. What became known as the Battle of Leyte Gulf, which began on Octo- ber 23 and was waged in three separate locations, is the greatest naval en- gagement in world history, involving 282 ships and more than 200,000 men. Scores of vessels were sunk, hundreds of aircraft were destroyed, and thousands of lives were sacrificed. As one historian has noted, "Every aspect of naval warfare—air, surface, submarine, and amphibious—was involved in this great struggle, and the weapons used included bombs of every type, guns of every caliber, torpedoes, mines, rockets, and even a forerunner of the guided missile."[28]

On October 24, the *Cuhel* dropped anchor in San Pedro Bay, but Kil- lens and the 813th remained aboard for five more days. By October 26, the

Battle of Leyte Gulf had turned into a decisive victory for the Allies. Although they eventually secured Leyte itself, Japan still controlled the air in the vicinity, and repeated bombing and strafing slowed the Allied advance. During this period, the men of the 813th heard the round-the-clock air attacks and witnessed the crash of several enemy planes. Most of the Japanese planes that were destroyed had been shot down, but at Leyte Gulf, the Japanese officially unleashed kamikazes, who deliberately crashed their planes into Allied targets.[29] The kamikazes, a devastating weapon that would sink more American ships during the war than any other technique, failed to save Japan, but they signaled the desperation of a military that was by then operating at a distinct hardware disadvantage.

On October 29, the 813th landed on Red Beach, Leyte, the scene of MacArthur's arrival nine days earlier. After being caught in a typhoon, the company broke camp on October 30 and moved to San Jose, Leyte, amid intermittent bombing and strafing. Four days later, the men were again on the move, convoying to Tacloban, the capital of Leyte, and setting up a site along Cancabato Bay. On November 4, they witnessed heavy Japanese bombing and strafing—twenty-three red alerts over a twenty-four hour period. As Killens wrote in *And Then We Heard the Thunder*, "It was an uncomfortable business making trip after trip from the beach to the ships out in the bay with the bombs and shrapnel dropping all around you unconcernedly."[30] As if manufactured perils were not enough to cope with, the 813th was hit by another typhoon on November 8.

Despite casualties and other hardships, the Allied advance in the Philippines counted as a political success for Roosevelt: he garnered 53 percent of the popular vote in the election on November 11. Although the margin was the smallest in any of his four victories, the result was, given his political vulnerability, an impressive feat, aided immeasurably not only by MacArthur but also by Marshall. In addition to taking place when the loss of American lives in the war had reached the hundreds of thousands, the 1944 presidential campaign was the first one during which the debacle at Pearl Harbor and Roosevelt's connection to it could be placed on the campaign agenda. Roosevelt's main rival, New York governor Thomas E. Dewey, intended to press the issue of Roosevelt's foreknowledge of the attack. Such a tactic, however, would have involved official discussion of the nation's intelligence operations, activity that Marshall thought to be unwise. Marshall, normally nonpartisan, therefore prevailed on Dewey to abandon that aspect of his campaign strategy.

The 813th broke camp near Tacloban on December 8 and traveled eighteen miles to Tanauan, setting up a bivouac area along the beach between Tanauan and Toolosa. On December 20, amid another red alert, an enemy plane plunged into Leyte Bay, and events here inspired another passage in *And Then We Heard the Thunder*: "From under the truck you could still see some of the silver stuff flashing across the brilliant sky and going into dives and pulling out again and laying their eggs of death and the earth beneath erupting, and one of the silvery buzzards swooped toward a ship in the bay and dropped its egg and climbed upward again like a sea gull. It was a direct hit and the ship jumped fifty feet in the air with pieces flying everywhere and arms and legs and other debris and heads and bodies and settled back onto the water quietly and burning and disappearing into the bay."[31]

In the Philippines, Killens observed the numerous casualties that would lead him to describe his South Pacific experience as one of the "smell of blood and shit and suffering."[32] At one point he told Grace, "I'm writing from my old reliable fox hole. The planes have been coming in all day long. Tojo dropped two devastating eggs in our neighborhood's front yard—just about fifty feet away."[33] He also sent fiction manuscripts home, some delivered by his old friend Pierce Brunson, who was stationed in the Philippines and returned to the States before Killens did. Brunson made the trek to Brooklyn to deliver a bundle of pages written in longhand.

With 1944 drawing to a close, Killens wrote a ten-page letter, "With the Amphibians in the Philippines," in which he reflected on the fact that he had not seen his wife for the entire calendar year—what he described as an "unbearable separation." He was "counting on 1945 to be quite different, to bring us together again—never to separate. Good ol' 1945! Please be good to John O." He also inquired about his son, who had been visited by John's brother, Charles, and his wife and had seemed to take to them: "Well, that just shows to go you or goes to show that he definitely possesses discriminating taste. Either that or that he has none at all. You figure it out."[34]

Just prior to writing the letter, John Killens had seen the film adaptation of James Thurber and Elliott Nugent's play, *The Male Animal*. It was the first movie he had seen since his arrival in the Philippines. Although he had seen the film a few years earlier when he was a civilian, he expressed new appreciation for Henry Fonda's portrayal of the university professor threatened with dismissal for daring to read to his class an essay by Bartolomeo Vanzetti, who had been railroaded to execution with Nicola Sacco in 1927.[35]

Killens then turned to contemporary politics: "Sweetheart of mine, I certainly hope you're right in your assurances of a better America for us GI's to come back to, one devoid of fear, poverty and suffering and full of the four freedoms with another one added—freedom from racial discrimination. That's what the GI's are fighting for." He told of witnessing the Japanese bombing of a "harmless Philippino dwelling": "I don't believe I was ever any angrier. I was almost moved to tears. Why is the word justice in the dictionary? What's Webster attempting to put over on us?" He believed that the war was far from won but expressed cautious optimism: "We can ill-afford complacency from anyone at home or overseas. We must continue to win the all-important battle of production. There must not be the slightest let-up."[36] He closed by reminding Grace that he was "still in top shape" and facetiously speculating that maybe he was in love.[37]

On February 3, 1945, the forces of MacArthur and Krueger recaptured Manila. Allied strategists then eyed the home islands of Japan, whose leaders vowed to fight to the end rather than to accept an unconditional surrender. The subsequent capture of Iwo Jima and Okinawa, ferocious bombing raids, and a stifling naval blockade solidified the invasion plans. The 813th seemed destined to join another massive invasion convoy. The company viewed the Army film *Two Down and One to Go* on May 20 and watched *On to Tokyo* on June 28.[38] The immediate destination would be the Japanese home island of Kyushu. But President Roosevelt would not oversee the war's conclusion; after his death on April 12, that task fell to Harry S. Truman.

When Germany surrendered on May 8, Truman had to update his assessment of Japan's remaining strength and the intentions of an important ally, the Soviet Union. Seventy Imperial Japanese Army divisions, more than one million soldiers, were set to defend their homeland. Truman and most of his strategists figured that the fighting would be protracted and the loss of lives staggering. An invasion could cost more American lives than all the war's other battles combined. By June, Truman preferred the atomic bomb as an alternative, though he had at least one other motive beyond saving American soldiers. The Soviet Union, Japan's most feared enemy historically, was scheduled to declare war on Japan on August 8. Truman distrusted Stalin and considered excessive his demands in return for intervention; therefore, the U.S. president sought to force the Japanese capitulation before the almost certainly decisive Soviet entry.[39]

On July 17, while in Potsdam, Truman received word of the successful test of the bomb in Alamogordo, New Mexico. On July 26, the Potsdam Declaration, promising "prompt and utter destruction" in the absence of a surrender, was broadcast to Japan, while bombers dropped paper copies of the document throughout the home islands.[40] The Japanese were unyielding. On July 29, a Japanese submarine sank the cruiser *Indianapolis*, killing more than eight hundred U.S. crewmen. The loss could have been prevented, but American leaders failed to protect the cruiser because they underestimated the remaining strike capacity and resolve of a fighting force that barely resembled the once fearsome Imperial Japanese Navy. But the *Indianapolis* had already delivered the detonation device for the world's first nuclear weapon.

On August 6, U.S. forces dropped the atomic bomb on Hiroshima, instantly incinerating seventy-eight thousand people. On August 9, after the Soviet Union fulfilled its promise by declaring war on Japan, the Americans dropped another A-bomb on Nagasaki, immediately causing twenty-four thousand more Japanese fatalities. Five days later, the Japanese surrendered unconditionally.

Killens and the other soldiers in his outfit were immensely relieved to hear that the war had all but ceremonially ended. Fifty million lives had been lost worldwide. One soldier in the 813th advised Killens and his comrades, "The thing they should do now is dump the rest of those fucking bombs in the middle of the Pacific, destroy the formula, then round up all the bloody scientists who know anything about the formula and blow their fucking brains out!"[41]

CHAPTER FIVE

None as Radical as Mickey Mouse, 1945–1948

Sergeant John Oliver Killens was released from the military on December 3, 1945, exactly forty-one months after his induction. He was one month away from his thirtieth birthday. He came home to reunite with his wife and meet his son, who was almost two years old. Although he had been away from Grace much longer than they had been together, the two were definitely still in love. Killens created a stir, however, when he announced soon after coming home that he had changed his career plans. Rather than working as a lawyer, he wanted to become a professional writer, work that he believed could constitute a crucial part of his social contribution: "I had been turned by the war into some sort of half-assed revolutionary. With the stench of blood and shit still in my nostrils, I reasoned that a lawyer was not a revolutionary by the very nature of his position in society."[1] To his younger brother Richard, he simply said, "I want to tell the truth."[2] Family and friends tried to dissuade him from making this vocational shift: his distressed father-in-law gently reminded Killens that Paul Robeson had completed his law degree. But Grace supported her husband's decision, and hers was the only other voice that really mattered. In retrospect, she explained to poet Michael Harper, "I don't think I would have wanted John to be a lawyer. You know, with that kind of security, because it makes my life more interesting when you're taking chances, and when you're doing things you really want to do. I mean, becoming an artist is a very hazardous thing when you're trying to raise a family. But I think it's more rewarding in your life if you're able to do exactly what you want, even though you don't have [security], even though it's a struggle."[3]

Killens returned to Washington and on February 1, 1946, reported for work at the National Labor Relations Board, where he was assigned to the Supplies Section as a property and supply clerk, grade CAF-4, at an annual salary of $2,232.[4] After three months, he was reassigned to the Administrative Statistics Section as a statistical clerk. But much of his real work took place after hours, when he grappled with the prose he had generated during his tour in the army.

The writing was clearly of apprentice quality. His descriptive abilities did not yet approach those of his primary model, Richard Wright, and Killens's work lacked the poetic flair for which he would become known. He relied too heavily on dialogue to develop characters and scenes. Plotting emerged as his strength. With a bit more revision, "Things Might Have Been," a story written in the legal ledger he sometimes favored, might have drawn favorable comparisons to Wright's "Long Black Song." Narrated from the son's point of view, "Things Might Have Been" explores the character of the mother, Dollie, who suffers from alcoholism largely as a consequence of constraints imposed on her in a racist and sexist environment. Dollie's drinking habit leads her to an undesirable hangout; her husband, George, eventually arrives to take her home. A white man, Robert Jackson, accosts Dollie; George defends her honor. When the incident turns violent, George kills Jackson in a clear case of self-defense but is nonetheless convicted and executed. George is certainly a victim, and Dollie's actions directly contribute to his death, but the reader is also left to ponder how much George influenced Dollie's character. Forecasting his published work, Killens depicts the brutality of southern racism while avoiding strictly black-white, Manichaean conflict and gestures toward African American female interiority. Thus, the contours of the story resemble Wright's tale, in which Silas is killed after a chain of events set in motion by Sarah's tryst with a white salesman. That the son narrates Killens's story portends another feature of the author's published fiction that distinguishes it sharply from Wright's: children are generally central.

Killens sketched other vignettes and character studies involving southern racism; he also wrote about male-female romances and his military experiences. He felt especially drawn to revisit and refine drafts about his war experiences but knew he hovered too close to the material emotionally to try to craft it extensively at that point.[5] For his most sustained composing, then, he focused on accounts of his childhood and union activism.

Robert Travers occupies the center of one major story. More commonly referred to as Bobby, he is an African American youth in Gibbsville, Alabama, who belongs to a close-knit family. The story re-creates episodes from Killens's childhood, including the battle at the crossroads. Heightening the dramatic tension, although the scene is underdeveloped overall, Killens portrays Bobby as one of the children beaten by his mother and indicates how that action breaks the bond of trust between son and mother. When Bobby subsequently is mistreated by Hawkins, the white proprietor of a grocery store, and retaliates by throwing a tomato in his face before fleeing, the boy is reluctant to tell his mother, Laurie, what has transpired. On this occasion, however, Laurie fully backs her son. When Hawkins demands that Bobby be beaten, Laurie refuses. Hawkins threatens her, but she seizes an iron and stands her ground, thereby regaining her son's trust, and he eventually blossoms into a trade union leader.[6]

While Killens attempted to shape his various scenes into a novel, the pull of activism as well as his day job slowed his progress. He faced a contradiction with which he would wrestle for the next forty years: the perpetual need for solitude to write and his insatiable desire to participate concretely in social movements. He aimed to be both a writer and an activist who would help on the front lines.

One point of intervention involved soldiers who returned from the war. Although Killens enjoyed relative security at the National Labor Relations Board, he remembered his vow to fight for a better America. This meant, in part, agitating on behalf of beleaguered African American servicemen, and the treatment of Isaac Woodward helped to catalyze Killens's efforts. South Carolina police accused Woodward, an African American soldier en route from Fort Gordon, Georgia, to North Carolina, of public drunkenness and beat him severely, blinding him. The ensuing publicity, which included a protest by the National Association for the Advancement of Colored People and condemnation by President Harry S. Truman, spurred Killens; his brother-in-law, Thomas Russell Jones; prominent journalist George B. Murphy Jr.; and future Detroit mayor Coleman Young to form an interracial advocacy group. More than four hundred veterans convened at the National Conference for a National Veterans' Organization held on April 6 and 7 at Chicago's Du Sable High School, with white activist and veteran Bertram Alves serving as chair, and heavyweight champion Joe Louis as honorary chair. Provisional committees issued a "reveille" proclaiming, "Fascism is not dead! It threatens us right here at home! In Congress there are the Rankins, Bilbos, Ellenders, and Eastlands. They spread the foul poisons of Jim Crow, Anti-Semitism, Race Hate, and Lynching."[7] Attendees formed committees, conducted elections, convened discussion groups, and heard reports.

By the close of the proceedings, the group had adopted the name United Negro and Allied Veterans of America. Killens was named commander of the Washington, D.C., chapter and presided over a three-day conference there from May 31 to June 2. The Washington "reveille" echoed the one sounded the previous month in Chicago but added local notes: "Right here in Washington the returning veteran meets segregation and discrimination as he seeks living quarters at the War Housing Agency, or as he seeks a job at the United States Employment Service."[8] Killens reiterated these points during his keynote speech at the Vermont Avenue Baptist Church. As with nearly every group he had joined, the United Negro and Allied Veterans of America was subjected to red-baiting and other oppositional tactics that compromised the possibility of long-term effectiveness.[9]

But there was still the labor movement, which held prospects more exciting to Killens than clerking at the labor board. On August 13, he took a leave without pay to organize full time for unions such as the United Federal Workers of America and the United Cafeteria Workers under the auspices of the Committee for Industrial Organization (CIO), headed by John L. Lewis, president of the United Mine Workers of America. The CIO, founded in 1935, was a more progressive and political organization than the dominant American Federation of Labor, and the CIO's approach became the choice among African American workers, who believed that it represented the best chance for, in Alphaeus Hunton's words, "that complete unity of labor which in turn means a powerful labor movement." By 1946, the CIO totaled more than six million workers. Moreover, in addition to Hunton, Robeson and W. E. B. Du Bois supported the CIO, endorsements that carried great weight with Killens.[10]

During a blizzard that struck the East Coast during 1947, Killens and a coworker traveled to New York to meet with Robeson and ask him to give a benefit performance in Washington for the striking cafeteria staff at Howard University, whom Killens proudly labeled "militant Black women workers." After several days, Killens and his coworker connected with Robeson and were invited to his Manhattan apartment. When Robeson agreed to do the concert, Killens offered to have the union cover the cost of his travel and living expenses. Robeson declined, explaining that he would get to Washington on his own and knew many places where he could spend the night. He then told Killens and the other man that no thanks were necessary because he was doing it for himself. Killens was taken aback by Robeson's generosity but later reflected, "How many of us have reached this epitome of understanding? That when you fight in the interest of your people, you are fighting for yourself in the profoundest sense?" More than ever, Robeson became Killens's model of activism: "He was us and we were him, he was so much a part of his people. It was like Earl Robinson wrote of old Abe Lincoln, 'It was impossible to tell where the people left off and where Paul Robeson began.'"[11]

Despite Robeson's support, organized labor managed only Sisyphean progress. For the most part, unions gained strength after the National Labor Relations Act was passed and upheld. However, the Taft-Hartley Act represented a significant defeat. The law restricted the nature of union shops, forbade certain kinds of strikes and boycotts, exempted some employers from bargaining with unions, and required unions to declare that they did not support the Communist Party. President Truman vigorously opposed the proposed law, but Congress passed the bill over his veto on June 23, 1947. Exactly one week later, a politically cautious Killens resigned officially from the National Labor Relations Board, giving only "personal reasons" as an explanation.[12] He continued his work for the CIO.

On January 22, 1947, eight days after her father's thirty-first birthday, Barbara Ellen Killens joined the family. John Killens later described his daughter as bouncy, always running headlong into life. Killens was a good parent, attentive, supportive, and generous. He played with his kids, especially basketball with Chuck, and helped to monitor their schoolwork and overall intellectual development. He took pride in introducing his children to Robeson and Langston Hughes. In later years, he encouraged the teenage Chuck to become a literary critic, giving him the task of comparing the newly completed *And Then We Heard the Thunder* with the prior *Youngblood*. He was pleased when the boy concluded that the second novel beat the first.

By the end of the year, Killens had completed a typed draft of "Stony the Road We Trod," a 642-page manuscript dedicated to his mother, wife, and children and "to the never ceasing struggle against racial bigotry and fascism."[13] The manuscript resembles *Youngblood* enough to be termed a draft of the novel, featuring the fictionalized setting of his boyhood Macon; numerous autobiographical anecdotes; the idealized African American family of four at the heart of the story; the son who becomes central to the town's union movement; the exemplary progressive white unionist; and Mr. Myles, the northern-bred schoolteacher who is an intellectual spark plug (as well as Myles Killens's namesake). However, this early version differs significantly from the later novel in several important respects. First, "Stony the Road We Trod" is much more of a classic proletarian vehicle than is *Youngblood*. Whereas the plot of *Youngblood* is driven by a series of encounters that indicate the full range of black-white interaction in the Jim Crow South—issues of education, culture, and civil rights are highlighted as much as an economic agenda—the action in "Stony the Road We Trod" is dominated by labor issues. Although calamities and atrocities of Jim Crow life provide the background, the mission to bring a progressive trade union to Gibbsville, Alabama, is the overriding dynamic.

In a scene reminiscent of the Cocky Glover episode, the narrative of "Stony the Road We Trod" begins with a wild shootout between white policemen and Billy Johnson, a nineteen-year-old African American. But Johnson is more admirable politically than Glover. The authorities hunt Johnson after he retaliates physically against Ransom, Johnson's straw boss at Barkels Bakery, who harassed and assaulted Johnson because the youth had been organizing the African American workers at the bakery to protest "starvation wages."[14] After killing two policemen and fleeing the scene, Johnson is eventually captured and executed. The incident, which serves as prophecy, becomes one of the earliest memories for the story's young protagonist, Bobby Travers, whose fledgling grasp of racism thus becomes connected to an instance of worker activism.

A second prophetic encounter involves Rob Sweet, another African American martyr, who inspires seven-year-old Bobby to read the "right kind of books" and leaves behind a library of critical work. Bobby reaches intellectual maturity under the guidance of his mentor and study partner, Dick Myles. His mother, Laurie Travers, though not as learned as Sweet or Myles, instills in the boy a vision—also a prophecy that comes to fruition in the tale—of "leaders, white, black and yellow fighting side by side for the cause of freedom for everyone."[15]

The fight that Laurie foretells, which is largely a labor fight, intensifies as the mill workers who toil for Gibbsville's patriarch, Joshua Gibbs, begin to clamor for increased wages, shorter hours, and better working conditions. At the same time, rumors abound that the National Labor Brotherhood has targeted Gibbsville as part of a campaign to organize in the South. Management tries to dissuade workers with a typical response: "Do you know what else joining this radical communist organization would mean? It would mean having to open your doors to nigger membership. That's exactly what these goddam Yankee nigger lovers stand for!" Gibbs, however, has little to fear from the National Labor Brotherhood, a thinly disguised American Federation of Labor. Refusing to buck the South's racist mores, the brotherhood lacks commitment to an interracial union, the only sort that could break Gibbs's stranglehold on labor. After failing to convince visiting union organizers to pursue a strategy of uniting white and black workers, Myles sarcastically remarks, "Yes, that's what I like about these so-called radical labor organizations. Not one of them are as radical as Mickey Mouse."[16]

Radicalism comes to Gibbsville only in the form of the National Industrial Organization (NIO), a stand-in for the CIO, which challenges the National Labor Brotherhood's "smug complacency." Killens describes the NIO as "young and militant and . . . founded on the premise that the modern trend of industry calls for industrial unionism as opposed to craft unionism. It takes a firm stand on the issue of Negro workers."[17]

A study session marks the transition to the second half of the story, when Travers becomes a mill worker and union activist:

> They worked late that night. Dick's heart warmed at the eagerness with which Bob tackled the subject. The fire of youth, Dick thought. Here was a new thing to Bob. Industrial organization—vertical trade unionism. Let's look at this thing. How will it affect the trade union movement? Far into the night they talked about it—N.I.O.—Organized everybody.
>
> "How will the Negro workers be affected?"
>
> "New day for the Negro in the labor unions?"
>
> "What's the N.I.O. policy toward the black worker?"
>
> "—following a positive policy of non jim crow—integrating the Negro worker into the labor movement—"
>
> "—no more playing the role of the scab, the strike breaker—"
>
> "How about the south? N.I.O. coming south?"

"—Don't know—can't see how they can pass it up though. Lot of industry down here. Virgin field for industrial organization—they claim they're going to organize workers the country over. That means north, south, east, west."

"That's gonna be some union—no kidding!"

The NIO's Local 415, full of the spirit of "black and white, unite and fight," is thus born under the presidency of Oscar Grady, a forward-thinking white worker. Travers becomes cochair of the Action Committee. Solidarity runs high; workers perform such songs as "Union Maid," "Hold the Fort," and "Joe Hill" in the meeting hall. The National Labor Relations Board orders the disestablishment of the Loyal Employees Association of Gibbsville, a ploy by Gibbs to undermine real worker progress, after an election in which the workers at the mills chose the NIO over the Loyal Employees by a vote of 3,000 to 506.[18]

As in any good union story—and "Stony the Road We Trod" is a good union story though not a great novel—the most heightened drama involves the inevitable strike and the attempt to break it with guile, intimidation, bribes, frame-ups, violence, and racial division. However, the union survives, even triumphs. As part of the story's resolution, Travers instructs the membership, "White supremacy and exploitation. They are two cut from the same pattern. One sustains the other. The economic royalists exploit the ignorant myth of white supremacy to its greatest extent and then some. The southern tradition fosters a deliberate plan of divide and rule." John O'Hara, a white union organizer who, along with Myles and Travers, forms part of the author's ensemble alter ego, offers Bob a job in the North, but Bob casts his lot with the South's burgeoning labor struggle.[19] It is a story of unqualified success, a good deal more than the CIO and its Operation Dixie actually achieved during the 1940s.

A second major plot difference between "Stony the Road We Trod" and *Youngblood* is the interracial marriage between Dick Myles and Geraldine Gibbs, Joshua Gibbs's Radcliffe-educated daughter. At several points in the story, white antiunionists assert that integrated unions would be a precursor to miscegenation, with black men marrying Gibbsville's white daughters. The Myles-Gibbs marriage fulfills this prophecy, though ironically, since white workers had nothing to fear concerning their daughters and Myles. Only the boss's daughter—the symbol and potential continuity of the Gibbs regime—captures Myles's attention and personal affection. Killens thus disrupts capital's power in Gibbsville and presumably cuts off its lineage. Unlike Bob Travers, Myles and Gibbs could not reside in Alabama. Yet they represent one logical extreme of "black and white, unite and fight," and their child suggests a new order of being, progressive, antiracist, prounion—a socialist even by birthright.

As always with Killens's early fiction, a reading through the prism of Wright's work is instructive. Killens may have been engaging, in fact, in a specific rewriting of an aspect of *Native Son*. Geraldine Gibbs is very much a Mary Dalton figure, and Myles originally criticizes her as such. Mary's death at the terrified hands of Bigger Thomas leaves us with no way to know how progressive she might have become. Myles is the anti-Bigger who can live on, both in his own physical life and through progeny, and interact on an equal basis with whites.

"Stony the Road We Trod" is also different from *Youngblood* and linked to Wright's fiction by the prevalence of speeches. It is almost as though Max has escaped from the last book of *Native Son* to orate and write letters on behalf of the movement in Gibbsville. Killens's fiction always remained somewhat preachy and expository, but this early manuscript takes it to greater extremes than do later works. He still had much ground to cover in terms of developing his dramatic sense, his ability to deepen character and control pace. Joe Travers, Bob's father, is very passive and underdeveloped; Dick Myles remains one dimensional, without romance, for far too long. In addition, Killens, when his academic side dominated his vernacular sensibility, was still prone to using stilted phrases such as "the July sun asserted itself in no uncertain terms" and "no air at all bestirred itself."[20] However, insofar as such flaws were correctable through diligence, the massive manuscript, already the product of a long series of experiments, served notice that Killens had the talent and discipline to succeed.

During the final days of 1947, Killens received a note in response to a query he had sent to Leo Huberman, a noted labor activist and a founder of the *Monthly Review*. Huberman told Killens that he would find it difficult to secure a publisher. The book business was bad, but more problematic was the political climate, in which "a novel with social significance has very little chance." Huberman thought Killens's best opportunity lay with Boni and Gaer.[21] Joseph Gaer, a Russian-born Jew, taught at Berkeley in the early 1930s and served as editor in chief of the Federal Writers Project from 1935 to 1939 and as publicity director of the Political Action Committee for the CIO between 1943 and 1945 before becoming president of Boni and Gaer in

1946. But Gaer, though sympathetic toward Killens and his project, did not have the resources to take on a novel of that size.

Killens's stance toward his manuscript began to change. By the summer of 1948, he had become disenchanted with the CIO. The union caved in to pressure to purge itself of its more radical elements, losing its original promise and coming to resemble the American Federation of Labor more than Killens's NIO. *Youngblood* contains no specific mention of a union name.

As the CIO became more and more a sign of the splintering and collapsing Left, Killens took hope in the newly formed Progressive Party and the candidacy of Henry Wallace, to both of which, many observers believed, was tied the future of progressive politics in America. Wallace had helped to swing his native state, Iowa, for Franklin Roosevelt in 1932 and was elected vice president in 1940. Truman appointed Wallace secretary of commerce, but he often found himself at odds with the chief executive. On September 12, 1946, Wallace delivered a speech at Madison Square Garden in which he criticized the administration's uncompromising policy toward the Soviet Union. He thought that U.S. policy catered too much to Winston Churchill, who had made his famous "iron curtain" speech in Fulton, Missouri, the preceding March with Truman on the dais.

Truman subsequently asked Wallace to resign, and Wallace complied, eventually becoming editor of the *New Republic*. Early in 1948, Du Bois urged him to put journalism on hold and run as a third-party candidate for the U.S. presidency. Du Bois stumped for Wallace at Harlem's Golden Gate Ballroom in February and appeared with him at the Progressive Party convention in Philadelphia. The new political entity needed to pull a large chunk of the New Deal coalition voters to become a viable political force, with some estimates holding that Wallace would need to attract four million votes for the campaign to be successful and keep the positions of the Progressive Party a respectable part of public debate.[22]

Killens did volunteer work for the Wallace campaign but also felt an intense need to push forward with his writing. During the summer of 1948, he took two months off from the campaign and his increasingly tenuous union job. He traveled to New York and, utilizing GI Bill benefits, enrolled in creative writing workshops at Columbia University. One course was taught by Dorothy Brewster, an intellectually energetic sixty-five-year-old who had edited *A Book of Modern Short Stories* and with fellow faculty member Angus Burwell had cowritten *Dead Reckonings in Fiction*. Brewster also had worked with Ralph Ellison and Myra Page in the left-wing League of American Writers, serving with those two on the editorial board of the league's journal, *Clipper*. In addition, she knew Wright, who by then had published *Uncle Tom's Children, Native Son, 12 Million Black Voices*, and *Black Boy*.

In Brewster's workshop, Killens read a selection based on the fight between black and white children in which he had participated as a boy in Macon. Brewster told him it was a powerful scene but that its full potential was unrealized. Nonetheless, she acknowledged he had talent and compared his descriptive power to that of Wright. Such praise dispelled any doubts Killens harbored about his literary aspirations and made him manic about rewriting and improving. He was keenly conscious of the fact that he was thirty-two years old and that when Wright had published *Native Son* in 1940, he had been thirty-one. When the semester ended on August 13, Killens returned to Washington to gather his family and belongings. He had always preferred New York to Washington, and he decided that to realize his dreams, New York was the only place to be.

CHAPTER SIX

The Efficacy of Struggle, 1948–1949

The Wallace campaign failed. Despite the throng of fifty thousand people who attended a September 10 rally at Yankee Stadium sponsored by the American Labor Party—the party in which John and Grace Killens were registered voters—election results proved disheartening for the Left.[1]

No one expected a Wallace victory, but the Progressive Party candidate drew barely a million votes and was shut out in the Electoral College. Moreover, he did not even finish third in the popular vote. Strom Thurmond, the arch-segregationist and secessionist senator from South Carolina, outpolled him.

Killens expressed disappointment about the outcome but denied that he had had any illusions.[2] However, illusions are part of what gave him the zeal to tackle cultural and political problems. He took hope from the Harlem political scene. Meetings and rallies regularly brought him into contact with Paul Robeson, Alphaeus Hunton, W. E. B. Du Bois, Langston Hughes, and Ewart Guinier, who also had been active in the United Public Workers and the American Labor Party and who would mount a respectable challenge to Robert Wagner during the 1949 election for the borough presidency of Manhattan. According to Ossie Davis, "John was always in high gear, always headed toward some conflict. If you avoided John on one block, you'd run into [fellow activist writer] Julian Mayfield on the next."[3]

Under the influence of such noted African American leaders, Killens began to express keen interest in the African political scene. Like his mentors, he saw a link between the project to decolonize Africa and the African American liberation struggle. As Hunton taught, "Racial oppression and exploitation have a universal pattern, and whether they occur in South Africa, Mississippi or New Jersey, they must be exposed and fought as part of a worldwide system of oppression, the fountain-head of which is today among the reactionary and fascist-minded ruling circles of white America."[4] Proponents of this approach saw the masses of Africans and African Americans as natural allies in a battle against capitalism, imperialism, and Jim Crow. In the Old Left analysis to which Killens subscribed, these groups also had natural allies among the working class as a whole. But perhaps because he thought the labor movement had grown too conservative about interracial solidarity and because of the flameout of the Wallace campaign, the idea of subjugated African people in alliance with an oppressed nation of African Americans provided Killens with needed intellectual and emotional energy.

The Council on African Affairs (CAA) served as a focal point for his political efforts. Established in 1937, the CAA was the primary American entity bringing attention to Africans' problems and struggles. In addition to providing speakers, films, and reports, the council organized direct aid to Africa—for example, collecting funds for the families of twenty-six miners gunned down on November 19, 1949, during a strike in the coal pits of Enugu, Nigeria. Hunton had become the educational director of the council in 1943 while on leave from Howard University. The following year, he resigned from Howard and moved to New York to carry on the council's work full time. Killens worked with Hunton, distributing leaflets, doing clerical work, and participating in street rallies.

The council's work never proceeded smoothly. Chronically underfunded and harassed by McCarthyite forces, the organization also endured early internal power struggles, particularly between Robeson, Du Bois, and Hunton on one side and executive director Max Yergan on the other. A founder of the CAA who once hosted Communist Party leader Earl Browder in his home, Yergan had begun to reinvent himself politically in the face of anticommunist hysteria, some of which was aimed at the CAA. He charged that communists were running the organization, fired Hunton, and then tried to seize control from Robeson, the council's chair. After a series of moves and countermoves, Yergan, who committed several fiscal improprieties and later ranged so far to the right that he became an apologist for apartheid South Africa, was expelled.[5]

Around the same time, Du Bois was forced out of the National Association for the Advancement of Colored People (NAACP), partly because of his position on Africa. As a special researcher for the association, Du Bois was already at odds with its executive committee over several issues when he composed a September 7, 1948, memo explaining his refusal to provide executive secretary Walter White with a report outlining the various issues of interest to the NAACP that were likely to arise during a Paris meeting of the United Nations later that month, a gathering White was scheduled to attend. Du Bois thought that White had offered grossly inadequate feedback about prior suggestions concerning foreign policy, especially with respect to the "Darker Races outside the United States and particularly in Africa," and refused to attend a meeting with White, submitting the memo instead.[6] Du Bois subsequently moved his headquarters, which was also the center of his activities on the peace, civil rights, labor, and national liberation fronts, to the CAA, becoming vice chair in 1949.

Killens kept a copy of Du Bois's memo among his personal effects, although he never dared an attempt to get close to Du Bois. In Killens's view, "You, the great unwashed, do not call yourself a personal friend of the Patriarch, no matter how much you revere him. And that's the image he evoked for me."[7] In addition, Killens feared becoming a target of Du Bois's arrogance, impatience, and biting wit: when he found himself seated next to Du Bois during a banquet, Killens promptly switched to another table.[8]

The Harlem cultural scene also held fascinating possibilities for Killens. He floated among a group of contemporaries that included Frederick O'Neal, Harry Belafonte, Alice Childress, Maxwell Glanville, Ossie Davis, Ruby Dee, Sidney Poitier, Charles White (Killens's favorite painter), Ernest Crichlow, Roy Decarava, John Henrik Clarke, and Harold Cruse. Killens eventually joined the Committee for the Negro in the Arts (CNA), a group formed in 1947 and sponsored at least in part by the Communist Party. Killens called the CNA a "beautiful organization with Paul Robeson as the inspiration and guiding spirit for all of us."[9] Cruse later disagreed with Killens about the CNA's overall worth, construing the group as counterproductive and viewing Killens, Davis, Dee, and others as "intellectual prisoners" of a Harlem left-wing philosophical tradition.[10] Killens, however, had not been captured as much as he had pursued political positions and contacts, some of which he had been developing for years. Harlem leftists, and the Communist Party in particular, had never proven themselves effective or efficient jailers, if that were even an aim. No one—including Richard Wright and

Ralph Ellison—ever had to struggle to get away. Although much of Cruse's rather lengthy critique is vague and contradictory, he claimed explicitly that Killens and others, operating under the directives of the Communist Party, routinely denounced the NAACP. To the extent that Cruse commented on aesthetics, his observations about the limitations of socialist realism were certainly legitimate, but he overplayed the point by asserting that "what Killens, Robeson and their middle-class-leftwing ethos truly idealized were nice, upright Negro workers; who, even if they did go to church and worship God and not Russia, at least tilled the Southern soil as solid citizen sharecroppers; or worked in factories or service industries but were never, never anti-union."[11] He further argued that the characters favored by Killens and Robeson "always knew which American wars were progressive and just and which were 'imperialist'; instinctively loved all foreign-born whites and were never, never anti-Semitic; and (God forbid!) who never, but never, had a single nationalistic sentiment in their naïve revolutionary souls!"[12] But given that Killens was an NAACP member who in 1949 expressed written support for the organization's rank and file, and given that he subscribed to some of Harry Haywood's ideas about the "national question," Cruse, his astute comments about socialist realism notwithstanding, did not accurately represent his cultural adversary.[13]

That Killens courted patronage among the white left is no startling revelation. Many aspiring African American writers, including Cruse, did the same. For what other reason would Cruse appeal to the Harlem left wing to create a cultural oversight commission in Harlem if not to generate left-wing financial support for a separate group, the Harlem Writers Club, of which he was chair? Had he succeeded, would Communist Party support have meant conditioning and control? Cruse correctly identified "all the strains, ambivalences and conflicts over political loyalties that were characteristic of the Harlem postwar period," and those psychic issues were not restricted to any one Harlem cultural faction.[14]

Paul Robeson Jr., who considered Killens a mentor, views him in more charitable terms: "John was not a [Communist] Party type." Robeson cannot imagine Killens sitting through lengthy and numerous meetings or operating as a functionary. He concedes that Killens may have signed on at some point—FBI records link him to the Kings County branch—but considers him to have been part of the "independent black left" rather than a Harlem party official.[15] The CNA was supported by and to some extent supported the Communist Party but was not tied strictly to party doctrine.

Killens's political activities in Harlem coincided with his formal studies at Columbia, which he relished. Attending mostly in the evening, he completed twenty-four credits during the 1948–49 academic year, including work in grammar, composition, critical writing, and fiction writing. The grammar and composition work did not appear relevant or necessary and was maybe even useless with respect to his writing ambitions, and the courses were sometimes worlds away from the discussions about culture and politics in which he participated beyond campus. He likely enrolled in such classes solely to achieve full-time status and thereby qualify for financial aid. In any case, he parsed sentences by the hundreds and apparently mastered the strictness of the exercises. After Killens had completed dozens of grammar and composition assignments, his instructor, former Rhodes Scholar Allen Walker Read, assistant editor of the *Dictionary of American English*, commented, "Congratulations on an excellent set of graphics. You have reason to be proud of them."[16]

Columbia's main attraction for Killens was the chance to study further with Dorothy Brewster, and he took her courses during both semesters. He found another encouraging teacher in Helen Hull, vice president of the Authors Guild, who had been teaching at Columbia for thirty-two years and had published more than a dozen novels and two collections of short fiction. Hull was also a friend of writer Ann Petry. He took copious notes about theme, plot, situation, tone, character, setting, time, narration angles, and amount of exposition. On October 4, 1948, for example, the class discussed why some writers are more effective than others: "1) greater amount of reality—intensity, 2) plausible characters, 3) sensory impressions and details, 4) recreation of life, 5) good but selective memory of incidents & details, and 6) a tendency to beware of clichés." He read essays on writing by Samuel Taylor Coleridge, Allen Tate, and Virginia Woolf. He perused Somerset Maugham's *The Summing Up* and analyzed the similarities between Maugham's conceptions and those of Hull. He agreed with the assessment that, as he recorded Hull's words, "Writing is a full-time job and is not a vocation that can be successfully followed in 'leisure time.' Writing must be the main object of the author's life." In addition, Hull confirmed Killens's approach to imagination, viewing it not so much in terms of flights of fantasy but as a "recombining and rearranging of already familiar elements, dealing with experiences and impressions the writer already possesses."[17] She resoundingly justified his semiautobiographical prose experiments. Most important, Killens diligently wrote and revised, following what Maugham described as the "method of trial and error" by which authors produce the best oeuvre of which they are capable.[18] Further exploring themes of racial injustice, radicalism, and military life, Killens worked both on his novel and on short stories. He began to submit his short fiction to publishers and accumulate the almost de rigueur rejection slips. He entered a story, "Back Seat," in *Tomorrow* magazine's College Writers' Short Story Contest for 1948.

Previously titled "Southern Confusion," the story revolves around a racial epiphany, a violent outburst, and the subsequent jailing of the main subject, college student Jack Walker. In the final scene, reminiscent of *Native Son* and anticipating *Youngblood*, Walker does battle with a rat in his cell, the animal's insides splashing against Walker's face.[19] Killens did not place in the contest, and along with the results, editorial assistant Lenore Davison told Killens that the judges did not think "Back Seat" suitable as a regular contribution to the magazine.[20] Killens upgraded his rejections by submitting a story to the *New Yorker*, but the editors told him matter-of-factly, "We regret that we are unable to use the enclosed material. Thank you for giving us the opportunity to consider it."[21] More rejections soon followed. The short story would never be his forte. If, as Killens wrote in his class notes, the short story is one room, a novelette is a suite, and the novel is a whole house, then he was going to have to build a whole house.[22] Mikhail Sholokhov's *And Quiet Flows the Don* (1934) provided Killens with a prominent blueprint of how to build the house of socialist realism.[23]

As he worked on his construction, Killens wrote several book reviews and longer critical papers under the tutelage of Glenn H. Mullin. One review lavished praise on G.B.S.: *A Full Length Portrait*, Hesketh Pearson's biography of George Bernard Shaw, whom Killens greatly admired; another lambasted Arthur Koestler's *Darkness at Noon*, a fictionalized account of the Moscow trials, also known widely as the show trials, by which Stalin purged numerous political enemies. Mullin accepted Killens's embrace of the socialist Shaw but issued a concise rebuttal to his take on Koestler, a former communist whom Killens, harboring pro-Stalinist tendencies, termed a "rabid anticommunist."[24] Mullin judged the review a failure because Killens's polemic against Koestler removed the focus from an analysis of *Darkness at Noon* as a piece of fiction. Mullin conceded, however, that his student had made a telling comment when he argued that Koestler inadequately portrayed the Soviets despite having spent a year in their country: "Part of his failure to create real people is undoubtedly due to his contempt for people, which would certainly keep him from getting inside of them."[25]

Mullin offered effusive praise for Killens's review of Norman Mailer's *The Naked and the Dead*, judging the paper to be the best commentary about Mailer he had encountered, including that by professional critics. Killens had become fluent in the critical vocabulary learned in his fiction-writing courses and used it to good effect in assessing Mailer's novel. He thought Mailer had done an outstanding job overall but was lukewarm about the book's experimental narrative style, the shifting angles of narration, and felt that the author indulged a bit too much in stereotypes—of Gallagher's family, for example: "Had there been a Negro among Mailer's group, one wonders how he would have been treated. Would he have been shuffling and bowing and scraping all over Annopopei?" Conversely, he saw Mailer as a "giant in the field of sensory impression," adding, "I hear the screams of the big shells, the unusual noises of the jungle, the zing of a rifle bullet. When Mailer's soldiers trek into the heart of the jungle, I go with them. When it rains, I get soaking wet and bog down up to the knees in tropical mud."[26]

Killens saved the bulk of his critical energy to engage the work of Wright, the African American novelist who had made the greatest impact on American letters and exerted the greatest influence on most aspiring black fiction writers, including Killens. One did not need to slay Wright, as James Baldwin famously experienced compulsion to do, but one had to come to terms with his work.[27] In a nine-page essay, "Wright's Rebels," Killens lauded *Uncle Tom's Children*, which he believed "remains far ahead of anything else [Wright] has written." Killens especially appreciated the theme of "small people, individually and in the mass, fighting against oppression," and he applauded Wright's ability to employ "the most vivid style imaginable" and his penchant for wringing "every scene of its utmost possibilities." He thought each of the five stories in the collection bettered the preceding one; he called "Bright and Morning Star," which promotes the possibilities of communist organizing and portrays the heroism of a black mother, "one of the most blood curdling, realistic accounts of devotion, misery, oppression, bravery, understanding and courage." Wright, Killens felt, knew the people about whom he wrote and loved them passionately. But he also argued, "*Native Son*, though a stirring piece of fiction, does not live up to the expectancy created by those five stories of Negro heroism. Certainly *Black Boy* with its defeatism and great despair has no relation to Uncle Tom's 'Fighting' Children." Presaging Lorraine Hansberry's remarks regarding Wright's *The Outsider*, Killens suggested that Wright's relocation to France had diminished the author's literary fire and genius.[28]

Killens followed up with a paper in which he compared four of Wright's works: *Native Son*, *12 Million Black Voices*, *Black Boy*, and "Early Days in Chicago."[29] Killens was never as acerbic concerning Wright as Baldwin was but could not reconcile the description of a powerfully loving black people in *12 Million Black Voices* with the statement in *Black Boy* about the "strange absence of real kindness in Negroes," juxtaposing some of the conflicting passages in his essay.[30] He understood the literary license a novelist might invoke but could not fathom such contradiction in Wright's nonfiction. Mullin commented that Killens was "inclined to burn incense a bit too much" but allowed that the paper was good and informative and that to indicate Wright's inconsistent attitude toward black folk was a reasonable point.[31]

Killens's first published journal article appeared in the summer 1949 issue of *New Foundations*, a Marxist student quarterly. "For National Freedom" was a lengthy review of Harry Haywood's *Negro Liberation*. Haywood, once a prominent member of the Communist Party, lectured at the communist-affiliated Jefferson School of Social Science, another of Killens's haunts.[32] After citing Haywood's opening statements about the agrarian origins of the Negro question, Killens immediately endorsed Haywood's text as a vital contribution to progressive thought. Killens asserted that the problems of "superexploited" African American sharecroppers or tenant farmers, which were not identical to those of exploited poor whites, required land redistribution, the erasure of poor farmers' debts, and the equipping of new farms with the essential tools of production. Staying close to the Haywood line, he suggested that land redistribution should not be confused with socialism and pointed to the French Revolution as an example of successful land reform under capitalism. He was indeed a socialist but chose, as a practical matter, to defer such advocacy in his article: "To talk about socialism without combating the oppression of the Negro people in the Black Belt, without supporting their struggles and those of the exploited whites, is to talk abstract nonsense, is in fact to alienate and fail to mobilize a most militant force in the battle for democracy."[33]

Killens rearticulated Haywood's Black Belt Thesis—the concept that given the character of their historical oppression, African Americans in the South constituted a subjected black nation, which was evident when attributes such as economic life, territory, language, culture, and psychological makeup were considered. Northern blacks factored into the analysis as well, though the territory argument was weaker as a consequence of migration. Given black-nation status, African Americans thus had a right to self-determination. Killens argued, however, that such right did not necessarily imply separatism but could mean some form of federation. In the end, he emphasized a pluralistic alliance in which working class African Americans, the "Negro bourgeoisie," and white progressives combined to fight against domination by the corporate elites.[34]

Killens knocked the Garvey movement, a position he later reversed, and expressed support for such groups as the National Negro Congress, the Urban League, and the National Association of Colored Women. But his main organizational hopes lay in the NAACP's militant rank and file, which he hoped could overcome the conservative white bourgeois and black petit bourgeois leadership; the trade union movement, particularly "the more progressive unions of the CIO"; and "the growing influence of the Communist Party in Negro life" (his only explicit written embrace of the Party).[35] The ideas expressed in "For National Freedom" remained at the core of Killens's ideology, although the elements of Marxism, nationalism, trade unionism, and left nationalism—all compatible with burgeoning notions of Pan-Africanism—recombined in varying proportions over the years.

On the home front, the Killens family settled into an apartment in the Bedford-Stuyvesant section of Grace's native Brooklyn. John and Grace, as a team, set specific goals concerning everyday survival and worked assiduously to achieve them, with Grace handling a variety of clerical jobs along the way. They lived on the basement and parlor floors of a brownstone, able to feel the train line that rumbled directly underneath them. Killens later recalled, "The subway trains were shaking the structure of the house apart, especially at the window sections, so that the winter came in as if it lived with us, but would not chip in on the rent." The apartment became so chilly that he often worked at the typewriter in his overcoat and even tried to type while wearing gloves.[36]

Killens's "so-called" landlord, an elderly Jamaican immigrant named Webb who sought to maximize his profit at the expense of his tenants, once had a summons issued against Killens for nonpayment of rent. Following the advice of his brother-in-law, Thomas Russell Jones, a youthful radical turned attorney, Killens investigated and discovered that seventeen violations against the building were pending and that the rent exceeded the legal amount by fifteen dollars a month. When the matter wound up in court, the judge ordered Killens to put the rent in escrow until the violations had been addressed and reduced the amount owed to within regulations. Killens nevertheless felt sorry for Webb, believing "somehow that I was the exploiter and he the downtrodden and exploited." But when Killens offered to give the rent directly to Webb, he asked, "Where's my other fifteen dollars?" The standoff ended a few days later, with the landlord explaining that he had thought Killens intended to cheat him. On another occasion, Webb attempted to fix the Killenses' toilet but instead rendered the entire plumbing system unusable, forcing the family to obtain buckets of water from a neighbor until they could pay the thirty-five dollars for a professional plumber.[37]

Killens took his revenge in his novel, *The Cotillion*, where Webb could be found "in the full bloom of his life posing with an alias as the cunning Mr. Shyler." Of Shyler, Killens wrote, "If you asked him why there was no heat in the radiators, he would shake his head tolerantly, and say of the heat: 'It goes up, it goes down.' And then, philosophically, 'What goes up must come down.'" Killens ultimately described Webb as worthy and wrote of him with some fondness, but he also recalled that the time on Lafayette Avenue taught him and Grace "in every fiber of our understanding what Frederick Douglass meant by the efficacy of *struggle*," alluding to Douglass's comment, "If there is no struggle there is no progress."[38]

CHAPTER SEVEN

A Colored Man Who Happened to Write, 1949–1951

As John Oliver Killens was completing his academic year at Columbia, anticommunist Cold War fervor approached high tide. Not since the Palmer raids, when thousands of noncitizen immigrants were detained and deported in 1919 and 1920, had law enforcement officials so vigorously squelched opposing voices.[1] The Soviet Union was unalterably construed as the enemy, military intervention in Korea was judged necessary, and those who manifested a perceived lack of patriotism were subject to overzealous prosecution.

Killens witnessed firsthand the political hardships endured by his main triumvirate of mentors, Paul Robeson, W. E. B. Du Bois, and Alphaeus Hunton. Robeson and Du Bois had long been beset by criticism as the only two nationally recognized African American figures who bucked the gradualist trend of the civil rights mainstream. They became the objects of heightened attacks after their appearance at the April 1949 Paris Peace Conference, where Robeson declared, "Our will for peace is strong. We shall not make war on anyone. We shall not make war on the Soviet Union."[2] The comments were pretty standard antiwar fare and were echoed by several other participants. However, a wire service erroneously reported that Robeson also said, "It is unthinkable that American Negroes would go to war on behalf of those who have oppressed us for generations against a country which in one generation has raised our people to the full dignity of mankind."[3] Robeson's numerous political opponents seized on the alleged statement to brand him a traitor, and when he returned to the United States, he found his speaking engagements canceled and performance venues closed to him. Unable to pursue his usual means of making a living, he had to bargain that select associates possessed the guile and fortitude in the face of Cold War hysteria to create concert opportunities. No major events were scheduled until the Harlem chapter of the Civil Rights Congress, of which Robeson was vice president, scheduled an August 27 show in Peekskill, New York. In a signal moment of the Cold War, rioting right-wing whites, including local police, forced cancellation. The concert took place without interruption one week later before a crowd of twenty thousand, but observers realized that the debacle, rather than the subsequent success, indicated what was in store.[4] The State Department dashed Robeson's only remaining hope for substantial revenue—overseas employment—by voiding his passport in July 1950. Killens and other members of the Committee for the Negro in the Arts (CNA) and the Council on African Affairs (CAA) rallied to Robeson's side and continued to work to procure performance venues and enlist general community support, but such efforts achieved relatively little.

Later in the year, despite his diminishing personal funds, Robeson launched a newspaper, *Freedom*, to provide a forum for Harlem writers and serve as a vehicle for expressing his political views and grievances. Under the editorship and management of Louis Burnham and George B. Murphy Jr., Killens's colleagues from the Southern Negro Youth Congress and the United Negro and Allied Veterans of America, respectively, *Freedom* was housed in the same office suite as the CAA. In addition to Killens, key members of the *Freedom* circle included Eslanda Robeson, Shirley Graham, Lloyd Brown, John Henrik Clarke, Alice Childress, and Lorraine Hansberry, who had just arrived in New York City at the age of twenty after two years at the University of Wisconsin and a brief stint at Roosevelt University in her native Chicago. Killens spent numerous hours conversing with Hansberry and termed her a "one-woman literary warrior for change" and a "Pan-Africanist with a socialist perspective."[5]

Du Bois refused to denounce Robeson both during and in the aftermath of the Paris Peace Conference, and the eighty-two-year-old crusader was vilified in the press and targeted for government persecution. In 1950, Du Bois agreed to chair the Peace Information Center, an organization created to publicize the Stockholm Peace Appeal. This action made Du Bois subject to arrest for failing to register as an agent of a foreign principal within the United States.[6] By the time the organizers disbanded the center in October, Du Bois had become a candidate for the U.S. Senate from New York. Trying to draw votes away from the Democratic ticket in an effort to help incumbent Vito Marcantonio, the most left-leaning member of Congress, Du Bois ran on the American Labor Party ticket and eventually polled a respectable 4 percent of the statewide vote and 15 percent of the vote in Harlem. He was arrested the following February. The charges ultimately were dismissed, but the case proved how easily supposedly progressive leadership, including African Americans, could be compromised. An embarrassing number of people canceled their scheduled appearances at a February 23 birthday celebration for Du Bois to be held at Essex House. Killens reflected, "Many black folk who owed [Du Bois] so much failed him at this hour. Some were too busy scurrying for cover, only to find out ultimately that there really was no hiding place down here, nor is there now, nor will there ever be."[7] Organizers held a smaller affair, over which E. Franklin Frazier presided, at Small's Paradise in Harlem.

Although Robeson's subsequent poor health and Du Bois's increasing sense of alienation were repercussions of Cold War persecution, the hardest and most immediate fall around Killens might have been Hunton's. In addition to his vital, controversial, and exhausting work for the CAA, Hunton agreed to serve as a trustee for the Civil Rights Bail Fund. The Civil Rights Congress, which was founded in 1946 as a merger of the International Labor Defense, the National Negro Congress, and the National Federation for Constitutional Liberties, initiated the fund to provide support for leftists who faced legal problems because of their political beliefs. Writer Howard Fast noted, "Private bonding companies—companies which readily provide bail for drug-dealers, gangsters, pimps and thieves—refused to provide bail for progressives."[8] Along with Hunton, writer Dashiell Hammett, wealthy scion Frederick Vanderbilt Field, and Abner Green, executive secretary of the Committee for the Protection of the Foreign Born, administered the fund.

The Civil Rights Congress, to which Killens belonged, counted among its successes the legal defense of scores of union activists and other harassed citizens. But most important in the eyes of federal prosecutors was the fact that the congress had provided bail for the eleven Communist Party leaders who had been convicted in October 1949 under the Smith Act for conspiring to overthrow the government of the United States.[9] The defendants included Harlem councilman Benjamin Davis, who, running on the Communist Party ticket, had been elected to his seat in 1943. Regardless of the numerous theoretical swords crossed over the Communist Party's efficacy, Harlem voters and activists had proven themselves more interested in candidates who demonstrated the best potential to serve them well than in traditional party allegiances. Killens signed Davis's 1949 nominating petition. Davis, however, lost his seat in the ensuing election and subsequently was sentenced to and served four years in prison.[10]

After four of the eleven defendants in the Smith Act trial went underground while out on bail pending appeal, a federal judge, acting at the behest of the Justice Department, ordered Hunton, Hammett, Field, and Green to provide the names of all contributors to the bail fund. None of them complied with the demand, and they were found guilty of contempt of court. In July 1951, Hunton was sentenced to six months and remanded to the federal prison in Petersburg, Virginia. *Freedom*, on which Hunton served as a board member, ran an editorial comparing him with Harriet Tubman, Sojourner Truth, Frederick Douglass, John Brown, Denmark Vesey, Nat Turner, and Gabriel Prosser, whom it called "trustees of our bloody struggles for freedom. Add to theirs the name of Hunton."[11] Despite their organizing efforts, however, the members of the *Freedom* circle had no major impact. Du Bois authored a petition for the Special Committee on Alphaeus Hunton; it garnered a mere fifty-four signatures. Hunton would not break, nor would the government ease up except to deduct one month of time from his sentence for good behavior.[12]

In June 1951, the Supreme Court upheld the convictions of the Communist Party leaders. Buoyed by this legal victory, authorities initiated a second round of prosecutions, handing down twenty-one indictments on June 20, including one against James Edward Jackson Jr., who, like his wife, Esther Cooper, had been prominent in the Southern Negro Youth Congress. Holder of a graduate degree in pharmacology from Howard University, he was the former southern regional director of the Communist Party and an alternate member of the National Committee. After returning to the United States in February 1946 from military duty in the South Pacific, Jackson had resumed political organizing. He soon conducted a series of interviews with Du Bois and tried to recruit him into the party. In an attempt to avoid an almost certain prison sentence, Jackson and several others went underground after the second-wave indictments were issued.[13]

The FBI immediately placed Jackson's home under surveillance and began harassing his family. Agents trailed Jackson's two young daughters to and from school and interviewed the girls' teachers and staked out the locations of field trips.[14]

On August 29, agents interviewed Killens. An informant had connected him to Jackson the previous January by reporting that Jackson had left a message for Killens to contact him at Communist Party headquarters. Killens acknowledged that he had met Jackson in Washington in conjunction with the Southern Negro Youth Congress but added that he had dropped out of the organization when he came to New York to attend Columbia University and had subsequently run into Jackson only sporadically, perhaps at American Labor Party meetings, and not at all in 1951. Killens denied being aware of Jackson's whereabouts, having engaged in any communication with him or his wife, or knowing any of his friends. When pressed about his visit to the Jackson home in late June, Killens responded that he had made the trip only because he wanted to find out if Esther Cooper Jackson (she began using her married name as a show of support) needed his assistance. Killens said she had not been home and he had not returned. When asked bluntly if he would notify the FBI if he discovered James Jackson's location, Killens stated that the question was academic and that he "would have to cross that bridge when he came to it."[15]

But Esther Cooper Jackson had been home. When Killens visited, he quickly delivered an envelope filled with cash sent by Communist Party member Howard "Stretch" Johnson, who served as a defense witness at the Smith Act trials. Killens spotted the agents on stakeout, as had Jackson and her next-door neighbor, Doxey Wilkerson. Jackson and Wilkerson had developed signals involving window shades as a secret way of communicating. Jackson thought Killens's report to the investigators had been clever.[16]

In Harlem cultural circles, Killens was gaining a more significant presence. In Harold Cruse's estimation, the literature section of the CNA operated increasingly as the "Killens group."[17] A faction that included Cruse disagreed with this "Killens group" about aesthetics. Killens unapologetically pushed the case for socialist realism, buttressing his opinion with reference to Du Bois's 1926 essay, "Criteria of Negro Art," in which he declared, "All art is propaganda."[18] As critic Stephen Carey later argued, "Killens develops heroic leadership as highly educated, as directly interested in the 'uplift' of the common masses, and as intensely active in directly resisting racial oppression. His protagonists must meet Du Boisian standards."[19] Carey could have added the phrase "Robesonian standards," as Robeson, through the force of his personal magnetism and his views about scientific socialism, had the greatest direct influence on the CNA. Also influential were Wilkerson and Lloyd Brown, associate editor of *Masses and Mainstream*.

Whereas Cruse conceded that "there is nothing wrong with the art of protest or political agitprop *in its place*" and affirmed that "art, of course, is always a weapon," he felt that the CNA's exclusive focus on socialist realism helped to suppress nationalist creativity among young Harlem writers in service to a Communist Party agenda of middle-class interracialism. For Cruse, following the logic of Ernest Kaiser, the emphasis on socialist realism entailed a "blind spot on Negro psychology." Moreover, offered Cruse, "A literary point of view such as Killens' is the kind of middle-class puritanism that rejects the human dregs in the real *social* world of pimps, whores, perverts, Uncle Toms, number runners and race traitors from the purview of its practical politics."[20] However, though Cruse was right about Puritanism being a strand of Killens's literary sensibility, such writings as "Things Might Have Been," "Stony the Road We Trod," and "For Negro Liberation" reveal a practical politics not reducible to the often-vague opprobrium "middle class." In retrospect, the "real" social world of the streets obviously has not received short shrift in terms of cultural representation. A greater omission has been the seeming purge of socialist realist texts—both primary and critical—from African American literary canons.[21]

Rival views led to the formation of the Harlem Writers Club, a group chaired by Cruse that consisted of artists who were "instinctively anti-social realist" and "knew that in order to influence a broad audience, a Harlem literary and cultural movement had to use forms that were steeped in the popular idiom and images, yet as free as possible of alien political propaganda."[22] Tensions among writers in Harlem were exacerbated when Wilkerson published "Negro Culture: Heritage and Weapon" in the August 1949 issue of *Masses and Mainstream*. Wilkerson's analysis embodied a nationalist impulse: "The Negro Arts defy adequate and fundamental understanding unless they are viewed as the expression of a *distinct people* within the general population of the United States, reflecting their *special* relations to the society as a whole, giving expression to their *special* memories, traditions and aspirations."[23] Wilkerson's piece functioned as cultural complement to Haywood's Black Belt Thesis. Nonetheless, some observers perceived his article as another endorsement of socialist realism over competing nationalist work. Spirited discussion in local circles led to a conference at the Jefferson School of Social Science, where Wilkerson was director of faculty and curriculum. Killens described the conference's goal as to "hammer out a liberation ideology for Black writers." Aesthetically, Killens held the home field advantage over Cruse, though Killens was far from a chief spokesperson. Minimizing his participation, he allowed, "I felt like a neophyte among all those big time theorists"—Wilkerson, Brown, and V. J. Jerome, a leading communist cultural critic.[24] Their voices would prevail. Indeed, Brown delivered a stirring polemic in response to a speech by Kaiser, who in the pages of *Phylon* had criticized the aesthetic views of Brown, Wilkerson, and Du Bois. Kaiser had problems with "Du Bois in his *New York Herald Tribune* review of Wright's *Black Boy* and in his newspaper columns and magazine articles reprimanding ill-mannered, drunken Negroes, Doxey Wilkerson in his introduction to Aptheker's *The Negro People in America* and Lloyd Brown, a Negro editor of *Masses & Mainstream*, in his lecture on the Negro character in American literature to Contemporary Writers."[25] Brown's countering oration, replete with the damning charge of Trotskyism, effectively spelled the end of the Harlem Writers Club. It remains unclear, however, how one speech could crush a literary insurgency so completely or why the Harlem Writers Club thought support from Brown, to whom members appealed for resources, could be forthcoming.

Perhaps the depths of discord were overstated, more the result of intellectual disagreement than deeply held enmity. Harlem Writers Club members Walter Christmas and Kaiser, who later criticized Cruse, were flexible enough to move among different literary groups.[26] Soon thereafter, Christmas joined with Killens, Rosa Guy, John Henrik Clarke, and others to establish the Harlem Writers Guild. A variant story has Guy asking novelist Phillip Bonosky to start the Harlem Writers Workshop, which first met on October 23, 1951. Whether writers first met alone or with Bonosky, Killens and the others initially operated out of the offices of the CAA and *Freedom*. Only Clarke had published work as a creative writer—a book of poems, *Rebellion in Rhyme*, and one short story, "The Boy Who Painted Christ Black." Killens remembered, "John Clarke was our celebrity, and we were damn proud of him."[27] By all accounts, Killens soon became the dominant presence in the workshop, and he served as the Harlem Writers Guild's first chair. If white left-wing patronage existed as the guiding force behind the early guild, it had failed to deliver anything for the small group of African American writers who formed the new literary entity. With "Stony the Road We Trod," Killens had already spun out a lengthy, artistically passable, proletarian, black-and-white, unite-and-fight manuscript that he could not get under contract. Some of his friends suggested that as long as the McCarthy era persisted, he never would.[28]

At the first meetings, Killens read the opening sections of the novel on which he was working. The story begins on a January 1, 1900, when Laurie Lee, a measurably deeper character than she is in "Stony the Road We Trod," enters the world, symbolically prefiguring the new-century African American woman. The chapter describes Laurie Lee's early years in Tipkin, Georgia, with the requisite racial insults and will on her part to overcome. Unlike in "Stony the Road We Trod," a fictionalized Georgia Killens, named Big Mama, emerges in the early pages of the new tale. She is a source of Laurie's strength and defiance. Also appearing in the chapter is Joe Jackson, born on April 1 but no fool. The chapter ends with Joe's marriage to Laurie and their move to Crossroads, Georgia. Joe is far more voiced and developed than in "Stony the Road the Trod." He, too, has overcome racial travails, including being forced to labor on a plantation in Tennessee.

The last major structural departure from "Stony the Road We Trod" involves the introduction of the spirituals as a major motif and plot element. Although African American folklore and humor, Killens trademarks, are in the background in the earlier draft, the spirituals are absent altogether. Their insertion seems directly traceable to Wilkerson's essay. In addition to agitating writers in Harlem, Wilkerson had provided pointed commentary about the possibilities of the spirituals as material for further art, urging contemporary writers to employ the ethos of the spirituals—the righteous indictment, the nobility, the courage, the belief in ultimate liberation—to inform current political struggle. Wilkerson mentioned a series of songs, including "Steal Away to Jesus," "Go Down, Moses," "Swing Low, Sweet Chariot," "Children We Shall Be Free," "Before I'd Be a Slave I'd Be Buried in My Grave," "Walk Together Children, Don't You Get Weary," and "Didn't My Lord Deliver Daniel?"[29] Killens eventually worked almost all of these songs into his manuscript in some form or another. The opening epigraph of the published version is "Didn't my Lord Deliver Daniel / And why not every man?"[30]

The founding members of the Harlem Writers Guild were appreciative but pessimistic concerning Killens's latest literary effort. They thought that the literary marketplace, with an eye for sensationalism, would not fancy his type of truth, telling the author, "That's great stuff, John, but ain't nobody going to publish you."[31]

Killens marched onward. Along with his general ideas about progressive fiction, he worked with two specific shibboleths in mind: the declaration by Kelly Miller, a former dean at Howard University, "It is not the treatment of a people that degrades them, but their acceptance of it" and Frederick Douglass's observation, "If there is no struggle, there is no progress."[32] Killens incorporated Douglass's words verbatim into the manuscript. Killens also clearly responded to a conversation centered on the fall 1950 issue of *Phylon*, which assessed the current state and future of African American literature. The editors considered midcentury a pivotal literary moment for African Americans as a consequence of Gwendolyn Brooks's receipt on May 1 of the Pulitzer Prize for poetry. They solicited input from various writers, journalists, and critics, most of whom agreed that African American literature, especially the novel, generally lacked universality and that African American writers needed to reduce their emphasis on racial material and racial identity.

Novelist William Gardner Smith, for example, opined that the plight of African Americans was a "transient topic" that could not be the stuff of universalism.[33] Hampton Institute's Hugh Gloster adduced that the "preponderating use of racial subject matter" had handicapped the African American writer and "retarded his attainment of a 'cosmic grasp.'"[34] Charles Nichols wrote, "In his literary efforts the Negro is surely coming of age—though, happily, not as a Negro."[35] Alain Locke called for "universalized particularity" and asserted, "When the racial themes are imposed upon the Negro author either from within or without, they become an intolerable and limiting artistic ghetto, but that accepted by choice, either on the ground of best known material or preferred opportunity, they stake off a cultural bonanza."[36] However, Locke did not explain the difference between "imposed from within or without" and "accepted by choice." Nor did he elaborate on what exactly is a "preferred opportunity."

In an astonishing bit of reasoning, Thomas Jarrett punctuated his argument against racial didacticism by concluding, "Richard Wright makes it clear that Bigger Thomas could be 'white.'"[37] Perhaps Wright was brought into the nonracial fold because *Native Son* functioned as the gold-standard novel for these respondents, and they could not allow the black novel most heralded among them to be a case against their own position, though Wright would have pilloried their stance, as "Blueprint for Negro Writing" and the racially overdetermined Bigger Thomas indicate. Wright indeed exhorted African American writers to transcend narrow nationalism, but only through an in-depth, Marxist-influenced exploration of African American identity in relation to the larger culture. Unlike Wright, *Phylon's* proponents of universalism failed even to hint at a theory of racial formation and the implications of racialized identities as social variables within the context of internationalism.

Although Smith, Gloster, Nichols, Locke, and Jarrett remained unconvincing regarding the virtues of universalism, they were unambiguous in terms of the specific work they championed: mainly that of Wright and Ann Petry, if seen in nonracialized ways, and the "post-racial" novels of Frank Yerby and Willard Motley. Smith, Saunders Redding, and William Demby were among a wave of emerging novelists considered worth following. And Langston Hughes, who otherwise straddled the fence on the universality issue in his interview with the editorial team, forcefully touted Ralph Ellison, then putting the finishing touches on *Invisible Man*, as a "really significant talent."[38]

The most strident voice that ran counter to *Phylon's* mainstream belonged to Morgan State's Nick Aaron Ford, who implored African American writers to continue using racial themes and termed universalism "pure sophistry." Ford judged the postracial novels of Yerby, Motley, Petry, and Zora Neale Hurston markedly inferior to their earlier efforts, decrying inartistic uses of didacticism but suggesting the "use of social propaganda subordinated so skillfully to the purposes of art that it will not insult the average intelligent reader."[39]

Killens sided with Ford and continued to work accordingly. In contrast, Lloyd Brown, whose novel, *Iron City*, would soon be published, became more publicly vocal. He blasted several of the *Phylon* contributors, debunking the theory that the "writer-who-happens-to-be-a-Negro," an apparent success produced by integration, had to change course in pursuit of the greater artistic goal of a universalism in which form reigned supreme over socially specific content. For Brown, the main trouble with so-called Negro literature was that "*it has not been Negro enough*—that is, it has not fully reflected the real life and character of the people." He viewed the widely acclaimed spirituals as irrefutable evidence that African American cultural forms had universal appeal and added that one of the great universal themes was the "epic struggle, still unended, of the Negro people in our land." While noting the irony that virtues of integration were being espoused in a Negro quarterly published by a Negro university in Jim Crow Georgia, "in the state governed by Herman Talmadge and represented in Congress by white men dedicated to the principles and practices of lynch law," Brown pointed out that as he composed his essay on February 4, 1951, none of the book reviews in the *New York Times* dealt with works by African American authors. Nor were any of the *Times's* thirty-two best sellers or eight other recommended volumes written by African American writers or even, as Brown put it facetiously, "a-writer-who-happens-to-be-a-Negro."[40]

Killens closely identified with Brown's viewpoint, both in 1951 and in later years: "How in the hell could I be a writer who happens to be Black? I wasn't born pecking on a typewriter." He regarded the experiences, rhythms, and idioms of black life as artistic resources too valuable to be exchanged for the supposed distinction of being a "writer who happens to be a colored man."[41]

In the domestic sphere, the crisis of representation was reflected in Killens's October 23, 1951, letter to Lita Schwartz, who taught seven-year-old Jon Charles at P.S. 54 in Brooklyn. Schwartz had assigned *Children Everywhere*, which contained "The Story of Li'l Hannibal." Killens thought the story contained "many of the vicious, Nazi-like myths about Negro people, such as—laziness, unusual fear of the darkness and the use of dialect," which only appeared in the tale in reference to African American characters. Killens suggested, "The use of such a book and others of its kind serves to perpetuate ignorance and prejudices rather than to further enlightenment and education," and he asked Schwartz to "kindly assign another which does not hold the Negro people up to disgraceful ridicule as this one does."[42]

Schwartz agreed with Killens's assessment, writing to him, "My own feelings follow yours pretty closely." However, only the school's principal, Saul Bloomgarden, had the authority to remove the text from the curriculum.[43] Three days later, Bloomgarden wrote to Killens on Board of Education stationery that the principal and several teachers were "in complete agreement in condemnation of the story on the grounds indicated by you." He ordered that the book be removed from all classrooms, instructed teachers to be more vigilant concerning objectionable material, notified his superiors so that the book would be removed from the school listing, and wrote to the publisher to explain that no more copies would be purchased until the material in question was deleted.[44]

The Poetry, Energy, and Convictions, 1951–1954

As 1951 drew to a close, thirty-five-year-old John Oliver Killens often sat at his cluttered desk working into the wee hours of the morning on the way to producing a 994-page draft of what would become *Youngblood*. He said his characters kept telling him, "You've got to get us down on paper before we vanish and are no more."[1] In shaping his novel, Killens continued to draw heavily on his childhood memories, particularly his sense of place and family. Although the story is mostly set in the fictional town of Crossroads, Georgia (a reference to the "crossroads" episode of Killens's childhood), Terminal Station, Cherry Street, Pine Street, Evergreen Street, and Big Road are all actual sites in Macon. Pleasant Grove is the fictional counterpart to Pleasant Hill. The characters Uncle Leo, Richard Wendell Myles, and Little Brother bear names derived from the Killens family. The fun-loving Uncle Ray is probably based on Son Coleman. By the author's admission, his sketches of Big Mama, the dominant presence in the early pages of the novel, are modeled closely on his great-grandmother.[2] Cousin Joe, who worked at the turpentine mills in Glenwood, Georgia, was the prototype for Joe Jackson, though the Jackson couple is also an idyllic recasting of the author's parents. In general, Killens rendered characters more elaborately than he did in his earlier work and portrayed an African American community that was more deeply engaged and interactive. Under the guidance of Dorothy Brewster and others, he had developed a knack for sustaining tension. The fictional "crossroads" episode, for example, involves more intrigue than its real-life counterpart. Robby is not fighting merely because he has proved better at the dozens; he has come to the rescue of Jenny Lee, who is assaulted by a group of white boys while on her way home from school. His mother, following the lead of Big Mama, has taught him that resistance is appropriate. Regardless of the omnipresent danger for assertive African American males in the South, Laurie Lee concentrates on grooming Robby to become a man who is unbowed and unwilling to accept being treated as socially inferior. That she acquiesces to authorities and beats Robby constitutes a serious defeat that she and her son must transcend.

Killens mined African American vernacular culture more extensively in his evolving manuscript, at least partly as a consequence of the influence of Doxey Wilkerson and Lloyd Brown, although Killens's facility with the tactic derived from his prolonged immersion, like Zora Neale Hurston and Richard Wright, in the rich environment of black southern folklore.[3] Like Brown, Killens never shied away from an expressly political purpose for his prose and consciously worked against the notions of art for art's sake expressed in the *Phylon* symposium. Structurally an expansive sermon, his novel features highly polemical African American characters engaged in heroic family and community struggle against white supremacy over the first third of the twentieth century.[4] Killens explicitly deconstructs the notion of happy, contented darkies in the good old Southland. His idealized family—Laurie Lee, Joe, Jenny Lee, and Robby (his principal alter ego)—never loses sight of the need for group insurgence despite setbacks such as Robby's whipping. Joe's favorite song, which functions as his (and the story's) mantra, is the spiritual "Walk Together Children." Even as Myles, the schoolteacher, another Killens alter ego, discusses activism with Laurie Lee and Joe, Joe perceives that Myles's "book learning" essentially restates Joe's own heartfelt impulses and folk understanding.[5]

Because his Marxist edge had not been dulled, Killens extends beyond a story of black resistance cast only in racial terms, as he did in "Stony the Road We Trod." Black solidarity is considered necessary, but Killens illustrates that a progressive, interethnic coalition is the only hope against economic exploitation by the Bourbons. As he recalled the genuine commitment of his high school teacher, Lewis Mounts, he crafted Oscar Jefferson, a character some fellow whites considered a nigger lover, to symbolize the role whites could play in the struggle. Jefferson is the answer to the wry question Joe poses while listening to Myles expound on interracial activism: "Where the white friends at?"[6] But Killens promotes more than mere friendship. Jefferson properly identifies his class interests and on that basis casts his lot with African American progressives. Much as Killens articulated in "For National Freedom," white assistance should not stem from "humanitarianism or paternalism."[7] Jefferson completes the core alliance— noble, rock-solid, psychologically whole black southern family; northern, black, Du Boisian intellectual; the previously underachieving black masses; the white working class—that assumes the challenge of creating a more humane Crossroads.

Although a highly motivated writer with a tremendous work ethic, Killens still availed himself of various writing workshops. Milton Ost directed him to blacklisted screenwriter Viola Brothers Shore, who ran what Killens regarded as a "progressive workshop" at her home. Shore assured him that he was working on a "major classic."[8] He also enrolled in the Professional Writers Clinic at New York University, where he worked on fiction and television script writing with Shore and other instructors, including Elizabeth Pollock and Saul Bellow.

While Killens worked on his novel, Shore helped him with a less ambitious project, the publication of a short story in the left-wing *California Quarterly*. Although Killens had to pay fifty dollars to have the journal publish his piece, he finally made it into print as a fiction writer. The story, "God Bless America," opens with soldiers in full field dress parading along a thoroughfare, the white troops preceding the black ones, toward a white ship for departure to Korea. Joe, who is among the first wave of black soldiers with his sidekick, Luke Robinson, anxiously scans the crowd of civilians lining both sides of the street looking for his wife, Cleo, who is pregnant with their first child. As he searches for her face, his mind flashes back to the previous night and their conversation concerning his orders. Cleo could not see "what colored soldiers have to fight for—especially against other colored people." Joe disagreed, asserting that African Americans had a stake in the Korean War and noting, "They're integrating colored soldiers now. And anyhow, what the hell's the use of getting all heated up about it? I got to go. That's all there is to it." Joe thinks that he and Cleo will have an easier time if they both believe in the worth of the military mission.[9]

As his outfit nears the ship, Joe finally spots Cleo; she then accompanies him as far as civilians are allowed to go. As the last of the white soldiers

boards the ship, a band on board is playing "God Bless America." Joe hopes
that Cleo can hear the music and that it can persuade her that America is
justified in going to war. But he soon hopes his wife becomes momentarily
deaf. As the black soldiers reach the ship, the band shifts to "The Darktown Strutters' Ball." Some white soldiers snap their fingers to the music.
Luke speaks sarcastically, "We ain't no soldiers, we're a bunch of goddamn
clowns." He teases Joe, "Take that goddamn chip off your shoulder. They
just trying to make you people feel at home. Don't you recognize the Negro
national anthem when you hear it?" Joe refuses to answer. With his anger
rising, he wishes he could walk away from it all but chooses instead to keep
marching "towards the big white boat."[10]

In January 1952, Killens received a letter from Philip Stevenson, one of
the editors of the *California Quarterly*, in which he conveyed the journal's
inclination to publish the story but suggested several changes. Because the
story relied on "plot-point" rather than "character-exploration," Stevenson
wanted to trim the piece as much as possible while retaining its essence.
In particular, he felt that the scene between the lovers the night before the
sailing was overdrawn. This objection made sense inasmuch as the story
had been excerpted from a second novel in progress, though Killens had
spent relatively little time on the novel and certainly had not labored over
the prose as he had with his tale about Crossroads, Georgia. Stevenson also
thought that Luke Robinson intruded too much at the story's end, that Joe
got the point by then and should simply stare straight ahead and board the
ship. Overall, however, the changes were minor. Stevenson felt that had it
been possible for him to meet with Killens in person, they could have finalized the story in an hour.[11]

On January 28, Killens wrote back and conceded that the story was too
long. He assented to most of the changes but argued for retaining Luke
Robinson's role, although he affirmed the need to paint the scene with more
economy. A little more than a week later, Stevenson wrote with a couple
of inquiries. Not expert in the African American vernacular, he wondered
about the grammar of "these peoples is a bitch" and had never heard the admonition "Don't worry about the mule going blind." But the story was basically ready. Stevenson also sent regards to Shore.[12]

At this point Killens was halfway through his novel. Still disciplined, he
nonetheless could not resist being in the swing of things socially and politically. He continued to assist Alphaeus Hunton at the Council on African
Affairs (CAA), participate prominently in the literature section of the Com-

mittee for the Negro in the Arts, and chair the Harlem Writers Guild. Audre Lorde, an eighteen-year-old poet, began attending the weekly guild meetings. The youngest participant by far, she did not find the most comfortable fit given her age and still insecure racial and sexual identity, although she drew particularly close to John Henrik Clarke, the one published poet in the group, who served as a mentor and father figure.[13]

On April 6, members of the Committee for the Negro in the Arts hosted a Manhattan party to celebrate the publication of Langston Hughes's new book, *Laughing to Keep from Crying*. The event coincided with the beginning of heightened protests against apartheid in South Africa. Siding with those who opposed the fascist government of Prime Minister D. F. Malan, Hunton and Killens coordinated CAA support for the Campaign of Defiance of Unjust Laws, a movement waged by South Africa's nonwhites. In addition to disseminating information and raising funds, the CAA effort included symbolic gestures such as observing two minutes of silence at noon on April 6 in support of freedom in conjunction with a similar effort in South Africa.

Later that afternoon, at the Hughes party, Killens spoke passionately about the situation in South Africa and about the African anticolonial movement in general as well as the efforts of the CAA, which had scheduled thirty hours of picketing over the next five days in front of the South African consulate in New York. Clad in suit, tie, dress coat, and hat, Killens spent considerable time on the picket line wearing a sign that read "American Labor Supports Freedom for South Africa"; Hunton's sign read "No U.S. Support for South African Oppression."

After the demonstrations concluded on April 11, another, more cultural event distracted Killens from his novel. The following day marked the official release of Ralph Ellison's *Invisible Man*. Killens and Ellison could hardly have been more politically and culturally opposite: one procommunist, a joiner by nature, disposed toward direct activism, a literary realist; the other anticommunist, more insular, suspicious of radical mass movements, more expressionist and avant-garde. In no mood for Ellison's brilliant parodies of African American figures, including those in the Communist Party, Killens joined with Lloyd Brown to double-team Ellison in print. In the June 1952 issue of *Masses and Mainstream*, Brown lamented that Ellison conformed to the literary formula of sadism, sex, shock, and the "central design of American Century Literature, anti-Communism." He considered the book "profoundly anti-Negro" and lumped Ellison with two other defectors from the communist ranks, Richard Wright and Chester Himes, who shared a "bitter alienation": "Cut off from the surging mainstream of Negro life and struggle and creativity, they stagnate in Paris, wander on lonely crusades, or spit out at the world from a hole in the ground." Moreover, he added, Ellison would not be a part of the growing renaissance of African American culture.[14] The same month in *Freedom*, Killens matched Brown's disdain, if not his critical eloquence, accusing Ellison of following a publisher's dream recipe of sex, violence, sadism, red-baiting, Uncle Toms, Negro perverts, and African American traitors. Concluding that the novel was a "modernized 'surrealist' anti-Negro stereotype," Killens avowed, "the Negro people need Ralph Ellison's *Invisible Man* like we need a hole in the head or a stab in the back."[15]

Ellison's remarkable literary achievement deserved better, and Killens, despite several requests, never allowed his review to be republished. However, *Invisible Man* and its strategic championing of individual liberty represented a crafty, somewhat conservative entry into Cold War cultural politics. It could hardly have found a warm reception — old organizational disputes and literary aesthetics aside — from Brown, Killens, and their ilk, who, at risk themselves, had an up-close view of the heavy dues acquaintances such as Paul Robeson, W. E. B. Du Bois, Alphaeus Hunton, James Jackson, and Benjamin Davis were paying for their dedication to front-line collective struggle.[16] The seeds had been planted, but a large-scale rivalry between Killens and Ellison never took root. Ellison's attention lay elsewhere. Although only three years older than Killens, Ellison was on the verge of iconic status and would save his best rebuttals for Irving Howe, who judged Ellison's work inferior to Wright's.[17]

"God Bless America" appeared in the spring 1952 issue of the *California Quarterly*, along with segments of Pablo Neruda's *Canto General*, translated by Waldeen, and Aimé Césaire's "Textbook of a Return to My Native Land," translated by Miriam G. Koshland. In addition, Angus Cameron, one of America's leading book editors, who had recently resigned from Little, Brown, and Company, contributed an essay about what he called the crisis in books. Cameron called for publishing activity linked to distribution through the labor movement, arguing that the natural merger of artist and worker would form a formidable alliance. He considered literature a "social function, not a private therapeutic."[18]

Back at New York University, Killens received additional encouragement. On August 9, Elizabeth Pollock mailed him feedback on the courthouse chapter of his manuscript. She judged it to have "tremendous power" and felt that the pace was "magnificently sustained." Pollock acknowledged that her student possessed unquestionable talent and commended him on his openness to constructive criticism. She thus forecast brightly, "If you can achieve and nourish a deliberate, analytical discipline by which to 'try out' the product of your passionate and compulsive writing, you will, in time, become a truly great novelist. You have the poetry, the energy and the convictions."[19]

Killens hoped the Guggenheim Foundation would also recognize his potential. At the suggestion of John Henrik Clarke, Killens asked Langston Hughes to read a portion of the manuscript and perhaps serve as a reference for Killens's application for a foundation grant. Hughes did not receive the request in time to serve as a reference, yet the other names on Killens's application were impressive: Columbia's Helen Hull, Howard's Arthur P. Davis, and New York University's Warren Bowers, Millen Brand, Ralph Bates, and Saul Bellow. Bellow was on the verge of publishing *The Adventures of Augie March*, the book that made him famous and a volume that still sits on a bookshelf in the living room of the Killens home.

On October 15, Killens hand delivered his application to the foundation's offices. He summarized his project as making "a substantial contribution in the field of creative writing towards the illumination of Negro life in the United States, particularly in the South." Although other novels on the "Negro theme" had been written, Killens argued that the aspects he was covering had never been done adequately. He promised to deal more fully with the varied dimensions of the southern way of life and projected that he could finish the novel within a year with Guggenheim support.[20]

The following month, James Jacobson, an editor at Simon and Schuster, provided another option. After consulting with fellow editor Herbert Alexander, who worked for affiliate Pocket Books, and to whom Killens had been introduced by Shore, Jacobson offered Killens an advance based on twenty-two chapters. The failed teen writer, compulsive army scribbler, serious student, and tireless reviser finally had a book deal. Following Hull's advice, Killens wrote to Robert Landry, who chaired the membership committee of the Authors League of America, to seek advice about the contract offer and apply for an associate membership, which entitled him to all rights and services except voting privileges. He signed the contract shortly thereafter and carried it around in his pocket for weeks. He ran into Hughes and rambled on for half an hour.

On December 8, Sanora Babb wrote from the *California Quarterly* with more good news. Anne-Marie Comert, a representative of Authors and

Publishers International Agency, had inquired about publishing "God Bless America" in France. Babb informed Killens that the journal would gladly grant permission and give him a chance to earn money. Killens followed up by contacting Comert and delivering two book chapters to her Manhattan office, seeking a bigger foreign prize than a short story publication. Comert responded on December 29 that the Paris office liked the short story and could use it, though a different song title at the end was requested because it had been determined that the average French reader did not know "The Darktown Strutters' Ball." However, Comert found the language spoken by the characters in the book chapters to be "absolutely untranslatable in French," making publication in France impossible.[21]

In April 1953, James Mathias notified Killens that his application for a Guggenheim had been denied, but by that point, the blow was minor. By late spring, Killens estimated that he had written three-quarters of the book and would finish by the end of the summer. Seeking feedback from various channels, he had sent a copy of the manuscript to Maxwell Geismar, whose reply was favorable. On June 4, Killens thanked Geismar and commented on his *Writers in Crisis*, which Killens found "stimulating and perceptive." Most interesting to him was the section on William Faulkner, "The Great Hatred," which took its title from Maurice Samuel's 1940 study of anti-Semitism. In Geismar's view, Faulkner used degrading depictions of women and African Americans to express his disdain for modern American society, particularly as influenced by the North. Killens found Geismar's reasoning audacious, "what with everybody burning incense to the Great Man (almost everybody)." Killens agreed with Geismar's criticism of Faulkner's attitude toward African Americans and women, adding, "I go along completely with your estimate of him as an unreconstructed rebel."[22]

Geismar wrote back later that month, expressing his pleasure at Killens's opinion of "The Great Hatred." Geismar reported that the essay had brought him a great deal of trouble with the southern critics who dominated the field, most notably Robert Penn Warren. Nonetheless, Geismar maintained, he would proceed along his "solitary path of dissent." He also offered to go over Killens's full manuscript when it was done. Geismar, who later wrote the foreword to Eldridge Cleaver's *Soul on Ice*, advised Killens, "Do it *all*, get it out, then go back steadily, and cut / and cut / and tighten it, I'd say, & work for *people*, good and bad as they are."[23]

The final push was on, and his characters remained as impatient as ever. Killens continued to work late on many nights, sometimes writing at the home of Charles and Fran Blackwell, who lived near City College and were the first readers of significant portions of the novel. On other occasions Killens used a hotel room, affixing a sign to the door: "Do Not Disturb — Writer at Work."[24]

The central family was now known as the Youngbloods, a possible rejoinder to Trueblood of *Invisible Man*.[25] The author put his assembled revolutionaries, who had proven their mettle through the preliminary stages of the white supremacist, capitalist assault, through their final paces. For one, they enact an African American unity that will hold firm in the face of hardship and thus ensure the social bonding required by the collective struggle against racism. Second, they are willing to defend themselves physically as state repression escalates. Unity means little if it can be easily eroded by intimidation. Finally, workers of every persuasion prove adept at organizing in resistance to their economic exploitation, which means in practical terms, as in "Stony the Road We Trod," the establishment of a viable trade union.

Progress on the cultural front is symbolized by Jubilee, an annual concert of Negro spirituals presented grudgingly by the students of Pleasant Grove School. The students resent singing for the amusement of a largely white audience and feel betrayed when Myles, who they had thought might object, agrees to coordinate the show. Inspired by the Reverend Ledbetter, however, Myles develops a twist, incorporating into Jubilee a narrative explaining the messages of rebellion encoded in the spirituals. Robby Youngblood, the narrator, explains to the audience that "Swing Low, Sweet Chariot" and "Steal Away to Jesus" allude to escape via the Underground Railroad and that "Go Down, Moses" celebrates Harriet Tubman. Thus, Killens uses the spirituals as a mechanism of empathy, accessing a cosmology shared by the black community of Crossroads and by much of his envisioned audience.[26]

The reconstituted Jubilee proves to be a huge hit with the African American audience, although many whites in the audience exit midway through the program out of disgust and seek Myles's dismissal. But the program has its intended effect, the creation of a militant and unified African American voice that enables Myles to retain his job. In addition, a radical understanding of the spirituals still implies universal appeal, as Wilkerson argued. Oscar Jefferson is deeply moved by the performance and is not one of the whites who leaves early.[27]

The question of self-defense revolves around Joe Youngblood. Joe is wounded during a dispute after he is cheated out of his salary at the mill. Ku Klux Klan members attempt to intimidate the African American community but are chased from Rockingham Quarters by gun-wielding residents. Robby had previously dreamed of an Armageddon-like, black-white show-down, and his dream comes to fruition during the novel's closing pages. However, Killens would not settle for a purely racialized vision. The Klan finds no welcome in Rockingham Quarters, but Oscar Jefferson and his son are accepted as they arrive to donate blood in an attempt to save Joe's life. At the outset of the novel, Joe Youngblood wonders how he is supposed to live in the white man's world. Killens answers that African Americans can only begin to live meaningfully—and Joe's life and death *are* meaningful—when they live in harmony with one another and adopt a posture of self-defense.[28]

In another shift from "Stony the Road We Trod," the site of union activity is the Oglethorpe Hotel rather than the mills. As the Great Depression sets in, African American workers are afraid to make waves and risk their low-level jobs. White workers prefer to accept unfit work conditions rather than to unite and fight with blacks. They are willing to endure exploitation and work against their own economic interests as long as they can retain white privilege. The situation recalls some of the limitations of the cio's efforts in the South. Killens later wrote that black people in the South hailed the cio as the "Freedom Train," but the train became "derailed in the muck and mire of white supremacy." Killens credited his old employer, however: "To give the c.i.o. its due, it did not keep the Negroes *out*. The trouble was that it could not keep the white workers *in*."[29]

Rob Youngblood and Oscar Jefferson fare better. African American workers are skeptical of eventually joining forces with whites, as Rob implores, but eventually realize that they possess no better option. As Willabelle Braxton reasons, "If we don't use the crackers against Mr. Ogle, Mr. Ogle'll use them against us."[30] Oscar, though a less dynamic figure than he is in "Stony the Road We Trod," convinces several white workers that an integrated union beats none at all. Ultimately, the union successes are not as final or dramatic as in "Stony the Road We Trod," but they represent a closer approximation to the realities of Georgia in the 1930s.

During the labor movement section of the novel, Killens mischievously enters his own text. He had already written hundreds and hundreds of pages, much of it veiled autobiography. Why not the fun of a role for himself? When organizer Jim Collins, formerly known as Jim Kilgrow, returns to Crossroads after a long absence to promote union activity, Oscar Jefferson, who had been Kilgrow's childhood friend, recognizes him during a meeting:

"Excuse me folks," Oscar said, "It's been such a long time since I seen this boy."

"Boy?" Jim Collins said.

"Mr. Kil—I mean Mr. Collins."

"That's more like it," Jim said. He turned to the others. "Well let's get down to the case on the docket."[31]

Youngblood was scheduled for release in mid-May 1954—coincidentally, the same week that the U.S. Supreme Court handed down its decision in *Brown v. Board of Education,* the legal ruling against Jim Crow education that served as a catalyst for the modern civil rights movement. The artistic rendering by Killens took aim at Jim Crow and its attendant economic exploitation and ushered in a new era in American literature.[32]

CHAPTER NINE

Mr. Youngblood, 1954–1955

Of the scenes and characters in *Youngblood*, reviewers responded most often to the revamped Jubilee, which had been inspired by Doxey Wilkerson; the whipping scene, which had impressed Dorothy Brewster at Columbia University and Elizabeth Pollock at New York University; and the book-long development of Laurie Lee. Granville Hicks titled his review "Laurie Grows Up." Another critic commented that Laurie stood out as "one of God's noblewomen" and added, "The poetry-like way in which Killens tells her story sets her apart as one of the most finely-etched women characters in modern American fiction."[1] Harriet Jaffe reported for the *Pacific Coast Youth Recorder*, "Particularly through Laurie Lee Youngblood and her daughter, the historic role that Negro women have played and are playing in the liberation struggles of their people is made real."[2] Critics also embraced Joe, Robby, Richard Myles, and Oscar Jefferson. Killens's large, robust, powerful, 566-page effort, the first noteworthy American novel that took as its focus a southern, activist, African American family and its role in effecting cross-ethnic political struggle, was an artistic hit. According to the critical consensus, he had drawn a memorable ensemble cast and imbued his work with lyrical description and majestic scope. Jim Maloney of the *Beaumont (Texas) Sunday Enterprise* considered *Youngblood* an especially strong contender for the National Book Award.[3]

Killens felt validated as a writer because of *Youngblood*'s critical reception but had learned enough to know that much more of his energy was required to translate sterling reviews into brisk sales. When Langston Hughes received his advance copy of the novel, he invited Killens to his Harlem home. As the two writers sat sipping rye and Coca-Cola, Hughes's favorite drink at the time, the elder conveyed some of his experiences in the publishing business: "These white folks will publish your book but they won't promote. You got to do your own promoting."[4]

Dial Press claimed to try. Acknowledging that a disappointment of the book business is that good books by new writers often go overlooked, the company unveiled its "New Novel Promotion Plan" to benefit the three novelists published that spring: Augusta Walker, H. Gifford Irion, and Killens. Dial committed to spending ten thousand dollars on advertising and to lavishly distributing complimentary copies to reviewers. Therefore, the initial splash for *Youngblood* was probably as good as could have been expected, though Dial's follow-up efforts to promote the title amounted, in the author's words, to "practically nothing."[5] Hughes gave Killens a list of bookstores, libraries, and individuals that might invite him to lecture and help sell his book. Taking the advice to heart, Killens began to develop an additional list based on his professional dealings with unions and other political and cultural groups.

He also made an important visit to a nearby basketball court. Still fancying himself a ballplayer in his late thirties, he frequented the local playground to test himself against men many years his junior. One was six foot, eight inch Les Campbell, later known as educator and activist Jitu Weusi. Campbell was less interested in Killens's game and more taken with the fact that someone in the neighborhood claimed to be a writer. Neither Campbell nor anyone else at the court possessed a practical sense of what that meant until the writer showed up with free copies of *Youngblood*.

The sales push began in earnest at the New York University Writing Center, where a tea was given in Killens's honor on publication day, May 21. The author appeared later in the month at the National Association for the Advancement of Colored People (NAACP) Youth Council in Manhattan. June included a guest spot on radio station WNYC and appearances at Brooklyn College, Countee Cullen Library, and the First African Methodist Episcopal Zion Church, along with a rather elaborate champagne reception on June 6 at the Harlem home of entertainer Juanita Hall. The event, cosponsored by Dial Press and the Harlem Writers Guild, was covered by the *Amsterdam News*. Jean Blackwell, a librarian at the Schomburg, served as chair. G. James Fleming and Louis Burnham delivered speeches about the importance and relevance of *Youngblood*. Killens then spoke for approximately ten minutes before selling and signing books, which for the occasion were discounted to $3.50 from the usual price of $3.95.

On June 20, Killens was featured at a "Starlight Forum" at the home of Annette Rubinstein, chair of the weekly series. Rubinstein had first met Killens at the Jefferson School of Social Science and eventually arranged the publication of *Youngblood* in Germany. The forums were sponsored by the New York Council of the Arts, Sciences, and Professions, and other writers featured that summer included Yuri Suhl, author of *Cowboy on a Wooden Horse*, and Phillip Bonosky, who penned the acclaimed *Burning Valley*.

Such early promotional efforts clearly succeeded: by June 30, several thousand copies of the book had been sold. Killens usually took one day a week to catch up on his mail and write thank-you letters to people who sponsored events for him. Then he turned back to promoting. He spent a week in Washington, D.C., mining old connections, and returned home to make numerous appearances in the metropolitan area during the remainder of the summer. On July 19, he spoke at the Harlem YMCA. The Harlem Round Table Association, chaired at the time by Professor S. R. Williams, had been meeting every Monday at the Y for nearly five years. Joining Killens as a special guest was Margaret Ting, who worked at the New York University Book Store and had agreed to do promotional work for Killens.

Not all promotional efforts unfolded as expected, and sometimes the lessons learned were comedic. Giddy about the spate of reviews and feeling quite important, Killens eagerly accepted when he received a phone call inviting him to address something like the Tenth National Convention of the Coptic Church of the USA (he did not precisely remember). His visions of a large crowd were dashed when he nervously made his way to an auditorium near the Apollo Theater and found just seven people—the man who invited him and served as the group's national chair, his devoted wife, and their five daughters. Killens recalled, "I was fit to be drawn and quartered."[6] He eventually delivered his prepared thirty-minute speech but for a long time thereafter was careful to screen his invitations and communicate clearly about the nature of the proposed event. And he kept his speeches focused on what he knew best: literature, history, civil rights, and workers' solidarity.

In August, he was back on the airwaves. He visited WNYC again on August 5 and was interviewed by Allen Jay on *Around New York*. Five days later, he joined Mike Wallace, cohost with his wife, Buff Cobb, of *Mike and Buff's Mail Bag* on WCBS. Wallace thought *Youngblood* "powerful and engrossing." Within the following two weeks, Killens was interviewed twice on WLIB. He also granted an interview to the *Brooklyn Eagle*. At the end of the month, the Harlem Writers Guild organized a second reception, this time at the home of Clarice Taylor in Queens. On August 30, Killens wrote letters to James Maloney, Taylor Glenn, and Don Murray, thanking them for their supportive book reviews and noting that he was available to deliver lectures.[7]

By September, Killens had begun to receive a considerable amount of fan mail. The most significant letter arrived from Herbert Biberman, who directed the proletarian film classic *Salt of the Earth* and had been blacklisted as a member of the Hollywood Ten, who had refused to testify before the House Committee on Un-American Activities in 1947. In language that Killens considered quite moving, Biberman explained that he had read *Youngblood* while traveling back and forth on the train between New York and Washington, D.C., and that it had constituted one of his most memorable literary experiences. "It seems to me that in former eras in our country's life, when writers cared deeply about the people and had open throats and hearts which articulated them—there were other such experiences. One doesn't expect them today—and yet one more truly expects them more—for they are more sorely the protection of our future than ever before, and so desperately needed." He also mentioned that he had recently met in Chicago with African American staff members of the Packinghouse Union and expressed fervently his belief that stories such as Killens's must continue to be written by so-called minorities and members of the working class. Biberman added, "*Youngblood* is one of the most American novels ever written, as the Negro people are among the most American of our peoples, as you, representing them with such justifiable love and admiration are among the most American writers."[8]

Biberman proved catalytic in terms of opening up Chicago for Killens, who began to focus on a proposed book tour. He made a brief trip to the city in October to visit with his enormously proud father and to meet Richard Durham, who held the post of national program coordinator for the Packinghouse Workers. Durham, a transplanted Mississippian about the same age as Killens, was also an editor and dramatist, having produced *Des-*

tination Freedom, a landmark radio series that celebrated African American achievement. Killens also met with relative youngsters Oscar Brown Jr., who worked as a program director for the union, and Frank London Brown (no relation), a writer who became one of Killens's favorite people. Killens found the two men a study in contrasts: "Frank was mild and easy-going on the surface, a volcano underneath; Oscar, nervous and obviously impatient to get the show put on the road."[9]

Back in New York, Killens wrote to Durham on October 21 that getting together with his group had seemed like Homecoming Day, even though he had never previously met any of the members. Inspired by his direct reconnection with unionists, he added, "I should like to spend a couple of *busy* weeks in your city."[10] But much organizing had to be done before a trip could be finalized because Killens insisted that he at least break even on the trip. His prime imperative was to move books, but he had meager personal funds with which to do so. In addition, he figured that if he had to spend so much time promoting *Youngblood* instead of working on his next novel, he would have to make the venture as worthwhile as possible. The key, then, was to hit enough colleges, libraries, clubs, workplaces, and parties. As he wrote to Oscar Brown Jr. on November 9, when the trip was in jeopardy, "I dislike very much to belabor [expenses] unduly, but like with so many other things, it certainly isn't the principle of the thing, it's the damn economics. I've had to get tough—even with myself—on this question."[11]

He need not have fretted so much. Oscar Brown proved instrumental in paving the way. The future world-famous entertainer was then a twenty-eight-year-old activist with an eclectic reach. As a member of the Communist Party, he ran for the Illinois legislature on the Progressive Party slate in 1948. Four years later, he hustled onto the Republican Party ticket and ran for Congress. He negotiated with organizations as different as the American Civil Liberties Union and the Unitarian Church. Frank London Brown, then twenty-seven, had varied interests and connections as well. He and Oscar set in motion the busy fortnight Killens sought, arranging appearances before the Packinghouse Workers, the Chicago Branch of the NAACP, and the Emma Lazarus Women's Club as well as a visit to the offices of Johnson Publishing.

Before heading to Chicago on November 20, Killens attended to a few other professional matters. Although the *Library Journal* recommended *Youngblood*, Chicago's Central Library rejected the novel on the basis of an internal reviewer's opinion that the language was too strong and, more important, that the book was "unfair to white folks." Vivian Harsh of the

George Cleveland Hall Public Library had informed Killens of the situation during his trip to Chicago in October, which led him to a subsequent conversation with a staff member at Central who concluded that Killens was not "bitter or anti-white" and promised to read the book and reconsider it. Killens also had Dial Press forward copies directly to Harsh.[12] In addition, Lawrence Reddick at Atlanta University's Trevor Arnett Library requested that Killens donate the typescript and galley proof, which had been on loan to the Schomburg Library but were scheduled to be returned later in the month. On November 1, Killens told Reddick that he would be pleased to give the materials to the university and suggested that he receive an invitation to visit campus.

On November 5, Killens spoke at a Manhattan "Break the Ghetto" conference that sought to address issues of community relations, employment, and housing and was sponsored by Southerners for Civil Rights, chaired by Broadus Mitchell. The event featured Killens along with Richard Lincoln, public relations director of the Urban League of Greater New York; and Robert Carter, assistant special counsel for the NAACP. The following week, as he had two years earlier, he hand delivered his application for a Guggenheim Fellowship. Included were a promotional brochure for *Youngblood*, the additions of Maxwell Geismar, George Joel, and Herbert Alexander to his list of references, and the description, "I am at present at work on a new novel dealing with World War II in the South Pacific, and the relationship between Negro and white soldiers and the tedious growth of friendship and understanding between the two groups."[13] During this time he wrote several more communiqués to shore up plans for the Chicago visit and appeared at an assembly program at Brooklyn's Girls High.

Killens then headed to Chicago, where, along with his promotional events, he caught up with an old acquaintance, Larry Sperber, secretary of the leftist National Lawyers Guild, who had traveled from Los Angeles to attend the organization's convention in the city. Sperber had contacted Killens the previous October and was eager to support his work. Both men set their promotional sights on California, with Sperber taking the lead in developing a schedule of events. They targeted the latter part of January because Killens wanted to spend some time beforehand working on the new novel. While in New York, he hoped to confine promoting *Youngblood* to weekends.

When Killens returned from Chicago, he found an encouraging letter waiting for him from a second member of the Hollywood Ten, Albert Maltz, whom Killens had contacted at Biberman's suggestion. Maltz regarded *Youngblood* as "one of the best novels ever written on American life." He conveyed to the author, "I think you will (unfortunately) fail the talent and literary skill you already have if you do not in the years to come become a major, world novelist. I am sure you will." Unlike many critics of the novel, Maltz thought the book should have been one hundred or two hundred pages longer to allow for greater development of some characters, particularly Joe Youngblood.[14]

Maltz then turned to the matter of foreign sales. He had recommended the novel to several foreign publishers and asked Killens to send them copies. Maltz also expressed dismay about Killens's contract with Dial, feeling that the press inappropriately deprived Killens of 10 percent of the foreign rights and should not have the right to approve all foreign contracts. He advised that Dial would not interfere with publication in capitalist countries but might when it came to socialist ones. He warned Killens to fight hard because publication in the Soviet Union or the German Democratic Republic could mean large print runs and bountiful royalties. Maltz closed by reassuring Killens of his artistic ability: "You are not only a good novelist, but a big one, a very big one. Neither Gorky nor Chekhov began so well."[15]

Killens next turned his attention to the California trip. His primary host in Los Angeles would be attorney Leo Branton, an emerging force in the legal world who had represented Smith Act defendants.[16] On January 21, *The Los Angeles Tribune* announced Killens's arrival with a brief item that termed his novel "sensational" and a large photograph of Killens and Branton.[17] Branton and his wife, Geri, hosted a large party for Killens, with attendees including Branton clients Nat King Cole and Dorothy Dandridge. Dandridge's film, *Carmen Jones*, had premiered four months earlier, and she was the toast of Hollywood. She subsequently called the Killens home several times to discuss possible projects, attention that did not thrill Grace Killens.

Dandridge was not the only woman who expressed an interest in Killens, though Grace generally chose to disregard such instances, weighing in only when forced to do so. On one occasion during the war, John wrote to his wife that a woman he met in the Philippines reminded him of her. Grace, who to this day wears both her and her husband's wedding rings, sent a third ring to her husband to aid him in his meditations about how far down that path he wanted to travel. Later, an Australian woman visiting the United States called John Killens, who spruced himself up and then went out to meet the woman, returning several hours later. Grace recalled,

"And that was it." Given John Killens's extensive involvement in cultural and political activities, which gave numerous women reason to contact him, Grace believed that becoming overly jealous, given her husband's bottom-line commitment to her, would have been self-defeating.[18]

Also on hand at the Brantons' party was an FBI informant. The occasion was cosponsored by the Hollywood branch of the National Council of the Arts, Sciences, and Professions, a group that, though declining in significance, still comprised the most important left-wing cultural organization in Los Angeles. Among the guests was another blacklisted dues payer, John Howard Lawson. A third member of the Hollywood Ten, the sixty-year-old writer, activist, and theorist had served as the first president of the Screen Writers Guild and headed the Hollywood section of the Communist Party. Considered an "aesthetic hard-liner," Lawson conversed easily with Killens, somewhat of a hard-liner himself.[19] Lawson, who scripted *Cry, the Beloved Country* under a pseudonym, was working on a play about Nat Turner, *Thunder Morning*, and asked Killens to read it after its completion. He also congratulated Killens on his "epoch-making" novel. On June 12, Lawson sent the manuscript to Killens for feedback. The novelist admired the dramatic attempt but did not think the Turner character had been developed sufficiently.[20]

During the first week in February, Killens moved north to work the Bay Area. On the evening of February 4, he took the train from San Francisco to San Jose for a 7:30 engagement with a black women's group. He spoke on the role of the African American writer and the impact of Frederick Douglass on his work. The audience was enthusiastic, and the affair continued longer than Killens had expected; he began to worry about missing the last train back to San Francisco, which departed at 11:00. At 10:50, he "rudely" began gathering his materials and heading for the exit, finally spurring the event's chairs into motion. He missed the train, and the women dropped him at the bus station to await a 2:30 bus. It finally arrived at 3:30, but it was a local, making numerous stops along the way to San Francisco.[21]

Dick Bancroft, whom Killens had known as a union organizer in Washington, D.C., picked him up around 10:00 in the morning. Two hours later, he spoke in Oakland before Men of Tomorrow, an African American civic group, before moving on to a party given by a black women's club. "The place was jammed and the people enthusiastic," Killens recalled, "and I was half asleep." The mistress of ceremonies began an overblown introduction during which she suggested that she was a dear and long-standing friend of the author and had predicted his success. But then she forgot her guest's name. When she turned toward him for help, Killens turned away, thinking, "Let her lie her way out of this embarrassment." The woman introduced him as Mr. Youngblood.[22]

Rose Eden, a friend of Killens from before the war, hosted an event at her home on the evening of February 5. According to an FBI account, Killens told those gathered, "A meeting such as this would probably be called a Communist meeting, but why worry about being called a Communist when you are fighting for the freedom of the Negro people."[23] Another member of the Hollywood Ten, Alvah Bessie, who was present at Eden's, agreed. Born in 1904 in New York City, Bessie worked as a fiction writer and journalist before migrating to Hollywood and the Communist Party in the 1930s. At the age of thirty-three, he fought in Spain on behalf of the Republican forces before returning to Hollywood, where he achieved modest success as a writer. He received an Oscar nomination for his original story contribution to the 1945 film *Objective, Burma!* After refusing to testify before the House Committee on Un-American Activities, he was jailed, serving his sentence in a Texas prison along with Biberman. Bessie was unable to secure work in Los Angeles after his release and moved to San Francisco, where he worked for the International Longshore and Warehouse Union and shied away from formal affiliation with the Communist Party, though not from leftist figures such as Killens, of whom Bessie became a huge supporter.[24]

By the middle of February, Killens was back in New York but still being publicized in the Bay Area. It was Negro History Week, the first such observance since the *Brown* decision, a point made on February 15 by radio personality Jim Grady during his KCBS program, *This Is San Francisco*. Grady pointed out, "It was only last year that the supreme law of the land took notice of the fact that the so-called 'separate and equal' status of segregated schools was, in fact, a violation of the civil rights of the Negro people in this country." He then recounted Killens's explanation of the significance of Negro History Week:

> Now how do you think my boy—and millions like him—feels when he
> looks into his school books—and sees no Negroes, looks into his TV and
> sees no Negroes, or goes to the movies and sees no Negroes? Or, if he does,
> in roles that he knows do not reflect his true life. Negro history is so impor-

tant because *not* giving equal emphasis to the work and contributions of the Negro people, their children are being deprived of the heritage that is rightly theirs. And this lack has great impact on the white children. For if they do not come to know and understand that Negro and white have a common stake in their country's traditions, they are vulnerable to all the misrepresentation and conflict that ignorance creates.

Grady concluded by asserting that Negro History Week should be a year-long program and advising his listeners that he would tell them about *Youngblood* on his next show.[25]

The following day, Grady spent a few minutes promoting the novel: "Most books are written either as entertainment or to make money. This is a book that had to be written, and it is that sense of necessity that gives it special impact."[26] The FBI was interested in the impact of Grady's show, and Killens's appearance was noted in the bureau's files.

On February 15, Killens visited New York's P.S. 25. Eight days later, he visited Cornell University at the invitation of Carl Yeargen and members of the Watermargin Club. These efforts interfered with his work on his new novel, but in early March, he told friends that he was determined to get to it: "Now that our history and brotherhood have been put in mothballs, for another year, it's back to the grind again."[27] Nevertheless, his attention remained divided. The novel would always be his preferred genre, a point he often stressed to his friend Loften Mitchell, who ceaselessly expressed preference for the play. However, Killens had committed himself to making a living, preferably a comfortable one, as a writer, and thus could ill afford to forgo assignments that would pay the bills. His standard of living would not be calibrated to his wife's wages, an arrangement that satisfied more than a few other novelists. He had achieved much of his high school fantasy—he had a pretty wife and children, and he was credit to his race. But although he was a political romantic, Killens was not romantic about the idea of being a poor artist. Moreover, Killens had begun a career-long practice of working on multiple projects simultaneously, an insurance policy against writer's block. If he could not make headway on one project, he could turn to another.

On May 15, 1955, one such side effort reached fruition with the airing of *Lamp unto My Feet*, a television show for which Killens had written the script. CBS paid Killens three hundred dollars to spin out a short tale involving a businessman, David Manning, who argues for stern prosecution when he is informed by the police that the truck thieves who have been plaguing his business have finally been arrested and charged not only with theft but with bribery. He changes his tune, however, when the ringleader is identified as his teenage son. He attempts to cover for the boy by telling the police he had authorized his son to pick up the truck, but this effort is thwarted because the stolen truck is not Manning's. At this point, Manning becomes belligerent and prepares to use his wealth and power to subvert justice. Manning's wife, Lizzie, then explains to her husband that his habit of covering for their son's past transgressions has led to his present problem. She even accuses Manning of modeling thievery by taking over his friend's trucking business: "You taught [the boy] everything in life could be bought." Lizzie suggests that they should now stress such qualities as brotherhood and genuine love in their dealings with their son. Manning's associate who is handling the matter then calls, and the ringing telephone jerks Manning's mind back to his plan to extract his son from trouble, while Lizzie protests, "No David—no—not that way." The script ends, "Hand poised he turns to meet her desperate look. His face registers his conflict as he lifts the phone." For the remainder of the half-hour show, the moderator, Lyman Bryson, and guest, Carlyle Marney, discussed the story's moral implications.[28]

During this time, Killens remained involved in political events and worked to formalize a set of rules for the Harlem Writers Guild. The group's immediate goals were to raise the level of criticism in the workshop and develop a forum or other public affair at least twice per year. The group also was to discuss the feasibility of creating a magazine and bestowing annual awards for journalism and fiction.

As the summer of 1955 loomed, Killens's stomach began to bother him. He blamed his ailments on the war, attributing them to something in the jungle, in the food, in the water, in injections, in the post-nuclear-blast air of Japan that had prolonged or delayed effects. But Killens was suffering from appendicitis, and as he was recovering from an appendectomy performed at Brooklyn's University Hospital, he received cheering professional news. The first printing of *Youngblood* had sold out.

CHAPTER TEN

Stalking the Truth, 1955–1957

His health restored—he also quit smoking after his surgery—
John Oliver Killens grappled once more with the contradiction
of his artistic lifetime: How could he remain isolated to write
but also promotionally and politically engaged? He could simply
turn inward and back to his drafts, especially the war material,
which was still a novel in waiting, and to other literary ventures
to help support himself and his family. He could also look for
the action outside, as he had done in varying degrees in Atlanta,
in Washington, in the military, and in New York. As the summer of 1955 wore on, the strongest pull was apparently external,
occasioned by the scheduled October publication of the pocket
book edition of *Youngblood*, which would open new opportunities for promotion, particularly among workers. Although the
Chicago tour was successful, Richard Durham suggested that
a book costing four dollars per copy was not the easiest item
to push among the unions. But the pocket book edition would
debut at only fifty cents. Attractive along with the price, Killens thought, would be the cover, which depicted the transfu-
sion scene involving Joe Youngblood and Junior Jefferson. The
author called it "a thing of beauty and great significance" and
thought that it would create a stir.[1]

On July 3, Killens wrote several letters designed to jump-start
promotion. He wrote to Durham about the prospects of pushing the pocket book edition among the Packinghouse Workers
both in Chicago and nationally. He sent similar letters to Frank

London Brown and to David Moore, who worked in Detroit for Local 600 of the United Auto Workers of America. With the West Coast in mind, he wrote to Dick Bancroft, a reliable supporter, and to Alvah Bessie at the *Dispatcher* in San Francisco. Killens asked Bessie, active on behalf of the International Longshore and Warehouse Union (ILWU), to explore the possibilities of promoting the book within the union. Bessie responded favorably and helped to land *Youngblood* on the ILWU Book Club List along with such titles as Bill Cahn's *Milltown*, Saul Alinsky's *John L. Lewis*, and Leo Huberman's *Man's Worldly Goods*. The ILWU advertised the novel by explaining that the host of characters included "sharecroppers and white 'aristocrats,' educated and uneducated whites and Negroes, teachers and ministers of the gospel and small businessmen." It then highlighted the Marxist angle: "All of them are here and the actual relationships which exist between them today are explored with profound understanding of the class forces in operation in the South."[2]

John Howard Lawson wrote from Los Angeles to thank Killens for his evaluation of the play and assure him that Lawson and Frances Williams, who were collaborating on production plans, were "studying your letter with care. . . . [E]very one of your comments will have a very real effect on my further work on the play." Lawson also inquired about the paperback edition of *Youngblood* and offered to assist in publicity efforts.[3]

Locally, Grace, deciding that Margaret Ting was peremptory and assuming and just too cozy with the boss, replaced her as John's secretary. Although she might have balanced the power dynamics in the home as she saw fit, Grace was not necessarily an upgrade as a secretary or agent. Neither she nor her husband proved a hard bargainer. She fielded numerous queries about speaking engagements for Killens in the New York metropolitan area and normally suggested a fee of seventy-five dollars plus expenses. However, any prospective sponsor with even the slightest negotiating skill could get him for twenty-five.

Despite his promotional activities, Killens did begin to work somewhat earnestly on his new fiction manuscript, and he confidently read a chapter at a meeting of the Harlem Writers Guild. Unimpressed, members accused him of buying into his own press clippings, trying to be slick, doing surface work just to get by. The criticism apparently stung. Killens's first response was to suspect that jealousy fueled his colleagues' remarks—he was the only guild member to have published a novel. He later realized, however, that the point was valid and that he had to address it if he were to remain honest about his craft. In fact, he ultimately came to appreciate the Harlem Writers Guild members' seriousness about writing and their forthrightness concerning critique. Those qualities, not sameness of political conviction, glued together the group, though political passion was also important. Killens remarked, "Some of us saw the writer as a hunter and this civilization as the man-made jungle. To stalk the truth in this jungle was to us the writer's mission. Not to kill the truth when we cornered it but to hold it aloft as a torch to set men free."[4]

While scrambling to prepare talks and revise prose, Killens took time out on the evening of July 19 to see Sidney Poitier in *Blackboard Jungle*, attending the film with his family, including his mother, now a member of his household. That night, Killens wrote his "first fan letter," telling the actor that the Killens family had been impressed, with eleven-year-old Chuck and eight-year-old Barbara cheering at the end of the movie: "You see, there is so little to cheer about in Hollywood these days." Killens also commended Glenn Ford, screenwriter Evan Hunter, and MGM. Referring to the movie's mixed critical reception, he offered that if the movie were not a good one, it would just have to do until a good one came along. He concluded, "Three rousing cheers to Sidney Poitier from the Killenses."[5]

During the first week of August, the Killenses were more somber when they had to make an unscheduled but not totally unexpected train trip to Macon. Carrie Coleman, age eighty-five and a major source of inspiration for John Killens, died on August 2. Funeral services were held four days later. Despite the tremendous loss, Killens relished the opportunity to visit members of his extended family and to renew friendships with Ballard alumni Lafayette Bonner and P. B. Brunson and with Lewis Hendrix Mounts. The former assistant principal subsequently sent Killens a thoughtful letter congratulating his old pupil and agreeing that the positive critical reception *Youngblood* had received was warranted. However, Mounts thought that the novel's portrayal of Macon's racial situation was too drastic.[6]

Word about *Youngblood* was spreading, as editions were published in Canada, Germany, Denmark, and Great Britain and as readers began to discuss the novel and the timeliness of its themes. On December 9, Killens traveled to Melrose Park, Pennsylvania, just outside Philadelphia, to participate in the Friday Forum, a community discussion group. He read from *Youngblood*, spoke about civil rights violations in the South, and promoted the National Association for the Advancement of Colored People (NAACP). In the lively question-and-answer session that ensued, an audience member asked about his view on the use of civil disobedience by Negroes, a tactic that some in the NAACP suggested was useful. Killens responded that he was "opposed to such policy, that the Negroes did not have enough power to make it effective, and that such a policy would lead only to mass retaliation by the whites and make conditions for the Negroes worse than they are now." He was also asked about New York congressman Adam Clayton Powell Jr.'s presence as an unofficial delegate to the Bandung Conference of African and Asian countries the previous April. The Eisenhower administration, particularly Secretary of State John Foster Dulles, had discouraged Powell from traveling to the Indonesian event because of the presence at the conference of communist leaders such as China's Chou En-lai and the suspicion that Powell would use the forum to make critical remarks about the U.S. racial situation that would damage the country's image internationally. However, according to the *Pittsburgh Courier*, Powell "showered American racial policies with saccharine praise."[7]

Powell also made disparaging comments about Paul Robeson, prompting Killens to label the congressman "strictly an 'Uncle Tom' type of Negro, . . . doing the Negroes a disservice, and . . . a traitor to the Negro people." He cited Michigan representative Charles Diggs, who had announced that he would challenge the seating of all members of Congress from Mississippi on the grounds that blacks had not been allowed to vote, as an example of a black politician "really fighting seriously for his people." When asked his opinion about the State Department's sponsorship of foreign performances of *Porgy and Bess*, George Gershwin's 1935 opera, Killens said that while he enjoyed the music, he thought that the show degraded blacks: "The Negroes who play in *Porgy and Bess* are opportunists who place their theatrical careers above the damage caused by the show to the Negro people as a whole."[8]

The following evening, Killens attended a party Langston Hughes hosted for South African writer Peter Abrahams, who was touring the country to promote his new book, *Mine Boy*. Abrahams had asked Hughes about meeting "some of our writers," and Hughes included Killens among about a dozen authors invited. Killens took great pride in the attention from Hughes, whom he had long idolized.[9]

As 1955 drew to a close, Killens had reached an activist crossroads. Criticisms of Powell and civil disobedience notwithstanding, much of the terrain had shifted. For the rest of his life, he remained committed to the idea of Pan-Africanism, but in domestic terms, the style of progressivism in which he had invested enormous energy for twenty years was all but extinct as a political force in the United States. The Communist Party that Killens viewed favorably in "For National Freedom" and whose ranks had once swelled to eighty thousand saw its membership drop to fifteen thousand or so during the postwar years and fall even further to just a few thousand following the revelations at the Twentieth Congress of the Communist Party of the Soviet Union and the 1956 Soviet invasion of Hungary. In New York, both the *Freedom* newspaper and the Council on African Affairs were forced to cease operations by the end of 1955. Robeson broke down physically, requiring prostate surgery and experiencing an extremely difficult recovery. Even the CIO reconciled with the AFL, and the two groups formally merged. The FBI was still a nuisance, but in a less repressive, if not less paranoid, context. McCarthy's power had been broken in the Senate, and the House Un-American Activities Committee operated with considerably more restraint. The FBI continued to watch Killens, however. On October 26, an agent used some pretext—perhaps the offer of a job, which was one of the bureau's stock ploys—to interview Killens at his home. Killens advised that he was self-employed as a writer and had no time for additional employment. Within the next few weeks, the bureau conducted another background check on Killens, obtaining academic, housing, police, and election records. And more FBI ruses and inquiries were forthcoming.[10] But by that point, the FBI probably had more informants than the Communist Party had members. There would be no return to the heyday of the Old Left. In fact, the symbolic death knell was just over the horizon in the form of Khrushchev's revelations about Stalin's butchery. Taking stock of the collapsing Left no doubt spurred Killens to increase his involvement in the NAACP, and he won election to the staff of the Brooklyn chapter as a member at large later that month.

The national gaze shifted to Montgomery, Alabama, where the specific type of organizing that came to dominate African American political initiatives for the next decade was now vividly and dramatically on display. The momentum that culminated in the historic December 1955 bus boycott had been building for months. In March, Claudette Colvin was arrested for violating Montgomery's segregation ordinance. Local activists including E. D. Nixon, a railroad worker who wielded significant influence inside the local NAACP chapter, decided that Colvin, an unwed pregnant teen lacking "refinement," failed to represent a suitable cause célèbre. Seven months later,

Mary Louise Smith was apprehended for refusing to yield her seat on a bus to a white passenger. As was the case with the Colvin incident, Nixon decided, based on Smith's less-than-sparkling family background, that the community would not rally around her case. Thus the stage was set for the unimpeachable Rosa Parks and her unique ability to inspire members of the city's working and middle classes; for Jo Ann Robinson and the rest of the fired-up members of the Women's Political Council; for Nixon himself, a leader of long standing; for the dynamic, twenty-six-year-old Martin Luther King Jr., who delivered his first sermon as pastor-designate at Dexter Avenue Baptist Church the same month the hardcover edition of *Youngblood* came out; and for Montgomery's resolute black community, like a cast of Killens characters, "walking together."[11]

Killens almost immediately sensed the full potential of the political and literary possibilities unfolding in the Cradle of the Confederacy. As he fulfilled engagements in the South in January 1956 and turned forty years old with little fanfare, he eagerly made the first of several visits to Montgomery for a firsthand look at the action and to visualize concretely the setting for a screenplay. He was impressed by the boycotters' solidarity and learned that a significant number of black men in the city had stopped riding the buses before the official boycott because they could no longer tolerate the debasement, including the disrespect shown to black women passengers, whom white bus drivers constantly referred to as "apes," "bitches," and "nigger whores." In Killens's view, the men had the choice of "castration, death, or tired feet."[12]

On February 23, Killens spoke in Baton Rouge, Louisiana, where he was hosted by Morgan Brown, a fellow 1933 graduate of Ballard and now a member of the faculty of Southern University's Department of Social Sciences, and Blyden Jackson, the head of the English Department. Killens addressed a humanities class of approximately 60 students as well as an audience of 150 or so freshmen and sophomores before meeting with the Pierian Club, a gathering of English majors, minors, and assorted specialists, including members of the staff.

On March 11, he read from his new novel at a Philadelphia event organized by literary newcomer Sarah Wright. The affair was the back end of an exchange orchestrated at least in part by Hughes. The previous week, the Harlem Writers Guild hosted a reading by Wright and Lucy Smith at Poitier's home. Wright and Smith had coauthored *Give Me a Child*, a volume of poetry Hughes described as "lovely indeed in achievement and in intent." Carl Van Vechten added, "I am enchanted with the contents."[13]

In Philadelphia, Killens read at length from his manuscript. He was warmly received overall, and he later conveyed to Wright how much he enjoyed the reception and appreciated the effort that went into it. In addition to recognizing the achievements of Wright, Smith, and Killens, the reception was intended to spark black literary activity in the city. Wright, in particular, envisioned a local writers' workshop comparable to the Harlem Writers Guild. Killens encouraged her experiments with fiction and helped to promote her poetry. As a result of Killens's efforts, Almena Lomax at the *Los Angeles Tribune* reviewed *Give Me a Child* in a fashion Wright considered "absolutely stunning."[14] Although Killens was not really an established writer, he had already begun to follow Hughes's model of generosity.

Later in March, Killens was a platform guest at Brooklyn's Concord Baptist Church as King spoke. Ten thousand people tried to crowd into the church, and the event raised four thousand dollars, including fifty dollars from Killens, for the Montgomery Improvement Association. Killens later expressed his support for the "fifty thousand who have shown the rest of us Americans how it can be done" and sent King a copy of *Youngblood*, which "tries to deal with many of the issues you and your colleagues are presently dealing with so ably in real life."[15]

King wrote back that he had heard of the "greatness and depth of *Youngblood*" but had not yet had time to peruse it. However, he said, "I am sure that it will meet a real need in my life." King noted that he and Killens were both Georgia natives and stated a desire to talk with the novelist in the near future.[16] The two subsequently met on several occasions, including a Killens visit to King's home in Montgomery, although they continued their respectful disagreement on the subject of civil disobedience. Despite the tactical success of the Montgomery Bus Boycott, Killens never embraced nonviolent resistance as an overarching strategy to defeat white supremacy. Killens later described King as a "beautiful human being. . . . [H]e joked, he laughed, he loved (and hated, I believe), he cried, he doubted."[17]

Killens's disagreements with King were mild compared to the author's rejection of William Faulkner's articulated gradualism. In 1956, *Life* magazine published Faulkner's "Letter to the North," imploring African Americans to go slow "for a moment."[18] Killens responded with "How Long Is a Moment, Mr. Faulkner? A Letter to William Faulkner and His Middle Grounders." Killens advised Faulkner that speediness, not proceeding slowly, was more to the point and urged Faulkner and his followers to tell federal and local authorities, "It's late, very late, but not too late for the government to do all within its capacity to unbrainwash the Southern mind with educational materials, pamphlets, books, forums, movies, T.V. scripts, etc., on the meaning and ways and workings of democracy." He zoomed in on Faulkner's comment that he had once opposed compulsory segregation and now just as strongly condemned compulsory integration. Killens believed that laws, propaganda, and terrorism are needed to keep people apart because their natural impulse is to get together; therefore, all segregation was compulsory. By the same token, he felt that when barriers were lifted, people would mix, so there would be no need to compel them do so. Stripped of modifiers, Killens argued, Faulkner's statement boiled down to "I was against segregation. I am against integration," which also meant, "I was once for integration but now am for segregation." Killens pronounced himself "utterly amazed when a person of [Faulkner's] literary stature, . . . proven facility with the written word, . . . world-wide prominence, comes up with such an ambiguous statement . . . on the most important issue facing the American people in this decade."[19]

Killens added a postscript when Faulkner later clarified his position by telling a *London Times* reporter that he would "fight for Mississippi against the United States, even if it meant going out into the street and shooting Negroes."[20] Killens wrote, "There was great hope for you in so many liberal-minded people's bosom, but, alas, you have deceived them. . . . You reveal yourself now in 1956 A.D. as an unreconstructed Southern rebel, ready to go to war, even as your great grandfather did before you, to save the holy cow of white supremacy."[21]

That spring, Killens worked the streets of Brooklyn in his role as a captain in the NAACP membership drive. He aimed to recruit ten people who would, in turn, serve as recruiters. He also chaired the Brooklyn branch's Cultural Activities Committee. As on previous occasions, his NAACP involvement helped to stall an FBI investigation. On June 15, New York bureau officials requested permission from J. Edgar Hoover's office to interview Killens formally about his past dealings with the Communist Party and some of its front groups as well as speak to his current inclinations and sympathies. On June 27, however, authority was denied: "It is noted that you have developed no evidence of Communist Party activity on the part of the subject. His principal activity has to do with the National Association for the Advancement of Colored People. He is employed as a writer and his books deal with the controversial subject of race relations."[22]

On July 16, after eight years on Lafayette Avenue, the Killens family moved into a three-story brick home at 1392 Union Street in the Crown Heights section of Brooklyn. Their residence ultimately became one of the city's key black cultural salons, a site of innumerable and spirited gatherings. Louis Reyes Rivera, Killens's son-in-law, remembers that at least three episodes of Gil Noble's acclaimed *Like It Is* stemmed directly from informal lectures John Henrik Clarke, with Noble in attendance, delivered in the Killens living room. Sarah Wright, who relocated to New York, recalled that at meetings of the Harlem Writers Guild, which Killens sometimes hosted, he would blare the music of Duke Ellington and then remark, "Now that the saints have arrived we can begin to work."[23]

Near the end of August, Killens received a letter from Alfred Duckett, a public relations representative for the multitalented Harry Belafonte, at the time on his way to becoming the most important black entertainer in America. Belafonte, Duckett reported, had read *Youngblood* several times and wanted an autographed copy. Duckett also declared himself "in complete agreement with Mr. Belafonte that *Youngblood* is a magnificent job."[24] Killens subsequently had lengthy conversations with Phil Stein and Charlie Katz, two Belafonte associates, about a number of film projects with which Killens might become involved. On the day after Christmas, Killens asked Belafonte for an update on those plans and wondered whether Belafonte would be willing to make an appearance at the Brooklyn NAACP. On April 25, Belafonte joined Ruby Dee, Ossie Davis, Sidney Poitier, Geoffrey Holder, and Carmen Delavallade onstage at the Manhattan Center as part of "The Night of the Stars for Civil Rights." Killens believed that a collaboration between him and Belafonte had boundless potential and looked forward to "spending a number of hours exploring and concretizing. There is so much to say to America, culturally speaking."[25]

Belafonte hired Killens to do a screen treatment based on the legend of John Henry, one of Killens's favorite folk characters. In early February, he received a five-hundred-dollar advance, half of the total fee; at around the same time, Katz sent Killens a contract to option *Youngblood*, and they finalized the deal later that month, with Killens receiving one thousand dollars to secure the option. Two weeks later, when Killens and Belafonte met in New York, the writer handed him the finished John Henry movie treatment. Killens received another five hundred dollars from Belafonte that spring in exchange for writing copy for the souvenir program for his upcoming summer tour. Killens wrote more than the fifteen hundred words for which he had been contracted, describing Belafonte in Robesonian terms without explicitly mentioning Robeson: "Mr. Belafonte is an artist of affirmation. His is not an art of negation. His art is an affirmation of the universal axiom that in all men the most impelling force is human dignity."[26]

On May 17, Killens joined Belafonte, Poitier, Dee, and the Robesons—Paul, Eslanda, and Paul Jr.—at a Prayer Pilgrimage led by Martin Luther King Jr. on the steps of the Lincoln Memorial to commemorate the third anniversary of the *Brown* decision. A week or so later, the Killenses held a dinner party, with guests including Belafonte, Poitier, and Dee as well as Killens's brother-in-law, Thomas Jones. As the diners discussed the prospects for black political progress, Jones jokingly disparaged current efforts with a version of the age-old "Negroes ain't ready" diatribe. His sister and brother-in-law could enjoy such a lively invitation to debate, but Jones had misread his larger audience, casting a pall over the affair. On May 31, Jones sent Killens a copy of a letter he had sent to Belafonte in hopes of repairing the damage and requested the addresses of Dee and Poitier. Jones told Killens, "I'm afraid in being too light and assuming too much about your guests, I missed the point and carried over too far. Please forgive me for the faux pas."[27]

To Belafonte, Jones apologized for his "too flippant and casual appraisal" and his "ill-fated excursion into the so-called Socratic device of making the other fellow prove and win his point by forcing him to consider the contrary view." Jones made the case that with the leadership potential of artists, writers, politicians, religious figures, professionals, and labor activists, African Americans had reached the most heightened state of readiness in their history with respect to seizing full citizenship rights. In addition, Jones explained, world conditions and opinion were on the side of African Americans. However, he stressed the need for mass preparation and education, the point he apparently had been trying to develop at the dinner party.[28]

On June 17, Killens heard again from Katz, who had reached the conclusion, based on his experience with movie studios, that the path to the screen for *Youngblood* ran through Broadway and that the novel would make an ideal play: "If the character of the young northern school teacher is telescoped into the son of the Youngbloods, we may develop a dramatic unity which would result in a patent three-act structure." In Katz's conception, act 1 would cover "childhood in the South—winding up with the beating by the mother of her boy at the command of the police." In act 2, "the son goes north and returns as school teacher [and ends with] the jubilee scene and its denouement." Act 3 would feature the "last one-third of the book with particular emphasis on the final gift of blood by the one decent 'cracker.'" Both the play and the film, Katz believed, should have as their "major inarticulate premise the message of the new Martin Luther King." To write the script, Katz suggested playwright Arnaud d'Usseau, who was affiliated with *Masses and Mainstream* and had achieved significant dramatic success during the 1940s when he collaborated with Paul Gow to write *Tomorrow the World* and *Deep Are the Roots*.[29]

In August 1955, Haskell Wexler, a rising filmmaker from Chicago who later became an Oscar-winning cinematographer and received a star on Hollywood's Walk of Fame, had initiated discussions with Killens about obtaining the film rights to *Youngblood*, but the project came to naught. In July 1957, before Katz's idea could take hold, Wexler again wrote to Killens, explaining that he had had serious intentions back in 1955 but was at the time "more susceptible to the cautions and reservations of my money-minded friends." Now relying on his own judgment about movie possibilities, Wexler asked if *Youngblood* were still available or if he could be involved as an investor and in some artistic capacity.[30] Wexler would have to negotiate with Belafonte, who still held the option.

Killens continued his mentoring of other authors. At the request of Louis Burnham he met with Eric Axalrod, author of *One Step Forward*, a novel about the lives and struggles of Florida citrus workers. He also reviewed the page proofs for Julian Mayfield's debut novel, *The Hit*, scheduled for release October 17, and sent positive comments to the publisher, Vanguard Press.

As plans for a production of *Youngblood* proceeded, Killens hoped to hit with "The Montgomery Story," an explicit King vehicle to be directed by Jeff Hayden. On September 9, in preparation for work to be undertaken in Los Angeles, Killens and Hayden visited the King home in Montgomery. Although King had just returned from an appearance at the Highlander Folk School's twenty-fifth anniversary celebration and engagements in Louisville and was preparing for a Montgomery Improvement Association board meeting to take place the following day, he and his wife, Coretta Scott King, hosted a relaxed lunch meeting. Also on hand was the Reverend Robert Graetz, pastor at Trinity Lutheran, whose home had been the scene of a dynamite blast during the boycott.

Killens then headed west to Hollywood, where he completed a competent, 129-page screenplay. The script is largely a documentary one faithful to the events of the bus boycott, though Killens took license to create dialogue and dramatize characters—in particular, Rosa Parks, Martin Luther King Jr., Martin Luther King Sr., Coretta Scott King, Ralph Abernathy, and E. D. Nixon. The elder King voices Killens's trademark ideas about manhood, telling his son, "If you achieve nothing else in all the schools you may go to, all the universities, remember, the most important thing is manhood, and in this white man's world the black man can't buy it with a million dollars." This flashback dissolves to a meeting in which Nixon issues a challenge to the city's African American preachers: "You ministers of the gospel, get off your knees to the white man. God almighty ain't got no color. And in these days and times, *boys* ain't got no business in the pulpit." King, remembering his father's words, speaks calmly and deliberately: "There are no boys here, brother Nixon. We are all men. I'll be at the rally tonight and do what this group sees fit for me to do."[31]

Also true to his personality and artistic nature, Killens injected a dose of humor into his portrayal of the black struggle. Sarah tells of an exchange involving her and her employer, Mrs. Thompkin: "Aunt Sarah, I'm just positive you ain't messed up with that boycott. You always been a good nigrah, just like one of the Thompkin family, and that boycott is the work of the devil just as sure as Heaven's happy." Sarah enjoys telling Mrs. Thompkin, "Indeed I ain't had a thing to do with that devilish boycott. I been walking every step of the way. In fact I told my children, 'Don't y'all go near that boycott long as it last. Walk everywhere you have to go.'"[32]

While Killens was in California working on the script, he was deeply touched by another of the signal developments of the modern civil rights movement. In September, President Dwight Eisenhower federalized the Arkansas National Guard and sent in troops from the 101st Airborne Division to enforce the integration of Little Rock's Central High School. When Killens saw pictures of the Little Rock Nine protected by military vehicles flying the American flag, he said Old Glory meant more to him than it had during his forty-one months in the U.S. Army.[33]

Although the writing in Hollywood went well in general, all did not proceed smoothly. Bayard Rustin enthusiastically submitted material for Killens's use, writing, "I feel that it is in excellent hands if you are connected with it."[34] However, Robinson, one of the leaders of the Montgomery movement, sought compensation for the material she painstakingly gathered for Killens's use. Robinson spent about a year gathering data, interviewing people, and recording her own experiences, saving Killens "many long hours of research . . . in attempting to construct the true origin and development of this great social upheaval. As you realize, too, I have recounted incidents that would take months to collect." Killens agreed with Robinson, acknowledging that her work had been extremely useful, but Hayden took a hard line, refusing to make Robinson what she termed "a reasonable offer." The project subsequently collapsed, and Killens termed the entire initiative a debacle.[35]

In mid-November, as the screenplay was becoming a point of contention, Killens traveled to Montgomery at the invitation of the Association for the Study of Negro Life and History to speak at a conference on the campus of Alabama State College, where Robinson worked. After greeting Robinson and others in the audience, Killens read Langston Hughes's "Notes on Commercial Theatre," which ends with an affirmation of African American artists' need to continue to push for self-representation, integrity, and control over their art.[36]

Killens then listed a number of problems that required the intervention of the type of art he envisioned. Referring to the recent launch of Sputnik, the first Soviet satellite, he spoke of the need to master human relationships on earth before conquering outer space. In addition, because African Americans faced a "new day in America and in the world," they needed to understand their historical and cultural background and their place in world affairs. In Killens's reasoning, art had to be a force to counter historical distortions and assaults on black pride and the resulting self-hatred and self-degradation. He argued for improving the media, telling of the pride his son felt when he received a copy of Hughes's *Famous American Negroes*, and of how intently his daughter peered at the television screen, waiting for black characters to appear. The dearth of African American characters, Killens warned, was detrimental to white children also because it gave them a distorted picture of a world populated overwhelmingly by people of color.[37]

Killens criticized William Faulkner and Lucy Daniels, author of *Caleb, My Son*, for their retrograde politics and for lacking universality: "Prejudice and provincialism are at the opposite poles of universality and brotherhood." He also called on writers to portray life in all of its dimensions, including humor, a quality that, in his estimation, Richard Wright, Chester Himes, and James Baldwin had forgotten. The impulse to laughter could not be stifled, Killens asserted, in prisons, ghettoes, on plantations, or even in Buchenwald. And he explained that he had written the Youngbloods to be "militant, re-evaluating their place in society and their self-respect, their importance in the scheme of things and their human dignity, and walking together with other Negroes in a greater unity and determination to be free within themselves and in the society of mankind."[38] Though Martin Luther King Jr. was away from Montgomery and could not attend the event, he wrote to the author two days later, "Coretta tells me that your address was brilliant. I am certainly sorry that a previous commitment made it impossible for me to hear you. I would appreciate it very much if you could send me a copy of your talk."[39]

CHAPTER ELEVEN

Rights and Rites, 1958–1959

On February 27, 1958, Thomas Jones wrote a letter to get the Soviets to pay. The Russian edition of *Youngblood* was being prepared for publication, and Jones informed Professor Mary Becker in Leningrad, who had requested a biographical sketch of Killens, that the author had not been consulted about translation, publication, or payment of royalties. The attorney inquired about the identity of the publisher, the size of the print run, and the format. Jones sent the same core message to the cultural attaché at the Soviet embassy in Washington, adding that he believed that the Soviet Union honored the "rights of authors to receive compensation for their original work."[1]

Weeks passed with no response. On March 17, Jones contacted Max Pfeffer, who had handled negotiations for the previous foreign editions but remained virtually irrelevant in this instance because the Soviet Union had not signed the International Copyright Convention. Jones sent another letter to the cultural attaché on April 16 but again heard nothing. Another letter followed on May 31: "It is assumed that the representatives of your country will treat intellectual workers of other nations with respect and consideration. I expect that you will regard my communications with your Government as worthy of response."[2]

On June 4, he finally heard back from Becker, who claimed that she had been away from Leningrad. Her only role was to write the preface, and she conveyed surprise that Jones seemed unaware of the Soviet stance toward copyright law. Nonetheless, she stated that the publisher, Inostrannaya Literatura, was willing to negotiate and suggested that he correspond directly with the publisher, located in Moscow. Jones thanked Becker for her response, indicated that he would send the biographical information requested, and said that his brother-in-law was pleased with the publisher's intent to negotiate. He also wrote to the publisher to obtain the specifics regarding its publication plans and to establish the fact that he would represent Killens in negotiations.

Two months later, Jones received a reply from Aleksei Krasilnikov, deputy director of publications for Inostrannaya Literatura, who explained that his company would consider payments to the author only after publication. Killens and Jones decided to press the issue, armed with research into Soviet publishing customs. After expressing gratitude to Krasilnikov for agreeing that royalty payments were appropriate, Jones claimed that Killens had written the "best expression in a generation of the dignity, courage and genius of the Negro people in their efforts to obtain their rightful place in the life of the American nation" and therefore qualified as an "author of the first rank in the United States." In accord with typical Soviet publishing practices, therefore, Jones proposed that his client receive a 35 percent advance on an agreed-upon royalty payment, with the remainder due within two months of printing. Although Jones had done his homework, he made no headway with Krasilnikov, who reiterated that no advance would be paid. In practical terms, the matter was closed for the time being.[3]

While Killens chased his characters into foreign lands, he also continued to try to shepherd them onto the silver screen. Although the screenplay about Montgomery had gone nowhere, Killens thought he still had a shot with *Youngblood* and could gain a solid foothold in racist Hollywood, something not achieved by Wallace Thurman, Arna Bontemps, or even Langston Hughes. But bringing a movie to the screen proved a much tougher proposition than publishing a book. As Hughes quipped, "Commercial white culture would rather allow a colored writer a book than a job, even fame rather than an ordinary, decent, dependable living."[4] But given Killens's alliance with Harry Belafonte and Haskell Wexler's exuberance, Killens seemed to hold as good a hand as any African American scenarist had ever been dealt.

In August 1957, Belafonte had formed Harbel Productions to pursue his own filmic vision, beginning in earnest the following year with *The World, the Flesh, and the Devil*. When Wexler sought control of the movie version of *Youngblood*, Belafonte agreed in hopes of accelerating progress. After somewhat complicated deliberations throughout the fall and winter, Belafonte assigned his option to Wexler. Wexler banked on Belafonte's continuing interest and planned to sign him to a starring role. Killens was unsure about whether Wexler would see the project through. Although Wexler was an "ostensibly honest-to-goodness YOUNGBLOOD fan," financial imperatives might supersede artistic concerns. If Wexler relied on his own funds, Killens believed, the work would go smoothly; however, he argued to Belafonte, if Wexler decided primarily to raise money from investors, he would become merely a "Hollywood organizer and operator, risking nothing of his own, but exploiting your name, our relationship and the property." Killens conceded that his "inferences [might be] exaggerated and unfair to Haskell" but expressed frustration at Wexler's indecisiveness: "He listens to everybody's opinion and allows these decisions to muddy the waters of his own conclusions and decisions. This is why he blows hot and cold at such frequent intervals."[5] Wexler's involvement nevertheless seemed promising.

Despite the new possibilities, Killens realized that devoting time to one screenplay would not yield the steady income he desired. He proposed that Harbel hire him as a writer, script editor, script scout, and script supervisor. He would read scripts and books that appeared to be good vehicles for Harbel and provide outlines and reports explaining dramatic potential. He would also read scripts already approved for production. He thought that *Odds against Tomorrow*, for example, a script by the blacklisted Abraham Polonsky based on William McGivern's 1957 novel of the same title, "might very well need the special skill and understanding of a Negro writer in terms of dialogue and psychological authenticity." *Odds* was the first of a half dozen movies—what Killens called the Harbel Six—that Belafonte planned to make under an arrangement with United Artists. Killens, flashing his pride, made it clear that he was looking for a job, not simply a favor. "I raise this question," he insisted, "only with the thought that a real essential service would be rendered. The need must be real as well as the service to be rendered. There can be no other basis."[6]

Killens had already drafted a play, *Lower Than the Angels*, based on a small segment of his first book, and he was working on a collection of short stories as well as the new novel. Yet the movie version of *Youngblood* was foremost in his dreams and appeared increasingly viable. Wexler provided reassurance about his commitment: though he was "squirming a little because of the gamble," he was "with it and you can rely on me."[7] Wexler also possessed a definite and worthwhile sense of how to make the genre transition from novel to film. In February, he made preliminary recommendations and began to arrange screenings for Killens, suggesting that *Grapes of Wrath*, *Ox Bow Incident*, *Red Badge of Courage*, *Les Miserables*, *Of Mice and Men*, and *East of Eden* represented good films derived from novels. Mostly practical, Wexler could also lapse into Hollywood shtick: "Marian and I found a pretty nice house with a lot of room. When you come out to receive the Academy Award for *Youngblood*, you and Grace and the kids will stay with us. There'll even be room for Tom and a few of the distinguished members of the bar."[8]

By May, Killens had completed the screen treatment for *Youngblood*, leading to another round of evaluations from Wexler and the beginning of an artistic rift. That too much had been squeezed into the treatment was uncontroversial. Wexler possessed a keen eye for cinematic technique. But he began to complain about the flatness of characters, particularly the white ones, and did not care much for Richard Myles. In a movie already threatening to be at least two and a half hours long, Wexler thought that there was no time to develop the character dramatically, as the novel did. Killens, in contrast, believed that he was presenting a black point of view, something in which Wexler did not believe. Moreover, Killens had tried to feature the Myles character because he and Wexler hoped that Belafonte would play that role, which therefore had to be substantial.

Killens collaborated with Arnaud d'Usseau on a rewrite, which the pair submitted to Wexler in September. He was impressed: "The overall problem of taking the wealth of material in the novel and organizing the best for motion pictures has been accomplished. This is the hardest task and the selection of the obligatory scenes is correct." Yet he also called Myles a "scenery bum," inflated with too much hot air. And although Wexler acknowledged that a single film could not tell everyone's story, he thought the "whites are flat-white."[9] On September 30, Killens and d'Usseau responded that although they felt they could address productively most of Wexler's critique, the issue of a black perspective remained a sticking point. This led to a meeting of the three in New York in October.[10]

At the same time, other projects beckoned. The Harlem Writers Guild thrived. In July, Ossie Davis dropped by the workshop to read from a draft of *Purlie Victorious*, finding the session helpful and inspiring and consequently seeking a closer association with the group. He had always imagined that a dramatic workshop or little theater group was the most productive situation for a playwright, but he shifted his opinion: "It occurs to me that a play is also a piece of literature, and can be judged as such."[11]

Sarah Wright had begun a novel about the struggles of African American women on Maryland's Eastern Shore. She had read several chapters to the guild, and she asked Killens to join Loften Mitchell, Langston Hughes, Almena Lomax, Arthur Spingarn, and Herbert Alexander in sponsoring her application for a John Hay Whitney Fellowship.

By the close of 1958, Killens and several other guild members were planning a two-day conference, "The American Negro Writer and His Roots," hosted by the American Society of African Culture (AMSAC). The writers did not know at the time that AMSAC, which had been formed with ample funding in June 1957, was a CIA front, a Cold War entity intended to monitor and, when possible, constrain black cultural and political discourse. Killens "never trusted AMSAC" but favored the idea of a literary gathering and chaired the Conference Planning Committee, which also included William Branch, John Henrik Clarke, Julian Mayfield, Loften Mitchell, and Sarah Wright.[12]

Adumbrating public challenges he would later make more forcefully, Harold Cruse wrote a lengthy missive to Killens proposing to address some "important and unresolved issues in Negro writing" in line with the conference theme. Cruse posed more than twenty-five questions about protest writing, socialist realism, integration, nationalism, and Marxism, at one point asking Killens his opinion of the case of Boris Pasternak, author of *Dr. Zhivago*, who, fearing government reprisals, had turned down the Nobel Prize a year earlier. Cruse proposed a resolution "in defense of Boris Pasternak as a symbol of the suppression of the creative writer by despotic authoritarianism" and wondered if Killens would support it.[13]

Cruse was rehearsing arguments that he would unveil publicly eight years later in *The Crisis of the Negro Intellectual*. He detailed that he left the Marxist movement in 1952 because of its policies concerning Negro writing. He vented about Stella Holt, director of the Greenwich Mews Theater, which had declined to produce a play he submitted but had staged Loften Mitchell's *A Land Beyond the River*, William Branch's *In Splendid Error*, and Alice Childress's *Trouble in Mind*. Cruse charged that Holt's incompetence had led to the closing of Hughes's *Simply Heavenly* and disclosed that he had changed his opinion of Hughes when he failed to protest vehemently: "This writer lost all respect for Langston Hughes because he revealed that backbone and principles mean less to him than keeping on good terms with paternalistic whitefolks in the Marxist movement." Cruse further argued, "In all of the Communist Party's 30 years of existence as a participant in the struggle for Negro liberation it has not developed an outstanding Negro writer and it never will. The demands placed on Negro writers by the Marxist movement serves, in the long run, to retard and often damage his career as a growing thinker and writer." He reserved explicit barbs for Lloyd Brown, whom Cruse dubbed the "favorite spokesman from the colored section of *Masses and Mainstream.*" Brown's *Iron City* was a "very bad novel" that attracted rave reviews from leftists as payback for "being good and taking his customary potshots at Richard Wright and Ralph Ellison." But since "history has proven that these two novelists, Wright and Ellison, were right in their criticisms of the Communist Party, it is wondered if Mr. Brown would have the guts to stand up and say so at this coming Negro Writer's conference." Cruse asked that his proposals be forwarded to Mayfield, whom Cruse already saw as an adversary. Mayfield was eager to see Cruse's suggestions and requested a copy of the letter. Cruse probably also saw Killens as an adversary but did not yet take a confrontational tone toward him.[14]

Cruse was not aware that Killens worked hard to get Richard Wright to the conference, a feat that would have constituted the "scoop of several decades." Wright had been in touch with Killens and had sent him a comedic play, *Daddy Goodness.* The younger (though steadily balding) writer felt honored that Wright had even heard of him. But Wright did not specify what he wanted Killens to do with the manuscript, a satire about religion adapted from Louis Sapin's *Papa Bon Dieu.* Killens recognized Wright's characteristic power but saw little comedy: "I wasn't sure he had a sense of humor." Killens did not envision Wright as the genial, laughing writer that he had met in Washington, D.C., years earlier. Killens sent a letter inviting Wright to the conference but received no response and followed up with a phone call. Wright declined to attend, citing a publication deadline for his new novel, *The Long Dream.* Killens subsequently contacted the volume's publisher, Doubleday, and learned that the editors would be more than happy to push back any deadline if it meant that Wright would visit the United States, a publicity boon for Doubleday. Killens again called Wright but was disappointed to learn that he still would not attend the conference because "it would be much too painful an experience."[15] Not even the death of Wright's mother on January 14, 1959—Killens's forty-third birthday— would lure Wright to the United States. Nevertheless, Killens's conference still had a big draw in Langston Hughes.

On February 28, 1959, Killens opened the conference before a crowd of several hundred. He suggested that the United States was enduring a national crisis unparalleled since the Civil War and Reconstruction, facing the central question of whether the rights of all individuals would be suppressed by a prejudiced and powerful few. He stressed black roots, heritage, and achievement. He then echoed W. E. B. Du Bois, Paul Robeson, and Alphaeus Hunton, positing that the American Negro's battle for human rights mirrored the broader struggle of colored peoples throughout the world against colonialism. Killens continued, "In the great drama unfolding before us, America is the stage, human rights is the universal theme, the Negro people are the protagonists, the audience is the entire world. WHAT KIND OF SONG WILL THE NEGRO POET SING?"[16]

The answer, according to the voices raised at the conference, was a painfully strained medley. According to William Branch, the conference included "American writers who are Negro, or American Negroes who are writers, or any of the many variations of these." As Mayfield recorded, "One would have thought that Negro writers, representing a tragic and unique experience in our national history, would be bound together by a dominant theme in their work. But if this is the case, it was not obvious."[17] Although ideologically diverse, most attendees could agree on the set of proposals to be submitted to the AMSAC general body, an agenda that included the establishment of publication outlets and literary awards, the creation of a reference database and lecture bureau, and the compiling and disseminating of bibliographies of African and African American literature.[18]

In the paper he presented at the conference, "Opportunities for Development of Negro Talent," Killens returned to a familiar theme—the production of positive, optimistic, affirming black literature. He felt that what an African American author had to say was more salient than the mere fact of ethnicity. Still smarting from the disappointment of "The Montgomery Story," he opined, "If a writer gives his agent a television story about Little Rock or Montgomery or simply a love story with a Negro background, it matters not whether the writer is Rod Serling or William Branch, Paddy Chayevsky or Loften Mitchell; the odds are ninety to one against acceptance and production." And a black writer's rejection slips were "symbolic of the rejection of the Negro as a cultural factor in American life."[19]

The most strident voices among writers at the conference belonged to Alice Childress and Lorraine Hansberry, whose groundbreaking *Raisin in the Sun* opened on Broadway less than two weeks later. They spoke militantly—more militantly than any character in Hansberry's play—about challenging white supremacy. Their speeches as well as Killens's opening remarks were omitted from the conference proceedings.[20]

While the AMSAC conference unfolded, the shooting of *Odds against Tomorrow* was under way. Killens's first major screenwriting credit was imminent, but he was not the author. Belafonte needed a front for the brilliant Polonsky, whose Hollywood career was curtailed when he refused to cooperate with the House Un-American Activities Committee in 1951, a loss that has been called "American film's greatest single loss to McCarthyism."[21] Polonsky's blacklisting meant that he could only be a ghostwriter on *Odds*, which is considered by consensus to be the last classic black-and-white film noir. Belafonte brought the source novel to Polonsky with the simple directive, "Fix it."[22]

Polonsky discarded the second half of the novel, in which McGivern's story—an attempt to explore race relations and redeem, at least in racial terms, petty criminal Earl Slater—descends from a promising crime thriller into a fatuous description of white hatred and black servitude. After a botched bank robbery, Slater, a racist, southern ex-con struggling with issues of self-worth, and Johnny Ingram, an African American card dealer who has run up a six-thousand-dollar gambling debt, hole up in an elderly couple's modest home in the autumnal, southeastern Pennsylvania countryside. While on the lam, Slater and Ingram bond and putatively transcend racial enmity, partly based on the fact they are both war veterans, though Slater continues to refer to Ingram as Sambo throughout the novel. At one point, while they are supposedly on good terms, Slater inquires, "You mind me calling you Sambo?" Ingram replies, "It's as good a name as any." The subservient Ingram becomes so invested in Slater's welfare that when he escapes back to Philadelphia, he follows through on the plan to locate Slater's girlfriend, Lorraine, and bring her and a getaway car back to the hideout. With law authorities closing in, Slater abandons a sick and weakening Ingram but then changes his mind and doubles back to rescue him, despite Lorraine's protests: "He was glad the odds against them were long; he wanted to show Sambo just how good he was. No guy should ever pass up a chance to show his best stuff. Why hide it, for God's sake."[23] When Slater returns, however, the police kill him before he completes the final gesture of his conversion.

Polonsky sketched Slater, played by Robert Ryan, much flatter and immutably racist but developed a macho Ingram as a worthy antagonist. Furthermore, Polonsky made unabated racism—Slater's barbs and Ingram's knee-jerk responses—a major factor that dooms the robbery and costs Slater and Ingram their lives. Rather than an escape and prolonged evasion, Slater and Ingram engage in a fight to the death at a nearby gas tank complex. After their errant gunshots cause an explosion, they are burned beyond recognition. In an ironic twist, the police and ambulance personnel cannot tell the white man from the black one. In the film, the term *odds against* specifically refers to the failure to defeat racial bigotry. The gritty realism of personal animus replaces sappy redemption.

In other departures from the source novel, Polonsky shifted the locales from Philadelphia and rural Pennsylvania to New York City and the fictional town of Melton. To create a meatier role for Belafonte, Polonsky gave Ingram a family (though a failed marriage) and cast him as a nightclub singer. And all the Sambo dialogue was dropped.

The subterfuge regarding authorship of the movie worked. A 1988 volume, *Contemporary Black American Playwrights and Their Plays*, describes *Odds against Tomorrow* as the "first major modern black-authored film," and Polonsky scholar John Schultheiss has suggested, "Given the form and content of *Odds Against Tomorrow* and the nature of [the] Killens profile, it would seem predictable, almost inevitable (if Killens were a screenwriter), that he would be the author of the film—his view of art as a medium of social protest, his affirmation of black manhood and the resistance to white intimidation, his advocacy of black violence as a response to white violence, his indictment of Hollywood's traditional portrayal of blacks, his association with Harry Belafonte."[24]

Nevertheless, Polonsky certainly wrote the screenplay, and the Writers Guild of America has now properly credited him. Belafonte explained Killens's willingness to participate by describing him as "not only already a rebel" but also "looking to skim the system. So he was invited in to become part of the illusion that we were creating." Moreover, according to Belafonte, Killens "went with 100% of everything Abe had written."[25] But this, too, is not accurate. Polonsky's diaries reveal that he spent the entire afternoon of March 22, 1958, discussing the project with Killens and Belafonte, and Killens offered several ideas that did not make the final cut.[26] As late as April 7, 1959, more than halfway through the shoot, he wrote to Belafonte, "I have one last suggestion to make." Dissatisfied with Slater's distrust of Ingram as the impetus for Ingram's final rage, Killens sought to have Ingram propose that they team up for a possible escape, at which point Slater would respond, "You ain't going with me nowhere, boy. If it hadn't been a nigger in the woodpile, I'd been fifty miles from this place by now." Killens elaborated, "It seems to me this is the kind of last damn straw which would set Johnny off and make him lose perspective of time and place and situation. This is also an almost inevitable step for Slater to take. He is the one who is completely blinded by hate, not Johnny Ingram. He has to blame somebody for the situation in which he finds himself and Johnny is there and obvious and Negro."[27] Slater's racial intransigence, in Killens's conception, finally spurs Ingram to fight him to the death. This dialogue was not used, although the film ends virtually as Killens suggested. He reportedly acknowledged that he contributed little to *Odds against Tomorrow*, but that he contributed any less than Nelson Giddings, who still has co-script credit, is doubtful.[28]

Part of the subterfuge involved a letter Killens wrote on November 24, 1958, to Harbel Productions to request payment of thirty-five thousand dollars (the fee Polonsky received) for writing the screenplay, with the funds to be paid to an accountant, Sydney Danis. In terms of Killens's career as a novelist, this letter was perhaps the worst move he could have made. Seeing his name connected to Polonsky's thirty-five-thousand-dollar fee proved intoxicating. To one who dreamed of riches and fame, the letter glowed like the green light at the end of Daisy Buchanan's dock, and no less than Gatsby could Killens refrain from the chase. To Killens's credit, he never betrayed his aesthetic beliefs in favor of money. But his principles ensured that even when he redoubled his efforts to crack the lucrative film and eventually stage markets, sacrificing his fiction in the process, he never achieved a big financial score.

In the April 7 letter to Belafonte, Killens turned to discussion of his own ambitions. He was due on the West Coast the following month to work on the shooting script for *Youngblood*, and he told Belafonte, "I want to discuss seriously with you about John Killens working on one of the Harbel Six. I am getting angry."[29]

Killens had to make a few cultural stops before heading to Hollywood. On May 10, 1959, Killens and the Harlem Writers Guild convened for an autograph party in honor of Frank London Brown, who had just published the novel *Trumbull Park*, about experiences in a public housing project in Chicago. Killens handled the introduction and fondly recalled how four years earlier, Brown had showed him a short story based on life in that setting.

He described Brown as "warm, fiercely honest and proud of being whatever he was" and asserted that Brown's writing had the "same warmth and the same fierce honesty and the same pride in being."[30]

The following week, Killens heard from his brother-in-law about the Russian-language edition of *Youngblood*. An undetermined amount, believed to be about twenty-five hundred dollars, would be encumbered for the author. The victory was only partial; the royalty would be paid in rubles and set aside in a bank in the Soviet Union, meaning that Killens could use the money only in that country.

The AMSAC gathering still resonated. Louis Burnham, who had attended the conference, penned an article in the May 4 issue of the *National Guardian* assessing the state of African American literature. Burnham sketched a brief history of African American literary politics before turning to several books — *The Book of Negro Folklore, Selected Poems of Langston Hughes, The Long Dream, The Long Night, Trumbull Park* — that he felt represented a "new blossoming." Yet some readers found the article perturbing. Sarah Wright complained to the *Guardian*, calling on "our fine writer" to deliver more of what he was known for: "truth, and credit given where credit is due." Wright took exception to Burnham's argument that "World War II and the post-war McCarthy period were not a congenial time for the artistic assessment of man's fate by Negro or white writers."[31] Burnham, however, had praised *Youngblood* and played a part in introducing the novel to the public.

Wright adopted a much more acerbic tone in a May 30 letter to the *Los Angeles Tribune*. The paper published an anonymous essay (undoubtedly written by Harold Cruse) that disparaged Hansberry and Killens — in particular, his relationship to Belafonte. Wright lamented the writing of a "camouflaged snake whose fangs drip poisonous ink" and admonished, "John O. Killens is the one Negro writer in New York City who is called at any hour of the day and sometimes late into the night (even though his phone is unlisted) by all the other anguishing, comfortless and seeking Negro writers who haven't achieved YOUNGBLOOD yet — and there are none."[32]

Killens arrived in Hollywood in mid-June. Holding a thousand-dollar advance against the twelve-thousand-dollar purchase price, he would earn roughly three hundred dollars per week to focus exclusively on getting the Youngbloods finally ready for the big screen. He stayed at the Montecito Hotel on Franklin Avenue before moving to the Chateau Marmont. However, other projects still intruded. He finished a major portion of his new novel and submitted it to Dial. Word came from Illinois that Myles Killens was experiencing foot problems that would require surgery. Grace, Chuck, and Barbara missed him dearly, and he them. They visited in August, but Willie Lee Killens did not want to stay alone in the Brooklyn house, so Son Coleman, her brother, came to keep her company; however, he stayed out so late at night that she hardly saw him. At least she could contribute to the script. When Killens needed information about midwives for the screenplay, his mother provided several anecdotes.

While in California, Killens received word from Angus Cameron, who had resurfaced in the corporate publishing world as an editor at Knopf. The author scribbled back, "My hearty and sincere congratulations! Your new job is good news and glad tidings for American literature." Contact with Cameron also laid the groundwork for a change of publishers, as Killens, never satisfied with Dial's promotional efforts, was more than willing to explore other options and promised to visit Cameron sometime in October.[33] Killens also sent good wishes to Paule Marshall, whose first novel, *Brown Girl, Brownstones*, was due for release on August 14 and who was expecting her first child in October. She told Killens, "At long last I'm really producing!"[34]

In the meantime, Killens grappled with the issue of a black viewpoint in his screenplay. He understood Wexler's gestures toward universalism but could not shake his instincts or experiences, which told him that a black psyche existed. His viewpoint was reconfirmed by a boxing match, often a telling indicator of American racial consciousness. On June 26, 1959, he went to a theater to watch a broadcast of Floyd Patterson defending the heavyweight title against Sweden's Ingemar Johansson. When it appeared that Johansson would take the title, whites cried, "Kill the nigger!" Killens perceived that, for whites in the audience, color superseded patriotism, and he later recalled that he felt as though he and Patterson were "aliens in a strange and hostile country."[35]

By October, a couple of weeks after Killens had intended to return to New York, he finished the shooting script. After establishing shots that capture the city of Macon in the fall of 1932, the action begins at the turpentine factory with a mild confrontation between Joe Youngblood and Mr. Mack that foretells the more serious conflict to come. The story moves quickly to Robby's classroom, where the Reverend Ledbetter, not Mr. Myles, is the teacher. Myles, the so-called scenery bum, has been cut out of the script altogether. The roles for white characters—in particular, Junior Jefferson—

had been expanded, but Wexler was still not mollified. If anything, Killens sketched some white characters as even meaner and more spiteful than in the novel. For example, when Robby is taken into custody, Laurie Lee is told to bring $15 to the courthouse. She has only $4.35 on hand, but her neighbor lends her the remainder. When Laurie Lee gets downtown, the police, surprised that she could obtain the money so readily, change the required amount to $25. When she cannot produce the extra money, she is forced to whip her son. Taking advantage of the medium, Killens indicates the need for a dissolve so sharp that the whip appears to strike Joe in the face while he is on the job and unaware that his son is being whipped.[36] After the courthouse scene, the script moves in a rather straightforward fashion to the climax and resolution. Significantly, the union angle does not make it from novel to final script.

After attending Game 5 of the World Series, in which twenty-three-year-old Dodger fireballer Sandy Koufax dropped a 1–0 decision to the Chicago White Sox, Killens flew back to New York with Wexler. *Odds against Tomorrow* had just premiered and was receiving solid, if not overwhelming, reviews. A postal worker from Macon, on vacation in Atlanta, smiled when he saw the marquee. Lafayette Bonner, Ballard Class of 1933, mused, "That's my friend."[37]

CHAPTER TWELVE

Journey to Genesis, 1959–1961

John Oliver Killens returned home to a request from Langston Hughes on behalf of the Afro-American Committee for Gifts of Art and Literature to Ghana. The ambassador from Ghana welcomed donations, vowing to facilitate shipment, exhibition, and eventual cataloging for scholarly use. Killens was instructed to submit material directly to Hughes's home and responded eagerly, having entered, as Sarah Wright commented, a marked Ethiopia-shall-stretch-forth-her-hand phase.[1]

Shortly thereafter, Maya Angelou breezed in from California. Killens had met the six-foot-tall nightclub singer with questionable pitch while he was in Los Angeles. His children spent time with her son, Guy, who was about midway between Chuck and Barbara in age. Although Angelou met James Baldwin in Paris in the early 1950s, Killens was the first published writer with whom she conversed in depth. She had been drafting vignettes, lyrics, and short stories, and Killens agreed to look at what he termed her "work in progress." Immediately recognizing her potential, he suggested that she move to New York and join the Harlem Writers Guild, an invitation Angelou called "oblique but definitely alluring." She wrote, "I had written and recorded six songs for Liberty Records, but I didn't seriously think of writing until John gave me his critique. After that I thought of little else."[2]

The thirty-one-year-old Angelou soon came to New York, staying at the Killens home for a couple of weeks until she secured an apartment nearby and prepared to send for Guy. At one point she painted and furnished the apartment by day and returned to the Killens residence at night. Late one evening, mindful of the militant conversation pervasive in the home, she asked her host about his seemingly perpetual anger: "I told him that while I agreed with Alabama blacks who boycotted bus companies and protested against segregation, California blacks were thousands of miles, literally and figuratively, from these Southern plagues." Killens answered, "Girl, don't you believe it. Georgia is Down South. California is Up South. If you're black in this country, you're on a plantation." Angelou reminded Killens that she had spent a year in New York, but he countered, "You were a dancer. Dancers don't see anything but other dancers. They don't see; they exist to be seen. This time you should look at New York with a writer's eyes, ears, and nose. Then you'll really see New York."[3] Killens construed his racial outrage not merely as anger but as commitment.

To ring in the 1960s, Killens attended a New Year's Eve party with several other African American writers, including Julian Mayfield, Loften Mitchell, and William Branch. Amid the din of noisemakers and horns, the writers talked optimistically about how the upcoming decade would usher in great change in the country, especially with respect to the situation of African Americans, and they believed that they would be integrally involved as voices for black liberation.[4] They had already done significant work: Killens argued that the 1950s had been the most fruitful and important decade for African American writers, with literary output exceeding that of the Harlem Renaissance "not only in quantity but in quality and profundity." He offered as evidence his own work as well as that of Mayfield, Mitchell, Branch, Paule Marshall, Pauli Murray, Lorenz Graham, Alice Childress, Frank London Brown, Louis Peterson, Lorraine Hansberry, James Baldwin, and Ralph Ellison.[5] But he and the other writers at the party looked forward to greater contributions in the 1960s.

Their optimism was jolted just a few weeks later with the unexpected February 12 death of forty-four-year-old Louis Burnham, one of the first people to address a public audience about the value of *Youngblood*. Burnham died of a heart attack while lecturing at the New York Intercultural Society on West Forty-eighth Street. Only four months older than Killens, the former editor of *Freedom* had been elected to the Communist Party's national committee the preceding December. Killens raised money and assisted in a memorial for Burnham—and the FBI noted Killens's efforts. Although the bureau no longer considered him to be active in the party, he still drew interest because of his associates, who included William Patterson, vice chair of the New York chapter. Killens had heard of Patterson as far back as the case of the Scottsboro Boys and had come to know him fairly well in New York, and as late as the early 1960s, several black activists still welcomed Patterson as their "Communist guru."[6]

Angelou's voice promised to achieve prominence in wider domains. She chose as her first reading for the workshop a play, "One Love. One Life," sharing her work with Sylvester Leaks, John Henrik Clarke, Sarah Wright, Mildred Jordan, and Marshall. Clarke, Angelou's harshest critic, judged the play to encapsulate "no life and very little love." However, he gladly welcomed her into the group while reminding her of the hard work writing required.[7]

Killens figured directly in several of Angelou's important decisions in New York. After she and Godfrey Cambridge attended a Harlem speech by Martin Luther King Jr., they organized a revue, later titled *Cabaret for Freedom*, to raise money for the Southern Christian Leadership Conference (SCLC). Angelou pitched the idea to the group's Harlem office, which meant approaching coordinator and publicist Bayard Rustin, Stanley Levison, and Jack Murray. Killens prepped her on the globetrotting Rustin's activist resume, which included prior associations with the Young Communist League, the Fellowship of Reconciliation, A. Philip Randolph, Mohandas Gandhi's Congress Party, the Congress of Racial Equality, Kwame Nkrumah, and the War Resisters League. And when the show opened an enormously successful run that spring, John and Grace Killens helped ensure a rousing start by attracting their "famous friends," among whom were Juanita and Sidney Poitier, Ruby Dee and Ossie Davis, and Lorraine Hansberry and Bob Nemiroff.[8]

At the end of June, shortly after *Cabaret for Freedom* closed, King forced Rustin out of the SCLC. Despite his keen intellect and tactical brilliance, Rustin had always been a potential political liability because of his communist background and his homosexuality, which was an open secret among African American leaders. Rustin had been jailed on a morals charge in Pasadena, California, in 1953. Adam Clayton Powell Jr., a master politician, cruelly exploited this political weakness while jostling with King for influence during the 1960 election season. Seeking to consolidate his position among mainstream Democrats, Powell tried to prevent a picket that

King and Randolph planned for the Democratic National Convention in Los Angeles. Through an intermediary, Powell informed King that if the picket were not canceled, he would inform the press that King and Rustin were having a sexual affair.⁹ Aware that the charge would be monstrously damaging, King in essence purged Rustin from the SCLC even though the move invited financial hardship. Rustin was the group's key fund-raiser in the North, from which flowed most of the SCLC's monies. Whoever replaced him would face, at least in the short run, drastically diminishing revenues. He tabbed Angelou as his successor. Honored by the offer to work with King but worried about her role in Rustin's departure and her ability to succeed, she consulted with Killens, who advised her to ask Rustin directly. "He's a man. Personally, I don't believe he would have suggested you if he didn't want you to take the job."¹⁰ Angelou's reportage, though, remains cryptic and somewhat kind. There would have been no need for her to fret about her role in Rustin's departure if his leaving entailed, as she described, simply a decision on his part to work once again with Randolph. In fact, Rustin turned down an offer to work for Randolph and the newly formed Negro American Labor Council and returned instead to the War Resisters League. If an ouster were in play, as it was, both Angelou and Killens either knew or could easily have guessed the reason. In any event, Rustin spoke explicitly in early July, declaring, "Congressman Powell has suggested that I am an obstacle to his giving full enthusiastic support to Dr. King. I want to remove that obstacle. I have resigned as Dr. King's special assistant and severed relations with the Southern Christian Leadership Conference."¹¹

Killens's coaching of Angelou implied that he still supported the non-violent direct action movement led by King. On March 7, the writer visited the home of Judge Hubert Delany to attend a meeting of the Committee to Defend Martin Luther King and the Struggle for Freedom in the South. However, he also turned his attention toward new developments internationally. Ninety miles from the U.S. mainland, an increasingly important government operated in Cuba under the leadership of Fidel Castro, whose startling achievement in seizing power energized what remained of the Old Left and helped to awaken the New. To counteract U.S. propaganda designed to undermine Castro's regime, a coalition of liberals and leftists led by Robert Taber and Edmonde Haddad formed the Fair Play for Cuba Committee, whose founding members also included Killens, Clarke, Baldwin, Mayfield, Frank London Brown, Norman Mailer, Truman Capote, Jean-Paul Sartre, Simone de Beauvoir, and Robert Williams. Williams, a prototypical Black Power advocate and head of the Monroe, North Carolina, chapter of the National Association for the Advancement of Colored People (NAACP), frequently visited Killens when in New York.[12] On April 6, the group used money raised at Harlem Writers Guild meetings in the Killens home to help fund a full-page *New York Times* advertisement headed, "What Is Really Happening in Cuba." The Communist Party and the Socialist Workers Party allegedly engaged in a subsequent struggle for control of the Fair Play for Cuba Committee, but neither group became dominant.[13]

Largely on the strength of his Fair Play for Cuba Committee activities, the Cuban government invited Killens as well as Sarah Wright, Mayfield, Harold Cruse, and LeRoi Jones (Amiri Baraka) to attend a celebration of the 26th of July Movement. Killens missed the trip because his paperwork was not processed in time, but Wright wrote to him that the journey to see Castro was "suffocatingly dusty, waterless, hot—uncompromisingly hot." Yet the Cubans considered these hardships insignificant in the face of their adulation for their president. Wright felt "that they would have to kill the entire population to conquer Cuba, that's how firmly behind Castro they were." After Castro spoke, the event featured a cultural presentation with dances and songs reflecting the islanders' African heritage.[14]

In September, Castro dropped in on Harlem. As the regular Monday workshop of the Harlem Writers Guild convened at Wright's Lower Manhattan home, they received a telephone call with the information that Castro and his entourage planned to check into the historic Hotel Theresa after having been turned away from the Hotel Shelburne downtown, their usual headquarters. The delegation allegedly killed and cooked chickens in rooms at the Shelburne, charges that were never substantiated. A verifiable source of dispute involved the exorbitant advance fees solicited by hotel management. The guild members hustled uptown in taxis to what they thought would be a small rally; instead, thousands of people stood in the rain, shouting, "Viva Castro! Viva Fidel!" Killens overheard one man say, "Yeah, I dig Fidel the most. Any time a man kicks Whitey's ass, he's okay with me!"[15]

Around the same time, Vusumzi Make of the Pan-Africanist Congress arrived for a lecture tour and to petition the United Nations on behalf of South Africa's antiapartheid movement. Killens attended a talk by Make before he and Grace hosted a reception for Make and Oliver Reginald Tambo, deputy president of the African National Congress. Inviting Angelou to the reception, Killens compared the relationship between the African National Congress and the Pan-African Congress to that between the NAACP and the Black Muslims.[16]

Killens invited more than he knew. Romantic sparks ignited between Angelou and Make. Grace noticed right away, as did Marshall. When Angelou informed Killens that she and Make planned to marry, he expressed grave reservations. She listened carefully and then went ahead with the wedding. Writing from England, where she and Make lived for a while, Angelou told Grace and John, "I'm happier than I thought it possible to be. Gloriously. Vus is the most wonderful man in the whole world. I'm sure I will have some argument from you on that score, but I'm prepared to offer proof. How about you?" She then specifically thanked John "for the influence you've had and are still having on my life."[17]

Alphaeus Hunton, who had nearly been broken by McCarthyism, reentered Killens's life around this time. Living in Guinea, where he was teaching along with his wife, Dorothy, Hunton wrote to Killens, offering insights into his work with African schoolchildren and an expansive analysis of African independence movements and the various pro- and anti-imperialist forces operating in the United Nations. Hunton, prompted by the fact that it was Thanksgiving, then waxed poetic about the African landscape and about how he missed friends in New York. Because Killens might not receive the letter until late December, Hunton also wished him a Merry Christmas and sent along his hopes for a fulfilling new year.[18]

By the close of 1960, the negotiations to film *Youngblood* had taken a nasty turn. Early in the year, Haskell Wexler decided to shelve the project to focus on other prospects. But Killens, along with Thomas Jones, proceeded under the assumption that there would be no appreciable delay between the completion of the script and the commencement of shooting. On March 4, Jones wrote to Wexler that it was "fair and reasonable," given the delay, to request another thousand-dollar advance against the payment to be made when production began, which Jones hoped would happen during the upcoming summer.[19] Wexler paid the advance the following month and suggested that a campaign had begun for *Youngblood* at United Artists.

An anxious Killens was less than thrilled with the latest news. Dealings with United Artists almost inevitably would be a drawn-out process likely to involve another round of criticism and, in Killens's mind, some loss of artistic integrity. He cited *Marty* and *Edge of the City* as examples of successful low-budget movies that had opened in art houses. In addition, production could not proceed on his play, *Lower Than the Angels*, until Wexler's contractual claim on that project was addressed, leaving Killens financially strapped.[20] Pat Fowler, who had served as stage manager for *The Seven Year*

Itch and Gore Vidal's *A Visit to a Small Planet* and who later coproduced *The Owl and the Pussycat*, had agreed to produce the play and budgeted the show at $125,000 with weekly operating costs at $17,000 and a weekly take of $40,000. She projected a two-year run in New York and a year on the road. And she estimated that the sale of the movie would bring in $350,000 because that was the purchase price of *A Raisin in the Sun*.[21] For the play to make the fall 1960 season, an agreement had to be reached almost immediately.

Lawyers swung into action, with Killens represented by Leo Branton. On June 20, an apparent agreement was reached, but Fowler and her backers decided they required more specific assurances regarding Wexler's claim on the material. Negotiations dragged through the summer, with little word from Wexler. Then Killens received a threat from Marshall Sevin, a Beverly Hills attorney, regarding a $150 airline ticket that Killens had charged to the travel agency of Haskell's brother and business partner, Yale. Killens acknowledged the debt but said he could not discharge it at the time.

By early October, a frustrated Killens instructed Branton to file suit against Haskell Wexler for blocking production of the play. Branton hesitated to do so because of the past relationship between the two parties. Legal deliberations ultimately were avoided, but Killens thought that the round of clarifying letters needed to reach that agreement consumed too much time. By the close of the year, it was obvious that the *Youngblood* script had little chance of being filmed. Worse, the language of the agreement between Killens and the Wexlers was still not specific enough to suit Fowler. After months of negotiation, there would be neither movie nor play, only a hassle about a plane ticket. On December 21, Killens wrote testily to Yale Wexler: "Due to the fact that your and Haskell's actions regarding YOUNGBLOOD and ANGELS have sabotaged my earning capacity and expectancy completely in 1960, I am not able to take care of this matter at this time."[22]

Over the next few months, Branton tried to obtain the language Fowler requested. He did not fully blame the Wexlers for the situation and told Killens that he was being "shafted" by Fowler's people. But Albert Da Silva, a lawyer for Fowler, insisted that Fowler remained interested in producing the play but simply did not want her hands tied in any way by Wexler's interest in the literary property.[23]

In early February, Killens learned that his delinquent travel account had been forwarded to a New York collection agency with instructions to "levy any interest" connected to *Youngblood* or *Lower Than the Angels*. Killens paid fifty dollars and promised to send more. In March, Pat Gallagher, Haskell Wexler's secretary, informed Killens that Wexler was in Brazil working on a film but was also pursuing new negotiations to get Killens's script to the screen.[24] Killens put little stock in the report, believing that the misgivings he had expressed to Harry Belafonte a few years earlier had been confirmed. Wexler could not be the risk taker Killens wanted him to be. As a filmmaker, Wexler was firmly behind *his* vision of Killens's vision. No compromise loomed that would make the film happen.

As the film and theater possibilities for his work seemed to go nowhere despite their allure, Killens kept plugging away on his second novel. After returning from California, he reconnected with Angus Cameron at Knopf and then submitted a draft of the manuscript to him. The editor's written response was favorable, and Killens informed Cameron, "There are no areas of disagreement in terms of story line, direction, plot or character development. Your notes were very helpful in crystallizing my own thinking in terms of the novel's climax and its denouement."[25] The author believed that five or six months of undivided attention to the novel would enable him to complete it, but he had difficulty maintaining such focus, as Cameron soon learned. The editor became a sounding board for Killens's various ideas and on one occasion wrote to the author, "Speaking of screenplays, let's speak of books."[26] Killens had at least one other novel in mind, floating the synopsis of a comedic story, "The Minister Primarily," in which an African American from the South is mistaken for an African dignitary. Despite the delays, Killens had nearly completed his sprawling war story by the spring of 1961. Knopf had already begun advertising, and Langston Hughes wrote to Killens in March to offer kudos.[27]

As Killens tried to apply the finishing touches to his mammoth manuscript, he was sidetracked once again. This diversion was unusual, however, because he would be able to fulfill his long-held dream of visiting Africa. Belafonte and Hank Raullerson, an official with the American Society of African Culture, suggested that Basil Okwu, Eastern Nigeria's minister of information, engage Killens as part of an effort to create thirteen half-hour documentary films about West Africa geared primarily toward audiences in Europe and the United States. The series, to be produced by External Development Services, would cover topics including history, geography, religion, agriculture, commerce, foreign policy, economic colonialism, Pan-

Africanism, and the place of the white man in Africa. The project required a black writer of stature because one of the intended angles was reporting about Africa through the eyes of an African American who would visit the land of his ancestors with a sense of nostalgia but also with an inquiring, critical mind. Killens had stature, if not much money, and readily accepted the assignment.[28]

On May 15, coproducer Martin Leighton wrote to Killens from London that they needed to arrive in Africa as soon as possible to stay ahead of the rainy season in Mali. Leighton wrote again on May 24 to inform Killens that arrangements had been made for him to depart New York in early June. He advised the writer to bring along clothes appropriate for the heat—he would have to eschew his customary suits—and to move swiftly to obtain the necessary visas as well as the required inoculations against smallpox and yellow fever. On his end, Leighton arranged for a brand-new Land Rover to be shipped from London to Lagos.[29]

In mid-June, Killens and Raullerson flew to London. Killens had been at Heathrow Airport for less than half an hour when he was paged over the loudspeaker. Waiting for him at the information booth was Make, who then gathered a group of South Africans, including Tambo and writer Bloke Modisane, for lengthy discussions in Killens's hotel room. The topics included African Americans' role in assisting the South African freedom struggle.

After a brief stay in London, Killens and Raullerson endured a turbulent flight to Lagos, Nigeria, with "the plane bucking like a wild mustang and the lightning flashing." But as soon as he landed, the forty-five-year-old writer knew that the hair-raising journey had been worth the trouble: "I thought about the Biblical story of the prodigal son. To be in a country where Blacks seemed to be in charge of everything. . . . It felt like I had been away on a long, long journey and had come home at last." He talked to people from various walks of life, including a number of artists and intellectuals whom Okwu had assembled. When called on to respond to Okwu's speech at a dinner in Killens's honor, the author claimed, "I was at my very best."[30]

Killens, Raullerson, and the British filmmakers, Leighton and director Wynford Vaughan Thomas, piled into the Land Rover for the journey from Lagos to Ibadan and then on to Benin City, Onitsha, Calibar, Port Harcourt, and Enugu, the capital of Eastern Nigeria. Killens felt strange traveling with the white men. People embraced him immediately but virtually ignored his traveling companions until someone would sense their discomfort and include them in the circle of conversation. Killens recalled, "Now they know how it feels to assume the role of Ellison's *Invisible Man*."[31]

In Enugu, the travelers met legislator Margaret Ekbo, the leading Nigerian feminist, who motivated them to consider adding to the project the topic of women in Nigeria specifically and West Africa in general. Exorbitant bride prices and female circumcision were particular practices that Ekbo, herself the victim of circumcision, believed needed to be eradicated.

While in Enugu, Killens also went to Club Lido to hear a jazz quintet led by an Ibo saxophonist who had been heavily influenced by Lester Young and Charlie Parker. After the first set, Killens stood outside bantering with the band members; he mentioned his upcoming trip to Timbuktu. When they learned that he was planning to travel by car rather than fly, they became skeptical, knowing, as Leighton did, the perils of attempting that drive during the rainy season. They wished him a safe journey.

Outside of Nsukka, Killens, Leighton, and Thomas parted ways with Raullerson and then more or less followed the Niger River north for the remainder of the day. Leighton did most of the driving, with Killens alongside him in the front seat. Thomas mainly occupied the back seat, chattering away. He had a great sense of humor and was supposedly studying Hausa to help out when the three of them inevitably, in Thomas's thinking, lost their way. Killens said he was never sure when to take Thomas seriously.[32]

In his notes on the trip, Thomas wrote, "All parties traveling through Africa—if they are to be pleasant—must create a fantasy amongst themselves." For Killens's group, Leighton was the leader: "To suggest for a moment that he can mistake the way is a crime. He *knows* Africa, we say. Forward with the leader. He will GET US THROUGH." Thomas facetiously dubbed himself the "Old Coaster," a paternalist, colonialist, member of a dying breed, he hoped, that ran counter to his true and progressive stance toward Africa: "The new Africa has no place for a Young Coaster." Killens was "the Candidate," "working to become the first President of United Africa. He waves frantically to everyone we pass—if they wave back he has won another vote. 'I am here,' he shouts to astonished Fulani or Hausas, standing with the minimum of clothing at the roadside. 'Killens is amongst you. Vote for Killens.'" According to Thomas, Killens's election rival was Louis Lomax, who came for a few weeks to Africa, cruised around hurriedly, and rushed a book into print. Killens considered anyone who failed to wave back to be a Lomax supporter.[33]

The travelers spent a night in the village of Yelwa, where they met the assistant district organizer, John Sampson, who was accompanied by a water engineer from Yorkshire who asserted that Africans had made no substantial contribution to civilization and that the entire continent would be back in the bush in five years if whites left. Killens responded with what he later described as an "angry lecture on African history fresh out of the books by Basil Davidson and W. E. B. Du Bois."[34]

On June 23, Grace wrote her first letter. Barbara, now fourteen, graduated from junior high school, looking "beautiful from top to bottom," while seventeen-year-old Chuck graduated from high school and was planning to attend the Newport Jazz Festival. Mayfield was celebrating the publication of his novel, *The Grand Parade*. Grace felt "terribly lonesome" without her husband and had trouble sleeping. Although Killens always welcomed her as a travel partner, she was often left behind because of her job, her children, or financial considerations. On this occasion, she ruled an overseas call out of the question for budgetary reasons even if it had been possible to track down her husband by phone. So their eighteenth wedding anniversary "passed unnoticed," but she "was happy because [John's] being in Africa was a wonderful anniversary gift for both of us." She instructed her husband, "Keep those eyes & ears open & get everything you can for all of us to know. It'll take months for you to digest & for us to get it out of you."[35]

On June 25, when the filmmakers reached Niamey, Niger, and were resting at the Grand Hotel du Niger, Killens wrote to his wife,

> In spite of the profound experiences I am having, I miss you very much. This is especially true today on your birthday, Grace. Extra especially true. Deeply true.
>
> So often while we are traveling through this great land do I wish for all of you to be here sharing my experiences. Some of them in Northern Nigeria seem to come right out of the biblical tales of old and out of the Arabian Nights. In Western Nigeria they are mostly Yorubas, in Eastern Nigeria mostly Ibos, but in the vast reaches of the North, you see the great cattle people, the Fulanis, and Hausas, some of them on their great handsome horses, the Hausas in their long robes and the horses bedecked in brilliant colors. The villages, most of them made of mud huts and straw and the families live walled in with a hut for them and one for their eternal goats. Great sweeping epic and romantic movies could be made of these places. The women shy and the children eager and friendly, and all in all, all of the people are warm, friendly and hospitable, even amongst the direst poverty. And there is poverty—so much poverty. The job the new leaders face is gigantic. So much to do. So little time. Where do you start? There

are schools all over the place. Governmental, Catholic, Protestant. Schools
Schools Schools. And bookshops. An unbelievable amount of bookshops.
For a people supposedly 90 to 95% illiterate, there are more bookshops in the
big cities and small towns of Nigeria per square block than in New York City,
not to mention the rest of television-watching America.[36]

The following evening, Killens and his party crossed into Mali. "One had
an overwhelming sense of déjà vu," he later wrote, "as if one were traveling back in time and steadily into the hopeful future. Gao! Songhai! And
tomorrow, Timbuktu!"[37] While they traveled the countryside in northern
Niger and southern Mali, he intermittently read Du Bois's *The World and
Africa*. After spending the night in Gao, the travelers went astray in the desert because they lost sight of the Niger River, the surest route to the fabled
city. After receiving directions from a traveler they encountered, they arrived in Timbuktu.

Over the next couple of days, in stifling heat, Killens, Leighton, and
Thomas talked with various residents and visited sites, including the Great
Mosque at Sankoree. When they headed back to the south, they encountered the heaviest downpour Killens had seen since his time in the South
Pacific. The Land Rover bogged down in the mud about twenty-five miles
south of Hambouri. Because few Malians had ventured onto the roads,
twelve hours passed before a group of Africans heading north in a truck
stopped to help. At one point, Killens found himself in conversation with
a Taureg educator, who asked, "Where do you stand on Paul Robeson and
W. E. B. Du Bois?" When Killens praised both men, the African hugged
him and said, "Then you are truly my American brother!"[38]

Killens, Leighton, and Thomas gave the educator, who was making a tour
of remote schools, and several other men a lift to Bori. As they bumped on-
ward along the bad roads, the Taureg excitedly posed numerous questions:
Was the American educational system still dominated by the ideas of John
Dewey? Was the United States going to give aid to Africa without any ties?
Why did the United States insist that African countries take sides in the
U.S./Russian political battle? The questioning continued until the vehicle
arrived in Bori well after midnight.[39]

The next major stop was the Malian capital, Bamako. The numerous fruit
bats that took off down to the Niger River in the evening reminded Killens of the skies over White Beach in the Philippines during an air raid.
Scheduled to spend four days, the travelers were stranded in Bamako for

almost three weeks after External Development Services, in a telling display of amateurishness, failed to provide the proper paperwork. After interviewing government officials, ordinary workers, and peasants, Killens, against the advice of white embassy workers, wandered the streets of Bamako alone late at night.

The travelers journeyed next to Ouagadougou in Upper Volta (now Burkina Faso). Then they drove south to Kumasi, Ghana, and eventually to Accra, the government seat of Kwame Nkrumah, whose concept of a United States of Africa appealed enormously to Killens, though he knew that some leaders in Ghana and in other African nations disagreed with Nkrumah. As Killens explained, "Foreign Minister of Nigeria Jaja Wachuku had told me in Nigeria that 'Kwame Nkrumah wanted to build the continent from the top of the pyramid down to the bottom. We must begin at the bottom of the pyramid and build our way to the top.'" Wachuku thought that independence for each nation had to be consolidated before federation could be considered. But, Killens wondered, "What if the U.S.A. had kept itself divided into Georgians, New Yorkers, Alabamans, North Carolinians, Californians? What if there were no United States of America? Would it be so powerful as a nation? Wasn't that what the Civil War was really about?"[40]

Near the end of July, Killens flew back to the United States for a story conference Grace had arranged with Angus Cameron. In addition, Haskell Wexler's option on *Youngblood* would expire on August 31. On July 26, Thomas Jones wrote to Wexler to gauge his intentions. Wexler immediately replied. He had been working in Brazil for four months, but while there he corresponded with a group that he thought could make *Youngblood* a film reality. However, Wexler received only discouragement from distributors, who told him, "Negro pictures don't make money," and raising production money was therefore irrelevant. The movie project was officially terminated.[41] The filmmaker specifically remembered meeting with Harry Belafonte, Sidney Poitier, and Max Youngstein, head of production and marketing at United Artists. After Belafonte and Poitier left the room, Youngstein, a civil rights supporter, waved Wexler closer and put the matter with a Yiddish twist: "Shvartzer pictures don't make money." He wanted to see how *A Raisin in the Sun* performed at the box office.[42]

While Wexler conceded defeat, he hoped to save his relationship with Killens. He told Jones, "I consider the argument between us a trivial combination of misunderstandings, tensions, and suspicions. I am quite willing to assume some blame for the deterioration of our friendship, and I hope

John will recognize some responsibility in this regard, too." And on August 7, Grace Killens sent Yale Wexler the balance owed on the plane ticket.[43]

During the middle of the month, Altina Carey, whose Educational Communications Corporation had received an Oscar nomination the previous year, contacted Killens about another film possibility. She had obtained the rights to Martin Luther King Jr.'s *Stride toward Freedom* and thought Killens would be a good choice to write the screen adaptation. She had approached King about playing himself in the film and reported that he was friendly to the idea. Outlining her vision of the film, Carey even suggested that Martin Luther King Sr. be cast as a "kind of Joe Youngblood, who was proud and resisted with all his manhood the demeaning of his person."[44]

Killens knew better than to become giddy about the prospects. Perhaps something good would come out of work already invested in "The Montgomery Story," but it did not seem likely. Most pressing, though, was his return to Africa for most of September and the early part of October. The itinerary for final scripting included another extended trip to Nigeria to visit markets, experimental farms, palm oil plantations, the Oron Museum, Christ the King College, Ibadan University, and a Shell installation as well as brief stops in Ghana, Liberia, and Senegal. Grace kept a map to chart his journey as accurately as she could. "It's tremendous," she wrote, "this continent of Africa!" She also sent along the most salient news from home. Barbara started classes at Wingate High. Chuck began his first year at Howard University. And there was a new addition to the Belafonte family, baby Gina. Less happily, Grace lost her job because her employer needed additional accounting services that she was not trained to provide. As always, she remained concerned about the Killens family budget, but she also resolved that things would work out.[45]

By the time Killens's African travels were over, he had logged more than twelve thousand miles in nearly a dozen nations. He sensed not only new possibilities for Africa but also a basic mistrust of the United States. Africans often asked him, "How can we believe your country's professions of good will to us, with whom they have not lived, when they deny human dignity to you who come from us and have lived with them for centuries and helped to build their great civilization?"[46] Killens understood this to be *the* question of the Cold War. The abysmal U.S. race record represented a liability abroad, if not an outright embarrassment, as both Eisenhower and Kennedy knew, though neither man had done enough on the civil rights or anticolonial fronts. Killens felt that the best diplomatic gesture the United

States could make in the so-called Third World was to ensure that freedom and democracy worked at home for African Americans. He continued a line of reasoning first taught to him by Du Bois, Robeson, and Hunton. Numerous latter-day activists were also beginning to theorize a connection between the African American freedom movement and decolonization. Prominent among them was Malcolm X.

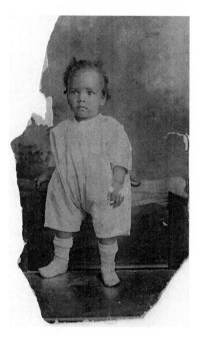

John Killens at about eighteen months old, 1917. *Courtesy of the Killens family*

Carrie Walker Coleman. *Courtesy of the Killens family*

Willie Lee Coleman Killens, ca. 1940s. *Courtesy of the Killens family*

Charles Myles Killens Sr., ca. 1953. *Courtesy of the Killens family*

John Killens (second row, third from right) at Pleasant Hill School, ca. 1922.
Courtesy of the Killens family

John (left) and Richard Killens, ca. 1927. *Courtesy of the Killens family*

Chuck Killens (right) and his cousin, Paul Wolfert, ca. 1946. *Courtesy of the Killens family*

Ballard faculty, including principal Raymond Goodwin von Tobel (top right); Lewis Hendrix Mounts, a key influence on Killens (top left); and Martha Logan (middle woman, second row), Killens's seventh-grade English teacher, ca. 1930. *Courtesy of the Middle Georgia Archives, Washington Memorial Library, Macon, Georgia*

Ballard Normal School on Forest Avenue in Macon, Georgia. *Courtesy of the Middle Georgia Archives, Washington Memorial Library, Macon, Georgia*

Ballard Normal School Graduating Class of 1933.
John Killens is back row, second from right.
Courtesy of the Killens family

John Killens in Monterey, California, 1943.
Courtesy of the Killens family

Charliemae Killens, 1951.
Courtesy of the Killens family

Charles Myles Killens Jr., ca. 1944.
Courtesy of the Killens family

The Hollywood Ten, 1948. Front row, from left: Herbert Biberman, attorneys Martin Popper and Robert W. Kenny, Albert Maltz, Lester Cole. Second row, from left: Dalton Trumbo, John Howard Lawson, Alvah Bessie, Samuel Ornitz. Third row, from left: Ring Lardner Jr., Edward Dmytryk, Adrian Scott. *Copyright* BETTMANN/CORBIS

Alphaeus Hunton after his release from prison, 1951. From left: Alphaeus Hunton, Dorothy Hunton, Paul Robeson, W. E. B. Du Bois. *From Dorothy K. Hunton,* Alphaeus Hunton: The Unsung Valiant *(Richmond Hill, N.Y.: Hunton, 1986)*

John Killens (left) and Alphaeus Hunton outside the South African Consulate, 1952. *From Dorothy K. Hunton,* Alphaeus Hunton: The Unsung Valiant *(Richmond Hill, N.Y.: Hunton, 1986)*

Dorothy Brewster, ca. 1930s.
*Photo by Associated News
Photographic Service. Courtesy of
Columbia University Archives*

Richard Wright, ca. 1950s. *Copyright*
BETTMANN/CORBIS

Langston Hughes. *Copyright*
BETTMANN/CORBIS

John Killens (right) and Mike Wallace, 1954. *Courtesy of the Killens family*

John Killens arriving at the annual convention of the National Association for the Advancement of Colored People, Atlantic City, New Jersey, June 1955. *Courtesy of the Killens family*

The National Association for the Advancement of Colored People's "Night of the Stars,"
New York, 1957. From left: Sidney Poitier, John Lewis, William Branch, John Killens,
Harry Belafonte. *Courtesy of the Killens family*

John Killens and Ruby Dee after
the Prayer Pilgrimage, 1957.
Courtesy of the Killens family

John Killens (right), Rosa Parks, and John Fletcher, ca. 1957.
Courtesy of the Killens family

Barbara Killens (front center); Harry Belafonte (front left); Killens's cousin, Paul
Wolfert (top left); Killens's aunt, Eleanor Wolfert; and Killens's cousin, Mark
Wolfert, ca. 1959. *Courtesy of the Killens family*

John Killens departing for Los Angeles to work on the *Youngblood* screenplay, June 1959. From left: Grace Killens, Barbara Killens, John Killens, Willie Lee Killens. *Courtesy of the Killens family*

Grace Killens, ca. 1963.
*Courtesy of the
Killens family*

Chuck and Barbara Killens, 1961.
Courtesy of the Killens family

Angus Cameron (left) meeting with Albert E. Kahn. *Copyright*
BETTMANN/CORBIS

Martin Luther King Jr. and
Malcolm X in Washington,
D.C., March 26, 1964.
Copyright BETTMANN/
CORBIS

Book party, 1966. From left: Val Pringle, John Killens, Godfrey Cambridge, representatives from Trident Press. *Courtesy of the Killens family*

Fisk University, April 1967. Seated, from left: Margaret Danner, John Killens, Gwendolyn Brooks, LeRoi Jones (Amiri Baraka), Lerone Bennett. Standing, from left: John Henrik Clarke, Ron Milner. *Courtesy of the Killens family*

Grace Killens working on manuscripts, July 1967.
Courtesy of the Killens family

John and Grace Killens in the Soviet Union, June 1968.
Courtesy of the Killens family

John Killens in Korea, summer 1970. John Cheever and Federico Cheever are to his left. Mary Cheever is at the head of the table. *Courtesy of the Killens family*

At the Guggenheim Museum for a Robert Frost centennial celebration, March 1974. From left: John Henrik Clarke, Robert Hayden, Daisy Turnbull Brown, Sterling Brown, John Killens. *Copyright Roy Lewis. Courtesy of Roy Lewis and the Killens family*

Wedding of Barbara Killens and Louis Reyes Rivera, November 2, 1974.
From left: Raymond Frost, Louis Reyes Rivera, Barbara Killens, John Killens,
Charlotte Herring, Thomas Russell Jones. *Courtesy of the Killens family*

Mabel Ward Jones, 1960s.
Courtesy of the Killens family

Barra and Kutisa, ca. 1980.
Courtesy of the Killens family

John Killens (left) at Yankee Stadium with author Piri Thomas and Detroit Tigers star Ron LeFlore, late 1970s. *Courtesy of the Killens family*

John Oliver Killens, ca. 1980. *Courtesy of the Killens family*

From left, Baron James Ashanti, Brenda Connor-Bey, John Killens, Doris Jean Austin, Arthur Flowers, Joan Cofer, ca. 1980. *Courtesy of the Killens family*

John Killens (left) and John A. Williams, ca. 1982. *Copyright Samuel F. Yette. Courtesy of Samuel F. Yette and the Killens family*

John Killens at the
Schomburg Center for
Research in Black Culture,
ca. 1982. *Copyright Paul
Mondesire. Courtesy of Paul
Mondesire and the Killens
family*

John Killens at the National Black Writers Conference, Medgar Evers College—CUNY,
1986. From left: Margaret Walker, Barbara Summers, John Killens, Elizabeth Nunez.
Copyright Eugene B. Redmond. Courtesy of Eugene B. Redmond and the Killens family

John Killens (left) and Haki Madhubuti, Chicago, 1986. *Copyright Eugene B. Redmond. Courtesy of Eugene B. Redmond and the Killens family*

John Killens (right) and Eugene Redmond, Chicago, 1986. *Copyright Eugene B. Redmond. Courtesy of Eugene B. Redmond and the Killens family*

John and Grace Killens with granddaughter Abiba, 1987.
Courtesy of the Killens family

The Killens family residence (right), 1392 Union Street, Brooklyn, 2009.
Copyright Kevin A. Browne

John Killens (left) and Tito Puente receiving honorary doctorates at the State University of New York, Old Westbury, May 31, 1987. *Courtesy of the Killens family*

CHAPTER THIRTEEN

Thundering Genius, 1961–1963

Back in the United States, John Oliver Killens agreed to a contract with the Educational Communications Corporation that
would net him four thousand dollars. The only major sticking
point between the parties was that Killens wanted no part of
working in Los Angeles. He planned to stay in New York and
complete the screenplay during the first eight or nine weeks of
1962, after the scripts on West Africa were done. However, that
project became imperiled, largely because of the inexperience
and ineptitude of External Development Services. Company
officials unrealistically expected Killens, who returned to the
States during the second week in October, to finish the thirteen
scripts by the end of the month. On November 13, Killens wrote
to Basil Okwu to explain that the snag resulted from External
Development's miscalculation about the amount of time and
creative effort required to produce quality films. Killens could
not participate in a "superficial quickie" for the consumption
of American and European audiences and sought advice from
Okwu about how to reignite the project.[1] But Okwu had been
transferred from his post as minister of information and no
longer held much influence over the film initiative.

Martin Leighton sided with Killens and supported the Eastern
Nigerian government's desire to control production. Leighton
urged External Development to abandon its role as producer, a
suggestion with which Wynford Vaughan Thomas agreed. The
director suggested that it would have been tactful for Killens to

turn over something in writing to External Development rather than refuse to proceed until terms acceptable to all parties had been negotiated.
But tact was not one of Killens's strong points. If tact were the only way he
could get films to the screen, they would never make it. Moreover, in light
of his previous screenplay adventures, he would only fully commit to a film
project he thought would actually be produced.

Killens received several reminders to attend to his novel. Alvah Bessie
wrote to him early in January, "Where is that second book?" By then it was
at least in production. A more powerful message arrived on March 12, when
Killens learned that Frank Brown had died of leukemia.[2] The news sent Killens spiraling into depression, unable to concentrate for days. As he wrote
to his cousin, Gus Savage, "Losing Frank is hard to take because he had so
much to give. A person of his integrity, enthusiasms and stamina is rare;
and he was very much needed by 'us.'"[3]

Killens's mood lifted when *And Then We Heard the Thunder*, the war
novel he had seemingly forever been promising friends and fans, finally
made it to galley form. Killens received the proofs from Knopf in April
with instructions to return the final copy the following month. While Killens could have reached this point much sooner had he not been chasing
Hollywood dreams, the novel would have differed substantially. *And Then
We Heard the Thunder* represents Killens's 1960s reevaluation of certain
communist positions and his ideological repositioning within Third World
Marxism.[4] Domestic class analyses still held considerable intellectual weight
for him, but he had become quite doubtful that legions of white workers
could ever transcend racism, identify their class interests à la Oscar Jefferson, and become progressive stalwarts. Therefore, Killens could advocate
no policy that subjugated antiracist struggle to the demands of a popular
front, which had been the Communist Party's line during World War II.
Moreover, the Soviet Union no longer served as a theoretical guidepost, as
it had when Killens criticized Arthur Koestler; thus, the novel concludes
by suggesting that Africa and Asia are humankind's hope.[5] It is not that
the earlier Killens had lacked a revolutionary nationalist or Third World
perspective, as demonstrated by his work with E. Franklin Frazier, W. E. B.
Du Bois, Paul Robeson, and Alphaeus Hunton; his reading of and continued association with Harry Haywood; and his reflections on the Bandung
Conference. However, although he had long felt a responsibility toward decolonization campaigns, not until the 1960s, with the growing national independence movements in Africa and his engagement with minds such as

Oliver Tambo's, did he articulate the tangible benefits decolonization efforts would provide for African Americans. *And Then We Heard the Thunder*, in fact, though definitely a World War II story, is also about several other wars—the U.S. Civil War, the Cold War, and Third World anti-imperialist revolutions.

The plot of *And Then We Heard the Thunder* is basically autobiographical. Law student Solly Saunders, Georgia-born but raised in Harlem, enters the army determined to make the most of the experience in terms of his personal ambition, which means getting along well enough to become an officer and making contacts that could be useful in white society. His new bride, Millie, overrides his mild protestations about black struggle, insisting that he should place the war against the external threat of fascism at the top of his political agenda—that is, be American, not Negro. Yet his racial yearnings haunt him. Ideally, he would like to "do my dancing in the Empire Room at the Waldorf but at the same time keep in touch with my folks who will still be stomping at the Savoy." Ironically, Solly experiences these thoughts while honeymooning in an apartment provided to him and his wife by a progressive white couple, a luxury that was not an option for many Harlem newlyweds. While asleep in the apartment, he dreams that the apartment owners come through the wall and the man says, "Millie is absolutely right. Americans have to forget their differences and stand together against the common enemy. A house divided—." The added irony is that Abraham Lincoln's injunction against enslavement, against half the house, was in itself a reason for war.[6]

Killens's invocation of the Civil War is also signaled by the novel's title, which is drawn from Harriet Tubman's account of a Civil War battle that serves as the book's epigraph:

> And then we saw the lightning, and that was the guns
> And then we heard the thunder and that was the big guns
> And then we heard the rain falling and that was the drops of blood falling
> And when we came to get in the crops, it was dead men that we reaped.[7]

Much as spirituals do in *Youngblood*, Tubman's text becomes *And We Heard the Thunder*'s formal outline. Part 1, "The Planting Season," chronicles Solly and his comrades' time in a segregated unit in the Jim Crow South. The comparison of the section to Civil War strife suggests the view that many African Americans occupy neoslave status and that the South itself is where it is found. The seeds sown in the soil of a racist U.S. Army will be grown and harvested over the course of the story. Part 2, "Cultivation," details events in California, where Solly and his unit are primed for slaughter in the South Pacific even as they are confined to the Booker T. Washington Post Exchange. As penalty for their antiracist activism in Georgia, they receive only four weeks—one-third of the normal time—to get ready for deployment as a special amphibian force. The section ends with a version of the 1952 story Killens wrote for the *California Quarterly*. Part 3, "Lightning—Thunder—Rainfall," portrays the action in the South Pacific, where black U.S. soldiers die at the hands of foreign troops. Part 4, "The Crop," in which African American soldiers die at the hands of their white U.S. counterparts—another Civil War—reminds readers that the scene Tubman witnessed led to only a partial victory over racialized persecution.

Killens refuses to let Solly ignore the call of the Double V. Solly distances himself from Millie's philosophy (she dies during childbirth to symbolize the rupture) and adopts the uncompromising black perspective of Fannie Mae, his second love interest and future wife, who exuberantly expresses the Double V slogan as "victory against the fascists overseas and against the crackers here at home." He stands in solidarity with other black men— Joseph "Bookworm" Taylor, Jerry Abraham Lincoln Scott, Jimmy "Quiet Man" Larker, and Randolph Greer—who see fighting racism not only as politically correct but also as manly and dignified. Saunders, Taylor, and Greer send a letter to the *People's Herald* that summarizes their view: "We Negro soldiers find ourselves in a hostile country in a racist-type undemocratic Army preparing ourselves to go overseas to lay down our lives in a world struggle against Racism and Fascism and for the cause of Freedom and Democracy. This is a bitter pill to swallow." After listing several specific grievances, they conclude, "Some of us feel that we do not need to go four or five thousand miles away to do battle with the enemies of Democracy. They are present with us here and now and spitting in our faces . . . riding on our backs and breathing down our necks. God only knows why we haven't taken matters in our own hands, or when we might."[8]

As the narrative moves toward the race riot in Australia, Killens comes to grips with aspects of his own political past. Even as he removed himself from direct involvement with the Communist Party, he never adopted a hypercritical tone as Ralph Ellison or Chester Himes did. When the rebels are called on the carpet before Captain Rutherford for writing the letter, which a number of newspapers have picked up, the captain pressures Sergeant Anderson to reveal all he knows about the document's origin, warning, "Don't be a fall guy for a couple of no-good New York Communists." Anderson replies that he would rather be a communist than an Uncle Tom and a snitch. While not retrospectively hostile toward communists, Killens embeds a full critique of the Popular Front in dialogue that takes place at a party in Australia organized by Celia Blake, a third love interest who nurses Solly after he is wounded in the Philippines. Dobbs, an Australian, says that he does not like Earl Browder's *Victory and After*. Steve, Celia's brother, chimes in, "Browder is a bloody fool." The commander of Solly's unit, Captain Bob Samuels, a Jewish liberal, then argues Browder's position that "progressive capitalism" is a legitimate U.S. goal. In Samuels's estimation, American corporate bosses can afford to provide workers with a high standard of living. But Dobbs counters with a crucial question: "What can you afford to give your Negroes?" Steve adds that most white American soldiers "swagger like the Nazis." A bit later, Solly, who has no faith in Samuels's liberalism or the current Communist Party line with which liberals could be so comfortable, says, "I'm putting my money on that large minority known as colored people, three quarters of the world's population." Steve turns his critical beam from Samuels to Solly, accusing, "You're not a Socialist. You're nationalistic and you're anti-white and you're reactionary." In practical terms, Killens was guilty of none of those charges, but he has Solly reply, "Just fine, thank you."[9]

When the race riot erupts in Bainbridge, Samuels concedes that Solly is right about Double V and fights alongside him in battle, killing white soldiers to save Solly's life. Solly terms Samuels a colored man, a label Samuels rejects, preferring to affirm that he is a white man capable of siding with African Americans—when racial justice is the issue—in deed as well as word. Although numerous casualties occur and no real physical triumph takes place at the end of the tale, Double V ideologically trumps the Popular Front. But even more salient is Killens's 1960s spin on liberation—that is, Solly's speculation about a "new and different dialogue that was people-oriented" that might come out of Africa and Asia. Solly also describes the small gathering of black and white soldiers after the cease-fire as the "place where the New World is."[10] Solly has reconciled personal angst and overcome obstacles posed by racism to posit or symbolize a liberating vision that is multiracial and socialist, though noncommunist, and seeks models in the East. The finale of *And Then We Heard the Thunder* recalls Du Bois's musings about Asia and perfectly anticipates and perhaps influences the conclusion of *The Autobiography of Malcolm X*, published three years later.

There, Malcolm speaks of the looming importance of Africa and Asia.[11] Solly ultimately reaffirms his decision to become a writer. As for Killens, writing had long been a "fierce obsession" for Solly, and he eschewed a law career to become a full-time author committed to the struggle for freedom.[12]

With the finishing touches being applied to *And Then We Heard the Thunder* and after reworking his earlier Montgomery script for submission to Altina Carey, Killens moved about more freely in public and met thunder of another type in Malcolm X. The author had admired Malcolm's success, under Elijah Muhammad's supervision, in rehabilitating black men who had been "relegated to the junk heap of obsolescence."[13] But Killens refrained from trying to establish a personal relationship because of Malcolm's religious fervor. But in the spring of 1962, the efforts of Ruby Dee and Ossie Davis began to change Killens's stance toward Malcolm.

Dee's brother, Edward, joined the Nation of Islam and began to pester his sister and her husband to visit a Manhattan mosque. The couple eventually met Malcolm and were impressed enough to invite him to their home. Malcolm came, accompanied by Herbert Muhammad, Elijah Muhammad's son. Dee and Davis also invited Killens, Sidney Poitier, Tina and Lonnie Satin, and a few others. The guests peppered Malcolm with questions: "What is your program offering black people, really? Do we all have to join and become Black Muslims to participate in your kingdom? Or is there a program that you have that affects all black folks?" They found Malcolm rather weak in terms of political theory and economic formulation. Malcolm could not or would not enter into a conversation about democratic socialism or Pan-Africanism, and his hosts thought whimsical his talk of government-sponsored separatism. Despite the ideological chasm, Malcolm came off as a compelling figure because of his charisma, quickness of mind, and intellectual promise as well as his apparent integrity and dedication.[14] The group became his firm supporters, and following his break with the Nation of Islam, he labeled an expanded version of the group "my braintrust."[15]

While Malcolm fished for converts to Islam, Killens and Davis in particular attempted to transform him into a youthful but post-Stalinist Paul Robeson, seeing him as an Up South complement to King. Despite his leadership role, King had never had strong appeal among the northern urban masses, especially young people, and his influence was slipping among southern student activists, the Freedom Riders and sit-in participants who in many instances were seizing the lead in the nonviolent direct action campaign. Moreover, if Killens, Davis, and others could get Malcolm to talk socialism, like King, they figured that the two leading black voices of the 1960s would end up on the same page in terms of economic advocacy. Then, they optimistically believed, the other differences between the "dream" and the "nightmare" could be worked out.[16] The question of nonviolence versus the right of self-defense already was more of a debate about tone and tactics than philosophy, a point King conceded to Robert Williams, though grudgingly and disingenuously.[17] A focus on economics would also shift the tenor of the debate regarding integration versus extreme nationalism, because a nation, though justifiable under the old Black Belt Thesis, remained a practical impossibility. Malcolm might be able to reach more people by acknowledging this fact. And integration under capitalism, which is what *integration* generally means in the American political vocabulary, would be bleached from the formula for freedom.

Malcolm became a new source of inspiration for Killens, his "main man" and "philosophical brother." They developed "a mutual admiration society." Killens came to see Malcolm as "Truly Mr. Everyblackman. Flesh of our flesh, blood of our blood . . . flotsam and jetsam of our Black experience."[18] Killens viewed Malcolm as shy and sensitive but also saw him hold audiences spellbound in small settings. As Killens recalled, "You'd walk in and look around and see a crowd, and there'd be that tall man standing in the middle of it. When he would come over to my house, there would be people there whom other people ask for autographs. And they would ask for *his*."[19] "I loved Malcolm," Killens exclaimed, "because he loved Black people and because he was the antithesis of Gunga Din. He had a Black sense of humor that would crack you up with laughter. He was an artist of the spoken word. And like all true artists he was self-critical."[20] Malcolm strained, as Killens saw, against Elijah Muhammad's stricture that Nation of Islam representatives could not become publicly involved in everyday political activities. Malcolm tried to transgress discretely in some instances, bearing witness on the periphery of the labor movement and taking interest in certain pickets and boycotts.[21]

As Killens awaited the publication of his novel and stayed politically active, he attended to several pressing personal/political matters. On July 25, he appeared at Hamilton House in Brooklyn to support his brother-in-law, who was running for the state assembly from the Seventeenth District. If successful, Thomas Jones would become the first African American to serve the district. The following month, Killens attended a wedding reception for Howard "Stretch" Johnson's daughter, Wendy Kay. Killens tried to get a contract with Knopf for Lorenz Graham, Shirley Graham Du Bois's younger brother, who had written a manuscript, "North Town." However, Angus Cameron did not think that the work was ready for publication, an assessment with which Graham ultimately agreed.

Recuperating from the amputation of one of his toes, Myles Killens was buoyed by a telegram from his grandson, Chuck. According to Myles, the boy's "paraphrasing was unique: the structure of his sentences, the subjects and predicates, the phrases and clauses were grammatically arranged with each sentence extending the thoughts in an orderly manner to the claim of the topic." Myles felt that Chuck, now eighteen, was alert and talented, with a "fine sense of values." But Myles was distressed that his grandson, who had not thrived away from home, had not returned to Howard for a second semester: "I hope we can keep him interested in school (a college education)." Myles wrote a long letter to Chuck, hoping to get him on track and giving him "a practical synopsis of the history of the United States, the greatest minds of our race, the forerunners of sit-ins and freedom riders, and why it is so important and necessary to avail himself *first* with a good college education, training, and intelligence." Myles appealed to his son for assistance in maintaining a correspondence with Chuck: "I want to give him my all—(experience) that part if accepted I know will benefit him." Myles also believed that Barbara could play a key role in persuading Chuck to stick with school.[22]

But Chuck already understood a great deal about the legacy his grandfather and parents embraced, and he returned to school in September, associating with the Nonviolent Action Group, whose members included Stokely Carmichael and Muriel Tillinghast, who later became key organizers in the Student Nonviolent Coordinating Committee. Chuck also wrote for the school newspaper, the *Hilltop*.

Knopf originally scheduled *And Then We Heard the Thunder* for a September release but pushed the date back to January, partly because Killens would not relinquish his grip on the galley proofs. The delay also resulted from the lengthy process of obtaining permissions from music companies to use song lyrics in the novel. After it became clear that the September 26 publication date could not be met, Killens pressed Knopf for a November date, but Cameron favored January because he thought that the novel would need serious promotion and did not want it overwhelmed in the fall competition for review space. In addition, postponing until January would allow the company to get quotations for the book jacket. He wrote to Killens, "If you have temporary dismay at the failure of a fall publication, call me for comfort, because I can give it to you."[23]

The author, always suspicious that the publisher's promotion efforts would be lacking, began beating the publicity drums. In June, he asked James Baldwin if he would provide a blurb. Killens subsequently made the same request of Daisy Bates; George Murphy Jr.; Dalton Trumbo, the most successful of the Hollywood Ten; Henry Lee Moon, director of public relations for the National Association for the Advancement of Colored People; James Hicks, managing editor of the *Amsterdam News*; and Cyprian Ekwensi of Nigeria's Ministry of Information. At Killens's suggestion, Knopf sent proofs directly to Ossie Davis, Ruby Dee, Lorraine Hansberry, Langston Hughes, Sidney Poitier, and Harry Belafonte. Nearly all responded favorably. In July, John and Grace Killens traveled to Los Angeles, where the author met with Altina Carey as well as with Dick Bancroft, who came down from San Francisco and expressed a willingness to promote the new novel in the Bay Area.

Back in New York, the Killenses continued to work publicity angles. Early in September, Grace wrote to Belafonte, who had not responded to the request for comments, and to Poitier, who had not provided remarks specific enough for Cameron. Poitier subsequently proclaimed, "This novel is a passionate shout for peace and freedom; let us hope the world will listen. *Thunder* is really one of the greatest books I've ever read."[24] Hansberry opined, "John Oliver Killens' *And Then We Heard the Thunder* is one of the most deeply instructing novels of our time. . . . It is an extraordinary experience. America will be finer and more a part of the present age if its message is absorbed. Thank God for writers like John Killens."[25] And Belafonte commented, "The powerful climax of this novel warns us that men *had better* come together. Killens' prose strikes lightning from page to page and we hear the awful thunder."[26]

By the end of the month, Killens was pressing Knopf to arrange for serialization of the novel, traditionally one of the best publicity maneuvers. *Playboy* seemed a reasonable option, but Frank DeBlois, an associate editor at the magazine, concluded that the material was similar to work already in the magazine's fiction inventory.

Speaking engagements were another channel through which to publicize *And Then We Heard the Thunder*, even if the book was not the sole focus of such events. His largest audience was the fifteen hundred students, faculty, and visitors—among them Malcolm X and Sidney Poitier—who filled a Howard University auditorium in early November to hear Killens, Baldwin, and Davis speak on "The Negro Writer in American Society." According to Baldwin, the writer's role was to "begin to excavate, almost for the first time, the real history of this country . . . not the history that one would like to believe about the Founding Fathers or the nobility of Abraham Lincoln, but to try to find out what really happened here . . . what really got us where we are." As older and more studious travelers on the left than Baldwin, Killens and Davis already possessed definite ideas about the emergence of latter-day capitalist, white supremacist America, but they seconded the mission of truth telling. Davis asserted, "I think that the time has come when we in this country, particularly the black man, must hang his harp on the willow and refuse to play it unless he can give the truth about himself, his people and the society in which we live." Weighing in last, Killens announced, "I, as a Negro writer, Negro artist, Negro teacher, Negro worker, ask America to listen to me. I am your conscience. Get right with me and you will truly be beautiful before the world." He explained that he wrote out of a frame of reference that was human, male, American, and black but that publishers and producers often asked him why he could not just write about *people*. Killens remarked, "Negroes are the only people I know who are set apart because of who they are, and at the same time told to forget it." He summed up his comments about the black writer's responsibility by reading Langston Hughes's "Notes on Commercial Theatre," with its closing resolve:

> But someday somebody'll
> Stand up and talk about me
> And write about me
> Black and beautiful
> And sing about me
> And put on plays about me
> I reckon it'll be
> Me myself
> Yes, it'll be me.

In the wide-ranging question-and-answer period that ensued, Killens declared, "We want the world to be different. This is what we do every time we type one line on a page. We are out to change the world, to make people live better with each other. I can state it almost that simply." He also touched on several topics, including Jean Genet's *The Blacks*, which for some people held "a kind of morbid fascination," and his trying times in the entertainment industry. "It is almost impossible," he argued, "to get a movie that will allow us to say something in this medium. If we have to wait until the South is ready for *Youngblood*, we will be waiting a long time."[27]

Stokely Carmichael "vividly" remembered the session. Even more memorable, however, was the impromptu, all-night party that followed at the apartment of Ed Brown (Rap's brother), Courtland Cox, and Butch Conn: "Our older writer brothers reasoned with us like family. We glowed, strengthened by their regard and evident concern. And these accomplished writers all seemed at ease in that small, raggedy student apartment."[28] At the age of forty-six, Killens had achieved the status of elder.

Although Belafonte had submitted a blurb for *And Then They Heard the Thunder*, tensions had arisen between him and Killens. On November 30, Killens wrote, "Grace and I were thinking about you folks the other evening, as we do quite often, and we wondered what has been the cause of the breakdown in communications between the two families. It's been almost a year to the day since we saw any of you. All of us have been busy, but how busy can you get?" Killens continued, "I regret very deeply that I have not yet been able to repay the loan you so generously made to me. The last year has been a rugged one for us, financially." Nevertheless, he promised to pay the debt in 1963, "PERIOD." He ended by demanding, "Goddammit give me a phone call this week" and calling Belafonte's proposed Pushkin film project "one of the greatest ideas you ever had."[29]

Two prominent voices apparently had not responded to Killens's earlier requests for help in promoting *And Then We Heard the Thunder*. On December 18, therefore, he forwarded to Baldwin comments made by Hansberry, Davis, Belafonte, and Poitier as well as a *Publisher's Weekly* review that described the book as "a very impressive novel about anti-Negro discrimination in the army in World War II. A fine job of writing, which rises to true eloquence in many scenes, it has such believable human beings, such action, and such cumulative impact that it fairly rivets the reader to the pages." A comment from Baldwin, Killens thought, "would surely round out the picture." The following day, he sent virtually the same package to Hughes, reminding him, "The time is nigh." Baldwin responded, "You have written a beautiful and powerful book." Hughes wrote, "Truth sounds like a brass gong or an angry trumpet playing notes of humor and tragedy on the scale of white-black soldier-civilian relations during World War II."[30]

On January 20, 1963, the Harlem Writers Guild and Knopf sponsored a party at the Carnegie Endowment Center for International Peace to celebrate the publication of *And Then We Heard the Thunder*. More than eight hundred people attended, and more than six hundred autographed copies of the hardback edition were sold. Killens was elated, as was Cameron, who thought the party the finest literary event he had ever attended. Among the notables present were Godfrey Cambridge, Carl Van Vechten, Maxwell Geismar, John Henrik Clarke, Walter Christmas, Abbey Lincoln, Max Roach, and Ernest Crichlow. Irving Burgie, the most commercially successful member of the Harlem Writers Guild, provided musical entertainment. Sterling Brown traveled from Washington to introduce the book with a review "as lyrical as one of his poems." Ossie Davis read the passage describing the beating of Solly Saunders and then remarked that the book "was tough and it was tender. It leapt out, it sang out, it screamed, it cried; it fought, it bled, it suffered—and it showed me love as [I] myself remember love to be." Ruby Dee read a scene depicting the relationship between Solly and Celia Blake. Dee had already described the novel's female characters as "people first then women. Passions are exact in times of death, and these women know life's measure. The white woman, for example, is drawn with great candor. She kicks over the goddess seat and screams for her share of all life's riches."[31]

Cameron was particularly moved by the appearance of Van Vechten, who moved so feebly at the age of eighty-two that Cameron had to help him to a taxi: "Somehow, to me, such an old and infirm man turning up for that occasion just to speak to [Killens] reflects a kind of valiance that I was quite touched by. It also reflects, of course, the depth of his feeling about the book." At Cameron's urging, Killens wrote Van Vechten a note thanking him for his positive comments.[32]

Lorraine Hansberry and Bob Nemiroff sent a telegram: "AND THEN WE HEARD THE THUNDER IS ONLY THE SECOND OF THE MANY STORMS OF TRUTH AND ART WE CAN EXPECT FROM YOU AND OTHERS LIKE YOU IN YEARS TO COME. BEST." Baldwin also sent a message, explaining that he was unavoidably delayed and would miss the party. And Langston Hughes telegrammed, "WISHING YOU A HAPPY PARTY AND MAY BLOCK BUSTING THUNDER BE A BOOMING HIT AND A BIG BEST SELLER."[33]

In some respects, the party was Killens's finest literary moment, symbolizing a triumphant return to his home genre after his frustrations with filmmakers. But the moment should have been much more. Knopf released the hardcover edition without using any of the blurbs that had been collected. And, in an ironic twist for the old union worker, his book was released in the middle of a 114-day New York City newspaper strike that had begun on December 8. The absence of mainstream newspaper coverage in New York, home to a disproportionate share of the nation's book sales, represented a major blow. Romare Bearden, an artist and Killens's comrade from the days of the United Negro and Allied Veterans Association, sent regrets that he could not attend the party but made it clear that he had ordered the book and planned to read it shortly. He added, "I hope that the newspaper strike is soon settled—I don't know about the effects of it on book publication, but attendance is way off at the art galleries. No one knows what's happening, else I'm sure I'd have seen a review of your book in the *Times*."[34]

And Then We Heard the Thunder nevertheless enjoyed a critical reception that its author deemed fantastic. Poppy Cannon White, writing in the pages of the *Amsterdam News*, termed Killens a "thundering genius" and asserted, "With the publication of his second novel *And Then We Heard the Thunder*, John Oliver Killens comes into his own as a giant on the American literary scene." "Even I," White averred, "who long ago made an almost-vow never to read another World War II novel found myself immediately caught, held, entrenched. I set aside all my work, broke engagements, devoured it from the first to the 485th page all in one blissful weekend. And savored every word!"[35]

In the *Saturday Review*, John Howard Griffin, author of *Black Like Me*, wrote, "In this big, polyphonic, violent novel about Negro soldiers in World War II, John Oliver Killens drags the reader into the fullness of the Negro's desolating experience." Griffin compared Killens's work to that of James Jones: "His battle scenes have the same hallucinatory power; his characters live and speak the raw language of the streets and the barracks."[36]

Crisis featured a lengthy review by George Norford, who had been a field correspondent in the South Pacific for *Yank*, the Army weekly, and a member of the Army Special Staff. Norford informed readers, "There should be gratitude for this book for it reveals how cynically personal and petty regional race prejudice can penetrate an Army dedicated to the fight for democracy and corrupt its fibre, subvert its unity and make its slogans seem a mockery and a fraud." Norford also suggested, "The author's skill in developing situations and moods of great intensity is superb. . . . Killens tells his story movingly, magnificently, and memorably."[37] The *Columbia Owl's* Molly Lucas wrote, "If you would gauge the temper of today's Negro, find the reasons for the growing persistence and scope of the non-violent demonstrations, or explanations for the sudden popularity of the Black Muslim movement, this book is a must. . . . [D]on't fail to read it—and pass the word along."[38] And when the *New York Post* restarted operations, Ted Poston affirmed, "This big, robust, readable novel more than fulfills the promise of Killens' *Youngblood*."[39]

Harlem Writers Guild members chimed in with clear respect if not always overwhelming praise. Louise Meriwether declared, "John Oliver Killens has done a tremendous job of writing here. His characters are unforgettable, especially bandyleg Scotty."[40] John Henrik Clarke expressed reservations about the perceived overuse of bawdy barracks talk, General Grant's pro-Japanese stance, and the love affair in Australia but decided that in the final analysis, "It is a major novel and only a major writer could have written it."[41]

Some of the most insightful remarks were contained in personal letters by known literary figures. Van Vechten wrote directly to Alfred Knopf, "You introduced me to Walter [White] and he introduced me to James Weldon Johnson, Langston Hughes and ever so many more and I eventually wrote *Nigger Heaven*. Well, what we started has eventually progressed to James Baldwin, John A. Williams, and JOHN OLIVER KILLENS." Van Vechten observed that *And Then We Heard the Thunder* was "a great book, a very real book, and a very true book."[42]

Killens made his biggest splash in the weeks following the publication of *And Then We Heard the Thunder* with his February 1 appearance on the *Today* show, hosted by Hugh Downs. Seen by millions, Killens shared the spotlight with James Baldwin and Louis Lomax, his friendly rival in Wynford Vaughan Thomas's imagined African election. Killens's cousin, Mark Frazier, wrote, "We are down here fighting so hard for equal rights and to see our own people having freedom of speech, it makes one feel proud of them."[43]

Back in Pleasant Hill, Killens's aunt, Louise Coleman Ketch, tuned in at 6:45 to ensure that she would not miss a minute of the broadcast: "All of the participants were good, but you, darling, were the best. . . . Gee I am happy. You looked so well and you were so composed and calm during your discussion." Many of Ketch's coworkers had noted the "striking resemblance" between her and her nephew. "I know you do have some of my ways," she offered. "One thing we have in common is that we are very determined to do what we want to do."[44]

And Then We Heard the Thunder was the only novel seriously considered for the 1964 Pulitzer Prize, but the judges chose not to give an award that year, reportedly expressing, with particular reference to Killens's novel, "criticism on technical grounds."[45] More crucial to Killens, however, was his belief that he had followed his muse and delivered a virtuoso message against racism and in support of progressive unity and self-defense. At the age of forty-seven, he had reached maturity as a craftsman, and in Solly Saunders the world could celebrate another African American hero.

CHAPTER FOURTEEN

It Doesn't Hurt to Review, 1963–1964

Shortly after the release of *And Then We Heard the Thunder*, Lee Nichols, a Defense Department official, arranged a meeting with John Oliver Killens at a lounge in midtown Manhattan. Over rounds of gin, Nichols lavished praise on the author, informing him that even attorney general Robert Kennedy had enjoyed the book. Nichols next asked about the writer's opinion of the army in 1963. Killens had given the matter little thought but could not imagine that the racial climate had changed substantially over the preceding twenty years. Nonetheless, he was invited to tour several military facilities and perhaps publicize any improvements he might perceive, a proposition he immediately rejected. Whatever betterment existed in the military's racial climate still measured far short of respectable, and Killens would not sign on as an apologist. During the following weeks, Nichols sent materials, including a book he had written about desegregation in the army, *Breakthrough on the Color Front*, and President John F. Kennedy's February 28, 1963, speech to Congress on civil rights. Nichols even called several times before figuring out that Killens "was not their boy."[1]

Killens eagerly accepted several other invitations, however. He had thrown himself into three new projects: a screenplay about slavery; a nonfiction book, *Black Man's Burden*; and a satirical novel, tentatively titled "The Minister Primarily," about the "red-carpet treatment they give a Georgia-born Negro whom they mistake for the Prime Minister of the newest, richest country (fictional) in all Africa."[2] But all of the writing projects had to compete for time against the usual run of political and social activities and the promotion of *And Then We Heard the Thunder*.

Killens helped to sponsor and publicize *Salute to Southern Students*, a show held at Carnegie Hall on February 1, the third anniversary of the Greensboro, North Carolina, student sit-ins. On February 13, James Forman, executive secretary of the Student Nonviolent Coordinating Committee (SNCC), wrote to thank Killens for his support and provide an update on the group's activities. Three members of the field staff were now working on voter registration in Selma, Alabama; most public facilities had been desegregated in Little Rock, Arkansas, and SNCC was now targeting Pine Bluff; and work continued in South Carolina, Mississippi, and southwestern Georgia. Later that month, Dorothy Burnham requested that Killens become a sponsor of a book party to celebrate the appearance of *A Star to Steer By*, a portrait of Captain Hugh Mulzac written by the late Louis Burnham and Norvel Welch. Mulzac was a political activist and artist who made history on October 23, 1942, by becoming the first African American captain of a merchant ship, the *Booker T. Washington*. The party would honor not only the book but also the captain's seventy-seventh birthday.

On March 1, Yuri Suhl, Killens's old buddy from the Viola Brothers Shore workshop, and his wife, Isabelle, hosted a book party for Killens in Lower Manhattan. On March 13, Killens spoke in Brooklyn at the Bedford branch of the YMCA. The following night, he joined Sterling Brown, John Henrik Clarke, Pauli Murray, William Branch, and African writers Bernard Dadie and Johnson Pepper Clark on a panel billed as "Afro-American Writers Meet African Creative Writers in the United States" at the Washington Heights branch of the New York Public Library.

Killens next made a quick swing through Chicago at the request of Evelyn Brown and the recently formed Frank London Brown Society, participating in the group's March 30 conference on "The Black Writer in an Era of Struggle." Killens sat on a conference panel with Lerone Bennett, an editor at *Ebony*; Clarke; and Hoyt Fuller, offering remarks that resembled those he had made at Howard University the previous fall.[3]

By the end of April, as he explored further speaking and promotional opportunities, Killens began to express dissatisfaction with Knopf's marketing campaign for *And Then We Heard the Thunder*. Sales were steady, primarily, he felt, because of his efforts and those of his friends. The publisher had yet to run a print advertisement, whereas Farrar and Straus had run what Killens termed a "fine" *New York Times* ad for *Sissie*, a new novel by John A. Williams. Killens had believed that Knopf would push his book just as zealously, featuring the quotations he had collected: "The advance comments are some of the most formidable ever collected. Not to use them in the *New York Times* is a crime against the book, morally if not legally. Why else were they collected?" Referring to Ted Poston's comment that in capturing the race riot, *And Then We Heard the Thunder* examines the best kept secret of the war, Killens suggested, "Apparently the publishers intend for my novel to be the best kept secret of 1963."[4] Cameron passed Killens's letter to the promotion and advertising department but noted that he had never planned a full-page announcement in the *Times*. Knopf had intended to run a two-column ad there but had expended the book's promotional budget on magazine ads during the newspaper strike and on the book party at the Carnegie Endowment.[5]

The symposium at Howard University had signaled a shift for Killens. Although he had always embraced the student element among civil rights protesters, he had continued to forge his sturdiest links with artists, professionals, celebrities, labor activists, and civil rights leaders. After appearing at Howard, however, he gushed for weeks about the intellect and passion of students such as Stokely Carmichael and Michael Thelwell, and he began to view the 1960s generation of student activists as a major force for social and political change. His budding collaboration with student activists resulted in a combined tribute to the author and SNCC benefit. The affair took place in Harlem on April 28, with Harry Belafonte, Ted Poston, Diahann Carroll, Diana Sands, and Abbey Lincoln among the notables participating. In the press release advertising the event, Killens stressed the connection between his writing and SNCC's activism: "Today's fighters in Mississippi and Alabama are carrying on the same tradition. Theirs is a struggle to make ours a land where human dignity is fact, not merely proclamation. Today's Freedom Fighters are writing a brand new book with their very lives for unborn generations."[6]

Killens increasingly celebrated student activists as he made his rounds. He spoke in Queens on April 30 at Hollis Unitarian Church and to the Brooklyn National Association for the Advancement of Colored People (NAACP), his old stomping grounds, three days later at the invitation of a cultural committee that included Shirley Chisholm. He traveled to Michigan, speaking at Western Michigan University on May 7 and at Wayne State University on May 9. Then he dashed off to Chicago.

Back in New York, he spoke on a June 15 panel that addressed "The Mood of the Negro in the North" and participated in another SNCC fund-raiser, "Harlem Salutes John Oliver Killens," a day later. On June 21, he addressed the Militant Labor Forum on "One Hundred Years of Freedom," a popular topic that spring. He spoke about how the freedom train had been stalled by racism, the most recent and dramatic example being the murder of Medgar Evers, head of the NAACP office in Jackson, Mississippi, who had been gunned down in his driveway during the preceding week. That same evening, Carnegie Hall hosted another SNCC benefit, "A Salute to Southern Freedom," featuring Mahalia Jackson as well as the Freedom Singers.

The following day, serious momentum began building toward the March on Washington for Jobs and Freedom. Perhaps the freedom train could be put back on track. President Kennedy had met with thirty civil rights leaders and had cast aside his initial opposition to the march. He encouraged the liberal establishment, including some members of his administration, to be supportive. Kennedy's blessing, though not unwelcome, spoke to what would become a sore point for numerous black activists: the degree of white liberal control over black political organizing. How black or radical could such activity ultimately be if it required white liberal permission and funding? Philanthropist Stephen Currier of the Taconic Foundation made available eight hundred thousand dollars to be divided among the major civil rights groups. On July 2—coincidentally, the day Evers would have celebrated his thirty-eighth birthday—key civil rights leaders (Martin Luther King Jr., Whitney Young, John Lewis, Roy Wilkins, James Farmer, and A. Philip Randolph, the first person to propose such a march) met in New York City to galvanize plans. After some haggling about the role Bayard Rustin, a Randolph favorite, would play, group members decided that Randolph would be in charge and would be free to turn over the primary orchestration to Rustin, whose fortitude and savvy became vital elements in making the march a watershed.

Two days later, the *New York Times* reported that Killens, Louis Lomax, and *New York Courier* editor Evelyn Cunningham had accepted invitations to visit Cuba to attend that year's July 26 celebration. Despite an official State Department ban on travel to Cuba, the trio reportedly would leave New York on July 23. But a bureaucratic delay again scuttled the trip for Killens. He did not receive permission from the State Department until after the celebration in Cuba was under way. Given the complicated process of obtaining a visa and securing travel arrangements in accord with the Cuban Assets Control Regulations promulgated by the U.S. Treasury Department,

Killens never really had a shot at the kind of experience Sarah Wright had described vividly three years earlier.

It was on to Washington—after a few other stops. On August 7, Killens participated in a Critics' Forum at Brandeis University. He sat on a panel with Edwin Burr Pettet, chair of the theater arts department, and Bryant Rollins, a staff reporter for the *Boston Globe*, to discuss Eugene O'Neill's *All God's Chillun Got Wings*, billed by forum organizers as a play that "flings out the challenge of prejudice and separation in American life. It opens the door for us to examine the nature of prejudice and discrimination and the barriers that separate man from his fellow man."[7]

The same day, his father wrote him a lengthy letter, typed rather than in his usual shaky handwriting. He thanked his son for sending a Father's Day gift and told him of his pride and devotion. Myles Killens also conveyed that his son should always keep his chin up and do what he felt was right. "There is no chance or destiny or fate," Myles wrote, "that can circumvent or hinder or control the firm resolve of determined souls." After granting that John was gaining a lot of compliments and fans in Chicago and that some people had come to regard him as a born genius, Myles observed, "You may have the instinct or you may be talented, but genius no." After citing Plato, Socrates, Aristotle, Quintilian, and Helvetius as figures who believed in the equality of minds at birth, Myles continued, "I do not believe in genius and declare that it is entirely a matter of education and training, that no knowledge is inherited and all must be acquired. This is the advantage that the children of people of culture, wealth and position possess: their parents knowing the value of culture impart its teaching to them in earliest childhood." Although Myles had lacked wealth and position, he had passed along culture and ideas. And he reminded his son to remember that because social intercourse is the prime condition of human life and is essential to happiness and progress—certainly Aristotelian notions—he should keep in sight that personal success is strongly related to achieving a good reputation among fellow men and women. Careful not to offend his son, however, Myles underplayed the intellectual content of his musings by closing with a Platonist twist: "Again, again and again the content of this letter is really not meant for advice and the substance is really quite so simple that all of it probably you will immediately recognize as having known before. But it doesn't hurt to review."[8]

On August 23, John Killens returned to Chicago with John Henrik Clarke at the request of the Amistad Society. Sterling Stuckey and Beatrice

Carpenter Young, both of whom were associated with the Frank London Brown Society, had established the Amistad Society as an outgrowth of the Emergency Relief Committee for Fayette and Haywood Counties, Tennessee. Beginning in 1960, the committee sent tons of food and clothing to African Americans trying to exercise the franchise. According to Stuckey, the Emergency Relief Committee "helped to create a Sixties atmosphere in Chicago, with its huge population of black migrants from the South." Stuckey and his colleagues thus saw it as fitting to have their organization present Killens and Clarke to an audience eager to hear their opinions. Stuckey already respected Killens's achievements and now embraced his manner: "John's modesty surprised me, for I was unknown. Still, he treated me as an equal, and that never changed." Stuckey also observed, "He carried himself with a degree of natural understatement, and yet was a man of courageous and compassionate convictions." Killens and Clarke joined Hoyt Fuller and Obi Wali, a Nigerian doctoral student at Northwestern University, for a session on "The Black Writer in an Era of Struggle." Political conflict subsequently proved deadly for Wali, a "poet of amazing eloquence," when he was murdered for protesting the Nigerian government's repressive tactics.[9] The night after the Amistad Society event, Gwendolyn Brooks and the Chicago Writers Club threw an autograph party for Killens. After flying back to New York, he attended an "On to Washington" rally at the Polo Grounds.

John and Grace Killens drove to Washington the day before the march and spent the night with John's brother, Charles, in the northeast section of the city. When they headed downtown the next morning, Killens saw that "the nation's capital was an armed encampment, a city under siege," with scores of nervous but ready policeman and National Guardsmen. "A quiet hovered over the city, a silence that was both frightening and deafening. Even the leaves of the trees were stilled as if holding their breaths in anticipation of some horrific holocaust. Perhaps Armageddon was at hand. The streets were empty of people except for the omnipresent federal militia armed to the teeth. It was strange, actually eerie, for the streets to be so empty on a week day."[10]

As Killens and other artists gathered in the lobby of the Willard Hotel awaited transportation to a premarch press conference, the news spread quietly but urgently: "The old man died." W. E. B. Du Bois, the chief emblem of racial uplift over the past sixty years, the man Killens called "Big Grand Daddy," died just as the civil rights movement he helped to inspire reached its symbolic apex.[11] As Killens reflected on the movement's old guard, a quarter of a million people listened to speeches by, among others, labor leader Walter Reuther, NAACP leader Roy Wilkins, and, of course, King. James Baldwin, with whom Killens was making the rounds of the lecture circuit, stood a few feet away. Standing shoulder to shoulder with Killens was Robert Ryan, costar of *Odds against Tomorrow*. On this day for dreamers, Malcolm X patrolled the sidelines, calling the entire spectacle a farce.

If the March on Washington represented in some ways a hard-to-script retrospective on Killens's political career, it also was one of his proudest moments as a parent. Nineteen-year-old Chuck had joined the youth contingent from the Congress of Racial Equality that walked from New York City to Washington. Killens was conversing with actor and director Frank Silvera when he spotted his son marching up to the platform. He recalled slyly wiping tears from his eyes as he pointed Chuck out to Silvera, who also had become misty-eyed. Said Killens, "It was that kind of day."[12]

Less than three weeks later, white supremacists murdered four African American girls—Denise McNair, Cynthia Wesley, Addie Mae Collins, and Carole Robertson—by bombing the Sixteenth Street Baptist Church in Birmingham, Alabama. The same weekend, also in Birmingham, police killed sixteen-year-old Johnnie Robinson, and white civilians killed thirteen-year-old Virgil Ware. At the joint funeral for McNair, Wesley, and Collins, Killens publicly objected to the philosophy of nonviolence. Before King delivered the eulogy, Killens addressed those in attendance and suggested that the Birmingham tragedies signaled the end of nonviolence in the black freedom movement: "Negroes must be prepared to protect themselves with guns." Denise McNair's father, Christopher, disagreed, asking, "What good would Denise have done with a machine gun in her hand?" For his part, King portrayed the girls as "heroines of a holy crusade for freedom and human dignity" and forwarded his argument about the redemptive force of unearned suffering. Killens brushed off McNair's point and conceded King's.[13] The author knew that nonviolence had its practicality and moral suasion but believed that African Americans' consistent willingness to engage in displays of nonviolence encouraged wanton acts of violence by white supremacists and created an atmosphere in which black children could be routinely martyred. In Killens's estimation, the germane issue was not what Denise McNair could have accomplished with a gun but how the willingness to wield guns strategically could have created a safer environment for her.

Back in New York, Killens presided over a September 20 memorial service for the girls, again expressing, in the presence of McNair's parents as well as Malcolm X, serious reservations about nonviolence as a strategy. Baldwin read an obituary and in the process criticized President Kennedy for being less than passionate about the civil rights struggle. Lomax delivered the eulogy. Odetta Gordon, Leon Bibb, and Don Shirley performed. Ruby Dee took an offering, netting $762 for the families of the slain children. Killens presented a statement formulated by himself, Baldwin, Lomax, Dee, and several others that called for the impeachment of Alabama governor George Wallace, the abolition of the phony investigation committee, the immediate apprehension and punishment of the murderers, and a boycott of Christmas shopping because "to celebrate Christmas 'as usual' this year would be a mockery to the memory of Jesus."[14] The money saved on gifts would be contributed to civil rights and religious organizations that furthered the moral and religious fiber of the nation. The audience unanimously adopted the resolutions, which were mostly symbolic. But a boycott of Christmas shopping, a move that King had used in Montgomery to some effectiveness eight years earlier, presented possibilities and drew media attention. The *New York Post* and the *New York Times* condemned the idea, while King, not surprisingly, supported the proposal, as did Adam Clayton Powell Jr. Killens and the others sought to formalize their activities, meeting at Odetta's home and at Baldwin's home to establish an "artistic adjunct" to civil rights organizations, which they first called Artists and Writers for Justice, soon changed to the Association of Artists for Freedom.[15] On September 28, Killens, Lomax, entertainer Dick Gregory, and former Manhattan borough president Hulan Jack led a rally at 125th Street and Seventh Avenue to advertise the boycott, attracting a crowd of about five hundred.

On October 11, Killens delivered a convocation address at West Virginia State College, speaking of the need for African American leaders to clarify their goals. From Killens's viewpoint, the civil rights movement needed to seek a better society, not simply integration for the sake of integration. Later in the fall, he also continued to converse with students whom he knew to be activists. In November, he and SNCC collaborated on another benefit, this one chaired by Julie Belafonte at Small's Paradise and featuring saxophonist King Curtis.

On December 15, Herbert Biberman wrote to Harry Belafonte to pitch a movie based on Harriet Beecher Stowe's *Uncle Tom's Cabin*. He had already broached the idea to Killens, and the two had joined heads to come up with a preliminary script. Biberman believed that none of the few 1963 plays or movies dealing with African Americans had been successful or of high caliber. (He excluded *Lilies of the Field* from consideration because it could have been played by a white actor with no effect on the story or its theme, although there would have been "a loss of charm, and beauty.") According to Biberman, the dearth of quality productions helped to prop up the myth that black subject matter generally could not generate theatrical success. Moreover, Biberman felt, the nation required powerful and truthful stories about the history, essential character, and situation of African Americans: "Every decent American, whatever his color, who works in the communications industries, must, if he is serious, review his role IN HIS MEDIUM, not merely in the broad Civil Rights field, if he wishes to gauge his contribution to America's most urgent need."[16]

During the previous year, Biberman had read a couple of books that focused his attention on *Uncle Tom's Cabin*. Harry Birdoff's *The World's Greatest Hit*, an account of the important productions of the novel from the 1850s to 1933, explained that the shows had so much influence that racists had to write plays and novels subverting and lampooning Stowe's book. Birdoff's work, along with Edmund Wilson's *Patriotic Gore*, showed Biberman that the power that *Uncle Tom's Cabin* held over six generations of American readers and audiences resulted from its emotional and intellectual grasp of American enslavement, "the consciously developed mendacious inversion of human relationships." Adapted to 1964 sensibilities and told from the viewpoint of the enslaved, Biberman believed, the story could again rouse people. He proposed making the film with an all-star cast and producing it independently so that no studio could destroy it. Biberman would direct the film, which he thought could be made for half a million dollars. Belafonte's association with the film would be of immense value, and Biberman offered to share supervision, including script approval, with the star. Biberman wanted the film released before the 1964 presidential elections because even though it would not directly touch on voting rights or other modern concerns of the civil rights movement, "it sets up a moral scale upon which—as a nation and as individuals—we MUST MEASURE OURSELVES. This art can accomplish. It is the totality against which the individual elements can be judged."[17]

Biberman assured Belafonte of his commitment to do battle against discrimination, citing the 1947 House Un-American Activities Committee investigation that had led to his imprisonment. "If I have a single conviction," he announced, "it is that the future in our country is in the hands of its com-municators—TO A DEGREE THEY DO NOT EVEN BEGIN TO APPRECIATE." Biberman predicted that the film would reach the artistic stature of James Baldwin's *The Fire Next Time* but would have more impact because it would reach tens of millions as opposed to tens of thousands. The chance to drive another movie vehicle in service of leftist politics, the possibility of cultivat-ing admiring multitudes, and the prospects of securing a significant pay-day in the process certainly invigorated Biberman. Killens, his collaborator, had stumbled down this path before, to his detriment as a novelist. Still, he could not resist.[18]

CHAPTER FIFTEEN

Statesmanlike Work, 1964

Public signs of a friendship between John Oliver Killens and Malcolm X existed well before the latter's break with the Nation of Islam in the wake of his chickens-coming-home-to-roost commentary following the assassination of President John F. Kennedy. On October 11, 1963, while visiting Berkeley, Malcolm was asked about Martin Luther King Jr.'s nonviolent direct action approach; he replied, "I'll let Jimmy Baldwin and John Killens and Lou Lomax, the writers, answer that," before quoting them.[1] It therefore stood to reason that Killens would become involved in Malcolm's efforts to fashion a better political role. As the chief spokesman for the Nation of Islam, Malcolm championed racial pride and uplift, but such exhortation remained wedded to a political philosophy of separatism and an organizational policy of abstention from black political initiatives by others. In 1964, he sought to create and participate in a broad-based secular entity that would push an agenda of African American political empowerment connected to a conception of the African American struggle as part of worldwide rebellion against oppression. Many observers saw this desire as marking the beginning of Malcolm's final, most revolutionary phase.[2] The operational vehicle would be the Organization of Afro-American Unity (OAAU), modeled on the Organization of African Unity (OAU), founded by African heads of state at Addis Ababa in May 1963. Malcolm was an observer at the founding OAU meeting, but John Henrik Clarke secured a copy of the OAU charter for use among the OAAU planning group.

Although Clarke never claimed much credit for the OAAU charter, both he and Killens played significant roles. They met with Malcolm on several occasions, including at Killens's home, to review ideas and language. Malcolm's new political emphasis represented music to Killens's ears. However, finalizing the charter would have to wait until June because of Malcolm's travel schedule.[3]

While the OAAU charter was being written, the FBI still chased communist connections, beginning a new investigation of Killens on January 27, 1964. In February, agents showed a photograph of Killens to their New York–area informants but failed to draw any hits. On February 26, agent Joseph McAleer made a pretext call to the Killens home to update the bureau's files on his residency and employment. After considering an interview, the agency decided in March against such action. Although the FBI remained interested in Killens because of his dealings with the Fair Play for Cuba Committee, the Socialist Workers Party, and the American Labor Party, he was now considered to be in a strong enough media position to embarrass the bureau.

Later that month, M. S. Handler, who was emerging as the main writer for the *New York Times* on black political developments in the metropolitan area and later wrote a controversial introduction to *The Autobiography of Malcolm X*, published an article featuring Killens. Killens had recently returned to old ideological territory, remarking, "If the United States is to be saved, Negro artists can do this by making white Americans look at themselves."[4] Killens remained interested in addressing all of America; Malcolm might have been his philosophical brother, but the two were not twins. Nonetheless, if a former communist and former Black Muslim could find common ground in the practical politics of black nationalism, then why not?

On March 12, Killens spoke at the New School for Social Research as part of a semester-long series coordinated by faculty member Daniel Anthony, former executive director of the Newark Human Rights Commission. The series on the "American Race Crisis" also featured presentations by Martin Luther King Jr., Robert Weaver, Whitney Young, James Farmer, Bayard Rustin, Roy Wilkins, and others. Killens subsequently agreed to teach a creative writing workshop at the school the following fall. As a zippy and impeccably organized forty-eight-year-old mentor, he would repeat to students lessons he had learned as an apprentice. For example, he was fond of quoting Polonius's advice to Laertes to be true to himself. Another favorite bromide he attributed to Irish writer George William Russell (Æ): "The important

thing about a writer is out of how deep a life does he speak?"[5] He used se-
lections from Hemingway to illustrate economy and conveyed what he had
studied at Columbia and New York University about time, space, narration angles, poetic quality, rhythm, language authenticity, conflict, drama,
irony, and paradox. But he replaced Helen Hull's housing metaphor about
the difference between short stories and novels with his own boxing metaphor, likening the short story to a one-round knockout and the novel to a
fifteen-round decision.

Killens strongly advised students to be clear from the outset about the
premise of their stories because he believed that doing so would help them
focus. He appreciated structure and style, sufficiently polished, but considered content primary. He remarked, "Some great novels have been poorly
written, meaning of course that it is sometimes possible to transcend
clumsy craftsmanship with profundity."[6] For Killens, Theodore Dreiser's
An American Tragedy exemplified a poorly written great novel. But, Killens
warned, elegance would not save writers who had nothing to say. Above
all, Killens emphasized the need for discipline. A writer had to produce
no matter how trying the circumstances and could not trade in excuses.
"So don't waste your time," he advised, "blaming your wife or husband or
your children or the telephone for not understanding your desperate need
for solitude and serenity. There is no such understanding anywhere on this
earth. It's up to you, entirely."[7]

Killens remained quite serious about his teaching, which not only provided him with an important revenue stream but was a natural extension
of his intense involvement in writing workshops such as the Harlem Writers Guild. In fact, before teaching at the New School, he had to address
a dramatic development at the guild. On March 29, the New York Times
ran an article in which Killens touted some of his guild colleagues. He almost immediately received messages from Atheneum, W. W. Norton, Random House, J. B. Lippincott, and George Braziller inquiring about the talent in the workshop. For several years, however, Killens had been steering
writers, including Sarah Wright, to Angus Cameron at Knopf. Although he
found the publisher's marketing department lacking, Cameron's editorial
presence was unassailable. But after Cameron favorably reviewed Wright's
novel manuscript, Knopf declined to publish it, communicating its decision
in what Wright, Killens, and the other guild members considered to be a
shabby manner. On April 12, the guild wrote to Knopf protesting the firm's
actions and suggesting that the guild members might need to reevaluate

their opinion of the publisher. Cameron understood the guild's reaction but was surprised that Killens signed the letter because the two of them had previously discussed Wright's novel and agreed about some of the manuscript's shortcomings.

Killens's relationship with Knopf grew testier. He had submitted seven chapters of "The Minister Primarily" in response to Knopf's right-of-first-refusal option and pressed for a decision. Publishing house staffers differed about whether Killens could handle a comic tour de force. In Cameron's view, "One has to walk that tightrope clear to the end and never get off on either side—that is, never fall off too far towards realism or too far towards farce."[8] In addition, he did not want Knopf's option to depend on a book that was off the typical Killens beat. On April 17, Cameron wrote, "John has given us a hard chance to handle here, I think, and I think he probably realizes it."[9] Cameron also wondered about Killens's work schedule, questioning how the writer could commit to a nonfiction book and give a viable delivery date for any new novel.

Before Killens and Knopf resolved the issue, personal and professional matters intruded. In early April, Killens's father-in-law, Thomas Sylvester Jones, died at the age of seventy-nine. After the funeral, Killens toured Savannah State, Morris, and Stillman Colleges. On April 19, he was back in Macon, where he was presented at Steward Chapel by the Women's Federated Clubs and the Homosophian Club. Pierce Brunson, his close friend and former schoolmate and now an educator, introduced him. Lillie Taylor, his seventh-grade teacher, more than ninety years old, beamed proudly from the audience. While in his hometown, he stayed on Ward Street with his aunt, Louise Coleman Ketch, and her husband, James.

Killens took the train from Macon to Nashville, where he appeared as part of Fisk University's thirty-fifth anniversary Festival of Music and Art. On April 24, he conducted a seminar on "The Creative Writer—His Roots and Inspiration." Arna Bontemps presided over the session, and one of Killens's future students, Nikki Giovanni, listened attentively.

Shortly after Killens returned to New York, he informed Cameron that he was leaving Knopf, a decision that left Cameron with a "strong sense of defeat." He thought Knopf could treat Killens as well as any publisher could. More important, Cameron had always been proud to be associated with *And Then We Heard the Thunder* and did not want to lose the creative relationship with the author. With respect to a reception Killens was trying to organize for Malcolm X, Cameron remarked presciently, "What a politician he is. I notice he went all the way to Mecca in order to find a rationale for not hating whites. That will serve him in the political operation he means to pursue in the future. A very shrewd man."[10]

On May 28, Cameron notified Killens that Knopf was releasing him from the option clause in his contract and wished him success in finding a publisher for "The Minister Primarily." The two men remained friends, and Killens continued to steer writers, including Cyprian Ekwensi, to Cameron.

On June 7, Killens reached his largest audience to date when the *New York Times Sunday Magazine* published his essay, "Explanation of the 'Black Psyche.'" The piece—one of the most controversial to appear in the magazine that year—functioned in essence as an elaboration on his and Arnaud d'Usseau's dispute with Haskell Wexler about a black perspective. Killens insisted that America had both a black psyche and a white one. He did not root his premise in biology but posited instead that the two outlooks had diverged for social, cultural, historical, and psychological reasons. Killens held a black psyche to be valid state of being, not something to be eradicated in a push for integration: "When we mean freedom, we mean freedom for us to be black, or brown, and you to be white and yet live together in a free and equal society." He extended an invitation to join him in working for radical pluralism: "Let those who truly love America join the valiant Negro revolt and change and save our country."[11]

Responses poured in from across the nation and from as far away as Ethiopia and Australia. The racist backlash was predictable. One reader recommended, "Why don't you stop kidding at least yourself? Negroes constitute a minority sub-culture. 10%. Most are garbage. Those of obvious virtue, goodness, worth and sincerity (that eliminates you) can not be ignored by whites."[12] A second objected, "I know of no contribution by the black man to our society in any field. If you spent half your time telling the black man what to work for instead of telling the white man what he has to give you we will all be better off."[13]

Letters also arrived from more thoughtful citizens, including some rather sharp youth. Claudia Viek of Bryn Mawr, Pennsylvania, wrote, "I am only fourteen and have not seen much of life, but I have my convictions and an open mind which yearns to learn about life and different people who make up this life, and your article has held a lot for me."[14] Edward Gottlieb, the principal at Manhattan's P.S. 165 observed, "The Negro, fired and tested, hammered and tempered, will hum with more power, drive with sharper insight, and soar with more spirit in the century to come. You prove it."[15] David Kimmelman, who saw his primary political job to be winning white allies, commented that Killens's piece was "hard-hitting, incisive, and clearly on target. This is indeed a Freedom Century."[16]

From fellow artists and friends, Killens received numerous plaudits. Elton Fax had said many of the same things as Killens during a recent State Department–sponsored tour of Africa. The black secondary and university students with whom Fax visited had no problem understanding that the denial of dignity for one challenges the dignity of all. But Fax believed that many white Americans in the audiences "were listening to a Negro speak with honesty for the first time in their experience; and their perplexity was matched only by the irony of a situation requiring of them a recognition of human values abroad with which they had never become acquainted at home." Fax concluded, "John Killens writes for them. Even more important he writes for the millions who will never work overseas but whose work in the muddled area of human relations right here at home is more than cut out for them."[17]

Len Holt, a civil rights attorney from Richmond, Virginia, wrote to Killens, "It had to be said. It has to be said. You said it—in the *New York Times Magazine*."[18] Hoyt Fuller wrote from Chicago that he thought the essay "a beautifully done piece."[19] Alice Childress added, "I completely agree with it and feel that this kind of mature and honest approach to our problems will prove the most rewarding in the long run, but rewarding or not, this is the truth."[20] Mildred Jordan acclaimed, "Henceforth my favorite essay!"[21] On June 11, Cameron brought the essay to work with him on the train. He wrote from his office, "I think this piece can be considered a kind of watershed for determining just where a white liberal stands in relation to the problem. I thought it was a very statesmanlike piece which managed that status without sacrificing anything of its razor-sharp edge. I congratulate you."[22]

On June 13, Killens, at the invitation of Juanita Poitier and Ruby Dee and accompanied by Malcolm X, visited the Poitiers' home for a summit meeting. Clarence Jones was on hand, along with A. Philip Randolph, Dorothy Height, Whitney Young, and Ossie Davis. Away from podiums and microphones, the group had a spirited but civil discussion about political possibilities and directions.[23]

Two days later, sparks flew more readily when the Association of Artists for Freedom sponsored a panel at Town Hall on "The Black Revolution and the White Backlash." The idea was conceived at a May meeting attended by Killens, Baldwin, Dee, Davis, Lomax, Odetta, and Clarence Jones—all of whom were founding members of the group—plus later arrivals Lonne Elder III and Wilbert Tatum. Grace Killens had also become active in the organization and worked with Jones, Mel Williamson, and Tatum, who was responsible for the overall logistics, to make the event happen smoothly.

The organizers had hoped to initiate a new dialogue between blacks and the white liberals about whom Angus Cameron wondered. Killens, Paule Marshall, Lorraine Hansberry, Ossie Davis, Ruby Dee, LeRoi Jones (Amiri Baraka), *Fortune* editor Charles Silberman, and *New York Post* editor James Wechsler were featured in a session moderated by David Susskind. Killens pressed the question of what white liberals would contribute to the black freedom movement, wondering how many whites, riddled with fears about so-called black extremism, would embrace liberal gradualism more firmly: "How many will be like Gideon's army? You know, Gideon was testing his army out, I believe. He asked for all—he put them through quite a few tests and when he got ready to fight, he only had about three hundred." More specifically, addressing a key debate, Killens demanded to know, "How many cold war liberals will desert our ranks when we assert the right of self-defense?" Addressing the idea of setting the plight of African Americans before the bar of world opinion, he argued vigorously against the "big happy family" approach: "We're not even one big unhappy family." In his view, the family approach discouraged activists from "embarrassing big daddy before the world." On a more affirming note, however, he added, "American black folk will with white assistance great or small change America if it can be changed and that's what it's all about."[24]

Silberman understood that black leadership was imperative and claimed that white liberals, especially those accustomed to being in charge of black affairs, needed to adjust. Of the whites on the panel, his politics, as indicated by *Crisis in Black and White*, which had been published that same year and to which Malcolm X had contributed a blurb, were the closest to those of Killens. However, Silberman was not completely comfortable with black rage or did not even hear it clearly. He described *And Then We Heard the Thunder* as a "weak novel but a powerful sociological tract"; the basis for its weakness, in Silberman's view, was that any white was the enemy by the end of the book. Silberman later reversed field somewhat by granting that Solly Saunders ultimately transcended racial hatred but argued that Killens hated and was suspicious of every white man. To Silberman, "Sometimes it seems as though Baldwin, Killens, *et al would* rather be angry."[25] However, one person's anger is another's passion and commitment. Killens did not conduct his private life in a rancorous manner. All who knew him even casually could speak to his pleasant and generous disposition. Silberman seemed to assume that Killens's professional and economic achievements should have militated against a sharp racial consciousness, a naive presupposition given that class mobility often exposes individuals to a wider range of prejudices, obstacles, and disappointments. Killens certainly experienced his bitter moments as he lost political and artistic battles, and he did not shy away from airing his grievances in public.

Wechsler, in some ways the voice of New York liberalism, resorted to a majoritarian and conformist argument. He cited a poll indicating that Lyndon B. Johnson was the most popular American among white Americans and black Americans alike and asserted that some readers of the *New York Post* considered criticism of Adam Clayton Powell Jr., a strain of discourse on the panel, "tantamount to a form of treason."[26] Wechsler pushed Gandhian tactics and explicitly supported King's brand of nonviolent direct action.

Hansberry, who seemed to set the left edge at these events, traced her family's embrace of gradualism in fighting racist housing covenants in Chicago; however, she pointed out, the city remained as segregated in 1964 as it had been decades earlier. Insofar as dialogue with white liberals was concerned, Hansberry felt, "The problem is we have to find some way with these dialogues to show and to encourage the white liberal to stop being a liberal and become an American radical."[27]

Susskind was no neutral moderator.[28] Jim Aronson of the *National Guardian*, which would publish selected proceedings, found Susskind obnoxious: "I was within spitting distance of David Susskind, but I refrained. I had a proper upbringing in Boston."[29]

Meanwhile, work on the OAAU's basic aims continued, with Killens and Clarke working on programmatic goals, Killens finalizing the wording, and daughter Barbara delivering copies from the Killens home to Malcolm's office in Harlem. On June 28, less than two weeks later, Malcolm X, with Killens on hand, presented the "Statement of Basic Aims and Objectives of the Organization of Afro-American Unity" at the Audubon Ballroom. The OAAU defined its members as "all people of African descent in the Western Hemisphere, as well as our brothers and sisters on the African Continent," and resolved to "reinforce the common bond of purpose between our people by submerging all of our differences and establishing a non-religious and non-sectarian constructive program for human rights." The charter stressed the right of self-defense, the need to counteract racist education by assuming control of schools in New York and other cities, the necessity for a massive voter registration drive to make every black person an independent voter with the goal of forming political clubs, running independent black candidates, and supporting blacks already in office who were responsive to the black community. Additional proposals included rent strikes, challenges to economic exploitation, a war against organized crime, initiatives to counter police brutality, rehabilitation clinics, orphanages, homes for senior citizens, a guardian system to set positive models for youth, and a "cultural revolution to unbrainwash an entire people," which would entail facilities and workshops in film, creative writing, theater, music, and history. "Basic Aims and Objectives" is infused not only with much of Malcolm's characteristic language about freedom, justice, and equality but also with Killens's omnipresent concern for black nobility. To make sure that no one who read the document would miss the Killens influence, the document concludes, "When the battle is won, let history be able to say to each one of us: 'He was a dedicated patriot: Dignity was his country, Manhood was his government, and Freedom was his land.'" The quotation was taken from *And Then We Heard the Thunder*.[30]

If Killens needed any more examples to clinch his point that white liberals and the civil rights establishment were out of step with the northern black masses, he could point a few weeks later to the Harlem Riot and similar outbreaks in Brooklyn precipitated by the shooting of African American teenager James Powell by New York City off-duty patrolman Thomas Gilligan. Powell had been traveling from his Harlem home to attend summer school on the Upper East Side when he and a group of schoolmates argued with a white man, who then sprayed them with a water hose. This set the scene for Gilligan's deadly intervention. Some Harlem residents subsequently pelted police officers with rocks and bottles. At one point, Rustin implored the crowd to stop, but the rioters ridiculed him, calling him an Uncle Tom and shouting that they wanted Malcolm X.

The Association of Artists for Freedom wrote a letter to the "Big Six" African American leaders—Farmer, King, John Lewis, Randolph, Wilkins, and Young. The members said that they deplored the rioting and looting but believed that such actions inevitably resulted from poor schooling, high unemployment, substandard housing, and police brutality. The letter continued, "We are resentful that our leaders are required to apologize for Harlem to the very people who make Harlem not only possible but profitable. No one has ever asked President Johnson to apologize for Mississippi." As a practical matter, they urged the civil rights leaders to push for the immediate suspension of Gilligan and more deployment of black officers in black neighborhoods.[31]

The FBI caught on to the connection between Killens and Malcolm X, observing that on August 9, in Malcolm's absence, the author spoke at the Audubon Ballroom on behalf of the OAAU. The turnout and response were lukewarm. Killens lacked the splendid rhetorical gifts and tools needed to enlist Harlem followers. If anyone was truly going to jump-start the OAAU, it had to be Malcolm.

In August 1964, Killens was in the process of teaming with Loften Mitchell to write *Ballad of the Winter Soldiers: A Musical Tribute to Freedom*, to be staged at Lincoln Center's Philharmonic Hall on September 28. Langston Hughes had introduced Mitchell to Killens years earlier at Michaux's bookstore. The two immediately began a long conversation that they continued down at Romare Bearden's studio. Killens became a devoted supporter and sometimes editor of Mitchell's work. At a reading of *A Land beyond the River*, Killens offered the author the line, "I'm responsible to my God and my congregation—and neither of them is white." Mitchell accepted. However, Mitchell's wife accused him of plagiarism because she later came across the line in *Youngblood*. Mitchell examined the text and called Killens to ask if he had heard the line. The novelist replied, "Man, that is in Act One of your play. That's when Graham Brown is telling off that white school superintendent and—" Mitchell interrupted and directed Killens to look at the relevant section in *Youngblood*. When the conversation resumed, Killens charged, "Why, you dirty thief!" Both writers roared with laughter.[32]

At any rate, when Dorothy Pitman and the Congress of Racial Equality (CORE) asked Killens to script the tribute to freedom, he sought Mitchell's assistance. The work went smoothly—once the two men managed to get on task. Mitchell held a script conference at his home during which the two writers barbecued and drank several rounds of scotch. When Killens called Grace, she immediately caught on to the fact that he was tipsy and furiously demanded to speak with Mitchell, who was in the same shape. Grace deduced that without the supervision of Mitchell's wife, who was not home at the time, things had escalated out of control. She decided that subsequent conferences would take place at her house and that the writers would be allowed one drink with the meal they were served. Additional drinks would be available only after the work session had been concluded. However, before Grace's plan was put into action, the two writers met at Mitchell's Harlem studio for another script conference. After working, they agreed to have one drink, a martini, at Frank's Restaurant on 125th Street. James Hicks, who had known Killens at Howard University and was the executive editor of the *Amsterdam News*, entered and began to order more rounds. Hicks had an ulterior motive: he wanted Killens and Mitchell to write his column while he was on vacation. Hicks told them the following week that they had agreed to do so. They wrote the columns as well as the script because Grace eventually took charge.

While sober, the writers drew on the words of Thomas Paine: "These are the times that try men's souls. The summer soldier and the sunshine patriot will, in this crisis, shrink from the service of their country. But he who stands it now, deserves the love and thanks of man and woman."[33] Presented by Pitman and directed by James E. Wall, the CORE benefit featured Diahann Carroll, Ruby Dee, Dick Gregory, Frederick O'Neal, Sidney Poitier, Robert Ryan, and Frank Silvera in performances ranging from a skit about Jewish resistance in Warsaw to a recitation of Margaret Walker's "For My People," which was Killens's favorite poem. By that time, CORE had become more militant and more to Killens's liking than the National Association for the Advancement of Colored People. The show was dedicated to the memory of CORE workers Michael Schwerner, James Chaney, and Andrew Goodman, who were murdered in Mississippi during the preceding summer.

Spurred by the reception his *New York Times* essay received, Killens spent much of the rest of the year crafting the other five essays to be published with "Explanation of the Black Psyche" (retitled "The Black Psyche") in *Black Man's Burden*. Grace informed inquirers that her husband presently could not accept any more speaking engagements because he was concentrating on his writing. Killens, always tempted by the movies, even backed off of a movie query from David Shepherd.[34] He did respond to a request by Eugene Gervasi, publicity manager at Knopf, for comments about Howard Zinn's *The Southern Mystique*, which was scheduled for publication on October 19. He also heard from Ellen Bandler at Knopf, who informed him that one thousand new copies of *And Then We Heard the Thunder* had been printed and bound. She added, "We miss seeing you here."[35] He wrote an essay on Hollywood for the *Nation* and attended to his class at the New School.[36] But as much as possible he kept his mind on the December 31 deadline.

Killens originally conceived *Black Man's Burden* as a scholarly tome and by the beginning of 1964 had identified more than fifty books—thirty of which he had read—that would help him with the project. Now he opted for the voice of the personal essay, mindful of Baldwin's best-selling success with *The Fire Next Time*, published at the same time as *And Then We Heard the Thunder*. In addition, scholarly writing was not his forte, and his more ambitious design at the very least would have taken the project long past the deadline.

In "The Black Writer vis-à-vis His Country," he repeated the call issued in the OAAU charter for African American artists to "assume an uneven load" because of their insights into America. Terming America the "land of the nigger-makers," where distorted images harmful to African American children circulated widely, he urged writers to produce a literature of heroes, legends, and myths. Killens took a special shot at the white avant-garde, which he considered "neither revolutionary, anti-bourgeois, as it sometimes makes pretensions of being, nor anti–white supremacy." He sought better from "white brothers" and was not promoting black exclusiveness or dominance: "I hope that colored men have watched Western men too long to commit the fatal folly of writing history with a 'colored' pencil."[37]

Killens returned to other favorite themes: the southern character, as he had explained to Maya Angelou, of the entire United States, the psychological castration of African American men, and the struggle for dignity. In "Downsouth-Upsouth," he explored how working-class whites clung more firmly to their whiteness than to Christianity or progressive traditions, a prime case in point being the failure of the CIO's Operation Dixie, during which white workers consistently opted for no union over an integrated one. Papering over what he felt were superficial differences between southern blacks and northern blacks, he suggested, "One thing the Negro Revolt has taught the Negro, North and South, is the universality of his degradation, that so long as human dignity is denied him in one section of this country, he will never achieve it fully in the other." The only solution was to "un-South the entire nation" and ultimately "build a society that will make sense for all the people, black and white." Killens translated this idea into an

anticapitalist agenda: "We, as a people, at this moment in the twentieth century, must determine once and for all which shall have primacy in our land,
the sanctity of private property or the dignity of man."[38]

Economic arguments also lay at the heart of "The Black Mystique; or,
Would You Want One of Them to Marry Your Daughter?" and "Black Man's
Burden." In the former, Killens dispensed with the expressed fear of miscegenation as nothing more than a smokescreen to divert attention from the
workings of a white, patriarchal, capitalist power structure. He compared
women's fight for equality and the plight of the poor in general to the black
freedom struggle. In the latter essay, the author proffered a multiethnic
vision of liberation in a nation that needed to emphasize free people over
free enterprise, humanity over profit. He queried, "If socialism is a dirty
word for so many of my countrymen, why call it socialism? If it conjures up
Russian bogeymen, forget it. Call it 'Africanism,' or 'true democracy,' if the
words taste better in your mouth.'"[39]

"The Myth of Non-Violence versus the Right of Self-Defense" directly
addressed the question of nonviolence. Killens acknowledged that nonviolent direct action possessed considerable value as a tactic in that it had rallied people and placed the African American struggle before the world—
most notably in the case of the Montgomery Bus Boycott. He also granted
that a certain power of moral suasion was ancillary to nonviolent protest.
But he felt that no one should ever waive the right of self-defense. In his
view, when nonviolence was championed as a way of life, it invalidated
other worthwhile strategies.

Although numerous scholars have dubbed Killens a nationalist during
this period, such a claim about his ideological stance at the midpoint of the
1960s is at once true and inconsequential. Nearly every African American
not suffering from racialized self-hatred is a nationalist of some sort because nationalism is more properly seen as a cluster of ideologies or a con-
tinuum ranging from Garvey-like separatism to surface-level cultural celebrations. By Killens's admission, he was more nationalist in effect by the
mid-1960s, but it is more important to ascertain what kind of nationalist
he was.[40] How much of his previous leanings had he retained; how much
had his prior leftist perspective shrunk? One answer is to examine the ways
he still differed from Malcolm X. Although several passages appear in both
the OAAU charter and Killens's essays, the latter versions all project a wider
political embrace. For example, section 6 of the OAAU document reads,
"We must launch a cultural revolution to unbrainwash an entire people. . . .

Culture is an indispensable weapon in the freedom struggle."[41] In "The Black Writer vis-à-vis His Country," Killens wrote, "A cultural revolution is desperately needed, here and now, to un-brainwash the entire American people, black and white."[42] In the OAAU passage, "entire people" refers specifically to African Americans, whereas Killens addressed his essays to a large multiethnic audience that he believed included whites. Killens's activism was often multipronged, and as he composed *Black Man's Burden*, he still thought enough of old colleagues, as the FBI recorded, to attend a November 19 fund-raising party for *American Dialog*, the successor to *Mainstream*.[43] And five days later, he attended the anniversary dinner for the *National Guardian*. In keeping with his mission since he had turned away from a law career two decades earlier, Killens remained a writer for freedom.

CHAPTER SIXTEEN

In Residence, 1965–1966

At the request of Fisk University president Stephen J. Wright, Arna Bontemps contacted John Oliver Killens to gauge his interest in spending a semester on campus as author in residence. Bontemps had known Killens for several years, and the two men "had a long session over literary matters" in the spring of 1962.[1] Bontemps suggested compensation would be in the neighborhood of $8,000, a princely sum to Killens, who scrambled to make a living. He had signed a contract to teach a second semester at the New School for $1,000, but an offer from Nashville at those higher numbers proved irresistible. When Killens wrote to Bontemps expressing interest in the position, Wright flew to New York to negotiate. The figure Bontemps quoted was inflated, but the $5,500 on which Wright and Killens agreed still represented a hefty salary boost. Killens's contract became effective February 1, 1965, though it was understood that he could not arrive in Nashville until the second week of classes. The arrangement seemed ideal: a chance at the highest steady income he had known, a light teaching load representing not much more work than he did with the Harlem Writers Guild during most weeks, a couple of hours per week of individual conferences, and plenty of time to work on his own writing with fewer distractions than in New York. Killens considered a full family relocation to Nashville, but, except for several visits, Grace remained in Brooklyn. Barbara, however, enrolled as a student at Fisk.

Before the promise of Nashville could unfold, several matters, some sad and shocking, remained to be faced in New York. Lorraine Hansberry died on January 12 at the age of thirty-four. Killens, listed as an honorary pallbearer, joined the throng of more than six hundred people who braved a blizzard to attend the January 15 funeral at the Church of the Masters. The day also marked the thirty-sixth birthday of Martin Luther King Jr., who sent a telegram in which he paraphrased *Romeo and Juliet*: "If she should die, take her and cut her into little stars and she will make the face of heaven so fine that all the world will be in love with night." He correctly predicted that Hansberry's "profound grasp of the deep social issues confronting the world today will remain an inspiration to generations unborn." Paul Robeson, who had returned to the United States accompanied by little fanfare and had maintained a relatively low profile, emerged to deliver a stirring eulogy. "As Lorraine says farewell," he told attendees, "she bids us keep our heads high and to hold on to our strength and power." Robeson was the subject of Hansberry's first script, a tribute written as a part of a 1954 fundraising effort. Malcolm X, who shared Hansberry's May 19 birthday, also attended, paying his respects to an artist with whom he had sparred over her interracial marriage but whom he respected profoundly. Malcolm spoke with Killens, Ossie Davis, and Paul Robeson Jr. about meeting the elder Robeson sometime soon.[2]

While still at the New School, Killens set in motion plans for a writers' conference to be held in the spring of 1965. That conference would now be a tribute to Hansberry. Killens no doubt thought of Hansberry when a Ford Foundation grant enabled his play, *Lower Than the Angels*, to finally get a reading at the American Place Theater on January 30. Loften Mitchell attended and later expressed dismay that dramatic works such as *Lower Than the Angels*, William Branch's *A Wreath for Udomo*, and Alice Childress's *Wedding Band* were being read on stage rather than produced. Allowing himself to dream, Mitchell envisioned the arrival of a young businessman turned producer who optioned scripts, founded a theater, and generated enthusiastic and concrete support in the African American community. Mitchell's fantasy continued: "*A Wreath for Udomo* is playing there, and so is *Wedding Band*, and *Lower Than the Angels*, and a recognized writer or a new writer has a place where his work is seen, not read."[3] At least Hansberry's work was still being produced. On February 2, Killens traveled by limousine with Robert Nemiroff to the Mineola Playhouse, billed as "Long

Island's only Broadway theatre," for the opening of *The Sign in Sidney Bru-stein's Window.*

As soon as Killens arrived at Fisk University, Dean George Redd urged him to address the student body at convocation. The author begged off, feeling a need to first get his "moorings and bearings."[4] Doing so proved difficult. He received another blow when Nat King Cole, a friend and Killens supporter since the publication of *Youngblood*, died at age forty-five on February 15. Killens felt a deep sense of loss for the second time in the space of a month.

The news did not improve. Less than a week later, on February 21, Barbara Killens phoned her father to tell him that Malcolm X had been shot. John Killens reassured her that the wound probably was not serious before frantically dialing New York in search of Grace, reaching her at her mother's home. Grace had already heard the initial reports and thought that Malcolm would survive, but while the Killenses spoke, the television flashed the news that he had not. John fell into a "deep depression," going around in a "daze for days." To add to his misery, he was separated from Grace and had to witness Barbara's distress as she experienced crying jags for more than a month.[5]

Malcolm's death particularly devastated Killens because in addition to their ties of friendship, he had the most potential—the best combination of charisma, intellect, curiosity, and integrity—to galvanize mass African American struggle. Malcolm was not "our own black shining Prince," as Ossie Davis famously dubbed him, simply because he represented black manhood.[6] He symbolized the possibility of a potent coalition that could achieve new levels in the black strivings for human rights. As Grace wrote to her husband on March 9, "The tragic situation that the bulk of the Negro people (especially in the North) find themselves in is that we have no mass organization through which we can function and be mobilized. This is what Malcolm was on his way to developing." She challenged John and members of the Association of Artists for Freedom to enlarge their voices and to avoid settling for being a fund-raising group for other civil rights organizations. She thought that they should pursue the purchase of radio and television time and try to become the "Voice of the People."[7]

In addition, Chuck, no longer enrolled in school, had received a notice to report for an army physical, an alarming prospect given the escalating events in Vietnam. Grace hoped that the possibility of being sent to war would motivate her twenty-one-year-old son to return to college.[8]

As mid-March approached, Killens, trying to steady himself emotionally, changed his mind and agreed to deliver the convocation address. "One doesn't feel much like stepping outdoors," he confided in a letter to Harry Belafonte. However, Killens's financial outlook was improving, and he had a new relationship with Trident Press, which would reissue *Youngblood* and publish his next three books: "I have finally found a big publisher who believes in me and what I have to say, and is willing to put his money (in terms of quarterly advances) where his mouth is." He sent Belafonte a check for one thousand dollars to pay one-third of a personal debt. He apologized for not being able to pay sooner and urged the entertainer, "Write or call sometime, you no-writing/no-communicating—."[9]

Standing at a podium in the chapel at Fisk, Killens first sought to establish a rapport with the students. He asked them to stand for a moment of silence in honor of Hansberry and Cole as well as musician Sam Cooke, who had been killed in Los Angeles three months earlier. As the audience of faculty and students began to rise, Killens added Malcolm X to the list, catching some white professors off guard. Several remained suspended "in the attitude of a baseball catcher, half standing and half squatting." Though they eventually rose, Killens sensed that he had fired the first salvo in a battle with liberal and conservative professors both black and white, much as his mentor, E. Franklin Frazier, had done at Fisk years earlier. Killens then tried to inspire the audience with the words of Frederick Douglass and Kelly Miller that had meant so much to him when he was younger. He offered a variation of his plea for a cultural revolution and suggested that writers should stand at the vanguard of efforts aimed against African American self-hatred and low self-esteem. Presaging a debate that would last decades, Killens urged all students to clean up their language and stop referring to themselves and each other as "niggers."[10]

Later that afternoon, a liberal white professor asked Killens to explain the connections among Hansberry, Cole, Cooke, and Malcolm. Killens responded that three had been his friends and all had been artists. The explanation did not sit well with the professor or with several of his colleagues in a group informally known as the Big Eight. But Killens had plans to bring allies to campus—Belafonte, Sidney Poitier, Ossie Davis, George Lamming, Stokely Carmichael, Miriam Makeba, and James Forman. In retrospect, he ruminated about the cultural battle, "I believe we won that one."[11] In doing so, Killens helped to foster a more militant student mood.

Fisk had long been a spawning ground for the civil rights movement. John Lewis, Bernard Lafayette, Diane Nash, James Bevel, and Marion Barry had been students at Fisk before assuming leadership positions in the Student Nonviolent Coordinating Committee (SNCC), the most important student activist group of the 1960s. James Lawson, another important SNCC leader, attended nearby Vanderbilt University. Indeed, the Nashville contingent loomed as one of the largest delegations at SNCC's April 1960 founding conference in Raleigh, North Carolina. Yet as SNCC was morphing from a focus on desegregation to participating in the New Left—becoming, in other words, "an amorphous body of young activists seeking new ideological alternatives to conventional liberalism"—the organization's influence declined on middle-class-oriented southern black campuses that had been crucial to its success.[12] In 1965, little of SNCC's militancy remained evident on the Fisk campus. Thus, according to Nikki Giovanni, Killens became instrumental in awakening or reawakening student consciousness.[13] During one class, when Killens began to speak of Paul Robeson, a student asked, "Who is he? One of them Uncle Tom niggers?" Killens told the student to visit the library to read up on Robeson, and he returned several days later and announced, "Brother John, that cat was a bad and militant dude long before it was popular!"[14] As expressed by Mignon Holland Anderson, a Fisk student who later earned a master's in fine arts from Columbia University and published the fiction books *Mostly Womenfolk and a Man or Two* and *The End of Dying*, the workshop's ethos was "steel forged in the furnaces of white hatred and the devoted love of our own folk who nurtured us, and, as such, we would continue to develop our voices, working with heartfelt study of craft while believing in the beauty and the strength of black America." Moreover, Killens was the "consummate teacher" who "wanted us to figure out who we were rather than being told who we were."[15]

On March 25, the modern civil rights movement reached its climax with the conclusion of the procession from Selma to Montgomery. The twelve thousand marchers, led by Martin Luther King Jr., who worried greatly that he would be assassinated in Selma, literally and figuratively completed an activist loop that had begun in Montgomery more than nine years earlier. After the boycotts, sit-ins, and freedom rides, the dramatic surge at the March on Washington, and the passage of the Civil Rights Act of 1964, all that remained of the main story line was the denouement of the Voting Rights Act of 1965 and several concluding years of largely ineffectual organizing up until King's assassination. Killens also closed the circle in a sense. As he had done in 1955, he traveled to Montgomery. This time he was part of a cast invited to perform at the celebration. The bill also included Harry Belafonte, Ruby Dee, Mahalia Jackson, Tony Bennett, Billy Eckstine, Pete Seeger, Bobby Darin, Joan Baez, Shelley Winters, James Baldwin, and Leonard Bernstein. Killens ran across novelist William Attaway, and the two discussed writing and Killens's new position at Fisk. The festive mood was quashed when white supremacists murdered activist Viola Liuzzo, the mother of five small children. Once again, although Killens applauded the success of certain nonviolent tactics, Liuzzo's death confirmed for him his hypothesis that white supremacist assassins become emboldened when they never have to consider reprisal.

In the April 1965 issue of *Negro Digest*, thirty-two writers contributed to a print symposium, "The Task of the Negro Writer as Artist." Reminiscent of the 1950 *Phylon* conversation and the 1959 American Society of African Culture conference, the presentation aimed to help readers and up-and-coming writers understand a long-running controversy. Each writer was asked, What is the task of the Negro writer concerned with creating a work of art in a segregated society, and how does his task differ from that of the white writer—if it differs at all? Although the question reprised the old debate about art for art's sake versus art as politics, which W. E. B. Du Bois, Richard Wright, and Lloyd Brown had already addressed memorably, the writers' responses did not divide neatly into camps. Frank Yerby and Gwendolyn Brooks came closest to articulating a "pure art" position. Yerby suggested, "I don't think that the color of the skin of a man engaged in the lonely task of creation matters at all . . . except to make it much more difficult for him to achieve the absolute, ironclad objectivity without which art lapses into propaganda." He deemed indisputable the justice of the African American writer's cause but felt that the black writer needed to pose to himself or herself such questions as, "Is the novel, short story, poem actually a means by which to obtain social justice? Or do I not risk having my fine *chef d'oeuvre* wind up as dead as the cause it is defending, when, through its inevitable solution by currents of change too strong to be denied, that cause becomes ancient history, as it will?" Brooks issued the shortest statement, reporting simply, "The task of the Negro writer in any sort of society is the task of every writer: to clarify his interior and to deliver, thoroughly and only, the 'messages' urged by that clarity." For his part, Killens offered what had become standard fare for him at that point: "The black writer's vision for society is basically anti–*status quo*. He is out to change the *status quo*, to create a new vision for mankind, because the *status quo* has ever been the bane of his and his people's existence."[16]

Also in April, Killens returned to New York for two cultural events. On April 22, he and Grace joined a crowd of two thousand people gathered to celebrate Paul Robeson, who had turned sixty-seven on April 9. Roscoe Lee Browne, Howard da Silva, Michael Babatunde Olatunji, Billy Taylor, Diana Sands, and Morris Carnovsky were among the entertainers who performed. In his remarks to the cheering throng, Robeson spoke of the universality of art, though clearly not in the sense of art for art's sake: he tied his comments to political activism, much as he had influenced Killens, who spoke briefly at the event, to do.

A few days later, Killens presided over the writers' conference at the New School. An annual writers' conference had been one of his announced goals since the 1959 conference. He still hoped to set such a series in motion, though he now imagined Fisk University as the location. Panelists at the event, "The Negro Writer's Vision of America," included Ossie Davis, John Henrik Clarke, Sarah Wright, Loften Mitchell, LeRoi Jones (Amiri Baraka), Walter Lowenfels, and James Baldwin. Killens tried to book Martin Luther King Jr. and Ralph Ellison. Neither effort panned out, but the absence of Ellison, who had an adversarial relationship with Killens dating back to his 1952 review of *Invisible Man*, was more telling. Moreover, critical remarks made at the conference, primarily by Clarke and white historian Herbert Aptheker, practically ensured that Ellison would never attend a gathering over which Killens presided. In response to positive comments about Ellison made by Herbert Hill, the labor secretary of the National Association for the Advancement of Colored People, Clarke argued that Ellison shunned other black writers and that Hill exaggerated the author's importance. Clarke acknowledged the craftsmanship of *Invisible Man* but wondered, "Whether Ralph Ellison will follow up, whether Ralph Ellison has grown up is open to question in many quarters starting with me." Aptheker added, "In terms of what [Ellison] has published and also his published assertions, he has made himself rather not particularly visible in the struggles of the Negro people."[17]

Baldwin received the most attention, both positive and negative. He held the audience in suspense with his keynote address, offering another revi-

sionist take on American history and insisting that artists had a moral ob-
ligation to fight for social justice. Nonetheless, by the close of the conference, Baldwin had been labeled an "extremely talented literary prostitute"
by panelist Myrna Baines, who was reportedly on the staff of *National Review*, a conservative publication edited by William F. Buckley.[18]

The New School conference was also memorable for the strand of feminist thinking articulated by Sarah Wright, Alice Childress, and Paule Marshall, ideas that many others would express over the coming decades.
Wright argued that in the quest for "manhood," American male writers, including African Americans, produced "so much slop concerning women in
the popular literature and advertisements of our day." Women had been so
sexually objectified, Wright reasoned, that they had been reduced "according to one of the most commercially successful films of recent times, into
being, and I quote, 'Pussy Galore' [from the James Bond film *Goldfinger*]."
Wright further asserted, "A virtual wilderness of the mind exists with respect to what it is to be a woman, a mother, a responsible-minded citizen, a
creator of significant and humanly meaningful work, a thoughtful person."
Marshall added that black women in American literature had been "strung
up on two poles and left hanging." They could be either a "nigger wench" or
"Negro matriarch." According to Childress, black women historically had
been largely overlooked for serious treatment in popular media "except for
the constant, but empty and decharacterized faithful servant" who had been
joined in more contemporary times by a woman "too militant, so domineering, so aggressive, with son, husband and brother, that [she] is one of
the chief reasons for any unexpressed manhood on the part of the Negro
man in America." Childress granted that some truth existed in the stereotype of the strong black woman, citing Baldwin's *Amen Corner*, Hansberry's
A Raisin in the Sun, and Childress's own *Florence* and *Trouble in Mind* as
legitimate explorations of the idea. Yet she also insisted that strong black
women were forged in the crucible of struggle against oppression and that
their presence certainly did not and could not undermine black manhood.
Childress concluded, "The Negro woman will attain her rightful place in
American literature when those of us who care about truth, justice and a
better life tell her story, with the full knowledge and appreciation of her
constant, unrelenting struggle against racism and for human rights."[19] To a
great degree, the discourse made public at the conference echoed conversations that had transpired within the Harlem Writers Guild. For example,
while Wright, Marshall, and Childress celebrated Killens's fiction, Wright

had raised questions in the workshop about the barracks talk in *And Then We Heard the Thunder*.

After the three-day conference ended on April 25, Killens traveled to Virginia to speak at Hampton Institute and then down to Alabama A&M to participate in an event, "The Negro Writer in Our Time," organized by lecturer in residence Rosey Pool. Other participating writers included Mari Evans, Hoyt Fuller, Owen Dodson, and Robert Hayden. Hayden's appearance was ironic because he had recently decided to resign from the faculty of Fisk University, partly because of Killens's presence. Hayden had been at Fisk for twenty years and felt he had earned a lighter teaching load. He thought the appointment of an outsider to the privileged position of author in residence was an unpardonable show of disrespect. After President Wright explained that the regulations governing the funds for the residency specified that an outside person had to be hired, Hayden withdrew his resignation.[20]

Killens, who had been reappointed for the 1965–66 academic year, next jetted off to yet another writers' gathering in East Germany. He received an all-expenses-paid trip to attend a conference celebrating the twentieth anniversary of the Nazi defeat. He arrived in Berlin on May 17 to join a gathering of almost 200 international guests and 133 East German colleagues. The most well known person among the American contingent was William Saroyan, but Killens's leftist friends Yuri Suhl, Phillip Bonosky, Walter Lowenfels, and Alvah Bessie also attended.[21]

Bessie and Killens tried to spark an international incident by visiting Volk and Welt, the house that, spurred by the recommendation of Annette Rubinstein, had published the German translation of *Youngblood* but had rejected *And Then We Heard the Thunder*. The publisher's chief Americanist gave as the reason for the rejection, "Too many Negroes in the novel were shown as not wanting to fight the war." Killens began to reply but noticed a photograph of William Faulkner on the wall and asked why it was there. Told that several staff members admired Faulkner and that the press was going to publish several of his books, Killens asserted that Faulkner was a white supremacist, paraphrasing Faulkner's comment about shooting down Negroes in the streets of Mississippi, stunning the Americanist. Bessie delightedly noted the exchange for publication in the United States.[22]

Back home, Killens turned to his writing projects and efforts to promote his work. An excerpt from *Black Man's Burden* appeared in the August issue of *Ebony* just as Watts erupted in riots. Killens's comments about African Americans' smoldering anger and the shortcomings of nonviolent resistance never seemed more persuasive than when a routine traffic stop by a California Highway Patrol motorcycle officer turned into an urban uprising much more dramatic and deadly than the one in Harlem, leaving thirty-four dead and more than a thousand injured.

Over the summer, Killens kept in touch with Bessie and read *Inquisition in Eden,* his new book about blacklisting in general and the Hollywood Ten in particular. Killens wrote to Bessie, "Together with its human and literary values, this work is important in that it vividly documents a disgraceful period in the nation's history. It also deglamorizes that phony flesh market of a city, Hollywood." Killens's wife and mother also enjoyed the book.[23]

Killens also explained his views on Claude Brown's stunning and popular *Manchild in the Promised Land,* which Bessie reviewed. Macmillan, soliciting comments, sent Killens two advance copies. But Killens decided that because he had nothing good to say about the book, he would say nothing at all for public consumption. In private, he compared Brown's memoir unfavorably to Bessie's, calling Brown's work "factual but untruthful." "If one didn't know Harlem, one would get the impression that it was made up of a half million dope addicts, pushers, hustlers, whores, etc. There are more churches in Harlem than anywhere in N.Y.C. Who keeps them going? The hard-working much-maligned people who make up 95% of its population—that's who." He saw Brown's book as in the same vein as Warren Miller's *The Cool World* and made it clear that *Manchild in the Promised Land* was not more palatable to him because the writer was "colored." "In Claude," he vented, "Mister Charlie has found a 'nigger,' who calls himself a 'nigger.' They have found themselves a diamond in the rough, a 'noble savage' at long last who sounds like he is the real thing. This is the meaning of the movie contract, book clubs, paperbacks, etc."[24]

In September, Killens had to address his status in the Harlem Writers Guild. He had resigned as chair on June 6 and was no longer an active member. The organization's new head, Sylvester Leaks, broached the topic of honorary membership, prompting the forty-nine-year-old Killens to reply, "With due regard and appreciation for the spirit in which the proposal was made, I have concluded that I have not lived long enough, nor have I contributed enough in life, to be an honorary member of anything, least of all the Harlem Writers Guild." Killens wanted to continue his regular membership until he could return as a fully participating member. He had obtained "many great harvests" from the guild and hoped to do so again when he was back in New York full time.[25]

Chuck was still at home, wrestling with depression and ballooning in weight. He was beyond Myles Killens's exhortations, even though his grandfather still tried. Myles complained to Grace, "He has not thought deeply enough about thinking." Myles wanted Chuck to examine some of the lessons in his own family: John's brother, Richard, who had better opportunities than his two older brothers but did not relish academic life, and his sister, Charliemae, who had the opportunity and desire but not the required determination. Myles said that if his health were better, he would go to college even though he was only a few days away from his seventy-second birthday.[26]

While Killens was back in Nashville, the FBI started updating his file, checking local police files and university records. On September 8, an agent ascertained that Killens did not plan to relocate permanently to Nashville. The Memphis Division was then asked to account for Killens's whereabouts and investigate the matter of the trip to East Germany.

Killens pressed on with his agenda. The September 20 issue of *The Nation* ran his "Hollywood in Black and White," in which he disparaged Hollywood's constant production of negative stereotypes, particularly those of Native Americans and African Americans. Killens claimed that "the Negro is the nation's mid-century protagonist" and had to be central to any fresh and dynamic tale about America, a saga that could be rendered most authentically only by African American writers.[27] In a companion article, "Broadway in Black and White," he pointed to the impressive stage, screen, and television accomplishments by Hansberry, Belafonte, Poitier, Bill Cosby, and Cicely Tyson. However, he believed that African American cultural contributions would have been much greater if not for the racism of the entertainment industry. Accordingly, African Americans needed to create their own cultural institutions at the same time that they pushed for further achievement inside the establishment.

Killens began the push for a writers' conference at Fisk, an effort that forced him to work with both Bontemps and Hayden. Bontemps was no problem, having gladly paved the way for Killens to come to Fisk. But the relationship between Killens and Hayden would only be strained at best given the institutional decisions about their jobs and their open disagreements about literary politics. Hayden decried Killens's black-oriented views and disapproved of the popularity of those convictions among the student body. Mindful of an earlier time, when writing by African Americans was sometimes described as "okay for a Negro," Hayden characteristically referred to himself as a poet who only happened to be Negro. Although he wrote several of the most distinguished poems about the black experience and social justice, including "Middle Passage," "Runagate, Runagate," "Frederick Douglass," and "Homage to the Empress of the Blues," he would never embrace any form of black cultural nationalism. Nevertheless, Hayden agreed to serve on the conference planning committee with Killens, Bontemps, Leslie Collins, Donald Graham, Ramona Hoage, Mignon Holland, and Katherine Mitchell.

Black Man's Burden was published on January 1, 1966. This time, Killens got a *New York Times* ad, which featured a photo of the author, a larger picture of the book cover, and Belafonte's description of the book in bold type: "Literary surgery cutting ruthlessly to the heart of American complacency." Also included were comments by cultural critic Nat Hentoff, Ossie Davis, and Allan Morrison of *Ebony*.[28] As was the case with Killens's two novels, critics generally weighed in favorably. Howard Zinn, in a review that combined *Black Man's Burden* with Gordon Parks's *A Choice of Weapons*, praised both volumes.[29] Earl Durham published a lukewarm piece, calling *Black Man's Burden* a "selective summation of the best of James Baldwin, Lerone Bennett, Malcolm X."[30] Durham failed to address the fact that Killens, Baldwin, Bennett, and Malcolm dipped into the same ideological reservoir to fashion a collective discourse. If Killens were summarily sampling, he was drawing on concepts he had helped to articulate.

Killens was linked with no writer more than Baldwin. They made their first significant splashes around the same time, since *Go Tell It on the Mountain* had been published only months before *Youngblood*. *The Fire Next Time* and *And Then We Heard the Thunder*, with their apocalyptic titles, also appeared at virtually the same time. And the two writers sat on panels and made other public appearances together. Many observers consider Killens the better novelist, while Baldwin is believed to be superior (to Killens and nearly everyone else) as an essayist. Alvah Bessie foretold such discussions when he made an extended comparison, biased toward his friend but nonetheless insightful, in *People's World*.[31]

Killens headed to another appearance on the *Today Show*, watched again by his aunt, Louise Coleman Ketch. On January 2, a reception was held at the Carnegie Endowment Center. The crowd was somewhat smaller than the one that had gathered to toast *And Then We Heard the Thunder*, but plenty of star power was on hand, including Poitier, Davis, Godfrey Cambridge, Sarah Wright, Ewart Guinier, and Loften Mitchell. Charles Myles Killens Jr. was there, as was Richard Durham, accompanied by world heavyweight boxing champion Muhammad Ali. Betty Shabazz and Flo Kennedy attended. Killens received several congratulatory telegrams, including one from John Lewis: "Your book is urgent and necessary reading for any serious student of contemporary human conflict."[32]

Killens was putting the finishing touches on yet another discussion of the conflict to which Lewis alluded—the prologue for *Harlem Stirs*, a pictorial book in the mold of Richard Wright and Edwin Rosskam's *12 Million Black Voices*. For *Harlem Stirs*, Fred Halstead wrote the text, and Anthony Aviles and Don Charles provided the photographs. In Killens's view, the book depicts Harlem as the hero instead of as the antihero or jungle, the prevailing description in recent books including *Manchild in the Promised Land*. *Harlem Stirs* recapitulates the history of Harlem with a focus on cultural contributions (the Harlem Renaissance and the Black Arts Repertory Theatre/School) and on struggles against exploitation (Marcus Garvey, rent strikes led by Jesse Gray, school strikes led by the Reverend Milton Galamison, Malcolm X, the riot of 1964). "The thing I like about this book," Killens wrote, "is that it has the courage to place the blame squarely and honestly where the blame belongs." He explained, "The 'jungle' and the jungle image is maintained because big white folk downtown and in Westchester and on Long Island eat high up on the hog because they make money and hold power based on the misery in the jungle." He correctly warned, as did many observers and analysts, that all signs pointed to the grim reality that additional urban disturbances were on the horizon.[33]

Amid the excitement of *Black Man Burden*'s publication and during the production cycle of *Harlem Stirs*, Killens turned fifty years old. Although he would have chosen to celebrate at home with his family, he spent the day visiting Coppin State College in Baltimore. Students took him on a tour of campus and to lunch. After a question-and-answer period with students and faculty, he commented on a selection of student work. Then he delivered a lecture, "What Negro Authors Are Saying—And Should Be Saying."

The following month, James Boggs and Grace Lee Boggs, who would emerge as two of the most insightful and articulate theorists of the Black Power era, wrote to inform Killens that their article, "The City Is the Black Man's Land," was slated for publication in the April issue of *Monthly Review*. The Boggses sought John and Grace Killens's help in disseminating the article to black militants nationwide because it "poses the perspective of black political Power in fundamental historical and programmatic terms and at the same time raises the question of how to organize to achieve it." The Boggses sought to make the concept of Black Power "as common, as universal and almost a 'popular prejudice' as the ideas of Liberty, Equality and Fraternity, National Independence, or Freedom Now."[34]

The article indeed broke new ground and remains an important statement in the development of a strand of revolutionary black nationalism that some observers even term *Boggsism*.[35] The authors began their analysis by noting that demographic predictions indicated that by 1970, fifty of the largest American cities would have black majorities, and important black blocs would exist in other cities, including New York, which had more African Americans than the entire state of Mississippi. Given those realities, the Boggses argued that African Americans were in line to seize leadership of municipal government, just as other ethnic blocs had done. However, the Boggses did not simply seek to argue for the proliferation of black public officials, many of whom they perceived as handpicked Quislings. Instead, the Boggses saw the political seizure of the cities as an initial step in a struggle against a nationally oppressive power structure, an endeavor that needed to be spearheaded by a black revolutionary organization and could hardly avoid an eventual confrontation with state force: "What, up until 1965, few black militants had grappled with is the fact that *jobs* and *positions* are what *boys* ask to be *given*, but *power* is something that *men* have to take and the taking of power requires the development of a revolutionary organization, a revolutionary program for the reorganization of society, and a revolutionary strategy for the conquest of power."[36] In specifying such a strategy, stressing historical process, and forwarding nonessentialist views of black nationalism—Grace Lee Boggs is Chinese— the Boggses' work represented an advance over the theorizing of Malcolm X, whom they admired, even while they were influenced more by C. L. R. James and Mao Tse-tung. In the Boggses, Killens found a revamped expression of his political carryovers from the Old Left. When he later took time out from explicit cultural commentary to speak about concrete political organizing, especially the relationship of the black working class to revolution, he aligned himself with Boggsism.

By early 1966, Chuck's health had deteriorated. He had stopped attending Howard in 1964, feeling the strain both of academic demands and activism. In New York, he had worked briefly and attended meetings of the Organization of Afro-American Unity. But he was now relatively inactive, and his weight had soared out of control. However, he fought to make a comeback. Grace reported to John that their son seemed to be in a better frame of mind, laughing at funny things on television and talking about his problems. And he was losing weight. Alluding to her son's stubborn streak, Grace conveyed, "*He* even admits he looks better!" She was obviously relieved.[37]

CHAPTER SEVENTEEN

Explaining Dissent, 1966–1967

The 1966 conference at Fisk centered on "The Image of the Negro in American Literature." Panelists highlighted conceptions about black consciousness, black affirmation, and politically useful art—some of John Oliver Killens's core values—and matched the prevailing mind-set of the attendees. Esteemed critic Saunders Redding, who had participated in the 1959 American Society of African Culture conference, served as the keynote speaker and charged some African American writers with developing an inappropriate line of characters, "making heroes out of heels." He specifically accused John A. Williams (*Night Song*), Chester Himes (*If He Hollers Let Him Go*), Rosa Guy (*Bird in My Window*), and James Baldwin (*Another Country*). While the remarks proved provocative and expressed sentiments not wholly shared or rejected by Killens, it was evident that the morally upright characters Killens created met with the approval of Redding and were his preferred prototypes.[1]

Redding's remarks did not surprise those, like Killens, who were aware of Redding's previous and consistent pronouncements about African American literature. As far back as 1945, in "The Negro Author: His Publisher, His Public, and His Purse," Redding had criticized Wallace Thurman (*Blacker the Berry*) and Claude McKay (*Banana Bottom*) for producing "empty, banal, pseudo-exotic tripe that is sometimes taken as the substance of Negro life in America."[2] Similarly, in his 1949 essay, "American Negro Literature," he had inveighed against negative stereotypes of blacks reflected in the writing of both black and white authors. He restated those ideas—often verbatim—in "The Relationship of the Negro Writer to His Roots," his address at the American Society of African Culture conference, and in the 1965 *Negro Digest* print symposium, "The Task of the Negro Writer as Artist."

Functioning partly as a counterweight to the thought and presence of Robert Hayden, Melvin B. Tolson voiced the most inspirational, strategic, and consequential articulation of the identity politics most promoted at the conference. Hayden, speaking first, knew he would be facing a mostly hostile audience, not as a poet—he was warmly applauded at the literary reading—but as a panelist because his basic argument amounted to, "Let's quit saying we're black writers writing to black folks. . . . [I]t has been given importance it should not have." Anticipating opposition, Hayden angrily stuttered as he proposed a more nuanced understanding of any writer's role and work. Not many in the crowd were swayed. In fact, the harried Hayden had merely warmed up the crowd for the dynamic Tolson.[3]

Although in his mid-sixties and battling the stomach cancer to which he would succumb only four months later, Tolson turned in an impressive performance. According to David Llorens, "The audience, now spellbound, listened as the man who might affectionately be called the grandfather of the conference spoke of the tridimensionality of man: 'A man has his biology, his sociology, and his psychology—*and then he becomes a poet*.'" Tolson then looked mischievously at Hayden and bellowed, "I'm a black poet, an African-American poet, a Negro poet. I'm no accident—and I don't give a tinker's damn what you think."[4] Tolson, a former dramatist and long-time debate coach, would have been too much of a match for Hayden rhetorically even if the audience had been neutral. In front of the assemblage that Killens had incited to be partial to Tolson's analysis, Hayden had little chance. Ironically, Hayden and Tolson were not very far apart aesthetically and were often grouped together as examples of technically excellent black modernists (a characterization that also drew Tolson, the more obscure of the two, some criticism from black aestheticians). And considerable mutual respect existed between the two poets, who had known each other for years. But the crowd at Fisk was not choosing between the two based on an assessment of their writing. In any event, Tolson's conception both echoed and prefigured words uttered by Killens. In the 1965 *Negro Digest* symposium, Killens wrote, "I am not just *any* American. I am a special kind of an American, known as the Negro, invented by America for the special purpose of exploitation. Therefore, I *am* different. I look at life from the vantage point (for better or worse) of being an American Negro."[5]

Although the following year's conference at Fisk is more legitimately regarded as the national debut of the Black Arts movement, the 1966 conference contributed directly to the success of a key Black Arts publishing outlet, Dudley Randall's Broadside Press, when Randall and Margaret Burroughs encountered Margaret Walker rehearsing a poem about Malcolm X. The three discussed the proliferation of tributes to Malcolm, talk that led to the volume *For Malcolm*, edited by Burroughs and Randall, which signaled Broadside Press's arrival as a significant independent publisher. At the conference's final session, Burroughs and Randall announced the plan to publish the book. Killens would provide a blurb.

Partly moved by the death of Malcolm X, Killens had begun a new novel, *'Sippi*, that begins in June 1954 and is virtually a sequel to *Youngblood*, which was released in May of that year.[6] Some of the material in *'Sippi* is drawn from the nearly two hundred pages Killens trimmed from the original *Youngblood* manuscript. Black solidarity and resistance are again central themes. The characters lack the near-perfect nobility of those in the earlier book, which makes them more realistic. Charles (Chuck) Othello Chaney, the most important figure, is a close approximation of Rob Youngblood and a hopeful version of Killens's son. His parents share most traits with the elder Youngbloods. The working-class African American community in Minksville is analogous to the one in Pleasant Grove, and a poorer community in the Bottom resembles the one in Rockingham Quarters. And the overall setting—Wakefield County, Mississippi, during the 1950s and 1960s—is every bit as racially segregated and harsh as Cross County, Georgia, in the 1920s and 1930s.

The primary difference between the characters' missions in the two novels lies in the specific nature of black political engagement. Whereas *Youngblood* focuses on the founding of a branch of the National Association for the Advancement of Colored People and the development of a labor union, *'Sippi*'s characters are working to seize political power through the ballot and eliminate the African American casualties at the hands of white supremacists. The Chaney surname invokes civil rights martyr James Chaney, and the first half of *'Sippi* testifies to the worth of the civil rights movement. The latter half is a call for Black Power. White supremacists have made it clear, particularly by the bombing murder of voter registration activist Luke

Gibson and his family, that violence is the language they best speak. As Chuck Othello explains to Mr. Wakefield, in phrasing the author himself later employed in numerous speeches, "Rocking the boat—why should we black folk be worried about rocking the goddamn boat, when we're not even in the boat, but drowning in the open sea? Our job is to capsize the boat—and build another one with accommodations for everybody."[7]

'Sippi, like Youngblood, concludes with the death of an African American male hero—in this case, David Woodson, who is reminiscent of Malcolm X—and the promise of heightened African American political involvement. Killens elaborately reorchestrates the optimism that inflects the final passages of his first novel. This time, instead of mentioning individuals, he lists organizations that will effect political change—the Student Nonviolent Coordinating Committee (SNCC), the Southern Christian Leadership Conference, the NAACP, the Urban League, the Congress of Racial Equality, the National Negro Labor Council, the Council of Negro Women, the Federation of Colored Women's Clubs, and the Deacons for Defense.[8] Although Killens became more nationalist in his activism over the latter half of the 1960s, this list offers a view that still suggests multiple possibilities for struggle. While Chaney banishes Carrie Louise Wakefield, the last prominent European American character in Killens's fiction, from the African American side of the civil rights movement—a sharp contrast to the fact that Oscar Jefferson sits on the executive committee of the hotel workers' union chaired by Rob Youngblood—Killens remained true to the idea of progressive pluralism or radical democracy. He simply was not terribly interested in integrating lunch counters, for example, and felt that the most important function for white activists was to educate and organize members of the white community.

Because some of the material for 'Sippi had been excised from the original Youngblood manuscript and the basic frames of the novels are so similar, the writing of 'Sippi flowed rapidly. Nonetheless, that Killens drafted another novel approaching five hundred pages in little more than a year also spoke to the relative isolation of Nashville, the fifty-year-old writer's sense of urgency, and the hyperfocus that sometimes accompanies trepidation about family—in his case, his worries about his son. As constructed in the novel, Chuck would definitely be all right. Killens remained his amiable and gregarious self in Nashville. He habitually opened his Nashville apartment so that people could socialize there. Although he held onto some of his reveler side, he kept things in balance. As Abdul Alkalimat, a young faculty member who briefly lived across the hall from the author, put it, "He was a *man* . . . who was responsible [but] who danced on the razor's edge."[9]

In early July, Killens struck the national racial nerve again when he published "Negroes Have a Right to Fight Back" in the July 2 edition of the *Saturday Evening Post*. The article resulted from Killens's attempt to have the publication adapt chapter 4 of *Black Man's Burden*, "The Myth of Non-Violence versus the Right of Self-Defense." John Hunt, senior editor at the *Post*, thought adaptation unwieldy and instead offered to pay two thousand dollars for a usable contribution to "Speaking Out," a provocative series of articles run by the magazine. Hunt explained that the pieces dissented from conventional wisdom "by definition and policy." He elaborated, "It is a popular theme that non-violence is a great idea, and is getting the Negro ahead just splendidly. Negroes preach this; whites agree. Mr. Killens says nonsense—and worse. Thus the dissent. And that is what we hope he will explain." Hunt continued, "In passing, the whole non-violence business has always struck me, personally, as sort of sneaky. It can sound so good. But if somebody recommended it to me, as the course I should follow, it would make me feel violent."[10]

Killens essentially composed a condensed version of arguments he had made before, particularly in *Black Man's Burden*. He mentioned again the crossroads incident that is at the heart of *Youngblood* and argued, "Moral suasion alone never brought about a revolution, for the simple reason that any power structure always constructs for itself a morality which is calculated to perpetuate itself forever." Killens stated, as he had earlier in *Harlem Stirs*, that if African Americans continued to be denied full rights, then longer and hotter summers loomed ahead.[11]

The *Post* received about seventy-five letters, with the sentiment running two to one against Killens's position. J. Hudson of San Gabriel, California, suggested, "When they decide to grow up and accept responsibilities of first class citizenship, then they will be entitled to it. Not before. And no dire threat of 'longer, hotter, summers' is going to change that. They will find the summers just as long and hot as we do, because we are just as tired of them as they are of us."[12] John Publius's remarks were more pointedly threatening—and Faulknerian. Writing from Alexandria, Virginia, he swaggered, "If the black man persists and continues to vent his frustrations in the streets, the white man will have no choice but to shoot him down like an animal."[13] R. W. Pierpont expressed amazement from suburban Philadelphia: "Ben Franklin would turn over in his grave at 6th and Arch if he could know what has happened to his original *Post* . . . printing and accepting the nigger's right to create another Watts, Harlem & Phila riots."[14]

But Robert S. Johnson, from Wayland, Massachusetts, a white Roman Catholic, appealed to a higher spirit than that of Benjamin Franklin. He thought that Jesus must have enjoyed Killens's article: "I have long suspected that Dr. King and many of the other non-violent Civil Rights leaders are trying to out-Jesus Jesus. Mistakenly so. It is one thing to turn the other cheek, and quite another to allow one's self to be devoured by wild animals without a struggle. If Jesus was able to work up some righteous anger and drive the money lenders from the temple, imagine how He would have conducted the present march through Mississippi."[15]

One of the letters most important to Killens did not come through the *Saturday Evening Post* mailroom. Lorenz Graham, who had rebounded from Knopf's rejection of *North Town* to publish the book and its sequel, *South Town*, had heard an African American commentator argue that Killens's article was "threatening and frightening, and should not have been published in a magazine of the *Post*'s stature." Graham disagreed and mentioned Arna Bontemps's review of *South Town*, which suggested that the action in the book would not receive Martin Luther King's approval. Graham informed Killens, "Man of peace that I am, Christian I hope, I am willing to shed my blood but not on a rather than theirs basis." Furthermore, he thanked Killens for "saying the thing so well."[16]

More fascinating to Killens, though, was another letter from Graham in which he discussed the overthrow of Ghanaian leader Kwame Nkrumah in February 1966. Graham, who had been in Ghana during the coup, told Killens that "the whole truth may never be known" and that "typical misrepresentation and outright lies have been published in practically all news media." According to Graham, the events represented not a people's uprising but "strictly a military coup." In the hours before the takeover, officers had told people that the Russians were in control of the presidential residence, Flagstaff House, and that Nkrumah had been sent to Vietnam to arrange for the Ghanaian army to go to war on the side of the North Vietnamese. Indeed, the United States, which wanted Nkrumah toppled, reported that Russians were killed and captured at Flagstaff House. But Graham maintained that while he was in Ghana, government officials admitted that not a single Russian—indeed, not a single white man—had been found in the compound. As for the crowds of people that were shown on television dancing in the streets, Graham said that a woman in the market had told him, "De guns was in dey back, dat's de ting. Guns was in dey back." Graham did not know the extent of the U.S. government's involvement in the coup, but he knew that American businessmen were spiritedly buying the enterprises established by Nkrumah.[17]

Nkrumah's Ghana had represented the most powerful symbol on the continent for Killens. The optimism he felt five years earlier, which had begun to wane seriously with Lumumba's assassination, had all but disappeared. If political independence in Africa bore some analogue to Emancipation and Reconstruction, then Nkrumah's fall seemed to cap the oppressive, post-Reconstruction restoration. Nonetheless, Killens remained intellectually and professionally, if less emotionally, committed to African freedom struggles. In his later years, he almost always wore in public an Africa-shaped medallion.

As Killens predicted, the United States faced another long, hot summer. In July, the Hough district of Cleveland exploded, and more than 240 fires were set. Four people died, and more than two thousand national guardsmen were summoned. The Cleveland uprising illustrated once again that nonviolent, gradualist, integrationist gestures failed to mollify all African Americans. There was no keeping the lid on either spontaneous or calculated expressions of black rage.

Killens received another invitation from the editors of *Negro Digest*, this time to participate in a print forum on "The Meaning and Measure of Black Power." He and Julian Bond, Eugene Walton, Anita Cornwell, Conrad Kent Rivers, Sterling Stuckey, Brooks Johnson, Francis Ward, Nathan Hare, Eloise Greenfield, Ronald Fair, and Dudley Randall were asked to address two sets of questions: (1) Is the civil rights movement at the crossroads, and, if so, what practical alternatives to it exist? (2) What is your reaction to the term *"Black Power,"* and why do you feel that the national press and the white public reacted as they did to the term? Killens responded that the civil rights movement had reached not a crossroads but a dead end and that an alternate strategy was required. Citing a growing schism between a black middle class, wayward in its complacency, and the black masses for whom economic conditions were worsening, he reiterated his belief that a black nationalist unity was a necessary prelude to the integrationist aims of civil rights advocates. He embraced Black Power, which was essentially a restatement of Organization of Afro-American Unity doctrine, but coupled the term, in a bit of *argumentum ad populum*, with the nation's supposedly cherished beliefs. Addressing African Americans' potential to elect responsive African American leadership as an alternative to unresponsive white leadership, Killens explained, "If Black Power means anything at all, it means 'one man, one vote.' It means an end to taxation without representation."[18] Although no one in the civil rights movement could object to a proposal to flex black voting muscle, Killens was too strident overall for mainstream activists. Martin Luther King Jr., for example, objected to Killens's comments about liberation preceding integration. By then, however, Killens had little contact with King. Killens was more in touch with Stokely Carmichael, who had become SNCC's chair in May and whose absence from the *Negro Digest* symposium represented a glaring omission since he had popularized the term *Black Power*.

While in New York for the summer, Killens took time out from his writing to handle a request from Burt Lancaster, with whom the author had spoken at the March on Washington. Killens examined the script for the satiric movie *The Scalphunters*, which he thought might even be another *Cat Ballou*, the classic Western spoof in which a teacher trainee turns into an avenging outlaw after corporate developers murder her father and seize the family land. But Killens had major problems with the characterization of Joseph Lee, describing him "just as obsequious as the typical Uncle Tom slave stereotype, with the exception that he doesn't speak with an Amos and Andy dialect."[19] Killens wanted to see the black character more human, more intelligent, and more interested in his own freedom. Although Killens's precise influence on the final project is unknown, Lee (Ossie Davis) certainly possesses a strong escape motive and shatters stereotypes about black men (though ones of drunken Indians are central to the tale) in his interaction with fur trapper Joe Bass (Lancaster). Lee quotes Aesop—"Better beans in freedom than cake in slavery"—when Bass suggests that Lee enjoyed more comforts under slavery than he would as a free man.[20] Lancaster biographer Kate Buford has accurately described Lee as an "erudite black slave who just wants his freedom."[21] *Cue* magazine termed *The Scalphunters* the "first black power western."[22] It was hardly that, but in the climactic fight scene with Bass, Lee captured the mood of many African Americans in the streets.

In the fall of 1966, Killens reached another milestone of sorts when the library at Boston University requested his help to establish the John Oliver Killens Collection. He left the details to Grace, who in October submitted a selection of manuscripts, work notes, and correspondence. The author, always pushing ahead, was more interested in building toward another writers' conference at Fisk.

Killens remained a popular campus speaker. On December 3, he attended a symposium on "The Writer and Human Rights" organized by Charles V. Hamilton, chair of the political science department at Lincoln University in Pennsylvania. The two had met through the mail when Hamilton, then a graduate student at the University of Chicago, wrote to Killens seeking an address for Paul Robeson. Killens spent an afternoon at Lincoln with Ron Milner, writer in residence; critic-essayist Wilmer Lucas, visiting professor of English; and Loften Mitchell.

In February 1967, Killens pored over the galleys for *'Sippi*. He had already started another novel, *The Cotillion*, a rather slight satiric vehicle. Although the combination of Killens and satire had scared Angus Cameron at Knopf, any serious read of *Youngblood* and *And Then We Heard the Thunder* reveals humor to be one of the writer's gifts. *Esquire* expressed interest, in fact, in the short story "Rough Diamond," a spoof (though not easily identifiable as such) of Claude Brown.

Not having given up on the film world completely, Killens also was in conversation with Clarence Jones and others, including Budd Schulberg, in an attempt to establish a company to produce independent African American films. On March 8, they met with David Holzman to discuss a proposal they hoped would pass muster with the Film Advisory Council and be funded by the National Endowment of the Arts.

Killens and Herbert Biberman, along with Philip Langner and Theatre Guild Films, were proceeding with the plan to make a film based on Harriet Beecher Stowe's *Uncle Tom's Cabin*. The project would be the first film for Langner, who codirected the Theater Guild, the distinguished company that evolved from the Washington Square Players and had been responsible since 1919 for numerous Broadway productions. Langner feared that another company would upstage his production and consequently sought to keep the news quiet until some casting had been done and the announcement could be buttressed with what the trade would consider saleable elements. Biberman cautioned Killens not to leak specific news about the production. He and Langner gave the project a temporary title intended as a code, "Till the War Is Ended."

With his film prospects on the upswing, Killens seemed to have dropped his grudge against Haskell Wexler. He and Grace wrote to congratulate Wexler for receiving an Academy Award as the cinematographer for *Who's*

Afraid of Virginia Woolf?: "It was beautiful seeing you dash up there to get the Oscar. Hope that this is just the beginning."[23]

Ultimately, however, the biggest project Killens tackled was a story about Alexander Pushkin. Killens had read about Pushkin, whose mother's paternal grandfather was born in Africa, in J. A. Rogers's *World's Great Men of Color*. Harry Belafonte consulted with Russian producers who wanted to do an English-language film on Pushkin starring Belafonte, and the actor suggested Killens for the script. Killens immediately went to the Schomburg Library and spent a week studying about Pushkin. Belafonte brought additional information from Europe. Although the movie project fell through, Killens became "hooked on Pushkin."[24] He was drawn to a vernacular artist who spoke the language of the Russian masses and supported revolutionary causes, but the key attraction was Pushkin's African ancestry and the chance for Killens to depict a black hero: "I had an Afro-Russian on my back and was loving it."[25]

CHAPTER EIGHTEEN

New Black, 1967–1968

John Oliver Killens's plans for a 1967 literary conference at Fisk paralleled the efforts of the Student Nonviolent Coordinating Committee (SNCC). In the fall of 1966, George Ware, the group's campus coordinator, arrived in Nashville to reestablish a strong presence for the organization. Killens's conference on "The Black Writer and Human Rights" was set for April, while Ware arranged for a Black Power conference, featuring Stokely Carmichael, to take place in March.

Fisk officials permitted the literary gathering to proceed despite the displeasure of conservative faculty. But the university banned Ware's conference, which ultimately was held in April at the Chapel of Saint Anselm, an Episcopal student parish directed by Father James Woodruff, a black clergyman who became a strong SNCC supporter. Other local civic leaders denounced SNCC, the conference, black militants in general, and Stokely Carmichael in particular. Carmichael recalled that all the publicity ensured standing-room-only attendance at the conference.[1]

Carmichael arrived in Nashville and spoke at Vanderbilt University on April 8 and gave the opening address at the Black Power conference the following morning before leaving town. A few hours later, the black proprietor of the University Inn, across the street from the SNCC office, called local police to remove a man from the premises who was behaving in an offensive manner. The man was not arrested. Instead, he made his way to the SNCC headquarters and rallied a dozen or so students to protest in front of the hotel. The crowd quickly swelled to several hundred, blocking an intersection. When the driver of a city bus forced his way through, students began hurling rocks and bottles, which propelled the police to open fire as well as attack students with clubs. Several Fisk students suffered gunshot wounds, and scores were driven back onto campus with clubs. More than seventy Fisk students were arrested over the next few days as the unrest continued.

The SNCC headquarters was raided on April 10. Police had issued a warrant for the arrest of Carmichael, who had returned to Nashville and now sought to escape. One of Killens's students tried to get the author to aid Carmichael, but the student told Carmichael, "Man, that jive, handkerchief-head Negro jes' scared. Man, wouldn't even talk to me." But Carmichael "told the brother to cool that. First of all, what do you expect them to do, all the propaganda that's been in the media? Besides, do you have any idea what that brother may have gone through during McCarthyism? Hey, the brother probably thinks his phone still tapped." Carmichael subsequently donned a disguise and escaped aboard a plane to Atlanta.[2] His assessment was correct: Killens was indeed wary, and he had reason to be. The FBI had been telephoning his house on various pretexts for years, and Killens often received invitations to participate in suspect activities.

As urban outbursts went, the events in Nashville never approached the deadliness of Watts, Newark, or Detroit. Yet they indicated the students' changing mood and explained their militant enthusiasm at the writers' conference less than two weeks later. Along with Killens, speakers included John Henrik Clarke, Ron Milner, Ronald Fair, Lerone Bennett, Margaret Danner, Gwendolyn Brooks, and LeRoi Jones (Amiri Baraka), the indisputable main attraction. The audience thus heard several speeches that continued the dominant, revolutionary tenor of the previous year's event and echoed the sentiments of Carmichael and Killens. Although *Negro Digest* underplayed the importance of SNCC, Carmichael's presence, and the protests of recent weeks, it reported on the growth of black consciousness on campus: "It is not possible to gauge novelist John O. Killens' direct influence on this phenomenon, but the writer's relaxed, informal manner, and his total lack of pomp and pretension, cannot but have proved a remarkable change for a faculty member on the campus."[3] Nikki Giovanni, who roomed with Killens's daughter and graduated from Fisk that spring, remarked, "At Fisk it was John who woke us up. For those of us at Fisk in the

early days of trying to be but not quite knowing what, John O. Killens gave
definition to our movement."⁴ Kalamu ya Salaam was an exchange student
from Carleton College who met Killens during the novelist's early days at
Fisk and "got the feeling he was someone you could talk to." Shortly thereafter, while in the army, Salaam read *And Then We Heard the Thunder* and
decided "this is the cat for now."⁵

Gwendolyn Brooks's "rebirth" at the 1967 conference widely influenced
discourses on African American cultural politics. Although the poet's work
had always reflected a deep concern for and understanding of African
American humanity, her artistic vision had been mostly connected, according to biographer George Kent, to the white liberal critical consensus. But
"suddenly," according to Brooks, "there was New Black to meet."⁶

Although not youngsters, historians Clarke and Bennett were among
the "New Blacks" who persuaded Brooks of the virtues of Black Power and
black nationalism. Clarke described enslavement as an assault on African
identity and asserted that slave narratives and other such literature were
survival oriented. He traced a movement from the slave narratives through
a literature of restoration (as typified by the work of W. E. B. Du Bois), a
literature of protest (as exemplified by the fiction of Richard Wright), and
neo-slave narratives (the writings of Killens, James Baldwin, and William
Melvin Kelley). In Clarke's words, "It is singularly the mission of the Black
writer to tell his people what they have been in order for them to understand what they are. And from this the people will clearly understand what
they must be."⁷ Two years earlier, Bennett had argued for a politically engaged art that would create new forms of expression and divorce itself from
the "white culture structure."⁸ He conveyed a similar message at Fisk, finding it astonishing that "an oppressed person would choose to address his
oppressors, primarily."⁹

Killens was perturbed that Brooks and fellow poet Margaret Danner were
introduced somewhat rudely on their panel by a student who suggested
that no African American poetry of relevance to the black freedom struggle
had been published between the Harlem Renaissance and contemporary
outpourings by black cultural nationalists. Both Danner and Brooks, who
had written during that alleged gap, took exception, but Danner, scheduled to speak first, reproached the student. Before her presentation, which
consisted mostly of reading poetry, Brooks issued a brief statement. Allowing that "race fed testimony" will find itself into black art, she avowed, "I
continue and violently to believe that, whatever the stimulating persuasion,

poetry, not journalism, must be the result of involvement with emotions and ideas and ink and paper." Then she quipped, "And that's all the vital prose that I have for you, Mr. Killens."[10]

Brooks's remarks were respectfully received, as were her verses, which included "Malcolm X," "Kitchenette Building," "The Mother," "We Real Cool," and "The Ballad of Rudolph Reed." She apologized for the fact that some of her poems treating the issue of social justice were too long to read. Students were more interested in Jones and Milner. Near the end of her performance, Brooks announced Jones's arrival in the hall, and "from that moment, the conference was in the hands of the more radical social critics and the visionary young."[11]

Brooks's immersion in the conference environment—proud and angry students denouncing integration—caused her to reconsider her specific notions of art and its relationship to the African American social and political struggle. She later wrote, "I didn't know what to make of what surrounded me, of what with hot sureness began almost immediately to invade me. *I* had never been before, in the general presence of such insouciance, such live firmness, such confident vigor, such determination to mold or carve something DEFINITE."[12] Back home in Chicago, she became active in working with young African American writers. Some, such as Don L. Lee (Haki Madhubuti), became important in their own right. She supported black cultural initiatives and ultimately severed her long-standing ties with Harper and Row, publishing with Broadside Press beginning in 1969. She put her manuscripts where her mouth was, and numerous African American writers and publishers have seen her as a model of commitment.

With another conference behind him and the semester winding down, Killens began another string of appearances. Although he seemed to be past his literary peak, his popularity surged, and he received far more requests to be a sponsor, board member, reviewer, or speaker than he could accept. On May 7, he spoke in Columbus, Ohio, under the sponsorship of the Catholic Interracial Council, sounding familiar themes from *Black Man's Burden* and opining that the church needed to join the new revolution. Four days later, he spoke at the Conference on Racism in American Education, organized by the Detroit Federation of Teachers and held at the University of Detroit. Then he was off to California. On May 13, he lectured on "The Negro Revolt and Vietnam" at the home of Mr. and Mrs. Richard Faust in San Jose. The next day at the San Francisco Negro and Cultural Society, the topic was "Negro Life and Literature."

Killens next attended the "Black Experience," a cultural and political conference held at Oakland's Merritt College, a hotbed of radical activism. Held
under the auspices of the Alain Locke Society, a group of Greater East Bay
"scholars and citizens" who shared a "common interest where black consciousness is valued," the gathering was coordinated by poet and English
instructor Sarah Webster Fabio. On May 19, Killens sat on a panel with Don
Hopkin, Kenneth Castellino, Norvell Smith, and Kenneth Good. The following afternoon he and Jones spoke during a two-hour symposium. Fabio
later wrote to Killens, "Everyone loved you here and even I must agree you
are a likeable person."[13]

On May 22, just after the conference, Langston Hughes died, depriving
the world of one of the most astute observers and recorders of black experience. "He loved Black people more than any other writer, before or after
him," Killens reflected on his first literary hero, an artist and mentor quick
to encourage, congratulate, and share.[14]

That same week, Killens thought of another generous friend. Because of
his recent fiscal stability, he was able to send another thousand dollars to
Harry Belafonte to repay loans. Then he turned to drumming up publicity for his new novel. Like Hughes and Belafonte, Killens still found time
to support other cultural workers. On June 15, he wrote to Hoyt Fuller in
an attempt to get Piri Thomas's *Down These Mean Streets* reviewed in *Negro
Digest*. While incarcerated, Thomas, who had since become a member of
the Harlem Writers Guild, found affirmation in *Youngblood*. A fellow inmate, known as Youngblood, obtained a copy of Killens's first novel and
introduced the book to Thomas by saying, "They wrote a book named after
me." Thomas read the book repeatedly over the next several days and then
decided that he, too, could write.[15]

Thomas was not the only notable inmate meditating about Killens's work.
In 1965, Eldridge Cleaver looked for Killens's works in the Folsom Prison
library but could not find them—or writings by a host of other notables,
including Ernest Hemingway, Norman Mailer, Albert Camus, Jean-Paul
Sartre, James Baldwin, Henry Miller, Terry Southern, Julian Mayfield, Saul
Bellow, William Burroughs, and Allen Ginsberg. Cleaver judged the facility "unsatisfactory to a stud who is trying to function in the last half of the
twentieth century . . . no action."[16]

The publication date for *'Sippi* suggested good luck for Killens, he thought,
because June 19, 1967, was his twenty-fourth wedding anniversary. And
early returns were encouraging; the first run was nearly sold out before

publication. But the book, as Killens grudgingly acknowledged, was a "criti-cal bust," despite the efforts of Ossie Davis and Geoffrey Cambridge and a positive review by John Henry Jones in *Freedomways*.[17] But critical observ-ers including Alvah Bessie knew immediately that the novel failed to mea-sure up to Killens's first two published efforts. Bessie, who considered Kil-lens a major American novelist, "if not THE major A.N.," had planned to review the book for a local newspaper. Instead, Bessie told Killens, "I could not get with it. . . . I *hope* you will forgive me."[18]

Whatever the critical reception, Killens promoted his novel with his usual energy both in and out of New York. At the end of June, he returned to Detroit for another Black Arts conference. At the event, Dudley Randall presented Betty Shabazz, a featured speaker, with an advance copy of the poetry anthology *For Malcolm*.

At the beginning of July, John and Grace Killens then headed back to California, traveling first to Oakland, where he spoke at the annual conven-tion of the Congress of Racial Equality. Other speakers included the group's founder, James Farmer, as well as Faye Bellamy, Ron Dellums, Lerone Ben-nett, Floyd McKissick, and H. Rap Brown. The Killenses then journeyed south to Los Angeles, where among his stops were the Los Angeles Urban League district office and Watts Towers, Watts Library, and the Imperial Courts Housing Project. By some measures, including local resident Lorenz Graham's reckoning, conditions had improved since 1965. But Graham and Killens figured that Watts could soon explode again.

Newark was on the verge. On July 12, as John and Grace were in transit back to New York, a traffic stop incident ignited another uprising. By the time the rioting subsided five days later, twenty-three people were dead, more than six hundred had been injured, and more than twelve hundred were in jail. Those arrested included Barry Wynn, Barbara Killens's boy-friend, who was picked up on weapons charges along with LeRoi Jones and Charles McCray. Twenty-year-old Barbara, however, was not among those arrested or hurt, having left Newark for the safety of Brooklyn.[19]

Less than a week after the Newark rebellion ended, Detroit exploded in the most dramatic of the 1960s urban riots. After a botched police raid on an after-hours location, nine days of conflict left forty-three dead and more than seven hundred injured. Almost eight thousand people were arrested, and the city sustained property damage in excess of fifty million dollars. In the turmoil's signal event, which became a national symbol of the racist and ultimately unpunished police brutality that was a major contributing factor to riots, Detroit police officers shot and killed three unarmed African American teenagers, Aubrey Pollard, Fred Temple, and Carl Cooper, at the Algiers Motel.[20] Killens and Rosa Parks, now a Detroit resident, participated in a mock trial in which the officers were found guilty, although they were acquitted in the official proceedings. As a consequence primarily of his relationships with James Boggs and Grace Lee Boggs and with the Reverend Albert Cleage Jr., Killens's ties to Detroit had begun to grow stronger.

In New York, much of the activist community buzzed over Harold Cruse's landmark *The Crisis of the Negro Intellectual*, and Killens was one of the book's main targets. He had criticized Ralph Ellison, William Faulkner, Adam Clayton Powell Jr., Martin Luther King Jr., and an array of Cold War liberals, and now it was his turn to bear the weight of an intellectual and verbal assault. Cruse disparaged all of Killens's writing—although no evidence indicates that he read much of it, and he certainly read none of it closely—and derogated Killens's political activities. Cruse declared that at the June 1964 debate on "The Black Revolution and the White Backlash," Killens, Lorraine Hansberry, and company "were accusing white liberals of not being radicals when they themselves did not compose a group with a radical Negro philosophy of any kind" and that the 1965 New School Conference was "painfully frenetic and pitifully rhetorical."[21] Although the bitterness of Cruse's tone might have been surprising, the complaints had been brewing since the days of the Committee for the Negro in the Arts and had been voiced in the lengthy letter Cruse wrote to Killens prior to the 1959 American Society of African Culture conference, at which point Killens probably should have given the Cruse viewpoint more attention. Whereas Lloyd Brown was the major Cruse target in front of Killens, Killens was arguably the major Cruse target in front of the world.

Julian Mayfield had been alert to Cruse's spiteful nature and had carefully written down Cruse's threats against Cuban officials while the two traveled on the island in 1960. Mayfield, also among the writers criticized in *Crisis of the Negro Intellectual*, was the first to issue a formal response. Aside from dismissing Cruse's book as a dismal failure despite its often brilliant economic analyses, Mayfield cited several expressions of petty jealousy, historical inaccuracies, and telling omissions. For example, he attributed the harsh chapter on Hansberry to the fact that Hansberry had refused to read the manuscript of a play Cruse had written. He accused Cruse of trying to pass himself off as a longtime black nationalist but failing to reveal that he had been a Marxist theoretician during the 1940s, a favored black son of the organized left wing in Harlem, and ideologically in league with many people he later scorned. According to Mayfield, when the two men were in Cuba, Cruse berated a Cuban aide, threatening, "You'd damn well better get us something to eat and drink or I'll go back to the States and write the worst things I can think of about you and your damned Revolution!" In Mayfield's view, such words spoke to an essential vindictiveness at the heart of Cruse's character: "The man who screamed that blackmail threat, merely for food and water, is the author of *The Crisis of the Negro Intellectual*, the political pundit who presumes to sit in moral judgment on almost every black person who has written and published a book, a play or a poem."[22]

Despite the vitriolic nature of *The Crisis of the Negro Intellectual* and its somewhat flawed analyses, the book still provides a valuable point of departure for a discussion of African American leadership. Killens reluctantly admitted as much in private, but he remained convinced that Cruse was a literary hatchet man working in the service of the establishment. The immediate problem for Killens, however, was that he had been verbally outmaneuvered, checkmated because he had not been paying close attention to the rhetorical board. To effectively refute Cruse's charges about his slavish adherence to Communist Party dictates, Killens would have had to reveal virtually all he knew of those dealings, which, in turn, would have meant divulging information about friends in the entertainment world whose careers could be adversely affected. The frustrated Killens apparently challenged Cruse to a fistfight. Askia M. Toure, who emerged as an important poet during the Black Arts movement and considered both Killens and Cruse as well as John Henrik Clarke to be mentors, likened the incident to two uncles getting out of hand. The bout never occurred, however, though Killens simmered. Ron Milner tried to console him: "Heard you let Cruse upset you. He got a little too much into personal, petty, vindictiveness. But overall it is (so far, haven't finished) a good thing. It isn't done for whiteie. And we do need ever so often critical re-evaluation of our group-thinking and intellectual (so-called) directions."[23] Nikki Giovanni adopted a similar tone, not only arguing that Mayfield was right but asserting, "It's time someone put Cruse into perspective."[24] James Boggs added, "It goes nowhere except back to where black people were in the late 30s. I call it a nigger book. But the book is the end of a period. It is another day, another season. Let it ride."[25]

Killens went back on the intellectual offensive in the wake of the fall 1967 publication and runaway success of William Styron's *The Confessions of Nat Turner*. Numerous African American readers and cultural observers, in-

cluding Killens, were outraged at Styron's depiction of the slave revolution-
ist, and Killens readily assented when Clarke solicited responses for an anthology, *William Styron's Nat Turner: Ten Black Writers Respond*, which was
published the following year. Other contributors were Lerone Bennett Jr.,
Alvin Poussaint, Vincent Harding, John A. Williams, Ernest Kaiser, Loyle
Hairston, Charles V. Hamilton, and Michael Thelwell.

In "The Confessions of Willie Styron," Killens suggested that the white
public loved the book because it confirms myths and prejudices about
black men and attempts to reduce Turner's stature as a historical figure.
Killens complained, "Nat Turner, in the tradition of most black Americans,
was a man of tragedy, a giant, but William Styron has depicted him as a
child of pathos."[26] In Killens's eyes, Styron should never have attempted the
novel because his paternalism and racism blocked him from understanding Turner's true motivations. Styron's Turner dotes on kindly masters, an
oxymoron to Killens, and is motivated more by lust for white women than
by slavery itself. Killens believed that Styron's book offered a clearly inferior
psychological profile of a black rebel than did *Black Thunder*, Arna Bontemps's historical novel about insurrectionist Gabriel Prosser. According to
Styron biographer Jim West, "To anyone educated to observe basic standards of logic and decorum, *Ten Black Writers Respond* is an appallingly
poor performance." But no professional literary critics were in the lineup.
Aside from any imposed sense of logic, decorum, or academic standards,
the writers were grappling over the mythic, as West understands, and reg-
istering their disgust with the mythic Nat Turner as rendered by Styron. In
this manner, they performed well.[27]

Early in 1968, Killens learned that producer David Wolper and director Norman Jewison planned to make a film version of *The Confessions of
Nat Turner*. He also learned that efforts to prevent the novel from becoming a film were being headed by the Anti-Black Defamation Association,
sponsored by Adam Clayton Powell Jr., Stokely Carmichael, H. Rap Brown,
John Henrik Clarke, and others, with Ossie Davis serving as the group's
national chair and novelist Louise Meriwether chairing the steering committee. Killens wrote to Meriwether, offering comments that she could use
to whatever effect she deemed advisable: "The first horror was for William
Styron to write the novel, which was a bastardization of art and history, a
story manufactured out of white supremacist wish fulfillment, signifying
nothing save the sickness of a slavemaster's grandson and the terminal sickness of the country. To make a film of this monstrosity is to compound the
felony."[28] The film was not made.

While the controversy over Styron's book raged, a rising literary star languished in prison on the other side of the ocean. In 1967, when author Wole Soyinka attempted to intervene to broker a peace settlement in the Nigerian civil war, the country's government, headed by Major-General Yakubu Gowon, arrested him. On November 19, Killens sent a telegram to Gowon on Soyinka's behalf: "AS A BLACK AMERICAN WRITER TWICE VISITING YOUR GREAT COUNTRY I AM DEEPLY GRIEVED BY CURRENT CIVIL WAR. ESPECIALLY CONCERNED WITH HEALTH AND SITUATION OF WOLE SOYINKA. URGE YOU USE YOUR OFFICE TOWARD AFFORDING HIM REGULAR VISITS FROM HIS FAMILY AND A JUST AND EXPEDITIOUS TRIAL." Despite the efforts of Killens and others, Soyinka was not released until the war ended nearly two years later.[29]

Chuck was also confined during this period, having suffered a breakdown that hospitalized him for more than a year. The diagnosis was schizophrenia, a setback Killens could not fix with fiction. But he continued his writing. On November 29, Killens wrote to Grace that he was flying home, up to his ears in work, including a new manuscript, *The Cotillion*. Killens wrote to Herbert Biberman around the same time that he did not think the script for *Slaves*, the movie based on *Uncle Tom's Cabin*, was ready for production: "It needs the insight, the focus, the deepening, the idiomatic truthfulness which only a black writer could give to it." If the script were going to be rushed into production, Killens asked to have his name removed from the project. He was willing to work more on the script—for two thousand dollars. Biberman sympathized with Killens's position but could not address it immediately, and he hoped to get Killens working on the project sometime in February. Early that month, Philip Langner agreed that Killens should do a "polish" on the script, working within the existing structure of story lines, scenes, and character relationships, which had been further developed by Biberman and Alida Sherman to a "point of excellent structural and story realization."[30]

As Killens attended to his end-of-the-year flurry of work, he lingered on the fallout from Cruse's book. On December 9, he wrote to playwright Charlie Russell, a fellow member of the Harlem Writers Guild who was serving as president of Onyx Publications, producer of *Onyx* magazine, whose advisory board Killens chaired. The magazine was sponsoring a book party for Cruse, prompting Killens to submit a letter of resignation to Russell and send copies to those from whom support had been solicited over Killens's signature. He said flatly, "I believe this book can only serve the enemies of black people. In my opinion, the book is a great disservice to the black movement, indeed the greatest in my memory—by a black man."[31] The following month, in what amounted to an extension of his remarks to Russell, he invited Mayfield to be the keynote speaker at the next Black Writers' Conference at Fisk.

Perhaps Killens was too thin-skinned. He certainly had the respect of his peers. In a *Negro Digest* poll of thirty-eight writers taken at the end of 1967, *And Then We Heard the Thunder* and John A. Williams's *The Man Who Cried I Am* were judged the most important novels written by African Americans since the publication of *Invisible Man*.[32] If Killens had a literary rival, it was apparently Williams, though their relationship was certainly a friendly one. And neither was considered the dominant African American literary figure of the day. That accolade belonged to LeRoi Jones.

In the first week of February 1968, Killens attended Wayne State University's "Black Symposium." Cleage delivered the keynote address on February 1; the following day, Killens spoke along with Milton Henry, Lerone Bennett, and John Conyers. Two weeks later, Killens was in New Orleans for Dillard University's Festival of Afro-American Arts.

Despite his hectic work schedule, Killens took time out to attend to a real-life relationship. Twenty-one-year-old Jackie Robinson Jr. had been arrested in Stamford, Connecticut, on marijuana, heroin, and gun charges and entered treatment for his drug addiction. His father received a letter from John and Grace Killens in which they reassured him, "The strength and stamina that helped you through your early career will see you through this period of despair." They enclosed a note for Jackie Jr.: "We last saw you when you were about 13 or 14 years old but we remember you as a fine young man. You have your whole life ahead of you and our people need the minds and energies of all of our young people and especially our young men, who are the future and especially one who has such fine parents as you have. Think of this time as a period that will pass so 'keep the faith,' because you are a much needed part of all of our lives."[33] The elder Robinson wrote back, noting that "family ties are strong and . . . with God's help we will come through this crisis." He added that he very much appreciated the words of encouragement and would pass along the message to his son.[34]

CHAPTER NINETEEN

We Must Construct a Monument, 1968–1969

"We marched along the streets of Atlanta to bid a final farewell to one of the most beautiful sons of Africa who ever walked upon this earth." John Oliver Killens's most poignant memory regarding the death of Martin Luther King Jr. intersected in his mind with a clear sense of anger. Recalling the ceremonies at Morehouse College, he wrote, "I remember a feeling of deep resentment at the hypocrisy that permeated the atmosphere. There were men and women of government, of the corporate world, who either by commission or omission helped create the atmosphere that in turn created the scenario for this great human tragedy."[1] For many African American youth who came of age in the 1960s, King's assassination marked a philosophical turning point. Those who agitated militantly, like Malcolm X, would be killed. Those who protested nonviolently, like King, would meet the same fate. A somber mood hung in the air when the 1968 Black Writers' Conference opened at Fisk University two weeks after King's death.

In his opening address, Killens exhorted his relatively small audience of two hundred, most of them students, to continue to fight for political and cultural change. "Make the revolution," he exhorted, "you can be rebels *with* a cause. A rebel-with-a-cause *plus* a program equals a revolutionary."[2] He made his familiar pitch for a literature of black legends, myths, and heroes, works that would incorporate historical reconstruction and visionary insight. The collective African American literary project should celebrate African American people and promote resistance against oppression, and this artistic outpouring should be presented in the African American vernacular. Proceeding unavoidably to the subject of King, he told the audience, "Martin was my valued friend. There were certain things about which we disagreed vis-à-vis the tactics of the Revolution. But I knew he was a revolutionary, and I loved him and respected him, and I am angry past description at the way we let him down. We must construct a monument, not built of stone and mortar, but forged out of [his] great vision, the vision for freedom and liberation; the vision that the disinherited shall inherit the earth."[3] Featured writers on hand who would also address the conference theme, "The Black Writer's Vision for America," which harkened back to the New School affair (*Black* replacing *Negro* to reflect changing linguistic and cultural consciousness), were Don L. Lee (Haki Madhubuti), gaining his first national exposure, Piri Thomas, Sarah Webster Fabio, and Julian Mayfield.

Mayfield had been abroad since 1961, residing in Ghana (a neighbor to W. E. B. Du Bois in the latter's final years) until 1966 and in Europe and Asia for another year. Prior to King's death, Mayfield might have used the platform to continue his debate with Harold Cruse (which certainly had been Killens's plan), but Mayfield focused instead on assigning meaning to the end of the King era. "The only way forward," he concluded, "is to destroy the system." Some people might still believe in the American dream, but "in their hearts they know that dream died a violent death two weeks ago." After citing a familiar catalog of the white abuses of power in American history and worldwide, Mayfield urged, "The duty of black writers is to harness the tremendous political power that was unleashed in the form of rioters after King's assassination." Although provocative, Mayfield cautioned against "senseless militancy," proposing in its place "black revolution": "Militants can get a lot of people killed. Black revolutionaries know how to use their power."[4]

The other speakers, including Killens, shared aspects of Mayfield's left nationalism. Lee represented the nationalist extreme, introducing himself as a separatist and declaring, "Blacks and whites can't live together and they can't work together." Because he felt that "White America has a case of double cancer—external cancer in Vietnam and racist internal cancer throughout the country," the only integration that interested Lee was that between "Negroes" and "blacks," and he thought that African American writers should promote this work.[5]

Despite the conference's defiant tone, the overall vibe remained some-what muted. Killens, in fact, was drained and nearing the end of his time on Fisk's faculty. Although he does not appear to have been forced out, he later complained about the conservative board of trustees and spoke of cer-tain black faculty "smiling in your face and whispering behind your back about how John Killens and that whole bunch was bringing the univer-sity down with that Black Power stuff."[6] On another occasion, he reflected, "After some of us left, the school began to go to pot (a realistic pun I fear), to go back to the old days when it sought to be *the* 'Negro Harvard.' Which meant we had not constructed a lasting leadership to carry on the struggle after we had split the scene. It might be almost designated as developing a 'cult of personality.' This is meant as a serious self-criticism."[7] Killens left his workshop in the care of Donald Graham, whom Killens thought had great promise. The week following the conference, Killens responded to a query from Frank MacShane, director of the new master of fine arts program at Columbia University, by recommending for regular admission Nikki Gio-vanni, Kathryn Mickins, and Deborah Toney. He recommended Graham for a special student category.

Later that spring, Killens appeared at a conference on "Arts and the Inner City" sponsored by Columbia College in Chicago. Recognizing that arts programs should be responsive to local communities, college president Mirron Alexandroff convened artists, sculptors, musicians, directors, and writers "from Harlem to Watts" to discuss program implementation. Kil-lens had been invited along with Piri Thomas; Robert Macbeth of the New Lafayette Theater in Harlem; Luis Valdez of El Teatro Campesino in Del Ray, California; Colin Carew of the New Thing in Washington D.C.; James Sherman of the Watts Writers Workshop; Gwendolyn Brooks, Ron Milner, and Haskell Wexler. Guests were asked (1) What standards and whose stan-dards for the arts in the inner city? (2) How can engagement with the arts, either as participant or audience, help individuals to self-esteem? To con-structive insight into self and society? (3) How can the arts bring people into meaningful group and community association? (4) Can the arts have a conscious, constructive relationship to social action?[8]

However, Alexandroff neglected black artists closer to home, causing members of the Chicago arts community to object and meet under the aus-pices of the Coalition of Black Revolutionary Artists (COBRA). Members of the Organization of Black American Culture, which had established a considerable presence in the city and functioned on this occasion as a part of COBRA, contacted Killens before the conference and expressed the feeling of the local artists. When Killens arrived in Chicago, he gathered most of the other conference speakers in his hotel room and conveyed the local group's views. All of those at the meeting decided to support the local protesters. Although he had not thoroughly thought out his own appearance, Killens certainly did not want to get caught on the wrong side of the protest. He and other speakers signed a resolution agreeing to donate half their honoraria to COBRA and requesting that Columbia College match the total donation. The signatories further suggested that Columbia College demonstrate its commitment to change by establishing more realistic relationships with its surrounding communities—"the Black community through negotiations with community people and the white community through direct action aimed to combat racism implicit in the culture and which is inevitably expressed in its arts as well as in aspects of the culture."[9]

At the conference opening, visual artist Jeff Donaldson took the floor. Killens admired Donaldson: four years earlier, he had written to solicit Killens's response to a mixed-genre manuscript, confiding that *Youngblood* had helped him resolve some of his bitterness.[10] In Chicago, Donaldson denounced the conference and shut down the proceedings. Two caucuses, one led by blacks and one led by whites, met to draft formal resolutions to end the conference. The conference dinner, however, was permitted to take place so that activists could confront keynote speaker Deton Brooks, an African American who headed the Chicago Committee on Urban Opportunity, which had provided funding. Mexican artist Luis Valdez presented the resolution for artistic self-determination and local control, though Valdez, like Killens, was one of the outsiders: "Therefore, the conference which was called 'Arts and the Inner City' and sponsored by Columbia College of Chicago had to fail, and all other conferences of that nature must fail. Black, Brown, Mexican, Puerto Rican, and other colonialized artists will refuse to participate in this kind of exploitation of themselves and their people."[11] Although Valdez's pronouncement was ironic, it indicated the theorizing on the fly that often took place. Keeping the national or global picture in mind was important, but so was adjusting based on local realities and sensitivities.

At the beginning of June, John and Grace Killens landed in the Soviet Union to attend their first Alexander Pushkin Festival. Earlier in the spring, Irakly Abashize of the Soviet Writers Union telegrammed an invitation to visit the country. Expenses would be paid out of Killens's royalties for the translation of *And Then We Heard the Thunder*. Tanya Kudriavtseva followed with the suggestion that the Killenses make it to the Pushkin festival in Mikhailovskoye on June 4.

Hosts bearing flowers met the Killenses at the Moscow airport and drove them to the Peking Hotel, where they rested before boarding a midnight train to Leningrad. There, they visited the Moika Embankment and the old Pushkin residence, watching as people poured through the site to pay homage to the Father of Russian Literature. In the courtyard behind the apartment, the Killenses lingered at the statue of Pushkin before continuing on a guided tour into the field where Pushkin was mortally wounded in a duel.

The Killenses proceeded to the nearby town of Pushkin (formerly Tsarskoye Selo) and then on to Mikhailovskoye, the site of Pushkin's great-grandfather's estate, where thousands of people had gathered. Performers wearing folk outfits honored Pushkin with singing, dancing, poetry, and speeches. Killens addressed the crowd and spoke about his interest in Pushkin, his developing manuscript about the Russian writer, and his and Pushkin's "mutual African heritage."[12] Before the festival ended, the Killenses attended a memorial service at the Pushkin grave site. Critic Addison Gayle labeled both Pushkin and Killens "people's poets" whose revolutionary concern exceeded the desire for personal wealth and accolades and thus made them symbols for other "revolutionaries/romantics." Gayle surmised that when Killens stared down at Pushkin's crypt, "two centuries of history merged and one poet reached across the vast expanse of time and distance to embrace another."[13]

Back home, aside from a late-July trip to the University of Notre Dame to speak on the "Dynamics of Contemporary Education," Killens busied himself with the Pushkin project and other revolutionary/romantic writings. But he also had to square a debt with the man who had put him on the Pushkin trail. Harry Belafonte requested $1,200 that Killens still owed on loans extended over the previous eight years. Killens responded within a week, sending a cashier's check for $1,250 along with a note informing Belafonte that he had miscalculated by $50. Killens soon replaced the money, agreeing to write the novelization of *Slaves*, which Pyramid Publications would issue to coincide with the release of the movie the following spring. The deadline was tight; the manuscript had to be finished by January 15.

As he attended to his writing, Killens also shouldered some of the day-to-day weariness and dreariness of reform politics. If no real revolution was taking place at the moment, revolutionaries might as well leverage the vote as best they could. He became involved in the campaign for the seat in the newly created Twelfth Congressional District in Brooklyn. However, rather than support Shirley Chisholm, who would become the first African American woman elected to the U.S. Congress, Killens backed James Farmer out of respect for his history of activism and that of the Congress of Racial Equality. Killens served as a conduit for donations to Farmer, including four hundred dollars from Burt Lancaster. Killens also distributed fliers showing Farmer leading a 1964 march in Bogalusa, Louisiana, visually suggesting that Farmer, despite beatings, jailings, and threats of assassination, had never tried to evade the heat of leadership. Farmer spoke to the need to end "plantation politics in Brooklyn," to extract the nation from "this ugly war in Vietnam," to "dispel the shadows of both crime and despair," and to protect children both black and white from being victimized by a "destructive school system."[14]

Farmer's pollsters, and perhaps Killens as well, thought he would win the election handily, but his campaign faced two sticking points. One, the district was 90 percent Democratic, and Farmer underestimated the degree to which the Democratic machine could deliver for any Democratic candidate in the district, a task made even easier when the person in question was someone as impressive and capable as Chisholm. Two, Farmer had secured the endorsement of the Republicans. Although he ran as a member of the Liberal Party, he had invited both major parties to run him on their tickets as well. The Republicans leaped at the chance because Farmer's candidacy seemed to promise at least a respectable showing in a district they had written off. Farmer had no qualms about running as a Republican because he believed that African Americans should market their vote strategically. And Killens certainly had no allegiance whatsoever to the Democrats. But Farmer did not want to be allied with Richard Nixon and was concerned about "the possibility that I might drain away enough votes from Hubert Humphrey in Brooklyn to throw New York State to Nixon in a close presidential election. That possibility I found unconscionable." So in the strange world of Brooklyn politics, the Republican-Liberal Farmer called a press conference to endorse the Democratic Humphrey, which angered Brooklyn's Republicans and led them to delay and withhold financial support. Farmer lost by a margin of 2.5 to 1, a strong showing on Democratic turf. And he made history as well: as a friend reminded him, he was the first African American man in the nation's history to lose to an African American woman in a congressional race.

Killens left Brooklyn the day before the election, flying to San Francisco to begin a week of engagements in the Bay Area. He spoke at Merritt College, where numerous fliers urged people to vote for Black Panther and Peace and Freedom candidates: Eldridge Cleaver for president; Peggy Terry for vice president; Paul Jacobs for the U.S. Senate; Huey Newton for Congress; Bobby Seale and Bob Machado for the California Assembly; and Mario Savio for the state senate. Killens's next stop was Sacramento State College; then it was on to San Francisco State, where the Black Students Union had initiated a student strike a few days earlier as part of a push for black studies programs and special admissions. Killens expressed solidarity with the student activists, and his talk transpired without incident. He then flew on to lectures in Los Angeles and San Diego.

Killens briefly stopped in New York before heading south to Washington, D.C., for a Howard University conference, "Toward a Black University." Other participants included James Turner, Stokely Carmichael, Floyd McKissick, Sarah Webster Fabio, David Driskell, Sonia Sanchez, Nathan Hare, Ron Karenga, Max Roach, Harold Cruse, LeRoi Jones, Harry Edwards, Ossie Davis, and Loften Mitchell.

For the spring semester of 1969, Killens began teaching a graduate seminar in black culture and a creative writing workshop at Columbia University, where he had been a student twenty years earlier. He attracted ample young talent to his classes, including Askia M. Toure, poet and actress Saundra Sharp, poet and playwright Carole Gregory, and George Davis, who later wrote the novel *Coming Home*. Toure recalled that Killens possessed a "Dickensian sense of humor that was fabulous" and "would criticize you hard but rein you back in. He had a genuine curiosity about what the young writers thought and had extraordinary patience with students."[15] Gregory remembered his "dress-to-go-to-church clothes" and his habitual misbuttoning of his coat.[16]

Killens again found himself paired with Ralph Ellison, who assumed a teaching post at New York University in 1970. Gregory, who taught with Ellison, found him "not a friendly man at all," and she discovered that he held a low opinion of her instructor uptown.[17] Whatever ill will existed was one-sided, but Killens could hardly complain. He had started it.

Approximately a month after Killens returned to Columbia, he sat for an interview with reporter Earl Caldwell. In Killens's opinion, "Generally speaking, most black writers have decided to move from the realm of social protest to the realm of affirmation and revolution. What's being done is more positive. It's not just a protest of how bad white folks are treating us." But, Killens noted, black writers, who were often antiestablishment, had to go to the establishment to be published, a problem that could be solved by the creation of black publishing houses.[18]

The same week as the interview with Caldwell, Killens met with literary agent Ronald Hobbs to discuss the formation of Crosstown Books, a company designed to be controlled and directed by blacks. According to Hobbs, the matter had been discussed with Carter Smith of Time-Life Books, Ed Miller of World Publishing, Arthur Wang of Hill and Wang, and Virginia Matthews of the American Book Publishing Council. The plan required three years of initial investments of between $150,000 and $250,000 per year. One-third of the money would come from black businesses, one-third from Time-Life, and one-third from banks and coalition groups. On February 25, Hobbs wrote a summary memo to Killens and others involved, including John Henrik Clarke, Floyd McKissick, and Vincent Harding. Crosstown Books never took off, however.

Killens had other irons in the fire, too. The previous December, Jay Martin, a faculty member at the University of California, Irvine, had informed Killens that the director of the school's writing program, James Hall, was leaving. Martin, a member of the committee searching for Hall's replacement, had read Killens's writings, had worked with a student at Yale who had been greatly influenced by him, and had spoken to Herbert Biberman, who highly recommended Killens. In response, Martin had drummed up interest in Killens and was in position to make a "firm request" that he come to Irvine to teach.[19]

In March 1969, Killens made a three-day visit to Irvine, meeting with Martin, Howard Babb, Galway Kinnell, and other faculty members and spending time with members of the Black Student Union. On March 13, he delivered a lecture in the Writing Center, for which he received a $250 honorarium. By the time Killens returned to New York, however, he had probably already decided not to accept the position. He was not inclined to make a permanent move to California, and the idea of such a long commute made the offer unappealing despite the $20,000 salary and the full professorship. While in California, he suggested Ossie Davis, among others, as other possible choices for the director's position. Martin nevertheless sought to persuade Killens to accept the job, writing to him on March 20, "I don't have to repeat again how much I hope that you will come here—but I will repeat it as often as I can. The students here have been telling me how much they feel that they need you here." Despite such entreaties, Killens turned Martin down.[20]

Killens had already agreed to be considered for the position of John T. Dorrance Visiting Professor at Trinity College in Hartford, Connecticut. The Dorrance professorship brought two visiting faculty to campus each year, usually for six months each. Killens would be free to teach on any aspect of black culture and would not be tied to a specific academic department. Compensation would be between eight and nine thousand dollars plus a furnished apartment. Moreover, the school's proximity to New York meant that the position would not interfere with Killens's appointment at Columbia, for which he would receive fifteen thousand dollars during the 1969–70 academic year. Killens's tenure as the Dorrance professor ultimately began in January 1970. Killens also turned down a 1969–70 visiting professorship at Harvard University's Graduate School of Education.

As Martin had indicated, Killens made a strong impression on students. Nikki Giovanni, for one, wrote that Killens's workshop at Fisk offered "a place to meet that validated our spirits."[21] In March 1969, the Fisk graduate made a literary splash in New York City as she promoted her new volume of poetry, *Black Judgement*. Killens helped to sponsor an event at Lloyd Price's Turntable, at which three dollars gained patrons admission plus an autographed copy of Giovanni's book. On hand to perform were Jaci Early, Larry Neal, Barbara Ann Teer, Piri Thomas, Lorenz Graham, Jimmy Radcliff, and a relatively unknown thirty-two-year-old actor, Morgan Freeman.

On May 6, *Slaves* had its world premiere in Baltimore, an event that doubled as a benefit for the Baltimore Urban Coalition. Despite its $950,000 budget and a cast that included Stephen Boyd, Ossie Davis, Dionne Warwick, Barbara Ann Teer, Gale Sondergaard, and Julius Harris, the movie received mostly bad reviews, although it did good early business in both white and black neighborhoods, raking in $400,000 the first week in New York City and $60,000 in one week in one theater in Detroit. In Philadelphia, the second week beat the first. The same was true in Chicago, where the film outgrossed *The Wild Bunch* and *True Grit*. In the long run, however, critics' negative opinions could not be overcome, and the film did not have the impact for which Biberman had hoped.

Killens's novelization fared little better. According to *Publisher's Weekly*, the story reads "like the black answer to *Mandingo*"—that is, Killens had countered a simplistic, psychologically underdeveloped tale of black sexual animals lusting more after whites than after freedom with an equally simplistic, psychologically underdeveloped tale of slaves obsessed *only* with freedom.[22] But some proponents of the black aesthetic considered such countering a strong literary move. With William Styron's Nat Turner still on their minds, they supported an expanded fictional treatment, regardless of how stylized, of Killens's point that slaves' main preoccupation was emancipation rather than lust for whites or servile adaptation to the fact of enslavement. Although the story, like the movie, did not live up to Biberman's grandiose claims, *Slaves* furthered Killens's fiction project, begun in *Youngblood*, to render the southern experience with his sense of historical accuracy.

The story is a slender version of Stowe's novel.[23] Because of impending financial ruin, Mr. Stillwell separates Luke from his family and sells him, along with his sidekick, Jericho. They end up on a cotton plantation in Mississippi owned by Nathan Mackay and labor under physically harsher conditions than had existed on the Stillwell horse farm in Kentucky. Nonetheless, Luke's pride and spirit are never broken, even by beating. Spurred by the birth of a girl whom he helps to deliver and names after his wife, Esther, Luke plans an escape with Jericho. They would take along Cassy, Mackay's long-standing but now rebellious mistress; Evaline, his recent purchase; and the baby girl. The plan is discovered, and Mackay kills Luke, although the others escape. But despite the simple plot and the generally accepted evil of enslavement, ethical issues lie at the heart of the story.

As the novel opens, Luke, the head slave on the Stillwell farm, is returning to Kentucky after his master has sent him to Ohio on business. Luke voluntarily returns from the North to the South, a decision that puzzles Jericho, who dubs him the "slavest slave of all."[24] Even Luke's wife questions his decision to forgo his best chance at freedom, believing that he has acted irresponsibly. Luke explains his return by saying that his kindly master has promised to manumit him and his family. But the master's economic self-interest supersedes his good intentions, and Luke is not only separated from his family but sold south.

A second issue involves the slave's view of the sanctity of black life under slavery. As in *Uncle Tom's Cabin*, Cassy kills her child rather than have it grow up a slave. Years later, after a decade as Stillwell's house mistress, her senses dulled by a steady supply of rum, she has not relented in her view, at least not during the early stages of the novel. She shows no sympathy toward baby Esther, who is Mackay's daughter, and sees no point in the birth.

Slaves contains Killens's fullest commentary in fiction on Christianity. He recognizes that it is the most powerful system of values and beliefs among African Americans, so he chooses to encode his appeals for resistance within a more revolutionary interpretation of the Scriptures than Stowe managed. Indeed, the rhetoric of and about Christianity serves as the binding structural element, with the evolving Gospel of Luke (Stillwell) at the center. At the outset of the novel, Luke takes solace in the fact that he lives on a so-called Christian plantation. All the Stillwell slaves have been baptized. Luke does not perceive, as Jericho (walls come tumbling down) does, that slavery is wrong in the absolute and always must be actively opposed. Jericho believes that if the basic message in the Bible is to be subservient, then the God in the Bible is the Massa's God. When Luke recalls that the Bible says, "Servant, obey your master," Jericho rejoins, "If the Good Book say that, I don't need to learn to read." When Mr. Stillwell's faith crumbles under economic pressure and he sells Luke, Mrs. Stillwell protests, reminding her husband that as Christians they promised never to sell slaves to the South. He replies, "Christianity is one thing—slavery is something else altogether. . . . I have no intention of having my son come home from college to find I've let them take Stillwell Farms away from him." Luke takes his Bible with him to New Orleans. Several weeks later, on a Sunday morning, with church bells ringing all over the city as backdrop, Luke and Jericho are auctioned, along with Evaline, to Mackay.[25]

Mackay makes no pretense at being Christian: "I don't believe in villainy or virtue. Only in reality." After interrogating Luke, Mackay remarks sarcastically, "Taught you to read, gave you the Bible, then took and sold you down the river. That's a Christian for you. . . . Here. I'm giving you the Bible too, but *I'm* going to keep you. Understand?" Only when Luke's faith evolves to the point where he can be as realistic as Mackay does he stand a chance of changing his condition. Jericho has insisted all along that if they are to embrace God, they must also embrace the idea, as generations of African Americans have been taught, that God helps those who help themselves.[26]

While Luke is recovering from a brutal beating administered by overseers, he begins to gravitate more toward the Old Testament—in particular, the story of Moses leading the Israelites from bondage. Luke doubts that he could be a Moses, but he views Esther's birth as a providential sign and vows somehow to make a good life for her. Luke is further motivated after he works a party at the Big House, where he overhears Mackay lecture to his friends, "I took artists, sculptors, and turned them into niggers. And you got to keep them niggers twenty-four hours a day. You got to make them believe deep down in their hearts and souls they're niggers. The moment they stop thinking of themselves as niggers, you're in trouble. I wouldn't tolerate slaves on my farm that wouldn't call each other nigger."[27]

Later that night, down in the slave quarters, Luke acknowledges that Jericho has been a true Christian all along because he never tried to be a "good nigger" and never believed in "good massas." "You a Christian," Luke tells him, "cause you always knew slavery was the Devil's workhouse, and you always worked to bring the building down."[28] In this spirit of understanding and brotherhood, the insurrection is planned. Luke becomes a martyr, but Esther, Jericho, Cassy, and Evaline leave the plantation with the help of several slaves and white sympathizer Mrs. Bennett. As in his other novels, Killens defines success for African Americans, even that laced with tragedy, as resulting from communal action and belief in common ideals. If Christianity is to be prominent among those ideals, then Killens clearly aims to promote a Christianity that is revolutionary.

Several other aspects link *Slaves* to Killens's earlier fiction. Jericho is the resident folk wit. Luke is cast physically in the Youngblood-Chaney mode, "tall and straight and handsome-black." Cassy imagines him as an Ashanti warrior, a man of supreme dignity, and this image, this fearlessness, awakens her feelings of love and admiration. Cassy is described as "black and comely. . . . She was lovely, she was statuesque and queenly." Cassy is sustained in part by the collection of African masks, a link to the African past, kept in the Big House.[29]

Killens preferred his novel, which elaborately details Luke's movement from a sort of Uncle Tom to insurrectionist, to the movie. He acknowledged that Biberman was a "pretty good man" and "committed guy" but thought that the director became too fascinated with the Stephen Boyd–Dionne Warwick (Mackay-Cassy) connection, which diminished the focus on Ossie Davis (Luke).[30]

As *Slaves* in both forms began to circulate as part of public discourse, Killens took another shot at helping to construct an African American infrastructure in the arts by following a concept traceable to the American Negro Academy, founded by Alexander Crummell in 1897. A group that included Romare Bearden, C. Eric Lincoln, Oliver Cromwell Cox, Robert Hooks, Martin Kilson, Benjamin Quarles, John A. Williams, and Killens had met in New York City during the closing months of 1968 to sketch the parameters of what would become the Black Academy of Arts and Letters. With a three-year startup grant, fifty members formally founded the academy on March 27, 1969, in Boston. Lincoln, then a professor of religion and sociology at Union Theological Seminary, was elected president. Killens was elected vice president, with Alvin Poussaint as treasurer and Doris Saunders as secretary. These officers would serve as initial directors along with Vincent Harding, Charles V. Hamilton, Charles White, John A. Williams, and Robert Hooks.

In his founding address, Lincoln stated, "If what is black can also be excellent, the Black Academy of Arts and Letters is long overdue." When asked by a reporter if the group were separatist, a litmus test for some liberals, Lincoln replied, "It does not conceive of itself as separatist or integrationist or anything of the sort, but as a society for the promotion of black arts and letters."[31]

Although Killens was now in his mid-fifties, he continued to develop as a writer, though he never again reached the artistic heights of *And Then We Heard the Thunder*. He finished a story, "Rough Diamond," in which he displayed a black vernacular voice that also infused one of the novels on which he was still working, *The Cotillion*. Although Killens had employed such discourse as a significant feature in his prior novels, particularly with respect to dialogue and folklore, such discursive practice was framed by or entwined with naturalism or social realism and was never the dominant stylistic feature of those texts. He had written what Gayl Jones terms "composite novels."[32] In "Rough Diamond," he freed his voice and devoted his complete literary canvas to showing off urban black orality.[33] This development squared with the ideas espoused in his address at the previous year's Fisk conference. After having lived and worked in Harlem and Brooklyn for more than two decades, his ear had become finely attuned to the black urban rhythms that surrounded him.

The story centers on Bill Yardbird, who wins the National Book Award in 1964 for a book on Harlem in which he mostly trades in social pathology and shows "that jungle in all its true savagery and degradation." Reminiscent of Killens's 1952 review of *Invisible Man*, though ironically Yardbird is Killens's Rinehart, the author has the narrator exclaim, "I went Ellison one better, baby, ten times better. The father of the hero of my book had knocked up his wife, his mother, his three daughters, all in the same damn month." The black press denounces Yardbird as an Uncle Tom or a Gunga Din instead of an authentic "diamond in the rough," and he is chased from the community. He lives in Greenwich Village while maintaining a Harlem address.[34] Yardbird, the ever-backward pseudo-militant, eventually ends up behind the Iron Curtain and in bed with Elsatanya, his Russian guide and interpreter. The inspiration for Yardbird is a real writer, whom Killens declines to name (though it is undoubtedly Claude Brown), who was on television talking about how he had to get away from the "niggers" in Harlem. The use of that word alone, especially when not assigned to a fictional character, was enough to prompt Killens to respond. He saw no positive place in the Afro-American lexicon for the word, which he termed the "alpha and omega word of our degradation." To revel in "niggerness," he added, "is to wallow complacently on the dunghill of our white-imposed degradation like a pig in a pool of mud."[35]

As 1969 wound down, Killens attended to a series of tasks that spoke to his still-considerable status as a literary figure, educator, and public intellectual. Maya Angelou's autobiographical *I Know Why the Caged Bird Sings* neared release, and on October 2 Bob Loomis from Random House wrote to ask Killens to examine the galleys. Sarah Wright, too, was joining the ranks of published book authors, as Delacorte Press was releasing *This Child's Gonna Live*, five years after the debacle at Knopf. After receiving an advance copy, Killens wrote of one of his most consistent supporters, "More than a hundred years ago the Eastern Shore of Maryland gave this country Black heroes and heroines like Frederick Douglass and Harriet Tubman. Now Sarah Wright, herself of the Eastern Shore, has given us a heroine of epic proportions in Mariah Upshur."[36]

Family life provided Killens with additional blessings. Barbara gave birth to his first grandchild, Abiba ("the beloved one" in the Ewe language), on July 31, 1969.

Although Killens had turned down Martin's offer to come to the University of California, Irvine, Joseph White, director of the school's Program in Black Culture, updated Killens regarding the creation of a program in comparative culture that evolved from the Department of American Studies and featured undergraduate concentrations in African American, African, Asian, Chicano, and American culture. A proposal for a doctoral program was in the final stages of approval, and White hoped that both Killens and Harold Cruse would join the faculty, although neither man did so.

On December 4, Killens dropped in on a course at New York University, Writers on America, taught by Ronald Gross. The semester's subjects included Robert Penn Warren, Kurt Vonnegut Jr., Joseph Heller, Nat Hentoff, and John Oliver Killens. A week later, he arrived at the University of Illinois at the invitation of Val Gray Ward, director of the Afro-American Cultural Program. Ward conducted a television interview with Killens, who also lectured. As he approached his fifty-fourth birthday, Killens returned to New York to see out the 1960s. The decade of "sit-ins, freedom rides, voter registration, Muslims, name-changing, Marches-on-Washington, assassinations, soothsaying, mystic cults, black revolts in New York, Newark, Watts, Chicago, Detroit, Nashville and the District of Columbia, spasmodic rebellions in the streets and on the campuses" was over.[37]

CHAPTER TWENTY

Champeenship of Blackness, 1970–1971

During the spring 1970 semester, John Oliver Killens shuttled back and forth between New York and Hartford, where he was teaching a course on "The Dynamics of Afro-American Culture," the same course he taught at Columbia University. Although the calendar had been flipped past the 1960s, his semester at Trinity College began with 1960s-style drama. Black students decided to bar white students from the course. The Trinity Coalition of Blacks later issued a statement expressing its sympathy to white students who were excluded: "White students can and should understand that the suppressed Black desire for a meaningful course could not allow that this course with limited enrollment be dominated by white students."[1] Killens did not express opposition to the move: although he could be an effective public voice, he often was ineffective when forced to decide specific conflicts among real individuals. When matters became complicated, when there were personal attachments on at least two sides, he was far more Hamlet than Laertes. As Wynford Vaughan Thomas had noted in Africa, Killens wanted to be liked by all of the people all of the time. At Trinity in 1970, the people were militant black students. And, just as he managed relative to the COBRA dustup at Columbia College, the fifty-five-year-old Killens avoided becoming trapped on the wrong side of the people's immediate struggle. So the author who wrote, "I hope that colored men have watched Western men too long to commit the fatal folly of writing history with a 'colored' pencil" declined to explain that concept fully to the African American student pro-testers.[2]

Unlike at the Columbia College conference, Killens had the power to-tally in his hands to decide the matter and should have resolved it in favor of all the students registered for the class. Trinity College failed to force his or the students' hands, though, to be fair, the situation must have looked far more complex than it does in retrospect. Conversely, Killens's friend King would not have made the same mistake: he would have refused complicity with the notion that any practice of separatism represented the moral high ground.

Student activists were also on the march again at Fisk University. On Jan-uary 8, Killens learned from Paul Puryear, chair of the political science de-partment, that he and student protesters were under pressure from the ad-ministration and that several students faced court action and expulsion. By the time the author telephoned Puryear, the situation seemed to be improv-ing, and on January 12, Puryear wrote to advise Killens that a compromise had been reached and the situation required no further action at the mo-ment.

Killens's writing workshop at Columbia proceeded more smoothly. Poli-tics was not foreign to the occasion, but the students were earnest in their creative efforts and embraced Killens's guidance despite his somewhat heavy-handed approach. Make sure you state that premise concisely and clearly at the outset!

Never ceasing to be a student, Killens became engrossed in the fiction ex-periments of Ishmael Reed, which meshed with Killens's attempts at more structural originality and satiric wit in *The Cotillion*. He requested and re-ceived a review copy of Reed's latest novel, *Yellow Back Radio Broke-Down*. Although the two writers were far apart ideologically—Reed could never tolerate the political and aesthetic prescriptivism of Killens or anyone else—Killens, focusing for the moment more on stylistic freedom than thematic rigidity, seconded Reed's declaration, delivered by his character Loop Garoo to Bo Shmo, head of the "neo–social realist" gang, "No one says a novel has to be one thing. It can be anything it wants to be, a vaudeville show, the six o'clock news, the mumblings of wild men saddled by demons."[3]

Just as the 1960s had begun for Killens with the loss of a valued colleague, Louis Burnham, the 1970s started in similar fashion. On January 13, Alpha-eus Hunton, the "Unsung Valiant," succumbed to cancer in Zambia at the age of sixty-six. Dorothy Hunton sent the news from Lusaka, where the couple had relocated in 1967. John and Grace Killens responded with a letter expressing both their condolences and a wish to see her soon.

Killens swept through a typical run of speaking appearances and other cultural and political activities. He visited Newark to attend a press conference and support the Committee for Unified Newark. On February 25, he spoke at Francis Lewis High School in Queens at the invitation of the Afro-American Society, delivering a strong, problack, pro-education, antidrug message that pleased both the students and principal Edward Kramer. On March 1, he returned to the Carnegie Endowment when the Harlem Writers Guild and Random House hosted a publication party for Maya Angelou. Soon thereafter, the guild threw a separate party. Guild writers were indeed having an impact, at least by their own estimation: Paule Marshall wrote to Killens from Haiti, "The Cultural Revolution at home is making itself felt even here. The other day I saw a young Haitian brother wearing a dashiki crowned by a lovely bush of hair. We're slowly getting our message of Black love and acceptance across."[4]

Benjamin Hickok wished to bring a bit of the revolution to Michigan State University. Early in March, he informed Killens that the Department of American Thought and Language sought to hire a "distinguished and fairly gregarious Black writer-in-residence" for the 1970–71 academic year. The basic salary was sixteen thousand dollars, but Hickok felt that the offer could go as high as twenty to twenty-five thousand dollars with the cooperation of the Center for Urban Affairs and the dean of University College.[5] Killens had no qualms about turning down sixteen thousand dollars—he had come a long way—but he considered the high end before eventually declining.

Shirley Graham Du Bois wrote from Egypt around the middle of the month. The U.S. government would not allow her to enter the country, and she therefore could not accept an invitation to join the Black Academy of Arts and Letters for a celebration of her husband's legacy and to her regret would not be seeing Killens and other friends. The seventy-three-year-old Du Bois was surprised by the government's actions: "One might ask 'How can they dare?' But, in view of what is happening in our world today that's a futile question. They think they can get away with anything! Not, however, forever! The struggle will go on."[6]

On March 26, the immediate issue for Killens was the education of children through literature. He attended the award ceremony for the Council on Interracial Books for Children, a group founded by Bradford Chambers and others concerned with promoting multiethnic literature. Private individuals donated the awards because the council had failed to attract funding from organizations. Killens served as a judge, and Walter Dean Myers, a recipient the previous year, made the presentations to the winners: Sharon Bell Mathis, Virginia Cox, Margot Webb, and the Reverend James Streeter. Not wanting to be "an idiot," Mathis did not approach Killens at the event but wrote to him a few weeks later to express her admiration and discuss publishers, agents, and grant proposals.[7]

Killens next turned his critical eye toward the military. As he crafted the fictional world of *The Cotillion*, he was reminded of the problems he had examined in *And Then We Heard the Thunder*. Private Frederick Coss wrote to ask Killens to intervene on behalf of African American soldiers in Vietnam. Cross cataloged the abuses he and other black soldiers endured, concluding, "This place is nothing but the playground for the Ku Klux Klan. And they control just about every post. And the few Blacks that hold rank are considered to be 'Colored Boys.'"[8] Killens responded by firing off a letter to Congresswoman Shirley Chisholm, who represented his district. She wrote back early in May, explaining that she was already involved in three or four cases concerning the "mistreatment, abuse and humiliation" of African American soldiers in Vietnam. Chisholm promised to call Killens to discuss the matter when she returned to New York but advised that such situations required "massive united action."[9]

Killens began final preparations with regard to *The Cotillion*, trying to finish the galley proofs before he left the country to attend the International Association of Poets, Playwrights, Editors, Essayists, and Novelists (PEN) Congress to be convened in Seoul at the end of June. He would appear as a guest of honor, all expenses paid, at the invitation of the group's Korean Centre. His days also remained busy with teaching and other events. On April 13, he appeared at Abraham and Strauss in downtown Brooklyn at a "Voices of Brooklyn" conference cosponsored by the retailer and the Brooklyn Public Library in celebration of National Library Week. As a part of the observance, the library created a set of six posters for display in all branches. One poster in each set displayed a quotation from *And Then We Heard the Thunder*: "He wanted to believe whatever was left of the world would come to its senses and build something new and different and new and new and altogether different. What other hope was there?"[10] Killens joined Marshall, Pete Hamill, Sol Yurick, Joe Flaherty, and Frank Conroy on a panel on "Urban Writing: The Brooklyn Experience." For his next class at Trinity, he brought along Charles V. Hamilton as a guest speaker, a move the dean heartily approved. Hamilton, by then a faculty member at Columbia with Killens, was known widely as coauthor, with Stokely Carmichael, of *Black Power*.

On April 20, the PEN American Center held a cocktail party to honor Killens, who served on the group's executive board, Elizabeth Longford, Jay Neugeboren, Ishbel Ross, and Tom Ungerer for their latest books. Earlier in the month, Beacon Press released *The Trial Record of Denmark Vesey*, for which Killens had written the introduction. The book was the first complete reissue of a volume prepared in 1822 at the direction of the court in Charleston to spell out the trial proceedings, which had been closed to the general public. The book represented no major effort for Killens, but it did focus his attention on Vesey, another hero. He planned to write more about Vesey before someone in the mold of William Styron beat him to it.

At the end of the month, Killens spoke at the New York Society for Ethical Culture, where Howard "Stretch" Johnson worked as an assistant to executive director Khoren Arlslan Jr. Johnson organized a series of lecture discussions on "The History and Future of Afro-America" and invited his old friend to address "Unresolved Issues of the Effects of the Civil War and Reconstruction on Black Culture."

By the end of June, the galleys of *The Cotillion* were complete. Readers and critics would soon decide if in choosing comedy, as he had with his early chapters of "The Minister Primarily" and with "Rough Diamond," Killens had made it to the end of the tightrope that worried Angus Cameron. Had he avoided falling off into either realism or excessive farce?

The genesis of *The Cotillion*, as with most Killens stories, was autobiographical.[11] Clubwomen tried to get his daughter to become involved in a cotillion at the Waldorf-Astoria, but Barbara preferred to be immersed in political protest activities. According to her father, "She was into demonstrating, picket lines, sitting down in front of trucks, getting arrested, etc."[12] Nonetheless, Killens seized on the scenario to turn out a satire of the black middle class and disingenuous black nationalism, set sometime after the assassination of Malcolm X but before the murder of Martin Luther King Jr.

The Femmes Fatales, a group of bourgeois black women who supposedly represent the "first black families of Brooklyn," have invited Harlem resident Yoruba Evelyn Lovejoy, the story's protagonist, to participate in the Grand Cotillion to be held at the Waldorf. Yoruba and four other "dis-advantaged" Harlem girls are slated to "benefit" from the missionary kind-ness of Mrs. Patterson and other members of the organization, all of whom reside in the relatively upscale district of Crowning Heights, a fictionalized version of the Crown Heights neighborhood in which Killens lived. Yoruba, however, is ambivalent about participating in the pageantry. Her budding black nationalist identity and aesthetic do not easily accommodate the role of black debutante, essentially seen as mimicry of white middle-class mat-ing rituals and standards of beauty. The pressure to participate, to which she succumbs, is applied by her mother, Daphne Braithwaite Lovejoy, a light-skinned West Indian mulatto who identifies much more with Euro-pean culture than with that derived from Africa. By contrast, Matt Love-joy, who bestowed the name Yoruba on his only child, is a Georgia-born, coal-black, frustrated nationalist who has no allegiance to white mythol-ogy and symbolism. He has no illusions about the value of a cotillion for African Americans. White folks, he understands, devised these events so that their daughters would have a chance to meet, mingle with, and perhaps snare desirable, wealthy bachelors. But he sees no benefit in slavish imita-tion that amounts to no more than "just some more white folks' foolishness that don't git Blacks folks nowhere except in debt."[13] Ben Ali Lumumba, Yo-ruba's boyfriend and the story's narrator, plays a crucial role in assisting her preparations for the Grand Cotillion, while she helps him clarify cultural and political conceptions and resolve some of his self-doubts about black identity and activism—his shaky reliance on symbols, for example, includ-ing the phony British accent with which he sometimes speaks. Lumumba is also the key agent in Daphne's eventual psychological liberation when she, Lumumba, and Yoruba work as servants at a white cotillion in South-ampton. He explains to Daphne—and Killens explains to readers—that he would attack the African American bourgeoisie only in the context of scru-tinizing the actions of the European American bourgeoisie.

Yoruba and Lumumba eventually decide to subvert the Grand Cotillion, to make it truly black and beautiful by using it as a platform to critique the festivities. They don African garb; Yoruba wears her hair natural for the first time. It is, as Fred Hord points out in *Reconstructing Memory*, the "cul-mination of their demystification of colonial cultural repression and their resistance to its dehumanization."[14] Charles Johnson describes *The Cotillion* as a "'positive' Cultural Nationalist comedy shaped entirely by radical black views on art."[15] Indeed, the book reads like a Black Arts prose poem, rather

removed stylistically from the social realism of Killens's first three novels—
and is only half as long as any of those books.

With the galleys securely in the hands of Trident Press, Killens flew to
Tokyo and then on to Seoul, where the main theme of the conference, "Hu-
mour in Literature East and West," aligned squarely with his recent work.
Key topics examined included regional characteristics of humor, the function of humor in contemporary society, and the role of humor in the theater. Killens's talk, "Humor and the Black Tradition," was received with a
mixture of enthusiasm and politeness. In fact, Killens thought politeness
was the dominant tone of the conference, although he did witness some
tension: "The naughty boys were the Lebanese delegation acting like the
Arabs they were and casting disparagement and negative insinuations on
the Israeli, who were deeply wounded and indignant."[16]

Away from the conference site, Killens paid acute attention not solely
to humor but to the poverty in Seoul, gazing into the narrow, desolate al-
leys while riding a bus through the streets. He was mindful that the conference was a luxurious gathering compared to the blight on display. He
also spent significant time with John Cheever and his family, whom he described as "a wonderful clan. John always being clever and ironic like in his
books, very New England, and or British, in his enunciation, working very
hard and relaxedly at being the life and wit of the party." Killens considered
Mary Cheever serene and intelligent. She was also attentive and seemed
especially interested in Killens's stories, including his recollections about
his stint in the segregated military. Killens also entertained Federico, the
Cheevers' thirteen-year-old son, who was friendly, poised, and articulate.
One night, Killens poured sake into the boy's tea; his mother did not object,
at least not out loud. Federico declared that hanging out with Killens was
the best fun he had ever had.[17]

In addition, Killens chatted with John Updike and his daughter, whom
he considered to be her father's spitting image. Updike had been published
in Korea and was received like a movie star but took his celebrity in stride
and was very graceful in his dealings with the locals. Killens thought Updike's speech was one of the best at the conference, touching on writers as
diverse as Cervantes and Twain.

More noteworthy than the Cheevers and Updikes, in Killens's eyes, was
the beauty of Korean women. He remarked after a folk festival, "Any dance
the Korean women do is OK with me." In particular, the *keinsing*, the Korean version of the geisha, impressed him. Back in Tokyo, Killens made a

rather extensive tour of the geisha scene, and he and Cheever hatched a joking plan to open up a geisha house in New York with an educational grant obtained from the Ford Foundation.[18]

Grace wrote to wish her husband well and keep him posted on developments at home. Chuck, now twenty-six years old and out of the hospital, was doing fairly well and had seen the doctor for his prescription and a consultation. Barbara, Barry, and Abiba were doing fine. One of his workshop students, Janet Tarver, had been evicted from her apartment and had subsequently ensconced herself in the Killens home. "Ensconced," Grace exclaimed, "I looked up the spelling."[19]

On the way back to New York, Killens spent time with Nathan Hare and his wife, Julia, in San Francisco. Hare had founded *The Black Scholar* the previous year and invited Killens to serve as a contributing member of the editorial board. The two men discussed having Killens write an article for the journal that drew on his experiences as an African American in the labor movement. "The brothers need to know such actual occurrences," Hare reasoned, "rather than just more grand theory."[20]

Back in the United States, the July 25 issue of *TV Guide* featured Killens's article, "Our Struggle Is Not to Be White Men in Black Skin," which provoked the sort of criticism he encountered whenever he published an opinionated piece in the national press. Although African Americans were no longer absent from television, he questioned whether genuine progress had occurred. He reported the opinions of several informants, including some members of his black culture seminar at Columbia:

> Miss L. said, "Ain't nothing happening."
> Mr. K. said, "All of them—*Julia*, Leslie Uggams, Della Reese, all those shows—are just White folks masquerading in Black skin."
> Mr. F. said, "That cat in *Mission: Impossible* is the natural end. He's the White folk's handy man. They should call the show, 'I Was a Stooge for the CIA.' I mean, like what you're always talking about, Brother Killens, he puts you in the mind of good old Gunga Din."

Killens argued that, in the final analysis, "the play is the fundamental thing, not the players," and if television were ever to render effectively the "great, throbbing, dramatic thing" that is life in the African American community, African American writers and other staff would have to be employed to achieve "Black conceptualization."[21] An anonymous writer from Los Angeles kept Killens in touch with an America he was certain he still knew:

"JOHN OLIVER KILLENS! JUST A NOTE TO SAY YOUR ARTICLE STUNK!!
BUT KEEP TRYING TO PERMOTE THE BLACK PEOPLE BECAUSE YOU WILL
SOON BE OUT OF WORK!! STOP PUSHING! WHY JOIN LUTHER KING."[22]

Killens dismissed such ignorant negative reactions, but he engaged in
an elaborate exercise of self-criticism at the request of John A. Williams,
who was working on the second installment of the journal *Amistad*. Williams had interviewed Chester Himes for *Amistad 1* and lined up Killens to
be the subject of an interview for *Amistad 2*. Williams then suggested that
Killens do the piece as a self-interview, and he agreed. In a wide-ranging
discourse—the published version runs forty pages—he covered such familiar ground as his decision to become a writer; his experiences with Langston Hughes, W. E. B. Du Bois, Paul Robeson, Martin Luther King Jr., and
Malcolm X; his appreciation of Margaret Walker's poetry; his belief in the
political, race-influenced nature of art; and his pride in the Harlem Writers Guild, which he felt had the best record of productivity of any writers'
workshop in the nation. He also commented on the shortcomings of some
of his political analyses, as represented, for example, by his youthful expectation that a multiethnic workers' alliance would, without the need for any
substantial appeal to nationalism, fundamentally transform the American
system. Mindful of attacks he had both levied and received and anticipating controversies about black political and cultural direction as part of the
battle for what he facetiously termed "The World Heavyweight Champeenship of Blackness," he asserted seriously, "I think I'm a man who has made a
helluva lot of mistakes in my time, but I have always been in there pitching.
I have always worked for Black liberation."[23]

While Killens enmeshed himself in reflection, Hare desperately wanted
the article for *The Black Scholar*, which remained unfinished. The piece,
"Black Labor and the Liberation Movement," proved polemical rather than
the memoir originally discussed, but it nevertheless was probably Killens's
best essay since those in *Black Man's Burden*. He argued the Black Liberation movement was running out of energy. The civil rights integrationist
organizations were, in his view, senile and obsolete, and Black Power advocates were powerless. He specifically addressed the "heroic resistance"
of the Black Panthers and their misguided championing of the lumpen element in the black community as the revolutionary catalyst. He also labeled
"revolutionary suicide," a phrase popularized by Huey Newton, futile—
"about as realistic in terms of furthering the liberation of black people as
Buddhist immolation by fire has been in ending the war in Viet Nam." Kil-

lens described the biggest weakness in current black political organizing as the failure to recruit the African American working class, which remained the most numerous and most potentially dynamic segment of the African American community. The working class outnumbered both the African American middle class, which according to Killens had set too much of the black political agenda, and the lumpen element romanticized by groups such as the Black Panthers. "The vanguard is beautiful, dramatic, inspirational and necessary," he wrote, "but the army is where it's at." After pointing out the historical failures of a labor movement hamstrung by racism and considering the extent to which Marxist thinking underplayed the influence of racism and the corruption of the white working class in industrialized nations, he cited the necessity of a national black congress, an organization whose "first loyalty and primary concern" would be to a black agenda—"Jobs, housing, education, culture, political and economic power, black control of black rank-and-file unions. In a word, black liberation."[24] Killens still saw much of the world in terms of a capitalism/anticapitalism dialectic, but by the 1970s, he had become certain that the best hope for black people lay in black political initiatives.

In October, just as "Black Labor and the Liberation Movement" appeared, a visitor from Australia, Stuart Sayers, asked Killens to refocus on literary matters, interviewing him over drinks at a bar during the World Series. Though Killens's attention kept shifting to the game, Sayers, who wrote for *The Age*, a Melbourne-based periodical, turned their conversation into an article, "With Color on His Mind," in which Killens discussed his career and plans and race relations in Australia. Sayers sent a copy to Killens along with the hope that "it expresses the spirit of our conversation."[25]

While Killens kept his name in periodicals and waited for the release of *The Cotillion*, he turned his attention to several matters involving the Black Academy of Arts and Letters. Following widespread protests by several members of Congress—Shirley Chisholm, Adam Clayton Powell Jr., Edward Koch, and John Conyers—as well as Senators Edward Brooke and Jacob Javits, Shirley Graham Du Bois received clearance to visit the United States. On September 20, she attended the academy's annual meeting, where she received a citation acknowledging her late husband's election into the group's Hall of Fame. At a November 1 follow-up meeting of the board of directors, which Killens attended, the academy took up the questions of W. E. B. Du Bois's grave site, which was already in ruins, and his papers, which needed a repository. Killens later discovered that his widow had paid her own airfare to attend the ceremony. Because the academy had invited her to appear, Killens believed that it should reimburse her. He wrote to fellow board member C. Eric Lincoln, who readily concurred, and by December, she had received a check for nearly eleven hundred dollars.

During the holiday season, Killens heard from the widow of another icon. Coretta Scott King's year-end letter extended her greetings and updated her friends on her thoughts and experiences during the past year. She spoke of the need for a "revitalized peace movement to complete the honorable task of ending, totally, one of the most tragic and unspeakable mistakes in American history." She optimistically sensed, with the 1970 elections, the "beginning of a new politics, a politics of government responsive to the people—*all* people." She saw the formation of a coalition of "black and white, young and old, rich and poor" that represented for her the best future for American politics in general and southern politics in particular. King offered updates on other matters, including the work of the Martin Luther King Jr. Memorial Center, the resumption of her Freedom Concerts, and her involvement with the Southern Christian Leadership Conference, Southern Rural Action, Local 1199, the National Committee of Inquiry, Clergy and Laymen Concerned about Vietnam, and the Commission on Economic Justice for Women.[26]

In January 1971, *The Cotillion* was published. The *New York Times* weighed in favorably—twice. Despite the reviewers' positive treatment, Killens objected to the statement by James R. Frakes that his book was not what "timid traditionalists" have agreed to call a novel.[27] The author seemed to want credit for both breaking and maintaining form. In the second *Times* review, Thomas Lask described the novel as "effervescent, bubbly, mirth-flecked, farce-studded, jumping" and "sober serious." He added, "What gives 'Cotillion' its special cachet is the author's attitude to the people in the book. It is sheer love. He loves them with their cro[t]chets, blind spots, hang-ups, vanities, weaknesses of flesh and intellect. They can be dead wrong but they are not evil." Lask compared Killens to Aldous Huxley but "without the older writer's acidulousness and intellectual despair."[28]

Jean Carey Bond gave the book a mixed review in *Freedomways*, a publication that never coddled Killens despite his in-group status. Bond applauded the "uproariously satirical moments" but found Lady Daphne problematic, a character of "blubbering idiocy," and thought Ben Ali Lumumba ultimately vacuous. Bond compared the novel to Chester Himes's

Pinktoes but stressed that Himes is never apologetic, whereas Killens wishes for approval, a weak trait in a satirist: "His uptightness is no more apparent than in the choice of a cotillion as the story's focus, an event that is ultimately able to redeem itself by turning black—a dubious turn of events if you think about it."[29] Loften Mitchell told the author that the book "is a song, a haunting, sweet song that runs the gamut. It is a song of sadness, a song of hope, bitter, bitter-sweet, sweet, clean, refreshing, vital, vigorous, emphatic, well-defined, well-orchestrated."[30] Novelist Sam Greenlee found *The Cotillion* uneven, with the superb treatment of Harlem life artistically dwarfing the Brooklyn scenes: "Presumably, the writer intended a contrast between the vibrant Harlem life style and the deadly dull fantasy lives of black bourgeois socialites. But as social-historical freaks, the characters, intended as comical, are simply not very funny. You can't parody a parody." Greenlee acknowledged that "the most jive word a book reviewer can lay on a book is 'uneven'—but *The Cotillion* is uneven for the best of reasons: The good portions make the rest seem much worse than they are. I'd settle for that any day."[31] Kay Greaves called the novel a "must-read" but cautioned, "Don't expect this to be another 'Youngblood' or ''Sippi,' or 'And Then We Heard the Thunder.' ... This is a whole new ballgame, written NOW for TODAY."[32] John A. Williams also noted and approved of the stylistic and thematic changes: "No doubt about it, John Killens' best so far in terms of content, style, and structure."[33]

The Cotillion stands as one of Killens's most successful books. Along with receiving critical acclaim, it proved commercially viable and was nominated for the Pulitzer Prize, and it offered Killens his best shot at commercial success on Broadway. Producers James and Joseph Nederlander bid on the play but insisted that Killens not be involved in the adaptation, thereby scuttling the deal. Motown Records then optioned the novel for a Broadway musical. However, disagreements about the Long Island scene soon arose. Motown executive Rob Cohen found the white cotillion "a bone in my throat. It is too extreme. Perhaps it should be eliminated altogether. We will need the fullest discussion of this point. We need something to convert Lady Daphne but it has to be more believable."[34] According to Killens, Cohen said that "to include the bash out on Long Island would make the ultimate Black cotillion at the Waldorf anti-climactic. Besides it would mean paying all those white actors to appear in one scene." But Smokey Robinson, who was slated to write the music, privately told Killens, "Bullshit! Bob just doesn't like the way you handled that white cotillion out there in Southampton." Killens reworked the script to have Daphne, Yoruba, and Lumumba parody the white cotillion after working it, but Cohen remained dissatisfied, complaining that while the black characters were treated with love, the white characters were treated like beasts. When Killens did not respond, Cohen continued, "Well, Mr. Killens, white folks may very well be beasts, but you can't say so on Broadway." Motown let the option expire, and Killens felt that the incident left him with a reputation for being intractable.[35] But the pattern was not new. He had had similar disagreements with Haskell Wexler and to a much lesser extent Angus Cameron.

Killens lent his usual energy to promoting the novel throughout the winter and spring of 1971. He returned to Fisk University on February 13 both to talk up the novel and to conduct a workshop, "The Hero Image in Black Literature," as part of a faculty development project in the teaching of black literature and creative writing. A day later, his new grandson, Barra, meaning "spirit of Ra," entered the world.

In March, Killens undertook a whirlwind West Coast trip coordinated by *The Black Scholar*. After landing in the Bay Area on March 7, he rushed to an Angela Davis rally and gave a ten-minute speech. He then proceeded to Dick Bancroft's house for drinks and on to a reception hosted by Jane Fonda. The following afternoon he lectured at San Francisco State before attending a dinner/book party and then a screening of the Muhammad Ali–Joe Frazier fight. Although Ali lost, Killens loved the way he immediately scrambled to his feet after the fifteenth-round knockdown. That was the fighting heart he cherished.

The next day, Killens gave a presentation at the University of California, Santa Barbara, staying there overnight before traveling to California State Polytechnic College, where Lorenz Graham, a member of the faculty, met him, and Killens spoke. The next stop was Claremont College, followed by Stanford University. Another dawn and Killens moved on to the Earl Warren Legal Center at the University of California, Berkeley. He flew to Portland, Oregon, the next day and lectured at Lewis and Clark College and Reed College.

The pace eased up somewhat when Killens returned to New York. On March 14, the Greenwich Village–Chelsea branch of the National Association for the Advancement of Colored People threw a party for him, with a Black Academy of Arts and Letters event following a week later. Killens was featured on *Black Pride*, Alma John's television show, on March 26 and was on hand for another reception on March 28. Killens invited Angus Cameron to attend, perhaps to chide him a bit. If he had fallen off the tightrope, it had not been too drastic a spill. But the editor could not make it; however, he wrote to offer plaudits: "I have seen two people on the commuting trains reading COTILLION and, of course, have been sharing your pleasures vicariously at the reviews."[36] Herbert Biberman and his wife, Gale Sondergaard, were reading *The Cotillion*, but Biberman's health prevented him from joining in any of the celebrations: "This will be the first of your book parties I will miss. And you may believe it, it hurts me much worse than it does you." Biberman also congratulated Killens on having "broken out of the confines of novel space into a 'free-fall' characterized by joyousness and, as one reviewer so magnificently pointed out, by the most intense love of those carrying the glowing quality of negritude."[37]

Columbia University president William J. McGill expressed his pride that Killens was a member of the university's faculty, but Killens had begun to make moves that would lead to his departure. Northwestern, Harvard, and Howard were bidding for his services. Northwestern offered him the option of teaching one or two quarters at eighty-five hundred dollars each during the 1971–72 academic year. Killens entertained the idea of commuting, but the dean of the school's College of Arts and Sciences frowned on the idea. Killens's old friend Ewart Guinier, head of African American studies at Harvard, spearheaded that school's recruitment effort. Guinier was the attraction at Harvard. But James Edward Cheek, Howard's thirty-eight-year-old president, argued, "I think you are a fine writer, but I think if you're going to be at a university, you should be at one where you will be in touch with thousands of Black students." Cheek's argument carried great weight with Killens because he often received reminders of his impact on African American students. Recently, for example, Benjamin Foster Jr., who had studied with Killens at Trinity College, had been inspired to found the John O. Killens Theater Group in Hartford.[38]

While he considered his next academic move, he was devastated by the news that his favorite protégé at Fisk, twenty-seven-year-old Donald (Dante) Graham, had been killed in an automobile accident on a Tennessee highway while returning to Fisk from a reading engagement. He expressed his sorrow to Graham's widow, Flora, who was due to give birth at the end of the year, reminding her, "You have Dante's and your child to live for and all the other children in the world. They are all your children and my children, and all of us work to make the lives of all the children in the world more worth living. This is the legacy Dante left us."[39] Flora Graham, in turn, wrote to let Killens know how much he had meant to her husband: "You encouraged Dante at a time when few saw his talent. You stood by him thru his trials and troubles. I pray that you know how much Dante respected, loved and trusted you, John.—you were a friend, colleague and the closest he ever came to having a father."[40]

Killens kept moving forward. He revamped his Vesey manuscript, scaling it down to an adolescent novel for quick publication. He obsessed over the Alexander Pushkin project. He subleased the apartment of Brock and Dee Dee Peters, who had engagements in Los Angeles, so that he could work more intently, and he prepared for a three-week trip to the Soviet Union to conduct research. Before leaving, he appeared on a radio program, "The Soul of Reason," hosted by Roscoe C. Brown Jr. and broadcast on WNBC-FM. He traveled by train to participate in a May 15 conference on "Unity through Communication" at the University of Delaware. He also made another trip to the University of California, Santa Barbara, one to UCLA, and one to Fisk.

Killens left for the Soviet Union in early June, describing the voyage as "cramped and tiresome. Close quarters, noisy, happy singing passengers. We stopped in London for an hour and a half. Arrived Moscow 4:15 P.M. Frieda and Laresa, an interpreter met me with flowers at the airport. . . . Left Moscow on a train at Midnite for Leningrad—Had 2 ½ busy days in Leningrad, then off to Pskov?, where I am writing this at 1 P.M."[41] To his audience in Pskov, he brought "greetings and fellowship from the Black writers of America who are dedicated to the same commitment as was Pushkin—that is—the liberation of mankind so that man everywhere can live in peace and freedom."[42]

The trip was much more of a chore than his earlier visit to the Soviet Union. There was less wonderment but more study and diligent observation. After visiting Novogorod and Kalinin, Killens returned to Moscow for ten days of research. He took copious notes, both from texts and from the social milieu. Every movement or sound, every landscape or social setting, every legend or fact of history had to be evaluated for its worth as material for the novel. Killens had previously spoken at length about Pushkin with Paul Robeson Jr. and while in the Soviet Union made use of information Robeson provided.

On his way back to New York, Killens spent a couple of days in London visiting with George Lamming. Killens then completed a three-part prison exposé for the *Amsterdam News*. Although the title asked "Brutalization or Rehabilitation?" the series did not result from open-minded investigative reporting. Before Killens toured the Manhattan House of Detention (widely known as the Tombs), the Brooklyn House of Detention, and Rikers Island, he already knew several of the major facts: an overwhelmingly disproportionate number of prisoners were African American and Puerto Rican; the New York City prison system had no program for curing drug addicts, despite an ongoing heroin epidemic; the recidivism rate was astronomical; and many of the victims of inmates released into African American and Puerto Rican communities were the residents of those communities. Moreover, Killens already agreed with his good friend, journalist Samuel Yette, that a conspiracy existed against America's "Blackpoor." "I have been told that I am paranoid," Killens offered. "But like I always say, a man who is apprehensive while walking in a rattlesnake farm is not suffering from paranoia. Those snakes are a reality."[43]

Later in the summer, Killens decided that he would move to Howard University. His initial appointment, brokered by Andrew Billingsley, vice president of academic affairs, would be for three years at an annual salary of twenty-five thousand dollars. He would stay on at Columbia at half his former load and salary. He neglected to inform Northwestern that he had accepted Howard's offer until August, although he told Harvard's Guinier in late June. Guinier responded with disappointment: "There's hardly another person that would bring on the things that you have. There are several students who will be deeply disappointed. They had looked forward so much to the writing course. And of course, the University as a whole will be worse off—except possibly the budgeters."[44]

Killens had also been lax in responding to Margaret Walker's invitation to participate in the Summer Institute in Black Culture for College Teachers that she planned to direct at Mississippi's Jackson State University. Walker was slated to teach the course on black American literature, with Killens, Saunders Redding, Dudley Randall, Loften Mitchell, and Alice Walker serving as consultants. Walker was counting on Killens, and he would not disappoint a woman he sometimes called the Empress of the Black Experience. Before going to Mississippi, John and Grace composed condolence notes to Jackie and Rachel Robinson on the death of their son, Jackie Jr., who had been killed in an automobile accident, and one to Sondergaard on Biberman's passing.[45]

Long-Distance Running, 1971–1974

John Oliver Killens's return in the fall of 1971 was part of Howard University's effort to create a major presence relative to contemporary African American culture. Not only was Killens employed as a writer in residence, working across the boundaries of the English department and the Institute for the Arts and Humanities with black culture seminars and writing workshops, but Haki Madhubuti was hired as well. Three days each week, Killens immersed himself in campus activities before driving back to New York in his brand-new Pontiac Le Mans to teach the writing workshop he maintained at Columbia University. He began teaching a series of courses that included fiction- and film-writing offerings. In addition to his own swelling collection of notes and *The Cotillion*, he drew on such texts as Lajos Egri's *The Art and Craft of Dramatic Writing*, Cleanth Brooks and Robert Penn Warren's *Understanding Fiction*, Lewis Herman's *A Practical Manual of Screen Playwriting*, Richard Wright's *Uncle Tom's Children* and *Native Son*, Margaret Walker's *How I Wrote Jubilee*, Ralph Ellison's *Invisible Man*, and John A. Williams's *The Man Who Cried I Am*.

Moreover, Killens's family and friendship ties made him just as busy in Washington, D.C., as in New York. His life certainly had grown no simpler or less stressful. He was back in New York on September 9, for example, for the official opening of Medgar Evers College, five blocks from his home. He also returned to pay tribute to his mother-in-law, who died in Brooklyn on January 30 at the age of eighty-one; he praised her dignity, humor, "great humanity," and "zest for life." She understood, in Killens's view, the essential paradox of life: "Life was essentially tragic-comic, and therefore one should take life seriously, but never to the extent of not being able to laugh at life sometimes, to laugh at one's crosses, to poke fun at adversity."[1] Either Killens read much of his own life into hers, or they had much in common.

After he established his presence at Howard, campus and community groups factored him into a steady stream of events. He was featured, along with psychiatrist Alyce Gullattee and journalist Samuel Yette, at a faculty forum held at the School of Social Work on "Black Survival and the Uses of Knowledge." He became involved with the Center for Clinical Legal Studies at Howard Law School and served as an officer at a public hearing on "The Administration of Justice in the District of Columbia" that fed into a later symposium on "Crime and Punishment in Minority Communities," at which Killens presented a paper.

As always, public involvement slowed but never derailed Killens's writing. He began looking for an outlet for the Pushkin story, writing to Dudley Randall about the possibilities at Broadside Press. Randall, primarily a publisher of slender poetry collections, could only dream about printing the novel, which ultimately was the longest book of Killens's career. However, Randall expressed interest in a Killens-authored children's book about Pushkin.[2]

Doubleday released Killens's adolescent novel, *Great Gittin' Up Morning*, which revolved around Denmark Vesey's 1822 insurrection in South Carolina. Killens was most intrigued by Vesey's status as a fairly prosperous free man whose wife and children were slaves. Killens portrays a hero whose love for family and brethren and absolute hatred of American slavery compels him to arms despite his relatively secure status. Vesey is a more commanding figure than the equivocating though ultimately heroic Luke Stillwell of *Slaves*. Vesey already has what Luke and the others seek—freedom—but risks it in an attempt to liberate masses of blacks.

Details of Vesey's early life are sketchy, and Killens takes license to create events and characters, depicting Vesey as uncommonly handsome and imposing, like all of Killens's male protagonists to date. However, the latter parts of the novel—the thwarting of the rebellion, the trials and hangings—remain quite faithful to the historical record and to Vesey's character and temperament as a Talented Tenth role model.

Reviewer Rosalind Goddard appreciated the history lesson but thought that the book came up short stylistically, labeling it verbose and not subtle enough, detracting from Vesey as a character. Killens was no stranger to such charges. Other readers offered ample support, however. After the author sent a copy of the book to Paul Puryear's son as a birthday present, Puryear replied, "*Great Gittin' Up Morning*—my, my my!!! What could a boy get for his 11th birthday that could be more dynamic, more rewarding, more pleasurable, more meaningful, more encouraging as he looks toward the arrival of his black manhood at age 12? Nothing could do all this except *Great Gittin' Up Morning*—which does all those and more." The boy, who had resisted his parents' earlier attempts to induce him to read books on topics other than sports, enjoyed the novel so much that he took it to school. Puryear also encouraged Killens to write more adolescent novels as pedagogical and ideological tools.[3]

Although the publicity push for *Great Gittin' Up Morning* amounted to only a tiny fraction of the effort on behalf of Killens's adult novels, the media still took some notice. On March 9, Pam Fields interviewed the author for radio station WBAL in Baltimore. The month also featured autograph parties in honor of both Killens and Chester Himes, whose autobiography, *The Quality of Hurt*, Doubleday had also just published. Killens described Himes's book as "the story of a Black American hero who refused to give up and his name will be remembered centuries after those who hurt him have long since been forgotten."[4]

On April 27, the film *Buck and the Preacher* had its New York City premiere. Killens thought that the movie constituted perhaps the most important African American artistic expression to emerge in a decade. "Here we had a flick," he reflected, "that taught us history, raised the question of land, raised the question of Black men and Red men, First World People uniting against the common foe. Here was a work of art that proved that art could teach even as it entertains."[5]

By then, Killens had picked a fight with Melvin Van Peebles over a movie released a year earlier. In "The Crisis in Black Writing," Killens criticized Van Peebles's *Sweet Sweetback's Baadasssss Song*, which is generally regarded as having ushered in Hollywood's blaxploitation era. Although the movie was in fact an independent production—no studio would finance it—its commercial success pointed the studios to the gold mine available in low-budget action films with predominantly African American casts. Killens's problem with *Sweetback*, in which a performer in a sex show improbably turns into a political outlaw and relies heavily on his sexual prowess to escape to Mexico, was the proliferation of what he considered to be negative images: "Who would have believed it possible that in 1965, in the midst of the era of our beautiful blackness (and now in 1971), we would still be looking at ourselves through the eyes of white America, that we would still regard ourselves as shitty, funky niggers?" Killens noted, "The great black prophetic writer, David Walker, did not write his *Appeal* to the 'niggers' of the world." After cycling through his familiar criticisms of the mainstream media and reissuing his call for writers to create noble and heroic dramas about the black experience, Killens refocused on *Sweetback* and observed, "Here is a sick-sick-woman-hating movie being hailed by some of our esteemed black critics as a cinematic breakthrough. Breakthrough for whom? Certainly not for black people." Killens went on to propose how black works of art should be evaluated: "Can we see and hear and feel the spiritual, poetic and idiomatic rhythm of black life and black expression? Does this work bring black people into artistic touch with that which is beautiful, unifying, humanistic, liberating and deniggerizing in the black experience?"[6]

Huey Newton offered an elaborate, well-reasoned, and sometimes brilliant defense of the movie that represented an affirmative response to Killens's questions, although Killens thought little of Newton's rationale. Newton argued that *Sweetback* exemplifies a positive community spirit and encompasses a liberating ethic, concluding that the character "is a Sweet Sweetback because he has come to understand that freedom, liberation, and the ability to love requires that first of all you have to recapture the holy grail; you have to restore your dignity and manhood by destroying the one who took it from you. When you do that, even if you do not completely escape, you are a dangerous man because after that the oppressor knows that you will no longer be submissive."[7] A film with the themes of African American dignity and manhood was precisely the sort of project Killens advocated, but his prudish side blocked him from viewing Van Peebles's effort in those terms.

On May 14, as part of the African Lecture Series at the American Museum of Natural History, Killens moved on to another topic, "The Significance of Black History." Later that week, he obliged Gary Simpkins and Cicero Wilson's request that he participate in a Harvard Graduate School of Education conference on "Language Problems and the Urban Child," joining outstanding thinkers George Cureton, Geneva Smitherman, Beryl Bailey, Ernie Smith, Grace Holt, and Walter Dean Myers.

Meanwhile, trouble brewed inside the Black Academy of Arts of Letters. The organization had made little headway toward achieving its goals—most glaringly, it had failed to purchase Langston Hughes's home, which the group sought to preserve and use as a headquarters. Although less than $200 from each academy member would have raised the money needed to purchase the structure, donations were not readily forthcoming. In April, academy president C. Eric Lincoln sent out a strong appeal for contributions, but over the next four months, only a few members ponied up, and only $3,485 was collected, with $1,250 of that amount coming from non-member Harry Belafonte.

Early in June, Killens heard from his former teacher, Dorothy Brewster, now almost ninety years old. Although Brewster did not keep up with contemporary fiction, she had read reviews of *The Cotillion* and hoped to read the book. She felt isolated from Columbia: her crowd had retired, moved away, or died. Nevertheless, she was pleased that Killens was at Columbia and doing well. Unfortunately, he was not doing as well as she imagined. On June 8, as Brewster's letter was being routed toward him, Killens left a hectic Black Academy of Arts and Letters meeting in Suite 518 at 475 Riverside Drive, not far from Brewster's home. He promptly fell down the stairs, having suffered a stroke. Killens was rushed to St. Luke's Hospital, where he was hospitalized for three weeks.

The get-well cards poured in, along with a series of demands and commands. According to Kristin Hunter, Killens had inherited Hughes's role as the "kindest and most helpful Black writer in America," but, she felt, he should become more selfish so he could continue writing *"for all our sakes."*[8] George Lamming wrote, "I believe I may have hinted to you in the past that your programme struck me as rather more than anyone should be carrying. But cool it for the time being, and try to keep it cool for as long as possible."[9] Hoyt Fuller weighed in: "Just want to say that you have no right at all to be risking your health and life. As a national Black resource, we who need you have to demand that you do what the doctors order."[10] Dudley Randall explained that Gwendolyn Brooks had had to give up commuting between Chicago and New York, and he urged Killens to ease up so that he could remain a living source of inspiration.[11] Ruby Dee said that she would not lecture about diet and so forth—*now.*[12] Romare Bearden reflected, "What with all the tensions of New York and modern living it's a wonder how we do manage to carry on as well as we do."[13] Harry Belafonte, Alex Haley, Verta Mae Grosvenor, Willie and Melba Kgositsile, and Pierce Brunson were among those who sent notes, as were Vincent Harding, William Strickland, and the entire staff of the Institute for the Black World. Amiri Baraka stated simply, "Distressed + upset."[14]

As Killens lay disabled, his father died in Illinois. Killens agonized that he could not travel to pay his last respects to the man who had been his greatest influence. No number of well-wishers could lessen the sense of loss, with which the author later grappled in fiction.

And FBI agents again were monitoring him. While in Jackson, Mississippi, during the summer of 1971, Killens had met and conversed at length with Imari Abubakari Obadele, president of the Republic of New Africa, a militant nationalist group that the FBI considered extremist. Although a May 1971 bureau memorandum concluded that "the available information on [Killens] does not indicate his association with any organization that would require any additional investigation at this time," an end-of-year donation of one hundred dollars to the Republic of New Africa rekindled agents' interest. Throughout the first half of 1972, the bureau fished through its snitch network to determine if deeper connections existed between Killens and the group but found nothing. The investigation concluded with a June 22 FBI search of the personnel records at Columbia University.[15]

To aid Killens's recuperation, Grace whisked him away to Barbados for three weeks, telling all who inquired that her husband would not be resuming regular activities for several months. Killens responded well to his time in Barbados but landed back in the hospital two weeks after his return when he suffered a slipped disc in his neck. He was released a fortnight later, still wearing a cervical collar, experiencing chronic pain in his neck and arms and unable to sleep well or type much. He had to pull out of the Paul Laurence Dunbar centennial celebration at the University of Dayton, where he had been scheduled to appear with Hoyt Fuller, Dudley Randall, Albert Aubert, Nikki Giovanni, Etheridge Knight, Audre Lorde, Paule Marshall, Gloria Oden, Raymond Patterson, Sonia Sanchez, Lorenzo Thomas, Alice Walker, Saunders Redding, Margaret Walker, and others. Furthermore, he had to take the fall semester off from Howard and Columbia because he could not manage the travel. George Davis and Derek Walcott covered his course at Columbia.

Restless at home, Killens wrote to Leo Branton in early October to suggest that they collaborate to bring five movies to fruition: *Youngblood, And Then We Heard the Thunder, 'Sippi, The Cotillion,* and *Great Gittin' Up Morning.* Far more reasonably, Killens wrote to thank Ishmael Reed for sending a copy of *Mumbo Jumbo,* "one of the maddest, craziest, angriest books I have read in a helluva long time."[16] The two writers had conversed on a number of occasions, but Reed "didn't know anything about the intellectual history of African Americans in New York, where I never quite fit in, or else my conversations with him would have been of greater quality. And I hadn't read much of his work including his masterwork, *And Then We Heard the Thunder*."[17]

By October 26, Killens had recovered enough to travel to the University of Notre Dame at the invitation of William Daley, acting director of the Black Studies Program. Killens spoke informally at the Black Cultural Arts Center before delivering a formal talk. Nevertheless, he still endured excruciating arm and neck pain: two visits to an acupuncturist relieved Killens only of his "hard-earned cash."[18] After seeking out further acupuncture treatment and expressing a willingness to travel to California and even China to find it, Killens was directed to a practitioner in New York's Chinatown who treated him successfully. Killens proclaimed acupuncture "the future in the medical profession and *it works!*"[19] At long last, he was again sleeping well, and he resumed work at his typewriter.

Friends continued to urge him to exercise caution with regard to his health, however. Shirley Graham Du Bois wrote from Cairo, exclaiming, "You young fellows better watch it!" She then invited Killens to come to Africa for three weeks or so of rest and restoration: "There comes a time, little brother," she advised, "when it's smart to drop everything and take off! Talk this over with Friend Wife."[20] Her son, David, was in the United States, becoming "so pleasantly involved" that Du Bois doubted she would see him for several months; therefore, his room and bath were available for the Killenses. Killens found Du Bois's offer tempting, but for six months his earning capacity "had been nil." Only if he could land lectures to help pay expenses could he luxuriate along the Nile.[21]

By the end of the year, Killens was back at Howard University. Sharon Bell Mathis and the D.C. Black Writers' Workshop arranged an event, "Spend an Evening with John Oliver Killens," which took place on December 14.

In the spring of 1973, Killens worked for four weeks on a script (completed with Walter Bernstein) for a multimedia cultural program celebrating Paul Robeson's seventy-fifth birthday. Held on April 15 at Carnegie Hall, the tribute was organized by Paul Robeson Jr.; his wife, Marilyn; producer Harry Belafonte; Julie Belafonte; Ralph Alswang; and several others. Speakers and performers included Dolores Huerta, Ramsey Clark, Angela Davis, Ruby Dee, James Earl Jones, and Coretta Scott King. Although Robeson did not attend due to poor health, he sent a two-minute taped greeting.[22]

The next day, Killens caught a plane to Washington to speak at a symposium on the status of the black arts held at Howard University's Institute for the Arts and Humanities. Although his doctor cautioned him against becoming overcommitted, he could not bypass an opportunity to present an award to Gwendolyn Brooks. In his keynote address, he stressed the historical continuity of black progressive art. He asserted that he had not waited until the 1960s to realize that he was black, that he had the examples of his parents, Robeson, Marcus Garvey, David Walker, Arna Bontemps, Langston Hughes, Martin Delany, Margaret Walker, Brooks, and W. E. B. Du Bois.

Killens also was the featured speaker at a celebration of the publication of Henry Lee Moon's *The Emerging Thought of W. E. B. Du Bois.* Killens noted the remarkable achievement of African American sprint athletes, but he felt that long-distance running was a proper metaphor for African American social and political struggle. Specifying a need for "one hundred year plans" and "two hundred year plans," he argued that short-term, hand-to-mouth efforts would not realize Du Bois's mission of "toppl[ing] this capitalistic white supremacy establishment." Moreover, he considered Du Bois the "most outstanding long distance runner of the twentieth century, or any other century for that matter." As "long distance running," Killens cited Du Bois's involvement with the Atlanta School of Social Work, the Niagara Movement, *The Crisis*, and the *Encyclopedia Africana* as well as Du Bois's vast library, "for with his books he had constructed an institution that would stand against the ravages of time, would inspire generations to come and help them to understand the task that lay ahead of them."[23]

Killens agreed to visit China for several weeks in July 1973 as part of a group of writers and teachers that included education activists Elizabeth Moos, who had been a colleague of Du Bois at the Peace Information Center, and Minnie Kennedy, who participated extensively in the civil rights movement and had worked with Martin Luther King Jr. Killens's flight stopped in Anchorage, Alaska, which Killens felt had a "frontier-western" aura: "White westerners were very much in control, much to the disadvantage and misfortune of the indigenous people." The party also had a brief stay in Tokyo, which Killens had visited three years earlier. He thought that with all its gaudy advertisements, the city increasingly resembled New York, especially Times Square. In addition, "to hear that beautiful Japanese women were having their eyes operated on in order to eliminate the Eastern look was terrible news indeed." The next morning, the group took a four-hour flight to Hong Kong, where Killens found "poverty and contradiction are in the air you breathe. On the one hand, the screaming evidence of opulence, the ostentatious display of fantastic wealth, modernistic high-rise apartments, vast villa-type estates; on the other hand, filthy shacks and filthier beggars." As in Africa, he did much of his deep thinking and most focused observing while walking the streets at night. When the travelers prepared to enter the People's Republic of China, Killens experienced chills and fought against a tide of emotion: "China! 'The Sleeping Giant!!' . . . 'You don't have a China-man's chance.' . . . My grandmother's admonition to us children: 'Eat every-thing on your plate. It's a sin to waste your food. Think of the starving people of China.' All the memories rushed in upon me. And then—the revolution of 1949. I remembered the words of W. E. B. Du Bois on his 91st birthday, when he called upon the people of Africa and all oppressed peoples to look to China, whose non-white people had been the wretched, yes, the despised of the earth."[24] He mailed a batch of postcards, including one to Nikki Gio-vanni that instructed, "Everyone should make this trip."[25] In fact, Killens had tried to persuade Grace to accompany him, and now that he was surf-ing the tide of excitement, he thought he should have insisted that the two of them had enough of a financial cushion for her to come along.

In Kwangchow (Canton), Killens visited communes in rural areas, light industry factories, a medical center, a dental clinic, a maternity ward, and a college and met with people in their homes. When a young Chinese student learned that he was an African American, she revealed that she was study-ing for a degree in English and had read a book in translation about a black soldier in Georgia who was beaten by police. When the woman told him that the title was *And Then the Thunder Was Heard*, Killens responded that he was the author, and she exclaimed, "You're John Keerins!"[26] Later, in Bei-jing, Killens met with Chinese publishers and discovered that he was widely read in China. The fact of recognition was good, but publication in China brought in no revenue because China did not recognize international copy-right law. Nonetheless, Killens left behind copies of '*Sippi, Great Gittin' Up Morning, Black Man's Burden*, and *The Cotillion*. He also provided a long list of black writers to be considered for publication.

After visiting the Great Wall of China, Killens wrote to Grace, "These people will not be defeated. They have put it together. And so can we!"[27] However, Killens did not ignore China's blemishes. The members of his group never received the tour of prisons they had requested, and the air pollution in the coal mining town of Fuison caused him to wonder how China would deal with the environmental effects of industrialization. In addition, he was disappointed that he did not get to meet with Chinese literary figures, as he had requested. Overall, though, he viewed his journey positively. Interested in Chinese-African alliances, he met with African students who spoke fondly of their experiences in China, and he read back copies of the *Afro-Asian Journalist*, a monthly magazine published in Beijing. Killens noted that China had assisted with the construction of the thousand-mile Tanzania-Zambia Railway, remarking, "Whatever the motivation, one thing is clear: the Chinese are working hard at establishing close ties and friendly relationships with the emerging nations of Africa, a relationship based on mutual respect and equality." He later advised, "Americans cannot hope to achieve this kind of fellowship with African nations so long as it denies full humanity and equality to the sons and daughters of Africa here at home."[28]

One of Killens's main reasons for going to China had been to study the country's example of cultural revolution. "Why," he wondered, "did it apparently have such a tremendous success, while our own Black cultural revolution, that bloomed so brightly during the Sixties, seems to be dying on the vine?"[29] The most obvious answer was that the cultural revolution in China had the backing of state power, though sometimes applied repressively, as Killens knew. Although no pure analogy could be constructed, he discerned the continuous effort required, the merger of political and cultural initiatives, the indigenous character, and a more progressive stance on gender than generally found among black cultural nationalists. And always sensitive to a project to "deniggerize," Killens suggested, "In the entire history of revolutions, I know of no liberated people who call themselves with the designation of the oppressors. Believe me, Sisters and Brothers, there are no 'chinks' in China."[30]

Back on home ground, Killens put in another semester of teaching, writing, and trying to create forums for the examination and development of cultural views and cultural agendas. He spent the autumn months working on an adaptation of *The Cotillion*, doing his final proofreading on Christmas Day. He also worked on an adolescent novel based on the legend of John Henry, a character with whom he had toyed since writing the television treatment for Belafonte years earlier. Little, Brown, and Company offered him a contract for the John Henry book, though the publishing house rejected the Pushkin manuscript because the editorial department did not feel that the work captured the era and personality of Pushkin in a way that made for successful historical fiction. *Youngblood*'s twentieth anniversary drew near, an occasion that would be celebrated with a party, but Killens could get no concrete encouragement from editors for the writing project about which he presently cared the most.

On February 4, 1974, shifting gears again, he appeared at Howard University with Harry Belafonte on a program sponsored by the Institute for the Arts and Humanities. The two men spoke after a screening of *Buck and the Preacher* and made their typical remarks about art and integrity and took shots at the "Superflies." Belafonte spoke for his old friend when he hit on a solution for the dearth of quality black films: "But we don't own the theaters and need to work from inside and outside the box office because there is so much more of black lives to be told."[31]

The Black Academy of Arts and Letters, becoming increasingly dysfunctional, would not seriously be involved in cultural efforts. By the spring of 1974, Lincoln had resigned as president; the office temporarily fell to Killens, who also resigned because he could not handle the load. Shortly thereafter, Killens joined eighty-one other summer fellows, including Alice Walker, in residence at the MacDowell Colony in Peterborough, New Hampshire. Killens worked on several projects, including the Pushkin novel, and set in motion plans for the first writers conference at Howard University that coming fall.

Also in the fall, Barbara Killens and writer Louis Reyes Rivera, who had met in 1973, two years after Barbara's separation from Barry Wynn, married at the Killens home on November 2, 1974. Among those in attendance were Rivera's mother, Amelia Pardo; his uncle, Gaspard Rivera, who stood with him; Charlotte Wong, who was at Barbara's side; and several relatives and friends, including John's brother, Richard, and brother-in-law, Thomas Russell Jones, who officiated over the nuptials, and Ewart and Genii Guinier, who traveled from Massachusetts for the occasion. Rivera, emerging as a prominent force on the New York cultural scene, particularly in black and Nuyorican poetry circles, now had more than occasional glimpses of the Killens household. In December, he had an extended conversation with Nina Simone, one of his idols, at a Killens party that was held to celebrate the twentieth anniversary of *Youngblood*'s publication. He did not, however, obtain the secret to his father-in-law's special martini blend, which would "bust you up," beyond learning that it lacked vermouth.[32] Rivera also did not have the recipe for one of the greatest sources of family pride, Killens's homemade biscuits, which he would whip up on Sunday mornings.

Rivera grew accustomed to tiptoeing around the spirited basement ping-pong contests between John and Chuck Killens. Rivera saw Killens fuss over his modest wine cellar and add to his extensive jazz collection. The two writers also talked at length about art and politics, and Rivera even accompanied his father-in-law on several morning jogs when the novelist, with his stroke not very far in the past, went through periods during which he would run before settling into his seat at the typewriter.[33]

I Always Said Class and Race, 1974–1977

Of all the Howard University conferences held between 1974 and 1978, the one held November 8–10, 1974, remains the most significant.[1] By the beginning of the 1970s, the ranks of African Americans still optimistic about social and political revolution had thinned. Much crucial black leadership had been eliminated—Far Left exemplars such as the Black Panthers, nationalist visionaries such as Malcolm X, and mainstream direct actionists such as Martin Luther King Jr. Their departures bred a belief that the oppressive establishment would always prevail. To demonstrate that black was beautiful could be done rather quickly, but more difficult was to authenticate that black was powerful and disciplined enough to sustain black beauty over the long haul. Even the symbolic black transformation of the 1960s was being reversed—fewer Afros, dashikis, tiki sticks, rallies, slogans—not that these elements alone, as John Oliver Killens depicted in *The Cotillion*, necessarily indicated progressive consciousness.

Killens directed this conference under the auspices of the Institute for the Arts and Humanities using the same theme as the 1966 conference at Fisk but changing the title to reflect new thinking about semantics: "The Image of the Negro in American Literature" became "The Image of Black Folk in American Literature." The Howard conference included thirty-two writers, far more than the eight or ten panelists who had attended the Fisk conferences. Howard hosted familiar participants such as Ossie Davis, Maya Angelou, Alice Childress, Piri Thomas, Paule Marshall, and Haki Madhubuti as well as writers who had gained prominence since the Fisk conferences—Ishmael Reed, Quincy Troupe, Kalamu ya Salaam, and Richard Wesley. In the conference brochure, Killens argued that Watergate corruption, presidential impeachment, wiretapping, and police state activities heightened the need for unity among black people and black writers, though he did not insist on a "dogmatic monolithic approach." He explicitly defended African American artists' right to individuality with respect to perception, style, and technique but stressed the necessity for "a unity of commitment, and that commitment is to the liberation of mankind, especially the oppressed of African descent where they may find themselves."[2]

However, the institute's planners could not achieve unity with regard to either the inaugural or subsequent conferences. E. Ethelbert Miller and Ahmos Zu-Bolton, for example, felt marginalized and frustrated in their efforts to get additional writers such as Ntozake Shange included on programs. Miller was less strident and less public in his criticism than was Harold Cruse but identified somewhat with Cruse's narrative of a Killens-led literary clique, though Madhubuti certainly emerged as an equal partner at Howard. Miller recalled, "I was always on the other side."[3]

According to Carole A. Parks, who covered the conference for *Black World*, the participants generally supported Killens's perspective on the hazards of negative images and the exigency of creating positive ones. Playwright-critic Eugene Perkins admonished, "Image-making should be a part of Black theater because from images we get models, from models, direction." But members of the group also expressed concerns, even disagreements, about how to disperse the magnificent images to be generated. Davis, who gave the keynote address immediately following Killens's welcome, declared that technical expertise, access to mechanisms of production, and a broad yet sharply focused political outlook were necessary so that the proposed creation of positive images could have maximum impact. He reasoned, "Seldom do we show our images connected with *power*. There is time for continuing to show how clever, how beautiful and talented we are. But we must have an international perspective on power." Despite such exhortations and the fact that between 250 and 600 people jammed the meeting sessions, fewer than 100 attendees showed up to discuss the most concrete organizational proposal made at the conference, the formation of a Black Writers Congress. Some undoubtedly were wary about which artistic tastes and policies would dominate in such an organization. Nonetheless, Ron Milner's comments rang ironically. Defending certain achievements of the 1960s, Milner argued, "Rhetoric was tested right in the middle of rhetoric. The fire burned off the fat, left the lean, so we knew what and who was real."[4] To Killens's dismay, what apparently was real was the lack of a collective will strong enough to establish a black writers' association.

A vigorous and intense debate transpired on an adjacent cultural and political front, as the *Black Scholar* became a site for the debate about black nationalism vis-à-vis Marxism-Leninism. The centerpiece was Haki Madhubuti's "The Latest Purge: The Attack on Black Nationalism and Pan-Afrikanism by the New Left, the Sons and Daughters of the Old Left," which appeared in September 1974. Madhubuti argued primarily that the critical shift to identifying systems such as monopoly capitalism and world imperialism as the primary problem of blacks removed the focus from white people as the oppressors of black people. Madhubuti felt that nothing productive could flow from a misidentification of the enemy and that Marxism was an insufficient tool for proper identification. As he stressed, "It is important to understand that *the ideology of white supremacy precedes the economic structure of capitalism and imperialism, the latter of which are falsely stated as the cause of racism. To believe that the white boy mis-used and manipulated us for centuries up until today for purely economic reasons is racist and void of any historical reality.*" With respect to the prospect of black-white coalitions, Madhubuti asserted, "Even for the liberal white socialist, there is no answer to why race, culture and ethnic separations divide people who on the surface seem to share a common political and economic interest. The race issue is the primary contradiction."[5] Madhubuti's theoretical decoupling of people from systems is questionable, as are his overall judgments concerning Marxism. Several responses to his article in subsequent issues of the journal spoke convincingly to both of those shortcomings.[6] Yet Madhubuti was correct on a major point of dispute between black nationalists and black Marxists. Forms of white supremacy and racism preceded the rise of capitalism, but doctrinaire Marxists insisted that racism, which is certainly a byproduct of capitalism, was *only* a byproduct of capitalism. White supremacy operates as a feature of capitalism but definitely can circulate independently of a capitalist economic base. But many intellectuals embraced an unnecessary binary in their search for correct theory as though all proposals for action could be evaluated only relative to a clear and simple analysis of racism's origin. In other words, they were overly concerned with whether race was the essential problematic.

Although the *Black Scholar* devoted considerable space to both sides of the question, publisher Nathan Hare resigned and distanced himself from all of the journal's activities, complaining of a "black Marxist takeover and seizure." According to Hare, this coup could only sidetrack the black freedom movement. After a decade of tutelage and instruction, he considered himself a serious student of Marx's ideas and appreciated the basic insights therein. However, his understanding of Marxism suggested that it had to be revamped (as he was sure Marx would have agreed) according to the specific historical contexts in which it was to be applied. But Hare felt that his thinking no longer dominated with respect to the journal, which he felt was moving increasingly toward a "narrow devotion to conventional Marxist interpretations and an ironclad intolerance for and resistance to opposing views" that was trapping the publication in a "deadly vice of progressive deterioration." Hare felt that his contributions were being "sabotaged and almost liquidated," and he compared his status to that of W. E. B. Du Bois within the National Association for the Advancement of Colored People under Walter White.[7]

Hare released his letter to a number of black media outlets, and by the second week in March, the *New York Times* had picked up the story. Hare further explained his charges to reporter Charlayne Hunter, attributing the shift in editorial policy to editor Robert Chrisman and managing editor Robert Allen's trip to Cuba two years earlier. The two men "were mesmerized by Cuba" and began to believe that "race had no meaning." Although Hare could find ample evidence, even in Cuba, to dispute this idea, he felt that in Chrisman and Allen's circles, "you could not criticize Russia or Cuba or Angela Davis." Hare claimed that an increasing number of articles were being solicited from Marxist and communist writers, but "when I protested that not enough black nationalists were getting into the debate, they tried to put out the idea that nationalists didn't have any new thoughts and I felt that way about the Marxists."[8]

Chrisman rejected Hare's reasoning, accusing his colleague of engaging in "old-fashioned red-baiting and smearing" and of fabricating the charges.[9] He explained that the majority of the contributing editors—a group that included Davis—were not Marxists. Chrisman, Allen, and business manager Glory Bevien issued another open letter in which they informed the public that the three of them had worked with Hare as a collective and between September 1972 and February 1975 had published the "full range of black ideological thought, as well as informative and critical articles on all aspects of the black experience." They vowed to continue the tradition: "We cannot, have not, and will not avoid Marxist thinking, nationalist thinking, reformist thinking or any kind of freedom-thinking. We believe that the black community must be fully informed of the ideological debates taking place among black movement groups."[10]

That the *Black Scholar* published Madhubuti's article seems to weaken Hare's position, yet Hare's analysis resonated with much of the advisory board. Charles V. Hamilton resigned immediately, and others followed. However, some interested observers did not appear overly concerned by the schism. As Abdul Alkalimat said, "It's the struggle for correct ideas that gets to correct ideas."[11]

In April, Hunter contributed a follow-up article in which she portrayed the debate about black nationalism and Marxism as the "chief development in black thought since the civil rights movement culminated in black power in the late nineteen-sixties."[12] She did not point out, though the title of Madhubuti's article hinted at it, that the debate was a virtual replay of arguments that went back at least as far back as the bitter Cyril Briggs–Marcus Garvey tussles of the 1920s. Although the latter-day camps were not entirely uniform, as Hunter was aware, she grouped Killens with the black nationalists. He did not object, though his political view was internationalist and his economic philosophy socialist, still Marxist-influenced. These positions do not necessarily accompany the designation *black nationalist*, though Killens was surely that as well. Experience made Killens a different kind of black nationalist than Madhubuti and a different kind of Marxist than the newly converted Amiri Baraka. Killens had been exploring Marxism and organizing since the 1930s, so he knew firsthand the obstacles of implementing interracial, class-based struggle, as those he labeled "instant Marxists" did not.[13] Thus, although he was not anti-Marxist, his attachment to Marxism was severely qualified as a consequence of his belief that Marxist thought did not adequately treat the corruptibility of the working class. He told Hunter, "With the unemployment problem becoming more crucial, I predict that white workers are going to shoot down black workers, fight them for the few jobs that are out there."[14] Conversely, he could not totally agree with a people-not-systems analysis that ignored or failed to emphasize economic structures and class distinctions, including class differences among African Americans: he had spent far too much time with E. Franklin Frazier, Alphaeus Hunton, James Jackson, Howard "Stretch" Johnson, and Harry Haywood.

Although Killens had no major problem with Hunter's characterization of him, he wrote to the *New York Times* to correct an "unintentional misquote" and to expound on the situation she described. Hunter had quoted him as saying "the absolute incorruptibility of the working class," a phrase that made no sense to him. Killens had actually said, "When Marx wrote about the 'absolute impoverishment of the working class,' he could not have possibly foreseen the phenomenon in the U.S.A., i.e., the 'absolute corruptibility of the working class.'" Killens declared that the American working class as a whole "has no class consciousness, is anti-Black and rent through and through with white racism." He explained that while he did not deny Marx's greatness as a philosopher or the relevance of Marxism to the black struggle, current conditions called for current analyses: "It is in this context that I insist that the Black question is both a class question and a race question. One can be both a Pan African nationalist and at the same time be an advocate of socialism. Certainly for an African country to achieve 'independence' at this historic moment and establish a capitalist economy would be a step backwards. Socialism is definitely the wave of the New World. But if socialism came to America tomorrow morning, we could still have white racism for the next one hundred years." Killens further suggested that a dialectical methodology should allow theorists and activists to reconcile the class-race contradiction. If a "great ideological split" existed in the black movement, an idea Hunter was playing up, "please count me out of it." He elaborated, "I feel no animosity toward Brother Baraka. I assume he has none toward me. Just as I openly disagreed on the question of non-violence with Brother Martin Luther King whom I loved and regarded as a friend, I assume that brother Baraka and I can disagree on this question and still be friends with a common commitment, i.e., ultimate liberation."[15] Killens concluded that the so-called ideological debate smacked of elitism and had little to do with the contemporary strivings of the black masses.

Amid the furor of the nationalist-Marxist debate, Killens welcomed another granddaughter, Kutisa—"spirit that shines," in the Kaamba language—on April 20 and published another novel, *A Man Ain't Nothin' but a Man: The Adventures of John Henry*. Although the book is an adolescent vehicle, partly as a consequence of Killens's growing grandchild-induced consciousness about what children read, the story should not be overlooked or minimized. It represents an important parallel to Killens's attempt to clarify his politics in his letter to the *New York Times*. In his clearest nod in fiction to cross-ethnic, working-class consciousness since *And Then We Heard the*

Thunder, Killens places John Henry, the black icon, within a multiethnic proletarian context.[16]

The most common and most tame John Henry tales paint the former slave as a proud and stubborn man who pitted his enormous strength and ability against a steam drill in an attempt to delay mechanization. By the 1970s, the dominant John Henry story was Ezra Jack Keats's *John Henry: An American Legend*. Keats's tale is not political with respect to the African American community. According to W. Nikola-Lisa, "John Henry's death symbolizes for Keats the waning of the prized American ideal of individualism. It is in this respect that Keats' John Henry gains widespread appeal, but at the price of ignoring the underlying racial tension inherent in the conflict between John Henry, an ex-slave, and white railroad bosses notorious for their exploitation of black laborers."[17] Killens knew the Keats version, but his John Henry, in the words of Brett Williams, "is clearly a black hero and a laboring hero. He does not represent dumb brute strength, but rather links his contest with the machine drill to human dignity."[18] Indeed, months before the book's publication, Killens privately described his protagonist as a "Black legendary working class hero."[19]

Although the notion of being a steel driver, like his father, has been on John Henry's mind from the time he was a toddler (as it must be in any full version of the legend), he chooses the vocation because it pays significantly higher wages than picking cotton on the plantation or rousting cotton on the waterfront. As such, the job increases the prospects that John Henry and his wife, Polly Anne, can purchase a farm. As he explains to her, freedom has to mean land.[20] That political power derives from landownership was, of course, a key principle of black nationalist discourse. What does not fit easily into that discourse, however, are the images of fellowship involving John Henry; Uncle Buddy; Ben Lawson, a white coworker; and a Chinese-American worker, George Ling Lee, who regularly dine together at John Henry's home. As an artist, Killens is still exploring both race and class. Ethnic differences nevertheless remain, and Captain Joe Brad exploits them by spreading racist rumors to drive a wedge between the workers, a sort of tension Killens had written about as far back as his unpublished "Stony the Road We Trod." Only Polly Anne's intervention prevents a confrontation between John Henry and Ben Lawson from turning tragic. As they subsequently talk in Lawson's home, John Henry discusses the limitations of ethnic alliances, telling Lawson, "When it come down to a test where a man really live at, you a white man first and a good man afterwards."[21] Lawson vehemently denies the charge, eventually arguing that he treats all men fairly regardless of color. He blames one of the captain's instigators, Will Hodge, for the trouble and plans to shoot him. John Henry counters that Hodge is merely a pawn of management. The more the men talk and understand management's tactics, the more the story turns back toward a transethnic leftist awareness reminiscent not only of "Stony the Road We Trod" but also of portions of *Youngblood*, *And Then We Heard the Thunder*, and *Black Man's Burden*. John Henry, Uncle Buddy, Lawson, and Lee understand how racism is employed to undermine working-class solidarity, with the result that management increases the profit margin at the expense of workers' well-being. As they wind up their session, John Henry reminds the others, "Just remember, a man ain't nothin' but a man, don't care what color he be. It seem such a hard thing to remember, especially hard for the poor white working folks."[22]

By the time readers get to the climactic challenge, the story is more complicated than the usual John Henry tale because of the merger of black nationalist and broader leftist sentiments. To prevent wage cuts or layoffs, John Henry tries to prove that a full complement of men is more economically expedient than machines. He feels a particular responsibility to save jobs for black workers, knowing that other job prospects for them almost inevitably mean a return to some plantation and a menial existence. After he wins the contest by drilling ten inches deeper than the drill, presumably saving the jobs, he admits as he faces his death that mechanization is inevitable. In his view, the enemy is not machines but rather the unwise use of them. The implied line of reasoning, of course, is that if economic inequality that damages blacks were to persist, it would constitute evidence that machines were indeed being misused. Therefore, Killens had placed popular fiction's most radical spin on John Henry. When taken as seriously as it should be, this tale unsettles the easy integrationist-to-nationalist orthodoxy relative to the Killens canon. Henry Hitz, a member of the fledgling communist Progressive Labor Party, grasped this point, writing to Killens, "I have no idea what your relationship was, or is, to the old [Communist Party], but it is obvious that you worked closely with them at one time, and it is equally obvious from your treatment of John Henry that the idea of a workers revolution is still alive for you."[23]

As the 1970s progressed, Killens seemed to be getting more honors than opportunities. He still had designs on seeing *The Cotillion* produced in some form and perhaps *And Then We Heard the Thunder* as well. He wanted to do an adult project about Denmark Vesey, probably a screenplay, and return to the novel, "The Minister Primarily," that he had started long ago and that had been at the center of his creative break with Angus Cameron and Knopf. Above all, he desired to see his Alexander Pushkin story in print. But the forecast was not optimistic except for developments with *The Cotillion*, a production of which, starring Taurean Blacque, Joyce Griffen, Hank Frazier, and Zaida Coles and directed by Allie Woods, ran for eleven days at Woodie King's New Federal Theater in New York during the summer of 1975. But Killens never succumbed to pessimism, always remaining certain that some of his major accomplishments lay ahead. So his mood was upbeat at the party thrown for him by the Institute of Arts and Humanities on January 14, 1976, his sixtieth birthday. Haki Madhubuti read a poem he had written in Killens's honor. Stephen Henderson presented the author with a plaque in recognition of his service to the institute and the university. In remarks to the attendees, Killens recalled his trip to China and the emphasis there on serving the people. He told his audience that he wanted them to make the same commitment.

The festive mood turned somber by the following week. Paul Robeson was gravely ill. On January 21, John and Grace sent a message expressing their "profound love and devotion to you and to the ideals for which you always gave the greatest measure of devotion." They recalled how Barbara had sat in Robeson's lap when she was two years old, and they tried to assure Robeson that he had been a constant inspiration to all of them.[24] Robeson never saw the letter: he died on January 23. Four days later, in the cold and rain, Killens squeezed in among the mourners at Harlem's Mother African Methodist Episcopal Zion Church, where Ben Robeson, Paul's brother, had pastored for more than a quarter century. The crowd was described as "Old Left and New, theater people and trade-unionists, white and black, Communists and conservatives, dear friends, old adversaries, complete strangers." Those gathered included A. Philip Randolph, Bayard Rustin, Betty Shabazz, Henry Winston, and Eubie Blake. The funeral began and ended with familiar Robeson songs playing over loudspeakers.[25]

On January 30, Killens spoke at the University of Cincinnati, where his host was William David Smith, head of the Department of Afro-American Studies. Killens visited three black literature classes, met with students, and delivered a lecture, which included a tribute to Robeson. On February 15, he spoke at a Los Angeles Robeson tribute; three days later, he did the same at Howard University.

The second National Conference of Afro-American Writers at Howard University transpired in April. Killens and Madhubuti participated along with Michael Harper, Audre Lorde, Bill Gunn, Amiri Baraka, Sonia Sanchez, Toni Morrison, and Hoyt Fuller, who delivered the keynote address. The conference theme was "Beyond Survival: Two Centuries of Black Literature, 1776–1976." Apropos of Killens's struggle with landing the Pushkin manuscript and the fact that *Black World* had just gone defunct, some speakers expressed concern about the state of black publishing. In fact, the *Washington Post* ran a story on the "Black Publishing Crisis," which the paper considered a dominant theme at the conference. For Fuller, black apathy, reassertion of white critical dominance, and black publishers' financial hardships represented the three major threats to the "further flourishing of black literature." Ahmos Zu-Bolton, who ran Energy Black South Press, noted harshly that only 2 percent of the $345,000 distributed to small presses by the National Endowment of the Humanities in 1976 went to black firms. Charles Harris, director of the Howard University Press, suggested that African American writers would do well to embrace projects of biography, technology, and general interest along with work in poetry, drama, and fiction.[26]

Beyond particular concerns with publishing, the conference produced the expected blend of aesthetic, social, and political commentary. Baraka presented a lengthy paper, "Not Just Survival: Revolution," in which he pushed a Marxist-Leninist-Maoist critique, excoriated the African American middle class for a lack of political consciousness, and blasted Russian-style communism and the Soviet Union's interference in African liberation struggles. Killens did not disagree. In fact, Baraka's talk contained little of substance beyond what Killens, following Harry Haywood, had written almost thirty years earlier in "For National Freedom."

Major new talent was developing in Killens's writing workshop. Student Bebe Campbell described the sessions as "the most beautiful and rewarding of times" and thought Killens a good teacher because he blended "criticism, good vibes, Blackness, and positivity."[27]

By the end of the year, Killens essentially had completed *Great Black Russian: A Novel on the Life and Times of Alexander Pushkin*.[28] His strong Africanist rendering is apparent from the outset as he stresses Pushkin's connection to his maternal great-grandfather, Ibrahim Hannibal, who was known as the Negro of Peter the Great. Killens portrayed this relationship with both negative and positive connotations. As Pushkin's father tries to persuade the budding poet to stop writing poems in Russian rather than French, he exclaims, "You little African bastard!" As the boy's mother urges him to be more like his little brother and sister, who do not look Africoid, she remarks, "He just has the devil in him. It's his African blood rising up in him." Positive comments about his African heritage come from his grandmother, who describes Hannibal with a favorite Killens phrase: "He was so tall and Black and comely." On several occasions, suffering from stress and loneliness, Pushkin conjures up visions of Hannibal, who apparently enjoyed a distinguished career in Czar Peter's court. The first apparition occurs when Pushkin is a student at the Lyceum, which he attended between the ages of twelve and eighteen. As Pushkin lies on his bed after a talk with his grandmother, "The tall Black man with dark eyes that seemed to pierce the darkness with their intensity came to his bedside and talked with him about times gone by, when he himself was a boy in far away Africa, a young Ethiopian prince." Shortly thereafter, Pushkin declares to a schoolmate, "I'm an African-Russian . . . A Russian with an African descendancy." He reiterates the point on several occasions.[29]

Because of his affinity for black heroes, Killens provides the most African read possible of Pushkin's life given the available data. However, many scholars have argued that Pushkin was far more Russian than anything else, a claim that Killens could not seriously dispute.[30] Moreover, the Pushkin name was one of the oldest among Russian nobility, traceable to the early fifteenth century, and although Pushkin was indeed fascinated with his Ethiopian ties, he was also proud of his father's lineage. He named his younger son Grigorii after the first known male in the Pushkin line. But Killens, defending his strong Africanist rendering, emphasized that Pushkin acknowledged and took pride in his African heritage, as is evidenced by the fact that Pushkin left behind an unfinished novel, *The Negro of Peter the Great*. In addition, that sense of pride apparently influenced his views on the plight of fellow blacks, including those enslaved in the West. Avrahm Yarmolinsky has observed that Pushkin spoke on at least one occasion of "my brother Negroes."[31] But Hannibal, who according to Killens owned a thousand slaves, cannot be credited as the source of his great-grandson's antislavery sentiment, which arose from the millions of peasants and serfs whose suffering a sensitive and sympathetic artist understood and detested.

Although Pushkin was not solely a black hero, he was enough of one to provide an appealing model for a Killens protagonist. He was not thoroughly committed and uncompromising, like Denmark Vesey, yet his influence was profound, an impact Killens understood well. To the extent that Russian workers read any poetry, they read Pushkin's. Subversives were often caught with copies of his poems in their possession. Masses of people responded favorably to his "Ode to Freedom," leading to his exile by Czar Alexander.[32]

Although born of nobility, Killens's Pushkin is less noble than the author's other tragic heroes. Despite his genius and impact, he is a brooding, often depressed talent who spends far too much time as a dissipater, playing cards, and being complicit in the exploitation of serfs. He is the product of a decadent family that has no particular commitment to social justice. He dies at the age of thirty-seven, not mortally wounded in the fight against racism and economic exploitation but as the result of a duel fought because of a love affair between his wife and a Frenchman, George Charles d'Anthes. Yet in Killens's hands, Pushkin remains as heroic as he ever could have been.

The author was convinced that *Great Black Russian* contained some of his finest writing, though much of the novel is overdrawn and stiff. Nonetheless, it is hard to imagine that a white writer of similar career accomplishments would have been unable to find a publisher for the novel. Killens nevertheless persevered: "I had done too much work on Pushkin to give in to the whims of publishers. I began a campaign to get Pushkin published. I made appearances on television and radio. I went across this country with Pushkin lectures."[33]

Pushing Pushkin, 1977–1982

On January 14, 1977, his sixty-first birthday, John Oliver Killens championed Alexander Pushkin on Howard University's radio station, WHUR, beginning a lengthy string of Pushkin-related appearances. He lectured at the New Muse Community Museum of Brooklyn and at New York University on "The Resurrection of Alexander Pushkin." Then he reprised the performance at Howard University. He visited the Federal City College Mount Vernon Campus on March 23. In early April, he went to Tufts University to address several literature classes on the Afro-American novel and to speak with the Russian Club about Pushkin. On May 1, he appeared on Gil Noble's *Like It Is*; the show ran again several weeks later.

As Killens worked feverishly to generate interest in *Great Black Russian*, other cultural matters crowded in. Harry Haywood had written in February to convey his sorrow about a December fire that destroyed part of Killens's home and his hope that Killens was "back on the beam again." Haywood was completing his autobiography, *Black Bolshevik*, and thanked Killens for his encouragement and suggested that he read the entire manuscript, which was in the hands of John Henrik Clarke, who was slated to write the introduction. To help with Killens's ongoing education about Africa, Haywood enclosed a copy of *IKWESI: A Journal of South African and Southern African Political Analysis*.[1]

Other colleagues continued to call on some of his other talents and knowledge. Roscoe C. Brown Jr., director of New York University's Institute of Afro-American Affairs, had developed a slide-cassette presentation on "Afro-American Culture in the Seventies: A Socio-Political Analysis" and asked Killens to visit his class and provide a critique, which he did on May 25. Around the same time, Virginia Spencer Carr recruited Killens for a Summer Writing Institute at Emory University. While in Atlanta, he met with Hoyt Fuller, who had launched a new publication, *First World*, and appeared with him at the Neighborhood Arts Center.

Killens retreated to Yaddo, the artists' community in Saratoga Springs, during the summer of 1977, tinkering with a few projects, including the Pushkin manuscript and a new story, "Run Like Hell and Holler Fire!" He envisioned he would develop it into another novel about the movement. He was not chained to the typewriter, however. He wandered a few times over to Saratoga Race Course, on one occasion catching a workout by the brilliant colt Seattle Slew. And, as had always been his habit, he placed a few wagers. Killens later admitted that he "lost a few pesos" but "all in all, had a helluva well rounded eventful time of it."[2]

He left Yaddo on August 28 and returned home to find a letter in which Fuller asked Killens to contact Jacqueline Kennedy Onassis, who was now a book editor at Viking Press and soon would be moving to Doubleday. The former First Lady reportedly had asked James Baldwin why he had not written a book on Pushkin, so she seemed a promising contact for Killens to pursue with his novel.

Paul Robeson, a play written by Phillip Hayes Dean and starring James Earl Jones, was in performance. Paul Robeson Jr. saw the one-man show in Louisville and thought Jones "played it like it was *The Great White Hope* or something."[3] Robeson issued a press release, claiming, "The play is a fictionalized and distorted portrayal of Paul Robeson that misrepresents the most important aspects of his life. His powerful message to all oppressed peoples and to Black Americans in particular is diffused and lost in a mass of confusion."[4] His outrage led to the formation of the Ad Hoc Committee to End Crimes against Paul Robeson and the promulgation of an open letter to the entertainment industry signed by Paul Robeson Jr. and his wife, Marilyn (although they did not initiate the document), as well as Killens, Lloyd Brown, George B. Murphy Jr., Alice Childress, Rosa Guy, Charles White, John Henrik Clarke, Ewart Guinier, Coleman Young, Irving Burgie, Paule Marshall, Gwendolyn Brooks, Alvin Ailey, Wilfred Cartey, Julian

Bond, Lerone Bennett, Loften Mitchell, Maya Angelou, Louise Meriwether, Ronald Walters, Quincy Troupe, and Nikki Giovanni. Giovanni signed only because Killens prevailed on her to do so, and she later expressed misgivings about her decision.[5]

According to Robeson, the petition had originated with Robert Nemiroff and his wife; Robeson's instinct had been to tell people to see the play and compare it to the information he was disseminating in radio appearances. He did not feel a need to attack Jones, who reportedly uttered, "I'm not a missionary; I'm a mercenary." Avery Brooks later performed a slightly rewritten version of the play and did what Robeson thought was a much better job.[6]

Later that fall, Killens flew back to Georgia for a conference at Georgia Southwestern College on "Black Politics in Georgia: New Responsibilities, New Challenges." Despite the suggestive title, this was not a gathering fueled mainly by heated ideological debates about such matters as nationalism or Marxism. Rather, the impetus was largely a presumed uncontroversial engagement with reform politics. Sponsored by the Georgia Association of Black Elected Officials, the Southern Center for Studies in Public Policy, the Institute of the Black World, and the Committee for the Humanities in Georgia, the generative questions had to do with the relationship between the emergence of a new black leadership class in Georgia and the conditions of the black masses; the responsibilities, if any, of blacks employed in high- and mid-level positions with regard to the overall black community; the resolution, if possible, of the conflict that members of the new black middle class might feel among their loyalties to their employers, the general public, the black community, and their personal aspirations; and the best political agenda for American society in general and for Georgia, especially African American Georgia, in particular. Keynote speakers included C. Dolores Tucker and Charles V. Hamilton. Panelists included Norman Underwood, executive secretary to Governor George Busbee; Carl Ware, president of the Atlanta City Council; and Thomas Murphy, speaker of the Georgia House of Representatives. On November 19, Killens joined fellow panelists Mack Jones, chair of the Political Science Department at Atlanta University; Creigs Beverly, associate dean of Atlanta University's School of Social Work; and state representative Hosea Williams for a session on "New Responsibilities and Obstacles Facing the New Black Middle Class," moderated by Melvin Williams, a member of the Macon school board.

Then it was back to promoting *Great Black Russian*—a lecture on "The Life and Times of Alexander Pushkin" at the Abyssinian Baptist Church in Harlem, an engagement at American University in Washington, D.C., and presentations at the Langston Hughes Library in Queens; the Afro-American Cultural Foundation in White Plains, New York; and the University of Maryland, Baltimore County.

The fourth National Conference of Afro-American Writers convened at Howard University on May 4–6, 1978, to discuss "The Impact of the '60s through the Prism of the Present." Participants included Sterling Stuckey, Larry Neal, Barbara Ann Teer, E. Ethelbert Miller, Quincy Troupe, June Jordan, Barbara Smith, and Sonia Sanchez. Nathan Hare delivered the keynote address. Killens joined a panel on the topic of publications, bookstores, and cultural organizations. He had yet to find a publisher for *Great Black Russian*, and he made familiar remarks about the need for an African American cultural infrastructure that would end black authors' reliance on the white publishing establishment.

The conference was noteworthy for two main reasons. First, it represented Killens's swan song at Howard. At sixty-two, he was leaving at the conclusion of the academic year and thereafter would teach closer to home, at Bronx Community College, where Roscoe C. Brown Jr. had assumed the presidency. Second, the cultural politics of sexuality came to the fore in a way that had not happened at previous gatherings. Hare declared that the white feminist movement threatened the unity between black men and black women, while Barbara Smith expanded the parameters of analysis. At the electric closing session, Smith charged, "There is no political movement to give power or support to those who want to examine black women's experiences through studying our history, literature and culture. When black women's books are dealt with at all, it is usually in the context of black literature, which largely ignores the implications of sexual politics." Smith also did not think that white women were qualified to deal with racial nuances in literature by black women. In closing, she wished "most of all for black women and black lesbians somehow not to be so alone." Smith received enthusiastic applause, but agitated members of the audience also voiced reservations about her feminist-lesbian stance. Psychologist Frances Cress Welsing stated, "An endorsement of homosexuality means the death of the race." Although no one voice prevailed, the various

pronouncements signaled clearly that at future major forums, the dynamics of gender and sexuality would not be suppressed by strict concerns with
race and/or class.[7]

Shortly after his departure from Howard University, Killens spent time at
Yaddo and visiting the Guiniers on Martha's Vineyard. Excited about producing new work, he quickly settled into a disciplined routine when he returned home. He typically began writing at dawn and continued until one
o'clock in the afternoon. He usually skipped lunch but would venture down-
stairs for juice or coffee and maybe an orange and then retreat to his office
to work until the six o'clock news. After dinner, he would watch television,
write more, or fulfill some social engagement. On Thursdays, he taught his
workshop at Bronx Community College, evaluating student texts and dis-
pensing advice: "One has to be specific in order to be universal. The tree of
universality has many branches. In order to live, it has to be rooted in speci-
ficity." Another aphorism of which he was fond but to which he did not
always adhere was, "You should have more respect for your characters than
for your message. If a reader believes in your characters, he will believe
in what you have to say."[8] As he had done at other schools, Killens began
bringing visitors to campus, most prominently Maya Angelou and James
Baldwin, and he floated plans for a writers' conference. Likewise, he continued to attract promising talent to his workshops—most notably Doris Jean
Austin, Terry McMillan, and Arthur Flowers, who had studied with him at
Columbia University.

   Near the end of the year, Killens and his wife headed south. They visited Soul City, North Carolina, a real estate development project headed by
former Congress of Racial Equality leader Floyd McKissick for which Killens served on the board of directors. From Soul City, he and Grace traveled to Atlanta to attend a meeting of the United Nations Special Committee against Apartheid. The next stop was the Macon Hilton, where Killens
met up with Pierce Brunson and Willis Sheftall for an extensive walking
tour. Macon had changed overall for the better, but Killens noticed that
African Americans seemed to own less property and fewer businesses than
had been the case during his childhood. Despite having made great strides,
blacks were still being left behind. While in Macon, Killens was interviewed
by Harold Michael Harvey of the *Macon Courier* and Yvonne Shinhoster of
the *Macon Telegraph*. Thinking again of the difficulty in landing his Push-

kin manuscript, Killens told Harvey, "When blacks stopped being in the streets, publishers stopped publishing black writers."[9]

Killens still received no interest from publishers, but Norman Loftis, a poet, novelist, upstart filmmaker, and former Fisk student, suggested a plan for producing a Pushkin film. Loftis imagined that Killens could get some of his talented friends to do a special that could be sold to a television network, with the profits then funneled into the Pushkin project. Loftis calculated, "If it costs $200,000 to produce the television show and the network pays $2,000,000 for it, we are $1,800,000 closer to doing Pushkin."[10] Though that plan never came to fruition, that fall, Killens received a ten-thousand-dollar National Endowment of the Arts Creative Fellowship Grant.

Although the shift from the 1970s to the 1980s did not represent as seismic an event in many imaginations as the previous transition from one decade to another, the moment was nonetheless expressed thematically in numerous publications and in conferences such as the one held on May 2–4, 1980, at Central State University in Wilberforce, Ohio. Haki Madhubuti, writer in residence after his departure from Howard University, selected the theme "Black Writers View the Eighties: Evolution, Stagnation, or Renewed Struggle?" Invited writers included Gwendolyn Brooks, Addison Gayle, Stephen Henderson, Hoyt Fuller, Mari Evans, Kalamu ya Salaam, Val Gray Ward, and Virginia Hamilton, and presentations addressed such topics as "The Poet as Prophet of the Eighties," "Current and Future Themes in Black Drama," "Images of Blacks in Children's Literature," and "The Cultural, Linguistic, and Critical Problems Facing African/Caribbean Literature in American Education." On May 3, Killens teamed up with Ayi Kwei Armah to address the issue of "Black Fiction as Social Commentary and Prophecy."

Six days later, with Grace looking on and beaming, Killens became the third recipient (after James Baldwin and Gwendolyn Brooks) of an award at the Langston Hughes Festival Tribute. Wilfred Cartey, Rosa Guy, and Addison Gayle were also on hand. Gayle, a critic who was always sympathetic to Killens, introduced him, and Elizabeth Catlett, an ardent Killens supporter, sent a congratulatory telegram from Mexico. Killens was also the guest of honor later that month at the fifth annual Lewis H. Michaux Book Fair, where he received the Lewis Michaux Award, bestowed by Harlem's Studio Museum.

But Killens longed to break back into print. On June 20, he wrote to Mad-hubuti to ask if his Third World Press might republish *Youngblood* with an eye toward reissuing his other novels and perhaps publishing *Great Black Russian*. Killens also asked Lawrence Hill whether the publisher would con-sider reissuing all four of Killens's adult novels—*Youngblood*, *And Then We Heard the Thunder*, *'Sippi*, and *The Cotillion*. Two months later, he broached the question of *Great Black Russian* with Hill, insisting that Killens's con-tacts in New York, Washington, D.C., Chicago, Los Angeles, San Francisco, and Atlanta would enable him to move an edition of four thousand cop-ies. These and further pleas were to no avail. As Hill explained to Killens toward the end of November, limited resources simply prevented him from issuing the novel despite its literary merit.

In February and March 1981, Killens asked Harry Belafonte to write to several editors on his behalf. In addition to Onassis, now at Doubleday, Kil-lens targeted Alan Rinzler at Bantam Books; Judith Riven at Avon Books, to whom Killens had been referred by writer and visual artist Barbara Chase-Riboud; and Carolyn Trager at A&W Publishers. He told Belafonte, "They say Richard Wright's NATIVE SON was turned down by ten publishers be-fore one publisher saw the light and it became a book-of-the-month best seller. They also said that YOUNGBLOOD could not and would not be pub-lished during the days of Cold War and McCarthy, but it *was* published. In any event, I have to try every tactic I can think of."[11]

On March 23, Riven turned down *Great Black Russian*, telling Killens that the literary rendering of Pushkin was not strong enough. Other rejections soon followed. Killens experienced mixed emotions, therefore, as he con-tinued to be feted for his past accomplishments. On April 11, accompanied by his daughter, Barbara, and before an audience that included Gil Noble, Piri Thomas, Amiri Baraka, Attallah Shabazz, Ruby Dee, and Ossie Davis, Killens received the first literary award presented by Brooklyn's Creative Arts Center, an entity dedicated to Paul Robeson.

Killens returned to Atlanta in May for a tribute to Hoyt Fuller, who had died that month at the age of fifty-seven. While there, Killens spoke with Toni Cade Bambara, who served on the advisory board for the University of Georgia Press, about convincing the press to republish *Youngblood*. In June, she was pleased to announce that it would. Although the Pushkin vol-ume remained without a publisher, the decision represented a step toward rebuilding his literary stature, and Killens gladly accepted. On June 14, he wrote to Bambara that his first choice to write the foreword was Gayle but that he would accept Angelou, Sarah Wright, Belafonte, or Bambara.

After another stint at Yaddo, the sixty-five-year-old Killens began yet another job. Even though Bronx Community College was much closer than Howard University, working there still involved hours of commuting. On December 15, 1980, he wrote to Richard Trent, president of Medgar Evers College, which was five blocks from Killens's home, about the possibility of joining the faculty. Both Trent and Wendell Clement, dean of academic affairs, were enthused about the prospect, and after a round of discussions, Killens was offered a first-year appointment in the Humanities Division at an annual salary of slightly more than twenty-six thousand dollars. Killens always held spots in his seminars for writers from the community, and several regulars in his Bronx workshop simply followed him to Brooklyn.

Killens tackled his new responsibilities with zeal. He teamed up with Zala Chandler to speak at a campus program on "Education in the 1980s." He participated in readings (usually selecting something from the Pushkin manuscript) with Chandler, Steve Cannon, and Robert Ford Jr. On October 5, 1981, he spoke at Brooklyn College, a couple of miles down Bedford Avenue, to help launch the City University of New York's twentieth anniversary celebration, which would include a yearlong black arts and literature series.

Killens also maintained his extracurricular activities. After his presentation at Brooklyn, he rushed into Manhattan to attend a benefit for the Conference in Solidarity with the Liberation Struggles of the Peoples of Southern Africa, which was held a few days later at Riverside Church. In early November, Killens was in Baltimore, where he spoke at a gathering of the Middle Atlantic Writers Association on "The Responsibility of the Black Writer to His Community," the same theme on which he was formulating plans for a conference. At Medgar Evers College, he met with Clara Alexander, acting chair of the school's Humanities Division, along with professor and author Arnold Kemp. Elizabeth Nunez, Steve Cannon, and Carla Burns also became involved. The conference was planned for May 21–23, and letters of invitation were sent to Alice Childress, Paule Marshall, Gil Noble, Amiri Baraka, Quincy Troupe, John A. Williams, Addison Gayle, Claude Brown, and Woodie King Jr. Articulating the need for the conference, Killens wrote that it is "a time of Reaganomics, police state activities, resurgence of racist organizations such as the KKK, the American Nazi Party and the so-called 'moral majority' and a time when it becomes increasingly difficult for our Black voices to be heard through the printed page and mass media." Tying the question of literary production directly to political engagement, he continued, "It becomes especially important that Black Writers, who are, presumably, the voices of our people, strive to achieve a unity of purpose and perspective among ourselves."[12]

However, writers were not the only voices of the people. Unhappy with the administration's response to some demands, student demonstrators, joined by several faculty members, Kemp among them, effectively shut down the college for several days. The conference was officially postponed, though it is doubtful that the resources were in place to hold the event in the manner Killens anticipated. Nonetheless, Killens remained busy with cultural affairs, including some involving writers who would have attended the conference. On December 11, he hosted a book party for Noble, who had published *Black Is the Color of My TV Tube*. On January 31, he joined Carlos Russell and Quincy Troupe at the Ferry Bank Restaurant in downtown Brooklyn to celebrate the eightieth anniversary of the birth of Langston Hughes. A few days later, he arrived back at Howard University for a symposium on Paul Robeson sponsored by the Afro-American Studies Department.

The news on Killens's book projects remained somewhat grim, however. *Youngblood* was in production, and Howard University Press had indicated its willingness to reissue *And Then We Heard the Thunder*, but *A Man Ain't Nothing but a Man* went out of print, and Norton, Harcourt Brace Jovanovich, Scribner, and Random House joined the list of publishers that rejected *Great Black Russian*. Anne Freedgood, an editor at Random House, wrote to Lawrence Jordan, a former Killens student at Columbia University who now served as his agent, "I'm just not very impressed by John Killens' writing."[13]

In March, Killens underwent abdominal surgery; while he recuperated, his dear friend Loften Mitchell, who was on the faculty at the State University of New York, Binghamton, extended his "hand across two hundred miles and a thousand miles of snowbanks and snowdrifts."[14] Killens proved resilient. As part of his recovery, he accepted an invitation from Ewart Guinier and his wife, Genii, to visit Martha's Vineyard. The seventy-two-year-old Guinier, whose permanent residence was in Queens, was struggling to write a memoir, and Killens tried to persuade him to join the Saturday writing workshop at Medgar Evers College, whose participants included Doris Jean Austin, Arthur Flowers, Barbara Summers, Terry McMillan, Elizabeth Nunez, James Yates, Tom Feelings, and Nicholasa Mohr.

Killens received an unexpected boost to his spirits when Ron Foster and Bill Benenson optioned *And Then We Heard the Thunder* for one thousand dollars and seemed determined to bring the story to the screen. Foster represented the New York–based Leslie Theatrical Company, and Benenson managed BBZ Films, which operated out of Venice, California. By now, Killens knew enough to remain only cautiously optimistic, but the Foster-Benenson venture marked his most solid film opportunity in years. *Thunder* on the screen would go a long way toward removing the sting of his inability to persuade anyone to publish the Pushkin story.

Foster and Benenson retained Robert Caswell, Australia's most celebrated screenwriter, to adapt the novel. However, Caswell expressed reservations about his ability to mold an epic novel with the power and range of *Thunder* into a screenplay for a ninety-minute film and still retain the story's integrity. He nevertheless began the process of revision, and one of his first changes involved altering Samuels's name to Morrison because he wanted the audience to identify with a WASP character.

Killens worked on several short pieces during the remainder of the year, including the foreword to the reissue of Sam Yette's 1971 *The Choice: The Issue of Black Survival in America*, which Yette considered the "most obvious improvement associated with the republication of the book itself."[15] A second piece, the contemplative "What Went Wrong?" was destined for the *National Leader*. Reflecting on the March on Washington nineteen years earlier, Killens suggested that many people had forgotten Frederick Douglass's admonition about the necessity and value of struggle. He then cataloged a series of problems that had arisen since 1963. Although the March on Washington symbolized a new plateau in the black freedom struggle, he decided that "too many of us mistook the plateau for the Promised Land." The traditional civil rights leadership had ceded far too much control to white allies, a fact exemplified as far back as the march itself when they threatened to withhold support if John Lewis failed to tone down the militancy of his speech. Too much black political direction, Killens concluded, had been controlled by a particular economic bloc: paternalistic northern liberals. Echoing the sentiments of William Mackey Jr., a writer who was Killens's friend and a fellow Brooklyn resident, Killens argued that in some

African American corners, desegregation had been confused with assimilation; African Americans subsequently failed to respond sufficiently to the need to create independent black political mechanisms, educational facilities, and cultural institutions. In Killens's analysis, whenever strides toward black self-determination occurred, white economic support dwindled, resulting in the relative absence of long-distance institutions. He saw recent years as analogous to the end of Reconstruction, with contemporary times marked by a "weird combination" of Democrats and Dixiecrats; the political backwardness of the members of the white working class, as evidenced by their strong show of electoral support, even in the North, for George Wallace; the resurgence of hate groups such as the Ku Klux Klan; and the "new respectability" of states' rights rhetoric in Congress and the White House. Concerning this perceived "new Federalism," Killens remarked, "Hayes—Reagan. The names of the actors change. But the scenario remains the same."[16]

Killens addressed the derailing of the black struggle by the FBI and the CIA and their infiltrating agents provocateurs as well as what he considered the deliberate flooding of black communities with drugs by the establishment. But he stressed that he reflected on past events only to suggest coping strategies for the 1980s and beyond. Above all, he maintained, the African American community must become committed to the idea of protracted liberatory struggle characterized by intellectual, strategic, and financial self-reliance; the construction of self-defense support mechanisms; and full equality for African American women.[17]

Shortly after the article appeared, Killens penned a follow-up statement, for he felt he had worked too hurriedly. Among his mistakes, he noted, was the failure to address the lack of participation by black labor. After summarizing, as he had on many occasions, the history of racism in organized labor and its negative impact on black political initiatives, he speculated, "Can you imagine what a liberated Black labor force could do for the Black Freedom movement? Can you imagine what a happening it could be if Black artists and Black labor got together regularly?" Killens envisioned a black labor movement that would spawn African American studies programs, voter registration drives, theaters, publishing outlets, and "communiversities." He acknowledged the difficulty of escaping the influence of the labor movement's "great white fathers," but he pointed to the fact that Local 1199 of the hospital workers' union had recently elected a black woman as its president as sign that white union bosses could be dislodged.[18]

Killens felt that black leaders did not pursue vigorously enough the issue of reparations for slavery but added that it was crucial for African Americans to simultaneously work toward a "time of clarity" for the white masses, who needed to understand that what benefited black people benefited the working class and nonworking poor throughout the country: "Surely if we, white and Black, learn nothing more from the Reagan administration, it is that when social services are withdrawn from Black people, that more whites suffer than Blacks. We must work toward a mutual understanding that just as we need allies in the struggle, they need us, fundamentally."[19]

For Freedom, 1982–1986

Harlem's Studio Museum buzzed with hundreds of guests who attended the autograph party sponsored by the eastern regional branch of the Ballard Normal Hudson Alumni and Friends on October 24, 1982. The crowd, with six foot, five inch Gil Noble towering above most of it, circulated throughout the gallery as the writer they had come to fete remained seated and signed copies of the University of Georgia Press edition of *Youngblood* with some spin on the basic inscription "For Freedom." Killens did not miss the irony of the fact that a place where he could not have attended school in his youth had brought his first book back into print. The sixty-six-year-old writer, coming off of another setback regarding his health, was somewhat frail by then, a bit underweight. Friends who stepped to the autograph table were as likely to inquire about his health as to congratulate him. He repeatedly insisted that he felt all right, though more than a few of the well-wishers remained doubtful.

Other parties followed over the next few months—at the Muse Community Center in Brooklyn, the Afrikan Poetry Theater in Queens, the New Muse back in Brooklyn. Although he appreciated the attention, Killens tried to focus on other projects. He now possessed a virtually complete draft of "The Minister Primarily." More Pushkin promotion remained to be done, and Killens wanted to edit an anthology, tentatively titled *Black Southern Voices*, for the New American Library. He also had other ideas: more novels, a short story collection, films, and a book on the teaching of creative writing. The one suggestion from which he always shied away, however, was writing an autobiography. To him, such an action spelled the end, artistically if not literally.

Shortly after the book party at the Studio Museum, Kenneth Peeples Jr., who attended the party and edited the journal *Community Review*, a publication sponsored by the City University of New York, visited the author's home to interview him. After covering familiar ground about the origins of his career and his motivation as a writer, Killens spoke optimistically about his Pushkin book and "The Minister Primarily," allowing himself to imagine the latter manuscript transformed into a movie with Lou Gossett playing the lead role.[1]

The 450-page manuscript of "The Minister Primarily," now set in the 1980s after various false starts since the 1960s, traces the personal and political intrigue that follows the discovery of inexhaustible beds of cobanium (a radioactive metallic element more powerful and effective than uranium) in the Independent People's Democratic Republic of Guanaya, Africa's newest independent nation. The find makes Guanaya the richest African nation, and its leaders must decide the most advantageous way to extract the wealth from the land and to ensure that the resource is used more for social advancement than for increasing weapons capability. Guanaya's problems interest the Soviet Union and the United States, both of which envision offering technical assistance and financial inducements to gain control over Guanayan cobanium. The United States makes the first pitch. But as the Guanayan delegation headed by Prime Minister Jaja Okwu Olivamaki (a surname that combines the names of Oliver Reginald Tambo and Vusumzi Make) prepares for its U.S. visit, it learns that an uprising is under way in Guanaya. Rather than postpone the trip and the crucial negotiations, the leaders decide to send an Olivamaki look-alike, folk singer James Jay Leander Johnson, who is working in Guanaya at the Club Lido (the name of a club that Killens had visited while in Nigeria in 1961), to impersonate the prime minister abroad. As Olivamaki reasons, "If we do postpone the trip, the world will know we're having difficulties and will think we are unstable. Great nations do not lend their money or technicians on this basis. And furthermore it will encourage outside interference in our affairs." Thus, Jimmy Jay and his "cabinet" are off on a comedic, raucous, somewhat farcical, and occasionally dangerous romp through Washington, D.C., New York City, and Jimmy Jay's hometown, Lolliloppi, Mississippi. Johnson "made his pilgrimage to the Motherland to find himself, and now he found himself on his way back to the U.S.A. as somebody else."[2]

Much of the action is lively and indeed funny, as Killens puts to good use the voice he honed in *The Cotillion*. In fact, with judicious editing, "The Minister Primarily" would be the better novel. Its plot is more compelling, and its scope is greater, subsuming the identity and cultural nationalist concerns of the earlier novel under a more encompassing Pan-Africanist, anticolonialist, socialist framework. On one level, the manuscript is a summary—even a collage at some points—of Killens's cultural and political journey. The deeper or continued exploration of certain social situations, political scenarios, and personalities such as Harry Belafonte is a plus. Having appeared in two previous Killens novels, Belafonte has become a serial character, a sort of Falstaff. But the mere repetition that often occurs in the story is a drawback. A section of the opening scene in *'Sippi*, for example, appears almost verbatim in "The Minister Primarily," as do passages from "The Half Ain't Never Been Told" (although they might have been written first for the novel). A looser association exists between the author's accounts of his 1961 trips to Africa and his descriptions in the novel, but the treatment in the story is far from fresh. Moreover, Killens is a character once again, appearing at a rally in one scene and described on another occasion as "an obscure novelist." Though this instance is amusing, as is his inclusion on Lumumba's bookshelf in *The Cotillion*, the technique becomes overbearing when Jimmy Jay berates Hollywood moguls for not turning *Youngblood* and *And Then We Heard the Thunder* into movies. Stale also are some of the sex scenes: the white vixen–black buck combination seems passé. At best, such scenes raise the question of how Killens could have been so critical of Melvin Van Peebles.

The writing is overdrawn and a bit suffocating, but Killens's trademark use of humor bursts through. In one scene, the Minister Primarily fields questions from reporters:

> "What do you think of the Cold War climate, Mr. Prime Minister?"
>
> "Too much weather," the P.M. cagily answered, even though he was distracted.
>
> "How does it feel to be in the Free World, Mr. Prime Minister?"
>
> "Oh, it's very nice indeed, and I bring you greetings from it. You should visit us sometimes."

The dialogue flows smoothly when the Minister Primarily befriends a drunken black man along a parade route and calls him comrade. A government security agent responds, "I don't know about all this comrade business. Sounds too much like commonism." The Minister Primarily replies,

"That's the trouble with you democratic capitalists. Everything halfway decent and humanistic, you attribute to communism. You sure give them a lot of credit. It's a wonder that more Black people don't join the Communist Party."[3]

Prior to landing in Africa, Jimmy Jay spends time in London, where he makes the political scene, on one occasion heckling a representative of the Workers Workless Party who has lambasted the Labor Party for selling out the working class: "What did your blawsted working class do about colonialism in Africa and Asia? What about the Nigerians? The South Africans? The Chinese? The West Indians? You and your bloody working class—the greatest sell-out artists of them all. You sold out your own damn class of people everywhere on earth. China, India, Africa, the Caribbean." Jimmy Jay later reveals an even broader perspective when he identifies with the struggles of the Irish and Lebanese.[4]

"The Minister Primarily" is an important and entertaining meditation on the modern global jockeying among nations for influence and power as connected to questions of freedom and peace, movement that speaks to the issue of African America and its relationship to Africa. The novel also addresses in political and personal terms notions of African tradition and African American retention and identity. If the manuscript were saved from being a greatest hits collection, streamlined overall with some of the name-dropping reduced, it would be Killens's third-best effort, behind *And Then We Heard the Thunder* and *Youngblood*, in that order.

Killens began looking for a partner on the anthology because the publisher had requested a coeditor who was an academic. Henry Louis Gates Jr., a thirty-two-year-old assistant professor of Afro-American studies and English at Yale University, was tabbed for the job. But Gates, always with a streak of businessman in him, had problems with the contract and procrastinated. Killens tried to reach him several times by phone and finally wrote in February, "I know that Black Visibility Month is a very busy time for all of us, but tempus is fugiting nevertheless. Is it that you have lost interest in the project?"[5] Two weeks later, Gates responded that he had been slow in recovering from the New Haven flu but remained interested in the project. He also suggested that if the contractual problems could not be resolved, Killens should find another collaborator. Jerry W. Ward Jr., an English professor at Mississippi's Tougaloo College, eventually assumed coeditorship. He and Killens "shared a belief that the writing of black Southerners is foundational in the evolution of African American literature. That belief, of course, deemphasizes the foundational contributions of New England writers and positions the South as the matrix for what is essentially African American—hang current anti-essentialist arguments."[6]

Killens spent part of the summer of 1983 at Yaddo. Grace drove up with him and returned to pick him up because he could no longer manage the drive alone. At the age of sixty-seven and in fragile health, he became drowsy after three hours behind the wheel.

Bill Benenson remained serious about filming *Thunder*. He showed some of Robert Caswell's writing to Robert Raymond, an Australian who was producing *Schindler's List*. Raymond expressed interest in the project, prompting Ron Foster and Benenson to extend the option. The producers seemed poised to deliver in ways Haskell Wexler had not, and Killens was itching to try his hand at the screenplay, as he had with his adaptation of *Youngblood*, but he did not press the matter.

That fall, Killens traveled to Morgan State University in Baltimore, where Andrew Billingsley had assumed the presidency, to attend a two-day conference on "Preserving the Literary Tradition of Black Colleges and Universities." Directed by Burney J. Hollis at Billingsley's suggestion, the conference was a response to the recent death of Nick Aaron Ford and paid tribute to Ford and another longtime Morgan State faculty member, novelist Waters E. Turpin. Writers and scholars including Sonia Sanchez, Addison Gayle, Margaret Reid, Eugenia Collier, and Richard Long drew crowds of several hundred. Killens delivered a lengthy luncheon address during which he hit on all of his familiar themes: writing to change the world, the inspiration of Frederick Douglass and Kelly Miller, the greatness of black people, the struggle-oriented tradition in African American literature, art as propaganda, the writer as necessary activist, the need for antisexism in the movement, revolutionizing the English language, and the imperative for long-distance runners. Commenting specifically on the current political scene and thereby explaining some of his recent actions, Killens argued, "To extend Malcolm's admonition to its logical fulfillment: from 'by any means necessary' to 'by every means necessary.' Altogether and simultaneously—Electoral politics. Sit-ins. Stand ins. Voter registration drives. Marches on City Hall and Washington, not in the hundreds, not in the hundreds of thousands, but in the millions." He turned his attention to President Reagan, "King Ronald," who, according to Killens, "labors under the illusion that the great gluttonous feasts enjoyed at the bounteous tables of oil moguls and Chrysler and General Motors somehow make the unemployed masses healthy and obese."[7]

The Killenses further spoke to politics during the ensuing holiday season. Eschewing Christmas cards in favor of an update letter, they "left out all of the obviously negative items like Reagan, Lebanon and those 'dangerous subversive Grenadians.'" Instead, they focused on the Killens family. Pushkin was "still seeking, stubbornly, a publisher." "The Minister Primarily" had begun to make the rounds, and a nonfiction book on creative writing, "Write On!" was "ready, willing, and able." The new edition of *Youngblood* had gone into another printing. The Killenses were less pleased with Mel Watkins's introduction to *And Then We Heard the Thunder* and with Howard University Press's overall handling of the republication of that book, believing that it would have been better off without Watkins's "faint praise" and that the sampling of lukewarm reviews included at the end could have been replaced by available rave reviews. But John and Grace were not "chronic grouchers," and they appreciated the fact that the novel had been reissued: "We must always think positively, and be thankful for small favors, it says here in fine print."[8]

In addition to assisting her husband, Grace had begun working part-time with a community group, Urban Strategies. She brought various cultural programs and artists to schools in the Brownsville section of Brooklyn. It was "an enjoyable experience for her as well as for the Black and Puerto Rican children who desperately need these kinds of cultural experiences which will help them to aspire to something positive." Chuck was "getting it together and doing well," planning to return to photography, one of his early interests. The Killens-Rivera combo was busy and productive, involved in a number of cultural, community, and educational ventures. Abiba thrived in high school; Barra pursued art courses; Kutisa proved a bundle of energy, whether the matter at hand was "school, dance classes, or just talking." And Ma Willie was also a match for most. As usual, she was at the Killens household for the holidays and at age eighty-seven was "ready for the round of parties."[9]

In 1983 and 1984, *Freedomways* published a portion of Killens's novella, "Run Like Hell and Holler Fire!" The plot revolves around three African American brothers, Charles Coleman, Richard Coleman, and Jeff Coleman. Jeff, an attorney, convinces his two older brothers, another lawyer and a doctor, to avenge the murder of their father, Moose Coleman, head of the Ludlow, Georgia, branch of the National Association for the Advancement of Colored People. Moose Coleman had been gunned down by Sheriff Hicks, who held a twisted infatuation for Coleman's wife. However, the characters are not developed enough to make such retaliation by the sons believable, and the framework of the story is not particularly creative. The opening passage, a funeral scene, is almost identical to the close of 'Sippi. As in 'Sippi, The Cotillion, and "The Minister Primarily," Killens inserts true-life figures as characters: Stokely Carmichael, H. Rap Brown, Ralph Abernathy, Coretta Scott King, Sidney Poitier, Harry Belafonte, James Farmer, Floyd McKissick, and Rosa Parks attend Coleman's funeral. The device is worn, as is some of the dialogue, especially those of Jeff's comments that Killens had already used. For example, Jeff argues that a lawyer can never be revolutionary and at best can only create an illusion that African Americans can get justice under an oppressive American system and explains that he supported Martin Luther King Jr. on nonviolence when used as a tactic but could not accept it as a philosophy.

The most interesting aspect of the story is the author's continuing response to family history. As a youth, Killens had longed for his parents to reconcile, and he later created fictionalized and idealized versions of them as a harmonious couple, particularly in parts of Youngblood. More than a decade after his father's death, Killens was still at it. The story is set in 1972, the same year Myles Killens died, and Moose and his wife are remembered as a perfectly loving couple with three admiring sons in a close-knit, nuclear family. Killens continued to control on the page what he could never dictate in life.

He no longer roamed as frequently or as far beyond New York City. By the mid-1980s, a formidable cast of younger and more popular African American writers competed for jobs, workshops, and speaking gigs, and Killens found himself in less demand. In addition, his health could not have withstood the challenges of his earlier schedule. He continued to make appearances, however, visiting Atlanta University—his native state was now the one that called him most—for an event sponsored by the Southern Collective of Black Writers and the Institute of the Black World. Readings from Youngblood were performed by Ebon Dooley, Alice Lovelace, and Malkia M'buzi. Soon thereafter, Killens visited a writers' and educators' workshop in Gary, Indiana, and was impressed with the energy of a gathering that included Mayor Richard Hatcher and writers Herman Gilbert and Shirley Lefore.

Although less visible nationally, Killens remained a valued local resource, speaking on a number of occasions, often to a new generation, though sometimes to disappointing turnouts. On January 15, 1984, the night after he turned sixty-eight, he ventured out into inclement weather to attend a Brooklyn book party for *Confirmation: An Anthology of African-American Women*, edited by Amiri Baraka and Amina Baraka. Killens made introductory remarks before readings by the Barakas and Rashidah Ismaili, Akua Leslie Hope, Geraldine Wilson, and Brenda Conner-Bey. However, he did not stick around for much of the show. Conner-Bey, an organizer of the event, noticed his early exit and later informed him that he had "missed Amina Baraka praising you, not only for being the gifted writer you are, but for being consistent in the struggle for black people's rights and how very honored she was that you had agreed to act as guest host."[10]

The next day, Killens again spoke in Brooklyn at the third annual Martin Luther King luncheon hosted by the New York Alliance of Black School Educators. Three days later, he lectured on Pushkin at the Harlem Library. He and Grace then traveled to Washington, D.C., where he chatted with Sterling Brown, whom he called the Original Strong Man, in reference to Brown's stirring poem, "Strong Men." Killens later suggested that Sam Yette pay the eighty-two-year-old Brown "a visit and bring along pictures you have of him. I got the feeling he was lonely for good strong creative conversation."[11]

Back in New York Killens appeared at the West Side YMCA on March 9 for "Writers from the Harlem Writers Guild," where he read along with aspiring novelists Grace Edwards-Yearwood, Jean Arnold, and Terry McMillan and veterans Brenda Wilkinson and Rosa Guy. Next up were appearances at Hunter College and the College of New Rochelle School of New Resources at the New York Theological Seminary. Near the end of March, he was featured at the Muse with Alice Childress and the up-and-coming Arthur Flowers as part of the lecture series, "From Fables to Novels: The Storytelling Tradition in the African World."

Flowers was in the midst of writing a novel that depended heavily on the myth of Highjohn de Conqueror. The myth was fair game, but Flowers's rendering of the character drew the ire of poet and fellow workshop member Baron James Ashanti, who accused Flowers of plagiarism. Workshop members took sides, and Killens was caught in the middle. After carefully reading the two writers' manuscripts, Killens invited them to his home to settle the matter. More decisive than he usually was with friends, he told

Flowers, "You've got to give it to Ashanti, he had it first." Flowers apologized, but Ashanti, who only wanted vindication, said, "*He* can have it."[12]

Not long thereafter, Flowers returned to the Killens home for another literary negotiation. By 1984, Flowers had taken over for Bill Ford as head of the Harlem Writers Guild, though Ford still aimed to serve as the de facto director. Following a verbal clash between Ford and McMillan, the guild split into factions. Flowers, who supported McMillan, was ousted from his position. Killens again stepped in, and with his blessing, Flowers and other writers, including McMillan, Ashanti, Joyce Dukes, and Doris Jean Austin, split off from the Harlem Writers Guild and formed the New Renaissance Writers Guild.

Killens's workshops were going well even though they typically enrolled almost thirty students. McMillan, Austin, and Flowers remained involved, joining Malaika Adero, Carol Dixon, Jacqueline Johnson, Elizabeth Nunez, Kay Brown, Barbara Summers, Cheryl Williams, Carole Gregory, and Conner-Bey. Killens diligently kept a notebook in which he responded to as many texts as he could manage. Nunez was at work on "October All Over," which would eventually become *When Rocks Dance*, her first published novel. Flowers neared the finish line with *De Mojo Blues*, his first novel, and was working on what would become his second, *Another Good Loving Blues*, using language Killens called "magnificent." McMillan too wrote portions of her first novel, *Mama*, but Killens was more immediately concerned with a short story she submitted, "The Monster." Killens also began another project, "The Exodusters," a book about black immigration to New York City, mainly from the South and the Caribbean, between World War I and World War II.

Although Killens was traveling less, he remained active. On March 31, 1984, the Killenses held a reception (soliciting twenty-dollar contributions) to support the election of delegates committed to Jesse Jackson. With Flowers as campaign manager, Killens ran as one of the Brooklyn Democrats for Jesse Jackson but was not chosen to attend the Democratic National Convention. Killens nevertheless was pleased with Jackson's strong showing in New York City and remained optimistic about possibilities for Jackson in 1988 and 1992.

Around the same time, Grace sent out an appeal to the couple's friends and acquaintances to garner support for the South African Drought Drive. While she waited for responses, she and her husband read manuscripts for

Southern Black Voices and prepared "The Minister Primarily" and the latest version of *Great Black Russian* for another round of submissions to publishers. In years past, Grace had made unilateral editorial decisions when working as her husband's typist, a practice that had caused friction. She was more cooperative now, and their working relationship was much smoother, though the work remained a handful. Both she and her husband were exhausted by summer's end.

News came from afar. Paule Marshall sent a postcard from Arizona, through which she passed while driving back to New York from Berkeley, where she had been teaching: "The country is lovely. Wish I could say the same about the politics."[13] George Lamming sent a note from Barbados reporting that Bayard Rustin "has been hanging around Barbados ever since the American invasion of Grenada. What would he be up to? He spent a few days here at the Atlantis Hotel where I normally stay. There's something very suspect about him. By the way don't reply in any way that might be confidential."[14] Rustin was in Barbados on behalf of Freedom House, an organization founded by Eleanor Roosevelt, Wendell Willkie, and others in 1941 that billed itself as an independent organization but was funded in part by the U.S. government and was invested ideologically in anticommunism.

Gerald Gladney, a staff member at Doubleday, sent Killens an advance copy of Mari Evans's *Black Women Writers*, to which Killens contributed an essay on Alice Childress. He had read her stories and seen most of her plays and had always found her work stimulating. Of his peers, Childress's career had most closely resembled Killens's in terms of politics and range of genre. He did not particularly care for her play, *Wedding Band*, since he did not identify with the heroine's struggle to preserve her relationship with a white man. He liked *A Hero Ain't Nothin' but a Sandwich*, though in the novel he wanted the hand of the oppressor more sharply drawn. He viewed *A Short Walk* as Childress's best novel and wrote that "perhaps her greatest gift, along with her satiric bent and the thematic accent on struggle, is the leitmotif of love for people, particularly her own people. I have come away from most of her writing mighty damn proud of the human race, especially the African aspect of it."[15] Childress subsequently wrote to Killens, "I thank you for your evaluation of my work. It gave me a fine feeling of pride and pleasure—and pause to think over the long years of our friendship— struggle in the Sun."[16]

Still bucking against the idea of writing his autobiography, Killens nevertheless completed a lengthy piece, "The Half Ain't Never Been Told," for inclusion in *Contemporary Authors Autobiography Series*. He concluded the essay by speaking proudly of his family, including his three grandchildren, his writing workshop at Medgar Evers College, and his hopes for publishing success: "I come home from the workshop, have lunch with Grace (my lovely wife), watch the madness of a football game, or basketball, or baseball. AND WISH AND PRAY FOR THE DAY THAT *PUSHKIN* WILL BE PUBLISHED."[17]

Killens continued his efforts to stage a writers' conference at Medgar Evers, collaborating at one point with philosophy professor Michael Fitzgerald on a proposal to the National Endowment for the Humanities. The grant was at first rejected, but after Nunez reworked it, the conference, to be held in March 1986, received an initial award of $20,480.

Friends and colleagues faded permanently from the scene with increasing regularity—the still youthful Julian Mayfield, the sickly Chester Himes, the elderly Harry Haywood. But at least one notable elder was doing well. On September 16, 1984, Killens participated in an event honoring Louise Thompson Patterson, who was both celebrating her eighty-third birthday and preparing to retire to California, where she would live for most of the next fifteen years. One of a rapidly dwindling number who could speak with firsthand knowledge about the Harlem Renaissance, Patterson had served as an editorial secretary for Langston Hughes and Zora Neale Hurston. Patterson and Hughes were among the group of artists and activists who visited the Soviet Union in 1932, and she toured the front during the Spanish Civil War. In subsequent years, her activism included serving as the executive secretary of the New York Committee to Free Angela Davis. Killens's tribute, "In the Great Tradition of Black Womanhood," noted Patterson's struggles in the face of the racism she encountered during her youth as well as her subsequent achievements—her 1923 graduation with honors from Berkeley, her teaching career in Arkansas and Virginia, and her work with the Urban League, the Council on African Affairs, the International Workers Order, and the American Institute of Marxist Studies.

Killens felt ill at the event and was diagnosed with a tumor in his colon. Doctors operated later that week, and Killens was told that he would need most of the fall to recuperate. This latest physical setback caused Killens to break several commitments, among them a September 22 meeting to discuss the formation of an organization to be called African Activists in America. However, he later submitted a written statement focusing on three points or suggestions: the need for overall unity, the participation of women as absolute equals in leadership, and a clearly defined program and role for youth. Another fledgling group that commanded Killens's attention was Art against Apartheid, which in October kicked off a series of interventions under the rubric "A Salute to Freedom Fighters in South Africa." Killens also had to postpone a benefit book party for the organization from October 27 until December 15. For a fifteen-dollar contribution, those who attended the affair at Abyssinian Baptist Church received an autographed copy of *Youngblood* or *And Then We Heard the Thunder*. The Reverend Calvin Butts welcomed the audience; Noble emceed; Aminata Moseka (Abbey Lincoln) sang; Ruby Dee read from *Youngblood*; and Ossie Davis read from *And Then We Heard the Thunder*. A stubborn and defiant Killens returned to classes at Medgar Evers College before the end of the semester.

In March 1985, Grace Killens engaged in a contentious series of exchanges with Lisa Jones, daughter of Amiri Baraka, who had interviewed John Killens for an article she wrote on Malcolm X for the *Village Voice*.[18] Grace objected to several inaccuracies in the piece and especially to Jones's characterization of John Killens as an avid integrationist who would not have been expected to show an interest in Malcolm's ideas. Grace made a clear distinction between desegregation (the term John had used) and integration (the term Jones substituted). She then irritated Jones by referring to her as a "young white woman."[19] Ron Plotkin, an editor at the paper, stood behind Jones's article, and Jones offered to let Grace hear a tape of the interview. Grace said she would be happy to listen to it because she was sure that there would be a mismatch between information on the tape and that printed in the paper. When Jones asked the difference between *desegregation* and *integration*, Grace told her that the answer was in the dictionary.

At the invitation of James Turner, Killens again hit the road for the National Council of Black Studies meeting, held at Cornell University on March 21–24. He and Grace then traveled to Winston-Salem to spend time at the home of Maya Angelou. By May, they were back in Killens's native state, this time at the University of Georgia, where Killens was featured at "Roots in Georgia: A Literary Symposium" organized by the *Georgia Review*. Billed as an official university bicentennial event, the gathering represented an unprecedented celebration of Georgia's literary history. Other featured writers included Erskine Caldwell and James Dickey. On the evening of May 16, Toni Cade Bambara introduced Killens, and he spoke about his Georgia roots and read from *Youngblood*. The following day he participated in a panel on "Southern Stereotype: Reflecting, Shaping, and/or Resisting." Killens enjoyed his time at the symposium, although he noted that the audience of five hundred contained at most twenty African Americans. Somewhat worn down again, Killens passed on the next temptation, a trip to accept a lifetime achievement award from the Before Columbus Foundation, instead sending a statement to Ishmael Reed to be read at the ceremony.

The author spent a month at MacDowell during the summer of 1985. He worked, as usual, on a number of projects, including the manuscript for "Blessed Obsession," an adult novel about Denmark Vesey. Fellow writer Elizabeth Michael cast him in a poem titled "Hiatus," describing him as a model of concentration, although such was not always the case. He fretted about his mother, who was slated to undergo a surgical procedure in Washington, D.C. He sought to reassure himself as well as the eighty-nine-year-old Willie Lee Killens when he wrote, "But a strong courageous woman like you will certainly pull through with flying colors." He promised to head for Washington as soon as he returned home from New Hampshire and advised his mother not to worry about her future care: "Whatever has to be done for you will be done by your children. You have done so much for us." He confidently revealed that a deal was in the works to film *And Then We Heard the Thunder*. Indeed, the producers were extending the option, and Foster and Caswell would be visiting him in New Hampshire. Killens optimistically wrote to his mother, "I am looking forward to the day when I shall escort you to the Grand Premier in New York."[20]

Also while at MacDowell, Killens anticipated finally bringing a major writers' conference to Medgar Evers College, though his role as director was largely ceremonial. A committee of faculty members, including Nunez as well as novelists Steve Cannon and Arnold Kemp, worked to orchestrate the biggest cultural event in the college's fifteen-year history. The theme, "The Social Responsibility of the Writer to the Community," was familiar yet timely. Discussions of stereotypes, which abound in African American literary circles, reached a new level of intensity after the release of the film version of Alice Walker's *The Color Purple* near the end of 1985. Prior to the movie's release, the debate about the novel had unfolded mainly among literary and academic types. When Kenneth Peeples had asked Killens if in giving Walker the Pulitzer Prize the jury had attempted to encourage more writing by African Americans, Killens responded, "I see this as an attempt

by publishers to say this is the way black writers should write about themselves. 'In this way you'll get prizes. We'll make sure you're on the bestsell-
er's list, etc. Don't write as if you love black people or that [black] people
are a great people, we're not interested in that.'"[21] But the film's widespread
popularity brought the topic into virtually all quarters of the black community and provided much of the explanation for the two thousand people
who attended the conference.

Conference preparations enmeshed Killens in another, potentially damaging, controversy. In the spring of 1985, Killens had promised members of
the Calabash Poets Workshop, an organization that had created much of the
literary activity and excitement in New York City over the previous fifteen
years and that included Zizwe Ngafua, B. J. Ashanti, Sekou Sundiata, and
Killens's son-in-law, Louis Reyes Rivera, that they would be represented
or involved in the conference. But Killens did not follow through strongly
enough on his promise with the conference committee, which perceived the
inclusion of these writers as a mild suggestion rather than a firm commitment. On November 5, several members of the group wrote to Killens and
Nunez to remind them of his promise. The bottom line: "YOUR CHOICE is
to correct this omission from the conference, & in so doing so, adequately
include us into the proceedings as representatives of the younger generation, particularly as befits both the poetry & fiction panels or be recorded
as having insulted our generation even further."[22] At that point, the group
considered disrupting the conference.

The protesters made a reasonable case, but the generation argument
never gained traction with the planning committee because some members were younger than most of Calabash writers and were not convinced
by the claim that those writers were the younger generation. In any case,
the committee would have agreed with Sundiata's self-criticism—that is,
that if the Calabash writers had done what they had been capable of, they
would be running their own major conference and making exclusion from
other conferences a moot point. A compromise was reached under which
Flowers, who was not a Calabash member although his name appeared
on the letter, was added to the fiction panel. Rivera remained unsatisfied,
sending his father-in-law a seventeen-page treatise on what "truly represents meeting our responsibilities to our community."[23] However, Rivera
overestimated Killens's influence on the organizing committee. Although
he did not object to the inclusion of the Calabash members and agonized

over the situation, he simply was incapable at that point of delivering more than he did.

In July, the University of Cincinnati, at the behest of Angelene Jamison, head of the Department of Afro-American Studies, had approved up to five thousand dollars to sponsor a two-week visit by Killens. He and Grace arrived on campus at the beginning of November. After opening the first week with a reception at the Faculty Club, Killens conducted three workshops and delivered an address on "The Responsibility of the Black Writer to the Community." During the second week, he ran two workshops and gave a lecture on "Incidents and Experiences of Growing Up in Georgia and Their Impact on My Writing."

Two months later, Killens again returned to Georgia as a writer in residence in his hometown. The Georgia Endowment for the Humanities had approved a $4,660 joint grant request from Mercer University, Macon Junior College, and the Middle Georgia Regional Library to bring in Killens to lead creative writing workshops and deliver several lectures. Maya Angelou savored the irony, writing to Killens, "But of course, my dear, Georgia has been waiting to admit you into its southern embrace. OK, so I admit it waited a damn long time. I also know that once in its embrace, you have to be very careful that it doesn't tighten up and start to choke you. Writer-in-residence in Macon, Georgia. Who'd have thought we'd live to tell that tale?"[24]

On January 4, the Killenses flew to Atlanta and then traveled to Macon by bus. After dinner with Joe Popson, chair of the Division of Humanities at Macon Junior College, and his wife, they were shown to their lodgings in the W. G. Lee Alumni House on the Mercer campus. Killens was impressed by the grand piano in the living room, the fifty-foot dining room table, the ostentatious chandeliers, and the most spacious bath he had ever used. He supposed that he and Grace were the first African Americans ever to stay there. Killens did an interview for the *Macon Telegraph* before spending the rest of his sojourn teaching workshops and lecturing. In addition, he visited Macon Junior College, Albany State College, Fort Valley State College, and the Central Correctional Institution.

The Killenses also spent time with the old Pleasant Hill crew—the Brunsons, the Pilgrims, the Bonners, the Lees. Walter "B. B." McElroy, who had graduated from Ballard with Killens, encouraged his daughter, Tina McElroy Ansa, a freelance writer and aspiring novelist, to attend the first week of workshops, though she could not stay for the second week. She brought along the pages of a manuscript and received inspiration and encouragement from Killens that helped her to turn the project into her first novel, *Baby of the Family*.

On January 14, Killens's seventieth birthday, he conducted what he considered a good workshop at the Washington Library. From just outside the library, the valiant writer-in-residence had a clear view down into Pleasant Hill. As Angelou posed the question, who really could have known?

Before heading back to New York, the Killenses stopped in Atlanta for several appearances sponsored by the Atlanta-Fulton Public Library. On January 23, he met with Michael Lomax's Afro-American literature class at Spelman College and lectured at Morris Brown College, where he had been a somewhat frightened undergraduate fifty years earlier. By the time he left Atlanta on January 25, Killens had been made an honorary citizen and had toured much of the city. It was the culmination of the most rigorous three-week stretch of activities that he had attempted in many years. He and Grace could think of little more than getting home to rest.

The writers' conference opened at Medgar Evers College on March 22, 1986. Killens greeted the invited writers, many of whom had long-standing ties to him or had participated in his previous conferences—Margaret Walker, Maya Angelou, Toni Cade Bambara, Ishmael Reed, Calvin Hernton, Phil Petrie, Samuel Yette, Sonia Sanchez, Quincy Troupe, Amiri Baraka, Lonne Elder III, Richard Wesley, Addison Gayle, and Mari Evans.[25] Killens began his welcoming remarks by telling the audience that writers, educators, and communicators had a responsibility to remain angry, though not despairing, about racism in the country. He spoke, as James Baldwin had at the 1965 New School conference, of the need to get America to face up to its history. Again he railed against negative depictions of African Americans in the mass media. Then, for what he knew might be the final time in the public gaze and was certainly the final time before a sizable audience, he turned forcefully to his favorite topic, one that had consumed so much of his life's energy and creative effort. Using his books as sources for anecdotes, he spoke of the centrality of African American literary heroes to social struggle: "Where are the novels, the dramas, the epics about Saint Harriet of the Eastern Shore? Saint Medgar and Saint Fannie Lou of 'Sippi?

Saint Rosa of Montgomery? Saint Malcolm of Nebraska? Saint Martin of Atlanta? The great Saint Paul of Rutgers?"[26]

At the conference, Walker, Angelou, Bambara, Evans, Sanchez, and others amplified Killens's call, urging black writers and cultural workers to show their commitment to the black community. Walker, who, like Killens, had entered her eighth decade and whom Killens had introduced as the "Empress of the Black Experience," noted, "Black writers are tied to the black world and are responsible to it." Walker's nationalism, like Killens's, opened onto a broader outlook as she forecast a "new people's socialism of the twenty-first century" and spoke optimistically of a "pluralistic people's world." She urged African American writers to "behold the vision and begin the task."[27]

Angelou spoke of a double responsibility: individual concern for one's artistic development and collective concern for the advancement of black people. Making veiled references to the controversy surrounding *The Color Purple*, she stressed that to progress as a group, African Americans needed to love one another. And she argued that the theme of love had always been a central although perhaps overlooked quality of African American poetry.[28]

Bambara and Evans directly addressed the disputes over *The Color Purple*. Bambara, who saw African American writers as responsible for reminding people of what they were pretending not to know, denounced the round of *Purple* debates as largely a diversion promoted by elements of the media to diminish efforts to dismantle apartheid in South Africa and mobilize protest against the MOVE bombing in Philadelphia. Evans suggested that those in attendance focus on what they could control—the building of a black cultural infrastructure, for example—and take proactive steps with respect to issues such as blacks' disproportionately high incarceration rates and the proper care of black children. Because African American artists draw from the group, she argued, they owe the group, and she cited W. E. B. Du Bois's "Criteria of Negro Art" (Killens could think of no better reference) as a rationale for self-consciously political literary works.[29]

In one of the conference's most moving presentations, Sanchez exhorted artists and others to form a broad progressive alliance to combat racism and economic exploitation. She mentioned the Middle Passage, the genocide of Native Americans, South African apartheid, the expanding U.S. prison-industrial complex, the invasion of Grenada, the danger posed by nuclear waste, the MOVE bombing, and the Atlanta child murders as political developments to which responses had been inadequate. Asserting that "Americonomics" (the economic policies of the Reagan administration) was a systematic attack on people to discourage activism, she called for the "building of institutions and consciousness not tied to the swing of capital." Alluding somewhat obliquely to the *Purple* brouhaha, Sanchez admonished, "If you are doing, you don't have time to talk about other writers."[30]

At that night's banquet in his honor, Killens thanked all those in attendance for their support and told them that such affirmation encouraged him in his efforts. Although he was visibly tired, he read from Langston Hughes's poem, "Mother to Son," and announced that he fully intended to "keep on keeping on." He declared that the powers that be, chief among them the media and the board of education, were engaged in a counter cultural revolution. As he had done at previous conferences dating back to 1959, he called for a permanent National Black Writers Conference, adding a reiteration of the idea of a writers' union and the question of forming an "amalgamated Black press" to ensure that black myths, legends, plays, and films were disseminated. He closed by reading from the greetings in the conference booklet: "We can take this beachhead and maintain it, if we work tirelessly, and fearlessly. We must push forward, for there is nought behind us save the open sea. The open sea and vicious sharks. And Moby Dick."[31]

Killens did not attend the conference closing, over which Arnold Kemp presided. He was already busy preparing himself for another literary event the same day during which he would again be acknowledged for lifetime achievement. James Brooks, chair of the English department at City College, was coordinating "A Decade of Celebration" in honor of those writers who had received tributes at previous Hughes festivals—Baldwin, Gwendolyn Brooks, Killens, Bambara, Marshall, Morrison, Sterling Brown, and Walker. Brooks and Brown did not attend but sent representatives. Ralph Ellison, who had been honored in 1984, was not involved with the event.

Dr. K's Run, 1986–1987

After the euphoria generated by the National Black Writers Conference subsided, John Oliver Killens invited several members of the planning committee to his home to brainstorm about a March 1988 sequel. He seemed relaxed yet energetic, at one point taking his guests on a tour of his home during which he lingered momentarily before the large print of Paul Robeson on display in the basement. Killens commented about how much Maya Angelou liked the poster. He also showed off a new novel that he was reading, Ishmael Reed's *Reckless Eyeballing*. He thought that Reed was a great writer but felt that he should slow down the pace of his narrative, not a surprising comment from an old social realist.

Although he had suffered his share of physical ailments, Killens felt that his mind was still sharp. He prepared to return to MacDowell for the summer. And fans still called, even if less frequently. In June, before driving to the hills of New Hampshire, he attended a writers' conference in Chicago that also included Herman Gilbert, Eugene Redmond, and Sterling Plumpp. Some in Chicago, including Gilbert, hailed Killens as the dean of African American writers. Based on accomplishment, engagement, height of profile, and influence, only Gwendolyn Brooks could challenge him for the title.

Bill Benenson, who still had not met Killens in person, sent a copy of Robert Caswell's finished screenplay for *And Then We Heard the Thunder*. Killens thought that the screenplay needed further work. Both Fannie Mae and Millie had been dropped, sacrificed in favor of a focus on the relationship between Celia and Solly. Caswell and Killens exchanged letters, with Caswell explaining his view that Saunders had to be kept "morally strong." He admitted that he had not reckoned with how his depiction of the Solly-Celia relationship would play in the American racial context. For Solly to be wrapped up romantically in Celia, without that affair being framed by the racial politics implied in the Solly-Millie and Solly-Fannie relationships, would not, in Killens's view, represent a strong moral move. Despite his criticism, he believed that the artistic differences were surmountable. Caswell agreed to tinker with the manuscript, and it looked like the film would be made. Robert Raymond agreed to coproduce; Stanley Kubrick was being courted to direct. *Variety* magazine announced that the movie was definitely in the works.[1]

Killens also became involved with another film project. Larry Clark and the Songhai Film group had contacted him about working on *Slow Boat to Moscow*, a film based on the true stories of African Americans—mainly George Tynes and others from Tuskegee, Alabama—who left the United States during the Great Depression and went to the Soviet Union to aid in the development of agriculture and make movies as a cultural statement. Killens quickly embraced another opportunity to depict African Americans making a contribution to the progressive movement of humankind. In August, Clark paid Killens a thousand dollars to begin research, advising him to consult Arnold Rampersad's biography of Langston Hughes because the section on Central Asia was interesting and informative, though Clark thought the Tuskegee group, not the Hughes group, was the more compelling story.

Any reflections about the Soviet Union reminded Killens to keep pushing *Great Black Russian*. In the fall, Gil Noble hosted a reception and reading for Killens at which he resumed his public campaign for a publisher. Despite his "dean" designation, he had not placed an entry into the adult market in more than fifteen years. Killens also returned to trying to drum up interest in a film version of *The Cotillion*, succumbing once again to the vision that Killens admirers would crowd movie theaters. He had a copy of the novel placed into the mailbox of Spike Lee, then a rapidly rising twenty-nine-year-old director.

Killens continued to support fellow writers, students, and friends. After the publication of Elizabeth Nunez's debut novel, *When Rocks Dance*, her mentor beamed proudly at an October 9, 1986, autograph party. The following day, Killens was back in Washington, D.C., to speak at a dinner honoring Samuel Yette, who was retiring from Howard University. The most familiar events, though, seemed to be the arrival of rejection letters. Random House/Ballantine was the latest to turn down "The Minister Primarily," although the publisher indicated it might be interested in reissuing *The Cotillion*.

As 1987 began, Killens received an upbeat holiday greeting from Stretch Johnson, who apologized for having fallen out of touch with the Killenses. Johnson had reunited with a former love, Ann Hitch, and they had relocated permanently to Hawaii. He had joined Alcoholics Anonymous and credited that decision with enabling him to become active again in radical movements. He was especially concerned with anti-nuclear-warheads and anti-apartheid issues, Hawaiian sovereignty initiatives, and the workings of the Afro-American Association. Johnson described the cultural life in Hawaii as "incredibly rich—polyglot, multi-ethnic, multi-racial—a crossroads of the Pacific." He had seen Whitney Houston, Wynton Marsalis, and Les McCann in concert and was looking forward to upcoming performances by Al Jarreau and Stevie Wonder. He also reported that on "Labor Day, I had the pleasure of meeting and hearing Andrea Young, Trummy's daughter, swing the blues in a style reminiscent of her dad. Nostalgia for days!"[2]

Stretch Johnson sounding so forward-looking and optimistic inspired Killens. But almost immediately he received a startling reminder of mortality when Pierce Brunson died. "I have known P. B. almost as long as I have known myself," Killens reflected to the man's family. "We have been more than mere close friends; he has been more like a brother to me. We have shared many experiences, got into a lot of mischief together in the county of Bibb. Although, and understandably, you and we are deeply saddened by the passing of this dear spirit, our attitude must be: 'Joy to the world! Pierce Butler Brunson lived. And because he dwelt upon this old earth, it is a fitter place for human habitation.'"[3] Willie Lee Killens's presence helped to lift her son's mood. She had come to town for a holiday visit that would extend three months. At ninety years old, Ma Willie was more than a mother; she was John's strongest symbol of hope.

Killens tried to convey a positive outlook to his brother, Charles, who had been diagnosed with diabetes. John and Grace knew several people who had "stayed on their feet and fought the good fight," and Killens knew that his brother could do so as well. As if to lead by example, Killens reported that 1987 might be one of his busiest years as a writer. He mentioned the contract for the film version of *And Then We Heard the Thunder*, a conversation with Quincy Jones about adapting *The Cotillion* for the screen, and "The Life of John Oliver Killens," a project being developed at the Henry Street Settlement. The plan was to dramatize excerpts from all of his books and prepare for an off-Broadway run and a tour of the college circuit.[4]

Despite his optimism and his grand plans, however, Killens could not change the fact that he had colon cancer. Killens seemed to think that he could will himself more days by launching new initiatives, as if ambition could ward off disease. He envisioned himself fulfilling a series of commitments over the next few years, both writing and otherwise, including a central role at the 1988 National Black Writers Conference. Even as his pace slowed and his stride shortened—the old man shuffle, as Arthur Flowers called it—he attended a January 27 book party for Terry McMillan's new novel, *Mama*. Beacon Press requested that he be a special guest at Roosevelt House at Hunter College to celebrate the republication of Alice Childress's *Like One of the Family* and Sarah Wright's *This Child's Gonna Live*, for which he had written an afterword.

Always with an eye turned toward politics, Killens and his wife tried to establish the Fund against Racism to defray the legal cost of racially charged cases pending against New York City. The couple acknowledged the legal efforts of the National Association for the Advancement of Colored People's Legal Defense Fund and the American Civil Liberties Union, but the Killenses believed that those groups emphasized cases of national importance or of special interest to the groups involved. The Killenses spoke of a lack of financial support for African American lawyers involved in recent legal matters, including police shootings of civilians and the Howard Beach assaults. To gauge interest in their effort, they sent out a letter that included a pledge form.[5]

On May 7, Killens spoke at Medgar Evers College as part of a Humanities Division open house. Other speakers included Edna Edet, a musician who collaborated with him on a student production of *The Cotillion*; George Cureton, whom Killens first met at Harvard; and Carole Gregory, a former student whom Killens had helped secure a faculty position. On May 10, he and Grace attended a party to honor Johnetta Cole, who had been selected as the first African American president of Spelman College. They gave Cole a sculpture by one of their favorite artists, Elizabeth Catlett. Thanking them, Cole remarked, "There is no greater gift than one which comes from the soul of our people. And of course that is exactly where Elizabeth Catlett's work comes from."[6]

Killens's own academic ceremony soon followed. On May 31, John, Grace, and their granddaughter, Abiba, traveled to the Nassau County campus of the State University of New York College at Old Westbury, where he would receive the honorary degree of doctor of letters. The university required that Killens attend commencement to receive the degree, and he did so although it was a struggle physically and Grace argued against the trip. At the same ceremony, Tito Puente received an honorary doctorate in music.

Another honor came Killens's way a week later, but he no longer possessed the energy to accept David Du Bois's invitation to join the advisory board of the recently incorporated W. E. B. Du Bois Foundation. Du Bois stressed that he wanted potential board members to do more than lend their names and reputations to the organization. He sought their participation in one of its ten divisions: (1) Publications; (2) Special Promotions; (3) Young People; (4) Fellowships; (5) Symposia, Seminars, and Workshops; (6) Monuments; (7) Cultural Activities; (8) Legal Aid; (9) Special Projects; and (10) Awards and Prizes. In some ways, the foundation spoke to the unfinished business of the Black Academy of Arts and Letters and was off to a more promising start. It had already accomplished the reinterment of W. E. B. Du Bois and Shirley Graham Du Bois in a tomb designed and constructed as a shrine on the grounds of the former Du Bois residence in Accra.

In July, Killens was hospitalized, though he still believed that he could recover and perform more work. There was, after all, the immediate example of David's uncle, eighty-four-year-old Lorenz Graham. After visiting more than sixty countries, including a dozen in Africa, Lorenz and his wife, Ruth, had recently made their first trip to the Republic of South Africa at the behest of the PEN Los Angeles Center. After touring much of the country and meeting with Alan Paton in Durban, the Grahams wrote a lengthy letter describing their trip. They expressed the belief that the racial oppression in South Africa was the worst they had ever seen or known and that black resentment was growing among the masses, who were strengthening in their will to resist. The Grahams believed that the more formally educated the masses, the better they would organize in their struggle for justice and that they would ultimately win: "We believe that an increasing number of White citizens of South Africa are convinced that the whole concept of apartheid is inhuman and support social philosophy based on justice, but white repressionists fear revolution and thus tighten up controls. And foster separation along racial, ethnic, and tribal lines. But blacks and whites are uniting in Christian fellowship, which was hopeful."[7]

Killens was on board with the vision of fellowship. At the core, he was always a radical pluralist. But he still struggled with the question of how tightly Christian any social effort should be. He attended church regularly nowadays, but maintained that he wasn't religious. He explained that he went to church because his people were religious and he desired to connect with them as much as possible.[8] Perhaps that was true, but certainly there could have been more to the matter. After all, in the end, few go as resolutely as Bigger Thomas and Monsieur Meursault.

For a fee of ten thousand dollars, the option on *And Then We Heard the Thunder* was extended through 1987. The money to make the movie had yet to be raised, and Caswell had not fully committed to revisions because he was working on the Meryl Streep film *Evil Angels*. But the producers remained on board, and a development deal with Columbia pictures seemed possible.

At long last, however, *Great Black Russian* was on its way to publication. Toni Cade Bambara, who served on the editorial board of Wayne State University Press's new African American Life Series, persuaded the press to issue the Pushkin volume.

Arthur Flowers described his final visit with Killens:

> The house was full of folks on the deathwatch. John was on the second floor, I went up to see him and was shocked. He was laying there all thin and wasted, a pale reflection of who I knew him to be, skin and bones and spirit. Still had spirit. Nobody else was in the room. We talked. He knew I was thinking about going to California and he was telling me to be careful out there, so weak he couldn't sit up in bed, still giving me the advice, "*Dont get lost out there*," he said, "*Dont ever let money rule the work*." Then he asked me to lift him up, put him in a chair that was sitting by the bed. I did, arms behind his knees and his back, and when I lifted him I almost stumbled, shocked by how feather light he was. I put him in the chair and arranged the blanket over him. "*Call Amazing Grace*," he said. That's what he called Ms

Grace, Amazing. I called her and she came upstairs and beamed at him sitting there so proud.

"*Im sitting up,*" he told her.

"*I see you are,*" she said.

"*I like to see what's going on around me,*" he said.

"*I know you do,*" she said.[9]

Killens died on October 27, 1987.

On October 23, Carla Hoke from the office of Manhattan borough president David Dinkins had written to inform the ailing writer of still another award: "Your work has been carefully reviewed by the panel of judges for the Manhattan Borough President's Awards for Excellence in the Arts. It is my pleasure to inform you that you are among the finalists selected in the Literature category." The ceremony took place on the evening of November 2, when Killens received the award posthumously.[10]

Several people who gazed upon Killens's body in its coffin remarked that it was the first time they had seen him without the medallion of Africa around his neck. But, they figured, he carried Africa inside of him, and all of America, too, along with all of the prophetic ideals about freedom and global democracy for which he had tried to gain a hearing with his cultural work. The chapel was packed for the funeral. Along with the family, those in attendance included Ossie Davis, Charles Fuller, Tom Feelings, Betty Shabazz, and John Henrik Clarke. Clarke seemed particularly dazed, and his wife, Eugenia, worried aloud about how her husband would cope with the loss.

The Harlem Writers Guild, whose members had published hundreds of books, held a memorial program for its founding chair on November 17. Davis, Rosa Guy, Clarke, Sarah Wright, and Wesley Brown were among the speakers. A similar event was convened at Howard University. Norman Loftis likened Killens to Ezra Pound in the sense that in addition to being important in his own right as an artist, Killens was crucial—as organizer, host, teacher, and mentor—to the development of many other careers.[11]

Major Owens, who followed Shirley Chisholm as the representative of New York's Twelfth Congressional District, read Killens into the *Congressional Record* on December 2. After reciting a carefully researched biographical statement, Owens intoned, "Killens and his family lived in Brooklyn, in my congressional district. He will be greatly missed by his family and friends, and those of us who were as inspired by his writings as he was by the established black authors of his generation. He has contributed a great deal to American literature, to black scholarship and literary art, and to current and future generations of writers, in this country and abroad. His genius and influence will leave a lasting impact for years to come."[12]

On January 16, 1988, two days after what would have been Killens's seventy-second birthday, a program honoring "our long distance runner" was held at Bethany Baptist Church. His family asked that any contributions be sent to the John Oliver Killens Scholarship Fund, which awarded a grant to a college-bound high school senior from Macon; the John Oliver Killens Chair at Medgar Evers College; or the Fund for a Free South Africa.[13] Louis Reyes Rivera read Margaret Walker's "For My People."

Much of Killens's work is now out of print, and none of his writings is included in *The Norton Anthology of African-American Literature*. According to Joseph Kaye, the husband of Sarah Wright, Wright and Killens do not make literary canons because they were unapologetically on the left.[14] Paul Robeson Jr. agrees: "Killens never got a chance to flower fully because of the prevailing cultural politics of the time."[15] But *Great Black Russian* was released in 1989, with *Ebony* reporting that the novel "stands as a great testament to two men who dedicated their lives to literature and the eradication of oppression—Alexander Pushkin and John Oliver Killens."[16] Jerry W. Ward Jr. finished the work needed to bring *Black Southern Voices* to bookshelves in 1992.

Killens has also received some well-deserved recognition. In 1998, he was inducted into the inaugural class of the Literary Hall of Fame for Writers of African Descent, founded by Haki Madhubuti, Bennett Johnson, and B. J. Bolden and housed at Chicago State University. Other honorees included W. E. B. Du Bois, Richard Wright, Langston Hughes, and Margaret Walker Alexander—all of whom were Killens's heroes. In 2000, he was named a charter member of the Georgia Writers Hall of Fame at the University of Georgia, joining Erskine Caldwell, James Dickey, W. E. B. Du Bois, Joel Chandler Harris, Martin Luther King Jr., Sidney Lanier, Augustus Baldwin Longstreet, Carson McCullers, Margaret Mitchell, Flannery O'Connor, and Lillian Smith.

Notes

Unless otherwise indicated, letters and other unpublished documents cited that pertain to John Oliver Killens are located in the John Oliver Killens Collection in the Robert W. Woodruff Library at Emory University. The Killens collection remains unprocessed; thus, I do not indicate box and folder locations. Researchers can find all material in this and other archives by using the appropriate finding aids.

Brief items from news periodicals are cited fully here in the notes section. Newspaper articles with bylines are listed in the bibliography.

Introduction

1. Glenn, "Books and Authors."
2. Clarke, review.
3. Hicks, "Laurie Grows Up."
4. John Oliver Killens to *Pittsburgh Courier*, October 19, 1954.
5. Killens, "Novel."
6. Richmond, "Novel."
7. Winslow, "More Film."
8. Petry, "Crossroads."
9. Peeples, "Artist," 14.

CHAPTER ONE: A White Man's Republic, 1915–1928

1. See Evans, *Black and White*; Ward, review.
2. Quoted in Schickel, *D. W. Griffith*, 270.
3. See W. T. Anderson, "Georgia Lynch Law!"
4. Robeson, *Here I Stand*, 25.

5. See Mary Jo Buhle, Buhle, and Georgakas, *Encyclopedia*, 310–12.

6. Killens, "Half," 285. Carrie Walker may well have been related to noted novelist Alice Walker, who was born in Eatonton, although no link has yet been discovered.

7. Iobst, *Civil War Macon*, 1.

8. Quoted in ibid., 53.

9. Dittmer, *Black Georgia*, xi.

10. Du Bois, *Souls*, 92.

11. The first English immigrants, led by James Edward Oglethorpe, landed in Georgia on February 12, 1733 (Hepburn, *Contemporary Georgia*, 2–3).

12. Du Bois, *Souls*, 101.

13. Quoted in Dittmer, *Black Georgia*, 121.

14. Clegg, *Original Man*, 10. Dittmer, reports that 505 lynchings of record occurred in Georgia between 1882 and 1923 (*Black Georgia*, 131). See also Walter White, *Rope and Faggot*.

15. *Macon Telegraph*, August 3, 1922.

16. Manis, *Macon*, 65; Killens, "Stony," 1–9.

17. Clegg, *Original Man*, 10–13.

18. Dittmer, *Black Georgia*, 189.

19. Ibid., 21.

20. National Register of Historic Places—Nomination Form, Historic District Information Form, both submitted to the U.S. Department of the Interior, National Park Service, copies in Washington Memorial Library, Macon, Ga.

21. Long, "Pleasant Hill's Rich History."

22. Quoted in ibid.

23. Thomas Bonner, interview by author, June 1, 2002.

24. *Macon's Black Heritage*, 39.

25. Killens, *Black Man's Burden*, 63–64, 101.

26. Ibid., 104.

27. Ibid., 102. According to Robert Williams (interview by author, June 24, 2004), the skirmish probably occurred around Hardeman Avenue in a section of the neighborhood that no longer exists as a result of the construction of Interstate 75. For the fictionalized version of the crossroads incident, see Killens, *Youngblood*, 163–76. See also Gilyard, *Liberation Memories*, 13–14.

28. Killens, *Black Man's Burden*, 84–85.

29. Several sources, including Killens's autobiographical essay, "Half Ain't Never Been Told," incorrectly refer to the church as Stewart Chapel.

30. Killens, "Half," 285.

31. Robert Williams, interview.

32. "There Is No East and No West" is the title contained in church records. Carson, lists an alternate title for the sermon: "A Realistic Look at Progress in the Area of Race Relations" (*Papers*, 46).

33. Killens, *Black Man's Burden*, 60.

34. In "Rappin' with Myself" (99–100), Killens noted that in his childhood he had been introduced to the work of Langston Hughes in the *Chicago Defender* and that both he and his father were fascinated by Hughes's irreverence. Killens later made similar remarks to Windham ("Long Distance Runner," 5), seeming to recall that Hughes wrote weekly either for the *Chicago Defender* or the *Pittsburgh Courier*, both of which were delivered to the Killens home. Though the basics of the Hughes story ring true, he may have come to influence Killens later in life than such stories suggest. Hughes published in the *Courier* during Killens's childhood but was not a columnist for the *Defender* until 1942, and in neither case did Hughes display a disdain for religion. Although Hughes wrote militant verse early in his career, a critical attitude toward religion was not apparent until such poems as "Christian Country" and "Goodbye Christ." If Myles Killens talked with his son about the most radical aspects of Hughes, he most likely did so when the boy was well into high school and within a broader discourse than the *Defender* or *Courier*.

35. Killens, "Half," 280.

36. Robert Williams, interview.

37. Killens, "Trouble," 2, 3.

38. Killens, "Half," 279.

39. Ibid.

40. Killens, *Youngblood*, 6.

41. Killens, "Half," 280–81.

42. Ibid., 284–85.

43. Ibid., 281.

CHAPTER TWO: Avoiding the River, 1928–1936

1. Titus Brown, *Faithful, Firm, and True*. General commentary about Ballard Normal School is drawn from this source.

2. For fuller discussion of the African American commitment to education in the South, see Holt, "'Knowledge Is Power.'"

3. Richard Leo Killens, interview by author, November 15, 2002.

4. Quoted in Pitts, *Reflections*, 49.

5. Ibid., 51, 52, 55.

6. Lafayette Bonner, interview by author, June 1, 2002.

7. Killens quoted in Pitts, *Reflections*, 54. Killens told several slightly different versions of his initial attempts to write a novel. In Windham, "Long Distance Runner," 5, he stated he that wrote thirty pages in the seventh grade before he gave up and then wrote about forty pages in the eighth grade. On another occasion, he related that he wrote about forty pages in the seventh grade and about fifty pages in the eighth grade (Peeples, "Artist," 8). In "The Half Ain't Never Been Told" (285), he recalled that both

early attempts occurred during the eighth grade, his first year at Ballard. The first was an effort of about forty pages; the second was fifty-five pages. Killens was more expansive in his own written remarks, and I thus choose to go along with the idea that his first attempts at a novel took place at Ballard.

8. Killens, "Armistice."

9. Quoted in Titus Brown, *Faithful, Firm, and True*, 115.

10. Ibid., 119.

11. Killens, "Half," 284.

12. Bonner, interview.

13. Killens, "Half," 284.

14. Valeria Williams, interview by author, June 22, 2002.

15. Quoted in Pitts, *Reflections*, 49.

16. *Macon Telegraph*, February 7, 1933.

17. Killens, "Half," 284.

18. Ibid., 285.

19. Ibid., 284.

20. Ibid., 283–84.

21. Killens, *Black Man's Burden*, 144.

22. *Macon Telegraph*, May 9, 1933.

23. Bonner, interview, June 22, 2002; Valeria Williams, interview.

24. Richard Leo Killens, interview.

25. Killens, *Youngblood*, 327–475.

26. Manis, *Macon*, 109.

27. Ibid., 108–9.

28. Ibid., 110.

29. According to Ferguson, the strikes against the all-white cotton industry spread throughout the South and had the support of four hundred thousand workers nationwide (*Black Politics*, 65–66).

30. *Macon Telegraph*, September 5, 1934.

31. Ibid., September 6, 1934.

32. Ibid., September 20, 1934.

33. Tucker, *Phoenix*, 7.

34. Ortiz, *Emancipation Betrayed*, xiv.

35. Ibid., 207.

36. Transcript provided by Barbara Killens-Rivera.

37. Thomas B. Jenkins to John Oliver Killens, June 8, 1958.

38. Ibid.

39. Killens, *Youngblood*, 135.

40. "Belafonte Becomes 'Big Business,'" *Ebony*, June 1958, 17–24; "Jungle Missionaries," *Ebony*, June 1958, 69–74.

41. Killens, "Stony," 272. I have no corroborating evidence that this passage is strictly autobiographical, but it is plausible. About his middle-age views on religion, Killens noted, "I was not and am not of a religious turn. If I have a religion, it is Black liberation. Black unity. Pan-Africanism. Sometimes it has been Brotherhood. . . . I believe that man is his own salvation. And that he must seek his salvation individually, but, more importantly, in unison with his fellow man and against his anti-fellow man" ("Rappin' with Myself," 118). In a 1972 address, Killens observed, "It has been said of Black people that we are a deeply religious people. If this be true, and the evidence weighs heavily in favor of that position, I see this as nothing at all to boast about" ("Trouble," 14). Some bridge had to be crossed from childhood skepticism to a firm antireligious persuasion, and the passage in "Stony" is the only place—in fiction or nonfiction—that Killens suggests how he first came to adopt the stance on religion that he later expressed in interviews and speeches.

42. Killens, "Stony," 273.

43. Manis, *Macon*, 115–16; *Macon Telegraph*, August 28, 1935.

44. Average wages for black workers were less than half those of white workers. See Manis, *Macon*, 122. See also Ferguson, *Black Politics*, 73–80, 90.

45. Manis, *Macon*, 119.

46. Jackson Davis to President William A. Fountain Jr., August 31, 1933. Rockefeller Center Archive, General Education Board, Series 1, Subseries 1. For the General Education Board's dominant tone toward the college during this period, see Jackson Davis to William A. Fountain Jr., June 7, 1933, A. W. Armour to William A. Fountain Jr., July 19, 1933, Jackson Davis to A. W. Armour, August 31, 1933, Walter B. Hill, memorandum, October 1, 1935, all in Rockefeller Center Archive, General Education Board, Series 1, Subseries 1.

47. Ferguson, *Black Politics*, 10–11.

48. Ibid, 61. I do not claim that Killens or a large number of students had read Du Bois's entire book, which was published in June 1935 and stretches more than seven hundred pages. But Du Bois had been developing and publishing portions of *Black Reconstruction* in some form or another for at least a quarter century, and those efforts and his overall contributions as the nation's reigning African American intellectual were certainly on the minds of students such as Killens. For contextualizing statements about *Black Reconstruction*, see David Levering Lewis, introduction.

49. Ferguson, *Black Politics*, 143.

50. Ibid.

51. These forums probably were organized by Emmet Johnson, an integrationist minister who headed the student YMCA at Emory University. See Robert Cohen, *When the Old Left Was Young*, 214–15.

52. Killens, *Black Man's Burden*, 81–82.

53. Killens, "Half," 286.

54. Manis, *Macon*, 117–20; *Macon Telegraph*, February 3, 1936.

55. National Labor Relations Board Personnel Files.

CHAPTER THREE: Mr. Killens, 1936–1942

1. Killens, *Black Man's Burden*, 66; Killens, "Half," 282.

2. Although Killens wrote in *Black Man's Burden*, 65, and "Half," 282, that he was nineteen when he first went to work at the NLRB, he was in fact twenty years old in April 1936.

3. Killens, *Black Man's Burden*, 67. A slightly different version appears in Killens, "Half," 282.

4. Killens, *Black Man's Burden*, 67; Killens, "Half," 282.

5. National Labor Relations Board Personnel Files.

6. For overall discussion of communist activity inside the NLRB, see Latham, *Communist Controversy*, 124–50; for specific commentary on the Smith Committee initiative against the NLRB, see 133–34.

7. For lengthy discussion of the Saposs case, see Latham, *Communist Controversy*, 134–40.

8. Fuchs voluntarily testified about his communist involvement before the U.S. House Un-American Activities Committee in 1955. Shortly thereafter, he was fired from his faculty position at American University.

9. Latham has argued that *communist* was an ambiguous designation because the party worked through people who were not official members. The phrase, "card-carrying member of the Communist party" is significant, Latham contends, but not definitive (*Communist Controversy*, 90–91).

10. Holloway, *Confronting*, 45.

11. Ibid., 50–58.

12. Killens, *Youngblood*, 136.

13. Hunton, *Alphaeus Hunton*, 30.

14. Haywood became acutely attuned to politics during a six-day Chicago race riot that occurred in July and August 1919 (during the nation's Red Summer). Drawn to revolutionary solutions, he joined the African Blood Brotherhood, the Young Communist League, and eventually the Communist Party itself. In the mid-1920s, Haywood studied in Moscow, where he tried to discern the best theoretical and practical connection between African American liberation and Marxism-Leninism. He was particularly interested in Lenin's "Preliminary Draft Theses on the National and Colonial Questions" and Stalin's "Marxism and the National Question." In 1927, a colleague of Haywood, known as Nasonov, suggested that African Americans constituted an oppressed nation whose struggle would become autonomous and result in an agrarian and democratic revolution in the South. See Haywood, *Black Bolshevik*, 231–32,

218–44. Haywood sought to rescue black nationalism, which he saw as a legitimate and likely recurring trend, from being diverted into Garvey-like separatism, which Haywood viewed as reactionary. In the acknowledgments section of his autobiography, Haywood lists John Killens, who would come to support much of Haywood's thinking, among a group of "veteran comrades and friends" who helped him to complete the book.

15. Platt, *E. Franklin Frazier*, 187, quoting Du Bois, "Social Planning." Du Bois had been expressing these views for several years before the article appeared in 1936.

16. Quoted in Platt, *E. Franklin Frazier*, 181.

17. Ossie Davis, *With Ossie and Ruby*, 117.

18. Participants at the conference included Harris, Bunche, Walter White, James Weldon Johnson, Houston, Frances Williams, Marion Cuthbert, and Roy Wilkins. The First Amenia Conference had been convened in 1916, shortly after the death of Booker T. Washington, as the NAACP sought to extend its influence among people who had been aligned with Washington.

19. Frazier, *Negro Family*, 474–75.

20. Platt, *E. Franklin Frazier*, 23, 189.

21. Hylan Lewis, "Focused Memoir," 22, 28.

22. Platt, *E. Franklin Frazier*, 104.

23. Killens, "Half," 282–83.

24. Platt, introduction, xvii–xix. See also Hoffman, *Race Traits*; Tillinghast, *Negro*; Dowd, *Negro*; Reuter, *American Race Problem*. I assume that any sociology course that Frazier taught in 1938 closely resembled his *Negro Family in the United States*, which was either in or near printing production in the spring of 1938.

25. Platt, introduction, xxix.

26. Frazier, *Negro Family*, 446; chapter 20 is titled "The Brown Middle Class."

27. Ibid., 475; chapter 21 is titled "The Black Proletariat."

28. Killens, *Black Man's Burden*, 114.

29. Ibid., 115.

30. Killens was twenty-two years old at the time of this trip, though he recalled being twenty ("Half," 289).

31. Ibid.

32. Ibid.

33. Ibid., 290.

34. Killens, *Black Man's Burden*, 5.

35. Killens, introduction to *Black Southern Voices*, 2.

36. Quoted in Duberman, *Paul Robeson*, 228.

37. Killens, "Half," 283.

38. *Barrister*, November 1940, 1.

39. Ibid., 6.

40. Percy Faison to John Oliver Killens, January 9, 1966.

41. For more on the relationship between Roosevelt and the AYC, see Robert Cohen, *When the Old Left Was Young*, 234–37.

42. McMichael, "Youth and the Nation," 7.

43. Tunney, "Youth Congress," 14.

44. Quoted in *Town Meeting*, 29.

45. Tunney, "Youth Congress," 15.

46. McMichael, a Christian socialist, had been mentored by Emmet Johnson at Emory and probably met Killens at one of the meetings sponsored by Johnson. Although McMichael certainly was cozy with the Communist Party, he was never recruited into the party, although former AYC chairs Waldo McNutt, Bill Hinckley, and Joe Gadden were. See Robert Cohen, *When the Old Left Was Young*, 234.

47. McMichael, "Youth and the Nation," 7.

48. Ibid., 8.

49. Quoted in *Town Meeting*, 17.

50. Cooper, "Free the Negro People," 12.

51. Ibid.

52. Killens, "Impact," 1.

53. Killens, "National Council," 7.

54. Killens, "Unfair."

55. Killens, "Brief," 1–8.

56. FBI file on John Oliver Killens.

57. Ibid.; Gellermann, *Martin Dies*, 151.

58. *Negro Will Defend America*, 3.

59. FBI file on John Oliver Killens.

60. FBI file on E. Franklin Frazier.

61. FBI file on John Oliver Killens.

62. National Labor Relations Board Personnel Files.

63. A. B. Hunt to Aviation Cadet Examining Board, May 16, 1942.

64. Herbert R. Glazer to Aviation Cadet Examining Board, May 18, 1942.

65. Sarah E. Wright to Almena Lomax, May 30, 1959.

66. Killens, "Eulogy to Mrs. Mabel Ward Jones," February 3, 1972.

67. Ambiguously addressing his and Grace's radical inclinations, Killens wrote that they met "in the student movement" ("Half," 287). In the same document, he wrote that he and Grace met in the "Youth Movement" (291).

68. Grace Killens, interview by author, October 14, 2005.

69. Ibid.

70. Information on Killens's military service comes from his personnel records at the National Personnel Records Center, St. Louis.

CHAPTER FOUR: Chasing the Double Victory, 1942–1945

1. See Voss, *Reporting*, 172–83.

2. Killens, *And Then We Heard*, 17, 174.

3. Ibid., 17.

4. Ottley, "Negroes," 212.

5. Ibid., 217.

6. Ibid., 216.

7. Quoted in Hope, *Racial Strife*, 26.

8. Ibid.

9. Ottley, "Negroes," 214.

10. Grace Killens, interview by author, October 14, 2005.

11. Ibid.

12. The argument here closely follows that of Saunders, who has written the best discussion of the direct connection between the riots in South Brisbane and the depictions in *And Then We Heard the Thunder* ("In a Cloud," 178–90). Aware of Killens's invoking of literary license, Saunders nonetheless concludes that Killens's account contributes mightily to an understanding of the events.

13. Poston, "Different Kind." However, Louis Reyes Rivera suggested that muckraker Drew Pearson wrote about the riots, but I have yet to locate the piece (Louis Reyes Rivera to author, July 26, 2009).

14. The report, written by Colonel C. H. Barnwell, is contained in Luszki, *Rape*, 157–59.

15. MacArthur to Marshall, March 29, 1942, Office of Military History, War Department Records, Operations Division, Executive Item 19D, National Archives, Washington, D.C.

16. Ibid., Executive Item 10D.

17. Saunders, "In a Cloud," 181–84.

18. Costello, *Pacific War*, 563.

19. Ibid., 561.

20. Killens, *And Then We Heard*, 456.

21. Ibid., 382, 403.

22. Information about all troop movements of the 813th Amphibian Truck Company is drawn from Monthly Unit Historical Summaries and Monthly Intelligence Summaries, National Archives, College Park, Md.

23. Cutler, *Battle*, 36.

24. Wouk, *War*, 924–25.

25. Cutler, *Battle*, 33–34.

26. Killens, *And Then We Heard*, 285–86. Herman Wouk articulated the historical and political ramifications of the invasion in his epic novel, *War and Remembrance* (926).

27. Wouk, *War*, 927.

28. Cutler, *Battle*, xiii.

29. Ibid., xii, 265–73; Costello, *Pacific War*, 517–18; van der Vat, *Pacific Campaign*, 350–51; Bergerud, *Fire*, 675.

30. Killens, *And Then We Heard*, 308.

31. Ibid., 280.

32. Killens, "Rappin' with Myself," 98.

33. John Oliver Killens to Grace Killens, ca. 1944.

34. Ibid., December 29, 1944.

35. Ibid.

36. Ibid.

37. Ibid.

38. 813th Amphibian Truck Company, Unit Historical Summaries, May 31, July 1, 1945.

39. van der Vat, *Pacific Campaign*, 391–94.

40. Ibid., 394.

41. Killens, *Black Man's Burden*, 122.

CHAPTER FIVE: None as Radical as Mickey Mouse, 1945–1948

1. Killens, "Rappin' with Myself," 98. Killens gives a similar account in "Half," 287, in which he attributes to a friend the reasoning that being a lawyer was not revolutionary.

2. Richard Leo Killens, interview by author, November 15, 2002.

3. Grace Killens, interview by Michael Harper, September 3, 1979.

4. National Labor Relations Board Personnel Files.

5. Windham, "Long Distance Runner," 6.

6. Killens, "Stony."

7. A National Conference for a National Veterans' Organization Souvenir Program.

8. Nation's Capital City Wide Veterans Conference Souvenir Program.

9. Daniel James, "Battle," exemplifies the anticommunist discourse that arose relative to veterans' organizations. James, a self-described liberal, addressed communist efforts to control the American Veterans Committee, of which he was a member, and the United Negro and Allied Veterans of America. James, however, failed to discuss the issues that members of the veterans group found pressing. Communists sponsored the group's activities—the contribution by black communist Claude Lightfoot in Illinois is an example—but communists did not create Jim Crow.

10. Hunton, *Alphaeus Hunton*, 28. For further discussion of the historical relationship between African Americans and organized labor, see Marshall, *Negro*, especially

chapter 2, "The Negro and the AFL," 14–33; chapter 3, "The Negro and the CIO," 34–52. See also Jacobson, *Negro*, especially Rosen, "CIO Era"; Hill, "Racial Practices."

11. Killens, "Paul Robeson," 3, 4. Killens referred to the musical tribute "The Lonesome Train," with music by Earl Robinson and words by Millard Lampell: "And you know who Lincoln's people were? / A Brooklyn blacksmith, a Pittsburgh preacher / A small-town tailor, a back-woods teacher / An old store-keeper shaking his head / Handing over a loaf of bread / A Buffalo-hunter telling a story / Out of Oregon territory / They were his people; he was their man / You couldn't quite tell where the people left off and where Abe Lincoln began."

12. National Labor Relations Board Personnel Files.

13. Killens, "Stony."

14. Ibid., 4.

15. Ibid., 33, 67–68.

16. Ibid., 182, 189.

17. Ibid., 264. On p. 603, Killens slipped and wrote CIO rather than NIO.

18. Ibid., 278, 329.

19. Ibid., 626.

20. Ibid., 30, 2.

21. Leo Huberman to John Oliver Killens, December 20, 1947.

22. Markowitz, "Progressive Party," 600.

CHAPTER SIX: The Efficacy of Struggle, 1948–1949

1. FBI file on John Oliver Killens.

2. Killens, "Rappin' with Myself," 122.

3. Remarks on the first day of the Harlem Writers Guild Fiftieth Anniversary Celebration, Schomburg Center for Research in Black Culture, New York Public Library, November 17, 2000.

4. Hunton, *Alphaeus Hunton*, 61.

5. See Duberman, *Paul Robeson*, 330–33.

6. W. E. B. Du Bois, Memorandum, September 7, 1948.

7. Killens, "Rappin' with Myself," 115.

8. Peeples, "Artist," 9.

9. Killens, "He Took His Art," 193.

10. Cruse, *Crisis*, 206.

11. Ibid., 236.

12. Ibid.

13. Killens, "For National Freedom," 258.

14. Cruse, *Crisis*, 228.

15. Paul Robeson Jr., interview by author, June 19, 2007.

16. Killens, "25th Session."

17. From Killens's notebooks.

18. Maugham, *Summing Up*, 120; for passages about Maugham's writing development that Killens specifically noted, see 18–20, 108–14.

19. Early in *Native Son*, Wright sketches the scenario involving Bigger Thomas, armed with a skillet, engaging in mortal combat with a rat, signifying Bigger's dehumanization within an oppressive environment (6). At a similar point in *Youngblood*, Laurie Lee recalls an episode involving her brother, Tim, after he had returned from a stint in a reformatory. When a field rat invades the Barksdale kitchen, the once squeamish Tim resolutely and repeatedly crushes the animal with his foot (13).

20. Lenore Davison to John Oliver Killens, ca. 1949.

21. *New Yorker* to John Oliver Killens, ca. 1949.

22. Killens's notebooks.

23. Windham, "Long Distance Runner," 28. In 1965, Sholokhov received the Nobel Prize in literature, though a controversy reigns over the authorship of *And Quiet Flows the Don*. Aleksandr Solzhenitsyn, for example, has argued that Fyodor Kryukov wrote much of the book, and Israeli academic Zeev Bar-Sela attributes the novel to Vinyamin Alekseevich Krasnushkin. Neither claim, however, has become definitive. Statistical analyses and an examination of drafts and notes support the contention that Sholokhov is indeed the novel's author.

24. Killens, "*Darkness*," 3.

25. Ibid., 6.

26. Killens, "*Naked*," 4, 2.

27. Hazel Rowley, *Richard Wright*, 414, notes that there are at least three versions of a rather famous argument that began at the Deux Magots in Paris in May 1953, one by each of the main principals—Richard Wright, James Baldwin, and Chester Himes. All agree that the argument stemmed from the November 1951 publication of Baldwin's "Many Thousands Gone," in which he was critical of Wright. Wright's version, according to Rowley, was given to an audience at the American Church in Paris only weeks before his death. In Wright's story, Baldwin, miffed because he felt Wright was condescending, screamed, "I'm going to destroy you! I'm going to destroy your reputation! You'll see!" Baldwin published his account in "Alas, Poor Richard," but he treats the incident vaguely, labeling Wright his "father" (191) and "spiritual father" (201) and describing himself, Wright, and Himes as three tense and egotistical people (198). In Himes's account, Wright set up the meeting with Baldwin, who had called to borrow money. At the meeting, Wright began attacking Baldwin, accusing him of ingratitude. Baldwin defended himself with passion. Himes recalled that the discussion went on well into the night, with Wright seeming to wear down. Himes remembered Baldwin saying, "the sons must slay their fathers" (*Quality*, 201).

28. Killens, "Wright's Rebels," 1, 2, 6, 9. Hansberry reviewed *The Outsider* in Robeson's *Freedom*, commenting with reductionist, Old Left bombast that Wright was

now an outsider, removed from "the reality of our struggle for freedom" and toiling "energetically in behalf of our oppressors" (7).

29. Richard Wright, "Early Days." Wright's memoir was originally titled *American Hunger* and dealt with his life through his days in Chicago. However, the Book-of-the-Month Club would accept only the portion concluding with Wright's departure from the South. Wright conceded, and his publisher printed the book as *Black Boy* in 1945. The rest of the manuscript was published in 1977 under the original title.

30. Richard Wright, 12 *Million*, 59, 61; Richard Wright, *Black Boy*, 33.

31. Mullin's comments on Killens, "Richard Wright, a Native Son."

32. The Jefferson School of Social Science, located at 575 Sixth Avenue, operated from 1943 to 1956. Associated with the Communist Party, it offered hundreds of courses and served up to five thousand students per term in its heyday. The school was directed by Howard Selsam, who had been fired from the City University of New York, as had a number of the faculty who taught at the Jefferson School.

33. Killens, "For National Freedom," 245–52, 253.

34. Ibid., 254.

35. Ibid., 258.

36. Killens, "Half," 292.

37. Ibid., 292, 293, 295.

38. Ibid., 295, 292; Killens, *Cotillion*, 54; Douglass, "Significance," 204.

CHAPTER SEVEN: A Colored Man Who Happened to Write, 1949–1951

1. For more on the Palmer raids, see Zinn, *People's History*, 374–76.

2. Quoted in Duberman, *Paul Robeson*, 342.

3. Ibid.

4. See ibid., 363–80.

5. Killens, "Lorraine Hansberry," 336–37.

6. Most useful on this episode is David Levering Lewis, *W. E. B. Du Bois*, 546–53.

7. Killens, introduction to *ABC of Color*, 12–13.

8. Fast wrote a series of *Crisis Papers* sponsored by the Civil Rights Congress and modeled on Thomas Paine's 1776 proclamation, *The Crisis*. The quotation in the text is from Fast's *Crisis No. 2* (1951), available at www.trussel.com/hf/crisis2.htm (accessed September 6, 2009).

9. The Alien and Registration Act of 1940 is commonly known as the Smith Act because of its sponsorship by Congressman Howard Smith of Virginia. The defendants in the 1949 trial were not charged with a particular conspiracy but with generally advocating and teaching Marxism-Leninism. Led by zealous anticommunist J. Edgar Hoover, the government indicted more than 140 Communist Party members until several Supreme Court decisions in 1957 turned the tide, most notably *Yates v. United States* and *Watkins v. United States*.

10. FBI file on John Oliver Killens.

11. Quoted in Hunton, *Alphaeus Hunton*, 85.

12. Ibid., 82–88.

13. Of Jackson's flight from prosecution, Du Bois biographer David Levering Lewis wrote, "In an utterly self-defeating gesture of contempt for capitalist justice that gave credence to the foreign-agents presumptions of a majority of Americans, Jim Jackson had followed a number of Party leaders in flight while on bail in 1951" (*W. E. B. Du Bois*, 555). On October 14, 2005, I asked Esther Cooper Jackson, in the presence of her husband, about Lewis's statement. She felt it was unfortunate that Lewis, who consulted with her and whose work she supported overall, placed that final construal on her husband's decision.

14. Hunton, *Alphaeus Hunton*, 84; Esther Cooper Jackson, interview by author, October 14, 2005.

15. FBI file on John Oliver Killens.

16. Jackson, interview.

17. Cruse, *Crisis*, 206–7, 212, 375, 498–500, 505, 508, 510, 512, 515–17, 562.

18. Du Bois, "Criteria," 296. Du Bois was using *propaganda* in the more neutral sense the word conveyed before the sinister connotations of the Cold War. Furthermore, his use of the term did not imply diminished artistry; he simply affirmed the persuasive aspect of art.

19. Carey, "Black Men's Du Boisian Relationships," 2.

20. Cruse, *Crisis*, 216, 221, 237.

21. Although not restricted to a concern with socialist realism as a literary technique, Washington voices a critique about the exclusion of radical viewpoints from many discussions of the historical development of African American literature. See, for example, "Desegregating the 1950s." She expressed similar ideas in "Other Black List."

22. Cruse, *Crisis*, 216.

23. Wilkerson, "Negro Culture," 5.

24. Killens, foreword, 7.

25. Kaiser, "Racial Dialectics," 299. For Wilkerson, the "safe" view of the Negro problem focused on attitude changes, and he saw in Myrdal's work "no more pretentious and dangerous an illustration" ("Negro Culture," 9). According to Wilkerson, "The 'decisive struggle' lies, not 'in the heart of the American,' as Myrdal would have us believe, but in the market place and factory, on the southern plantation, in the executive offices and legislative chambers of local, state and national government—in the ballot!" (10). Wilkerson made no specific comments about African American psychology, which I suppose was Kaiser's point. Kaiser understood (although I disagree) Wilkerson to suggest that all African Americans remained unwarped by oppression and were motivated and united to struggle against their class oppressors. In "Richard Wright Looks Back," Du Bois described *Black Boy* as "terribly overdrawn" and

lamented, "The Negroes he paints have almost no redeeming qualities. Some work hard, some are sly, many are resentful; but there is none who is ambitious, successful or really intelligent" (2). Du Bois also took issue with the passage about the "absence of real kindness in Negroes," the same description that Killens, undoubtedly aware of Du Bois's review, criticized while at Columbia University.

26. Kaiser, review. In this lengthy review, in which he pointed out numerous flaws in Cruse's analysis, Kaiser contended that Cruse was neither equipped nor qualified to write an academically rigorous book on African American political, social, and cultural thought and could not "even make a logical, consistent argument" (33). Kaiser sought to "dissociate my critical writing from its uses in Cruse's book," uses that Kaiser termed evil and destructive (33, 40).

27. Killens, "Write On!" 6.

28. Killens, "Half," 287.

29. Wilkerson, "Negro Culture," 8–9.

30. Killens, *Youngblood*, 1.

31. Killens, "Half," 287.

32. Peeples, "Artist as Liberator," 9; Douglass, "Significance," 204. The Douglass quotation was a favorite of Killens.

33. William Gardner Smith, "Negro Writer," 299.

34. Gloster, "Race," 369.

35. Nichols, "The Forties," 377.

36. Alain Locke, "Self-Criticism," 392.

37. Jarrett, "Toward Unfettered Creativity," 314–15.

38. Hughes and the Editors, "Some Practical Observations," 309.

39. Ford, "Blueprint," 375.

40. Lloyd L. Brown, "Which Way?" 53–55, 59–60; Lloyd L. Brown, "Which Way? II," 54, 53.

41. Killens, "Rappin' with Myself," 103.

42. John Oliver Killens to Lita Schwartz, October 23, 1951.

43. Lita Schwartz to John Oliver Killens, October 23, 1951.

44. Saul Bloomgarden to John Oliver Killens, October 26, 1951.

CHAPTER EIGHT: The Poetry, Energy, and Convictions, 1951–1954

1. Quoted in publicity material.

2. Killens, "Half," 285.

3. For a discussion of *Youngblood* in relation to the African American vernacular, see Gilyard, *Liberation Memories*, 26–35. See also Wiggins, "Structure."

4. For a synopsis of the novel, see Gilyard, *Liberation Memories*, 9–22. Lehman, "Development," was the first to point out the sermon structure of *Youngblood*.

5. Killens, *Youngblood*, 201–5.

6. Ibid., 204.

7. Killens, "For National Freedom," 249.

8. Killens, "Half," 288.

9. Killens, "God Bless America," 38.

10. Ibid., 40.

11. Philip Stevenson to John Oliver Killens, January 22, 1952.

12. John Oliver Killens to Philip Stevenson, January 28, 1952; Philip Stevenson to John Oliver Killens, February 6, 1952. Stevenson grasped the traditional meaning of the latter phrase when he asked, "Does it mean that a blind mule exposes itself to danger, and Joe has no intention of doing this?" These days one can still hear a familiar refrain uttered by the likes of my uncle, Steve Sherman, determined to handle his business, usually in a game of bid whist: "Don't worry about the mule going blind / Just sit tight and hold the line / Don't worry about the cow going po' / Just drink up the milk and ask for mo'."

13. See De Veaux, *Warrior Poet*, 38–39.

14. Lloyd L. Brown, "Deep Pit," 62, 63–64.

15. Killens, review of *Invisible Man*, 7.

16. An adequate and sufficiently balanced book on Harlem cultural politics of the 1940s and 1950s is yet to be written. The intellectual charge led by Harold Cruse against the organized Left, particularly against Robeson, Lorraine Hansberry, and Killens, remains influential despite significant flaws, though attacks on Wright and Ellison by Hansberry, Killens, and Brown lend a substantial measure of credence to the Cruse viewpoint. Lawrence Jackson's *Ralph Ellison* is wonderfully insightful and brilliantly composed, though a bit too pro-Ellison and inattentive to the worthwhile everyday efforts of Harlem leftists. Horne, "Comrades and Friends" is useful, as is Washington, "Desegregating the 1950s."

17. See Howe, "Black Boys"; Ellison, "World and the Jug."

18. Cameron, "Crisis," 16–19.

19. Elizabeth Pollock to John Oliver Killens, August 9, 1952.

20. John Oliver Killens to the John Simon Guggenheim Memorial Foundation, October 15, 1952.

21. Anne-Marie Comert to John Oliver Killens, December 29, 1952.

22. John Oliver Killens to Maxwell Geismar, June 4, 1953; Geismar, *Writers*, 179.

23. Maxwell Geismar to John Oliver Killens, June 1953.

24. Paule Marshall reminded Killens of the sign (Marshall to Killens, July 16, 1959).

25. Wald raised this possibility when he contrasted the two novels in "Trueblood versus Youngblood" (*Exiles*, 56–62). Furthermore, in poring over various drafts of Killens's novel, I have found no instance of the Youngblood surname being used before the publication of *Invisible Man*. The general line of argument here is drawn from Gilyard, *Liberation Memories*, 18–21.

26. Killens, *Youngblood*, 255–85.

27. Ibid., 285–98.

28. Ibid., 44–46, 443–75.

29. Killens, *Black Man's Burden*, 61, 62.

30. Killens, *Youngblood*, 404.

31. Ibid., 402–3.

32. Toni Cade Bambara, in her blurb for the 1982 edition of *Youngblood*, explained that the novel "broke starkly with the Wright school and opened a path for those novelists, poets and playwrights who comprised the neo–Black Arts Movement—a movement that recognized John Oliver Killens as its spiritual father."

CHAPTER NINE: Mr. Youngblood, 1954–1955

1. Glenn, "Books and Authors."

2. Jaffe, "John Killens' Powerful Novel."

3. Quoted in publicity material.

4. Killens, "Rappin' with Myself," 102.

5. John Oliver Killens to Ann Seidman, November 1, 1954.

6. Killens, "Half," 291.

7. *Courier* Theatrical Page, August 10, 1954.

8. Herbert Biberman to John Oliver Killens, September 5, 1954.

9. Killens, "Frank London Brown," 5.

10. John Oliver Killens to Richard Durham, October 21, 1954.

11. John Oliver Killens to Oscar Brown Jr., November 9, 1954.

12. John Oliver Killens to Vivian Harsh, November 1, 1954.

13. John Oliver Killens to Henry Allen Moe, November 10, 1954.

14. Albert Maltz to John Oliver Killens, November 24, 1954.

15. Ibid.

16. In 1972, Branton gained widespread notoriety when he helped defend Angela Davis against charges of murder, kidnapping, and conspiracy. His closing argument was so eloquent that Davis fell into a spell of "forgetting that it was *my* life at stake" (Angela Davis, *Angela Davis*, 385–86).

17. *Los Angeles Tribune*, January 21, 1955.

18. Grace Killens, interview by author, October 14, 2005.

19. See Mary Jo Buhle, Buhle, and Georgakas, *Encyclopedia*, 413–15.

20. John Howard Lawson to John Oliver Killens, June 12, 1955.

21. Killens, "Half," 291.

22. Ibid., 292.

23. FBI file on John Oliver Killens.

24. For a lengthy interview with Alvah Bessie, see McGilligan and Mate, "Alvah Bessie."

25. *Jim Grady Show*, February 15, 1955, transcript in FBI file on John Oliver Killens.

26. Ibid., February 16, 1955.

27. John Oliver Killens to Almena Lomax and Lucius Lomax, March 5, 1955.

28. Killens, "Alas," 17, 19.

CHAPTER TEN: Stalking the Truth, 1955–1957

1. John Oliver Killens to Richard Durham, July 3, 1955; John Oliver Killens to Richard Bancroft, July 3, 1955; John Oliver Killens to Alvah Bessie, July 3, 1955.

2. ILWU Book Club.

3. John Howard Lawson to John Oliver Killens, August 1, 1955.

4. Killens, "Smoking Sixties," xviii.

5. John Oliver Killens to Sidney Poitier, July 19, 1955.

6. Lewis H. Mounts to John Oliver Killens, September 24, 1955.

7. FBI file on John Oliver Killens; *Pittsburgh Courier* quoted in Haygood, *King*, 203.

8. FBI file on John Oliver Killens.

9. Langston Hughes to John Oliver Killens, November 28, 1955; FBI file on John Oliver Killens.

10. FBI file on John Oliver Killens.

11. For a gripping account of the Montgomery Bus Boycott and the events leading up to it, see Taylor Branch, *Parting the Waters*, 105–205.

12. Killens, *Black Man's Burden*, 109, 110.

13. Blurb for event brochure, March 11, 1956.

14. Sarah Wright to John Oliver Killens, May 5, 1956.

15. John Oliver Killens to Martin Luther King Jr., June 10, 1956.

16. Martin Luther King Jr. to John Oliver Killens, July 5, 1956.

17. Killens, "Rappin' with Myself," 120.

18. Faulkner, "Letter."

19. Killens, "How Long," 2, 6. Killens failed to convince publisher Max Ascoli to run the piece in *The Reporter*, a well-regarded liberal outlet, and it was never published.

20. Russell Howe, "New Civil War."

21. Killens, "How Long," 9.

22. FBI file on John Oliver Killens.

23. Remarks on the second day of the Harlem Writers Guild Fiftieth Anniversary Celebration, Schomburg Center for Research in Black Culture, New York Public Library, November 18, 2000.

24. Alfred Duckett to John Oliver Killens, August 22, 1956.

25. John Oliver Killens to Harry Belafonte, December 26, 1956.

26. Killens, brochure for "An Evening with Belafonte."

27. Thomas Russell Jones to John Oliver Killens, May 31, 1957.

28. Thomas Russell Jones to Harry Belafonte, June 1, 1957.

29. Charles Katz to John Oliver Killens, June 17, 1957.

30. Haskell Wexler to John Oliver Killens, July 17, 1957.

31. Killens, "Montgomery Story," 33.

32. Ibid., 71.

33. Killens, *Black Man's Burden*, 15–16.

34. Bayard Rustin to John Oliver Killens, October 2, 1957.

35. Jo Ann Robinson to John Oliver Killens, December 4, 1957; Killens, "Half," 289.

36. Killens, "Address."

37. Ibid.

38. Ibid.

39. Martin Luther King Jr. to John Oliver Killens, November 18, 1957.

CHAPTER ELEVEN: Rights and Rites, 1958–1959

1. Thomas Russell Jones to the Soviet Embassy, February 28, 1958.

2. Ibid., April 16, May 31, 1958.

3. Thomas Russell Jones to Aleksei Krasilnikov, October 6, 1958.

4. Hughes, "Writers," 45.

5. John Oliver Killens to Harry Belafonte, December 31, 1957.

6. Ibid.

7. Haskell Wexler to John Oliver Killens, January 3, 1958.

8. Ibid., February 27, 1958.

9. Ibid., September 23, 1958.

10. John Oliver Killens and Arnaud d'Usseau to Haskell Wexler, September 30, 1958; Haskell Wexler to John Oliver Killens and Arnaud d'Usseau, October 1, 1958.

11. Ossie Davis to the Harlem Writers Guild, July 25, 1958.

12. Grace Killens, interview by author, October 14, 2005.

13. Harold Cruse to John Oliver Killens, January 27, 1959.

14. Ibid. *Simply Heavenly* did not open at the Greenwich Mews Theatre because religious organizations that sponsored the theater objected to the content. Holt booked the play into the Eighty-fifth Street Playhouse, where it opened in May 1957. The production almost immediately encountered problems with breakdowns in the cooling mechanism, labor issues, and infractions of the fire code. Fire marshals shut the play down, although white shows had been using the building for years. The play went to the Forty-eighth Street Playhouse on Broadway and then to the Renata in Lower Manhattan, where it encountered additional labor issues. See Rampersad, *Life*, 265–76.

15. Killens, "Impact," 5, 6.

16. Killens, "Opening Remarks."

17. Mayfield, "Into the Mainstream," 33.

18. Killens, "Opportunities," 70; William Branch, "Marketing," 50.

19. Killens, "Opportunities," 64, 65.

20. Again, see Washington, "Desegregating the 1950s," 18–22. Although undeniably on target overall, Washington is reductionist in simply calling Saunders Redding and Arthur P. Davis, who were present at the conference, conservatives. Such might have been true of their literary tastes relative to some of the other conferees, but the label is not accurate—at least not from their remarks at the conference—as a description of their political positions, which were probably more liberal than conservative. See Redding, "Negro Writer"; Davis, "Integration." Hansberry's comments, "Negro Writer and His Roots," were published posthumously in *Black Scholar* (March–April 1981) and are included in Early, *Speech and Power*, 129–41.

21. Greenspun, "Screen." See also Paul Buhle and Wagner, *Very Dangerous Citizen*, 1.

22. Polonsky, *Odds*, 245.

23. McGivern, *Odds*, 178, 206.

24. Peterson, "John Oliver Killens," 293; Polonsky, *Odds*, 241.

25. Polonsky, *Odds*, 241.

26. Abraham Polonsky Diaries, vol. 42, March–July 1958, Abraham Polonsky Papers, Wisconsin Historical Society, Madison.

27. John Oliver Killens to Harry Belafonte, April 7, 1959.

28. Paul Buhle and Wagner (*Blacklisted*, 165) claim that Killens eventually acknowledged that he made only minor contributions to the script, but they cite no source for this contention.

29. John Oliver Killens to Harry Belafonte, April 7, 1959.

30. Killens, "Presentation."

31. Burnham, "Negro Writer"; Sarah Wright to the *National Guardian*, May 30, 1959.

32. Sarah Wright to Almena Lomax, May 30, 1959. Cruse had written a similar anonymous note about Belafonte to the *New York Post* three years earlier ("A Reader" to *New York Post*, November 1, 1956).

33. John Oliver Killens to Angus Cameron, September 7, 1959.

34. Paule Marshall to John Oliver Killens, July 16, 1959.

35. Killens, *Black Man's Burden*, 7.

36. Killens, "Youngblood Screenplay," 121.

37. Lafayette Bonner, interview by author, June 22, 2002.

CHAPTER TWELVE: Journey to Genesis, 1959–1961

1. Sarah Wright to Grace Killens, December 16, 1961.

2. Angelou, *Heart*, 22.

3. Ibid., 33. Angelou's experiences with discrimination in California belied her statement. For example, she had moved into a Laurel Canyon home only after her friends Atara and Joe Morheim served as fronts. Furthermore, Angelou encountered

racial prejudice in dealing with school administrators in Los Angeles, and she had been extremely nervous about booking into a Fresno hotel because of the racial climate in that city (5, 23–29).

4. Killens, "Smoking Sixties," xii.

5. John Oliver Killens to James Ivy, January 29, 1960.

6. Davis uses the term in reference to inviting Patterson to his home for a reading of *Purlie Victorious* (Ossie Davis and Dee, *With Ossie and Ruby*, 292). Others in attendance included Louise Thompson Patterson, Loften Mitchell, James Jackson, Esther Cooper Jackson, and Killens.

7. Angelou, *Heart*, 39–40.

8. Ibid., 67.

9. Behind Powell's threat was his knowledge or assumption that a photograph taken by an FBI informant depicted King bathing while conversing with Rustin. For discussion of Powell's actions relative to the convention, see Haygood, *King*, 265–69.

10. Angelou, *Heart*, 85–89. See also Taylor Branch, *Parting the Waters*, 314–16, 329.

11. Quoted in D'Emilio, *Lost Prophet*, 299.

12. See Tyson, *Radio Free Dixie*, 203–5.

13. FBI file on John Oliver Killens.

14. Sarah Wright to John Oliver Killens, July 29, 1960.

15. Killens, *Black Man's Burden*, 116.

16. Angelou, *Heart*, 106.

17. Maya Angelou to Grace Killens and John Oliver Killens, January 6, 1961.

18. Alphaeus Hunton to John Oliver Killens, December 1, 1960.

19. Thomas Russell Jones to Haskell Wexler, March 4, 1960.

20. John Oliver Killens to Haskell Wexler, April 27, 1960.

21. Pat Fowler to John Oliver Killens, September 20, 1960.

22. John Oliver Killens to Yale Wexler, December 21, 1960.

23. Leo Branton to John Oliver Killens, February 7, 1961; Albert Da Silva to Leo Branton, February 9, 28, 1961; Leo Branton to Marshall Sevin, February 24, 1961; Leo Branton to Albert Da Silva, February 24, 1961.

24. Pat Gallagher to John Oliver Killens, March 29, 1961.

25. John Oliver Killens to Angus Cameron, November 24, 1959.

26. Angus Cameron to John Oliver Killens, March 10, 1961.

27. Langston Hughes to John Oliver Killens, March 11, 1961.

28. External Development Services to John Oliver Killens, April 20, 1961.

29. Martin Leighton to John Oliver Killens, May 15, 24, 1961.

30. Killens, "Half," 299; John Oliver Killens to Grace Killens, June 25, 1961.

31. Killens, "Half," 299.

32. Ibid., 299–300.

33. "Notes by Wynford Vaughan Thomas on His Trip with EDS Scripting Team to West Africa, June 1961," 12–17.

34. Killens, "Half," 300.

35. Grace Killens to John Oliver Killens, June 23, 1961.

36. John Oliver Killens to Grace Killens, June 25, 1961.

37. Killens, "Half," 300.

38. Ibid., 302.

39. "Notes by Wynford Vaughan Thomas on His Trip with EDS Scripting Team to West Africa, June 1961," 22–23.

40. Killens, "Half," 303.

41. Haskell Wexler to Thomas Russell Jones, July 31, 1961.

42. Haskell Wexler to author, October 22, 2008.

43. Haskell Wexler to Thomas Russell Jones, July 31, 1961.

44. Altina Carey to John Oliver Killens, August 14, 1961.

45. Grace Killens to John Oliver Killens, September 25, 1961.

46. Killens, *Black Man's Burden*, 20. In *Black Man's Burden* (155), Killens wrote that he visited ten African countries, but then he listed eleven.

CHAPTER THIRTEEN: Thundering Genius, 1961–1963

1. John Oliver Killens to Chief Basil C. Okwu, November 13, 1961.

2. Evelyn Brown to John Oliver Killens and Grace Killens, March 12, 1962.

3. John Oliver Killens to Gus Savage, March 27, 1962.

4. I owe another considerable debt to Alan Wald because I developed this particular reading after consulting his discussion of the novel and its relationship to the Popular Front in his *Exiles*. This analysis is not intended to replace the discussion of *And Then We Heard the Thunder* in Gilyard, *Liberation Memories*, 37–57, which remains more detailed in terms of tracing certain textual patterns. Here I chart a course somewhere between my earlier read and Wald's. In addition, I recommend Jennifer C. James, *Freedom*, which frames *And Then We Heard the Thunder* as a military neoslave narrative (261–78).

5. Killens, *And Then We Heard*, 485.

6. Ibid., 5–6.

7. Lloyd L. Brown, "Which Way II," 53. Tubman's words are also included in Hughes's *Famous American Negroes*, which the author presented to Killens's son in the 1950s, probably around 1954 (Killens, *Black Man's Burden*, 36).

8. Killens, *And Then We Heard*, 79, 173, 174.

9. Ibid., 191, 386, 388, 392.

10. Ibid., 485.

11. Malcolm X, *Autobiography*, 387. Bill Mullen directed my attention to this particular passage in *Autobiography of Malcolm X*. Mullen also demonstrates how other activists, including Du Bois, drew on Asia in shaping their prophetic visions (*Afro-Orientalism*, 30). For a compatible analysis that includes Martin Luther King Jr. among those activists who gazed eastward, see Stull, *Amid the Fall*.

12. Killens, *And Then We Heard*, 56.

13. Killens, "Rappin' with Myself," 118.

14. Hampton and Fayer, *Voices*, 251–52.

15. FBI file on the Organization of Afro-American Unity.

16. A central argument in Cone, *Martin and Malcolm and America*, is that King's conception of an American dream and Malcolm's concept of an American nightmare were rhetorically and consciously juxtaposed by them, though, of course, King, too, sometimes perceived an American nightmare. Pivotal texts for Cone are King's "I Have a Dream Speech" at the March on Washington for Jobs and Freedom, August 28, 1963, and Malcolm's "Ballot or Bullet" speech at Cory Methodist Church in Cleveland on April 3, 1964.

17. Tyson, *Radio Free Dixie*, 192, 214–16.

18. Killens, "Rappin' with Myself," 118, 116.

19. Goldman, "Malcolm," 129.

20. Killens, "Rappin' with Myself," 118–19.

21. See Perry, *Malcolm*, 207–12.

22. Charles Myles Killens Sr. to John Oliver Killens, November 7, 1962.

23. Angus Cameron to John Oliver Killens, August 7, 1962.

24. Sidney Poitier to John Oliver Killens, ca. 1962.

25. Lorraine Hansberry to John Oliver Killens, ca. 1962.

26. Harry Belafonte to John Oliver Killens, ca. 1962.

27. "Negro Writer in America," 54, 56, 57, 58, 61–62; Hughes, "Notes."

28. Carmichael with Thelwell, *Ready*, 261, 262.

29. John Oliver Killens to Harry Belafonte, November 30, 1962.

30. Kitching, "Fiction Forecast," 43; John Oliver Killens to James Baldwin, December 18, 1962; John Oliver Killens to Langston Hughes, December 19, 1962; James Baldwin to John Oliver Killens, January 1963; Langston Hughes to John Oliver Killens, January 5, 1963.

31. Poppy Cannon White, "Thundering Genius"; Ruby Dee Davis to Angus Cameron, January 6, 1963.

32. Angus Cameron to John Oliver Killens, January 22, 1963; John Oliver Killens to Carl Van Vechten, January 30, 1963.

33. Lorraine Hansberry and Bob Nemiroff to John Oliver Killens, January 20, 1963; Langston Hughes to John Oliver Killens, January 20, 1963.

34. Romare Bearden to John Oliver Killens, January 22, 1963.

35. Poppy Cannon White, "Thundering Genius"; Killens, "Half," 295.

36. Griffin, "Color Line," 46.

37. Norford, "Search."

38. Lucas, "Color Line."

39. Poston, "Different Kind."

40. Meriwether, "From Cover to Cover."

41. Clarke, "Negro Men," 229.

42. Carl Van Vechten to Alfred Knopf, ca. 1963.

43. Mark Frazier to John Oliver Killens, February 4, 1963.

44. Louise Coleman Ketch to John Oliver Killens, February 1, 1963.

45. Khiss, "Pulitzer Prizes."

CHAPTER FOURTEEN: It Doesn't Hurt to Review, 1963–1964

1. Killens, "Rappin' with Myself," 134.

2. John Oliver Killens to Leonard Holt, ca. 1963.

3. Evelyn Brown to John Oliver Killens, March 19, 1963.

4. John Oliver Killens to Angus Cameron, April 28, 1963.

5. Angus Cameron to John Oliver Killens, May 8, 1963.

6. SNCC Press Release.

7. Brandeis University Critics' Forum, August 7, 1963.

8. Charles Myles Killens Sr. to John Oliver Killens, August 7, 1963.

9. Sterling Stuckey to author, October 16, 17, 2008.

10. Killens, "What Went Wrong?" 23.

11. Killens, introduction to *ABC of Color*, 9.

12. Killens, "What Went Wrong?" 23.

13. King, *My Life*, 226.

14. John Oliver Killens to Harry Belafonte, October 1, 1963.

15. Ibid. The association's document of aims and purposes elaborated its mission: 1. To be a cultural adjunct, and not in competition with, the existing organizations fighting for civil and human rights in our country; 2. To achieve a meaningful unity of all artists who are concerned with the great American moral and cultural crisis; 3. To conceive and sponsor and encourage cultural and artistic activities in the Negro communities in particular, and in the entire American community as well; 4. To help make art a part of the ordinary life of all people; 5. In the main, our activities will be neither political, nor legislative, but cultural. However, Ossie Davis expressed a specific political mission for the group when he filed a "Report to Association of Artists for Freedom." Davis spoke of the need for a political master plan.

16. Herbert Biberman to Harry Belafonte, December 15, 1963.

17. Ibid.

18. Ibid.

CHAPTER FIFTEEN: Statesmanlike Work, 1964

1. *1963 Live Interview with Malcolm X, Berkeley University* (video, Blacast Entertainment).

2. Breitman, for example, has noted that Malcolm admitted the possibility of solidarity with white allies (*Last Year*, 68). This "final phase," then, is allegedly marked by

Malcolm's more elaborate and mature statement of his black nationalism, what Breitman has described as a movement from "pure-and-simple black nationalism" to "black nationalism plus" (68). Breitman's view is hardly definitive. Dyson has argued that "the nature of Malcolm's thought during his last year was ambiguous and that making definite judgments about his direction is impossible" (*Making Malcolm*, 70). There is truth in both assessments, and as Marable has pointed out, attempts to analyze Malcolm's ideas are complicated by the absence of full and complete texts of his final writings and speeches (*Living Black History*, 163–77). Because Malcolm was involved with the Killens group of Old Leftists and Pan-Africanists, he likely seriously pondered some form of socialism as a platform. For a similar discussion of connections between Malcolm's advocacy and Killens's writing, see Gilyard, *Liberation Memories*, 59–68.

3. According to Peter Bailey, Killens was in Harlem at the first planning meeting, in December 1963 or January 1964, of what would become the OAAU (Hampton and Fayer, *Voices*, 250–52, 256–57). Gallen claims that Clarke took credit for getting the OAU charter as a model for the OAAU (*Malcolm X Reader*, 94). Sales acknowledges Killens's impact on the formation of the OAAU (*From Civil Rights to Black Liberation*, 60, 105, 155). According to FBI reports, Killens declined to sign the OAAU's incorporation papers; Lynn Shifflett reportedly told Betty Shabazz that Killens "chickened out" (FBI Files on the Organization of Afro-American Unity).

4. Handler, "Negro Novelist."

5. Quoted in Killens, "Write On!" 16. However, I have found no citation attributing the remark to Æ, and, as my colleague Mark Morrisson explained to me, the quote may originally be from the "Scylla and Charybdis" chapter of *Ulysses*, in which James Joyce has Æ say, "The supreme question about a work of art is out of how deep a life does it spring" (152). In *James Joyce*, Matthew Hodgart writes, "Frank O'Connor told Æ in his later years that Joyce had made him say in this chapter, 'the supreme question about a work of art is out of how deep a life does it spring,' to which Æ replied, 'How clever of Joyce: I might have said something like that.' 'He said it every day,' O'Connor comments" (95). Kathleen Raine reports in *Yeats the Initiate* that Æ "believed that the most important thing about a poet is finally this: 'out of how deep a life does he speak?'" (79). But she provides no citation. The quotation likely comes directly from Æ, although it may have originated with Joyce.

6. Killens, "Write On!" 40.

7. Ibid., 5.

8. Angus Cameron to John Oliver Killens, April 15, 1964.

9. Angus Cameron to Phyllis Jackson, April 17, 1964.

10. Angus Cameron to John Oliver Killens, May 11, 1964.

11. Killens, *Black Man's Burden*, 12, 22.

12. Raymond Johnson to John Oliver Killens, June 6, 1964.

13. Richard Bell to John Oliver Killens, June 7, 1964.

14. Claudia Viek to John Oliver Killens, June 7, 1964.

15. Edward P. Gottlieb to John Oliver Killens, June 8, 1964.

16. David B. Kimmelman to John Oliver Killens, June 8, 1964.

17. Elton Fax to editor, *New York Times Magazine*, June 8, 1964.

18. Len Holt to John Oliver Killens, June 10, 1964.

19. Hoyt Fuller to John Oliver Killens, June 8, 1964.

20. Alice Childress to John Oliver Killens, June 8, 1964.

21. Mildred Jordan to John Oliver Killens, June 9, 1964.

22. Angus Cameron to John Oliver Killens, June 11, 1964.

23. For more on the meeting, see Cone, *Martin and Malcolm and America*, 207–8; Taylor Branch, *Pillar*, 345–46.

24. Killens, Wechsler, and Hansberry, "Black Revolution," 442–43. This debate was part of a broader conversation about the Negro problem and liberals that included Miller, "Farewell," and Podhoretz, "My Negro Problem."

25. Silberman, *Crisis*, 61, 186, 191.

26. Killens, Wechsler, and Hansberry, "Black Revolution," 445.

27. Ibid., 447.

28. He blatantly showed his Cold Warrior colors when he was invited the following year to be a sponsor of a celebration of Paul Robeson's sixty-seventh birthday: "My reaction is that you must be joking—and what a bad joke it is" (Duberman, *Paul Robeson*, 528; David Susskind to *Freedomways*, April 2, 1965).

29. Jim Aronson to John Oliver Killens, August 27, 1964.

30. Malcolm X, "Statement," 559, 563, 564; Killens, *And Then We Heard*, 471.

31. Association of Artists for Freedom to James Farmer, Martin Luther King Jr., John Lewis, A. Philip Randolph, Roy Wilkins, and Whitney Young, July 29, 1964.

32. Mitchell, "More about John Killens," 2. The passage from *Youngblood*, spoken by Reverend Ledbetter, actually reads, "A Negro preacher is in a better, more independent position to serve his people than any other colored professional man in the United States. Two powers we have to answer to, and that's our congregation and God Almighty, and ain't neither one of them white" (261).

33. Paine, *The Crisis*, 712.

34. David Shepherd to John Oliver Killens, October 14, 1964.

35. Ellen Bandler to John Oliver Killens, October 30, 1964.

36. Killens, "Hollywood in Black and White."

37. Killens, *Black Man's Burden*, 26, 41, 43, 48, 54.

38. Ibid., 77, 79, 93.

39. Ibid, 166–67.

40. Joseph Walker, "American Author's Views."

41. Malcolm X, "Statement," 563.

42. Killens, *Black Man's Burden*, 26.

43. *Masses and Mainstream* became *Mainstream* in September 1956 and then ceased publication with its August 1963 issue. *American Dialog* debuted in the summer of 1964 under the editorship of Joseph North.

CHAPTER SIXTEEN: In Residence, 1965–1966

1. Arna Bontemps to Langston Hughes, May 23, 1962.
2. Tripp, *Importance*, 90–91. See also Duberman, *Paul Robeson*, 527.
3. Mitchell, "Three Writers," 222.
4. Killens, "Half," 296.
5. Ibid.
6. Ossie Davis, "Malcolm X," 153.
7. Grace Killens to John Oliver Killens, March 9, 1965.
8. Ibid.
9. John Oliver Killens to Harry Belafonte, March 8, 1965.
10. Killens, "Half," 297.
11. Ibid., 298.
12. Carson, *In Struggle*, 175.
13. Nikki Giovanni, interview by author, April 24, 2006.
14. Killens, "Black Culture," 24.
15. Mignon Holland Anderson to author, November 3, 2008.
16. "Task of the Negro Writer," 60, 70–75.
17. Quoted in Cruse, *Crisis*, 507, 508.
18. Talese, "Many Words."
19. Childress, Marshall, and Wright, "Negro Woman," 291–97.
20. Norman Loftis, interview by author, June 25, 2007.
21. Anna Seghers and Arnold Zweig to John Oliver Killens, ca. 1965.
22. Bessie, "Literary Conclave."
23. John Oliver Killens to Alvah Bessie, September 7, 1965.
24. Ibid.
25. John Oliver Killens to Sylvester Leaks, September 1, 1965.
26. Charles Myles Killens to Grace Killens, September 12, 1965.
27. Killens, "Hollywood in Black and White," 156.
28. *New York Times*, January 3, 1966.
29. Zinn, "Visible Men."
30. Durham, "Capturing the Negro Mood," 183.
31. Bessie, "We Need."
32. John Lewis to John Oliver Killens, January 2, 1966.
33. Killens, prologue, 5, 7. Blair offers an excellent assessment of *Cotillion*'s achievement (*Harlem Crossroads*, 242–44) but argues that Killens's involvement with *Harlem Stirs* was a major factor in the stylistic direction he took in *Cotillion*, which is set mostly in Harlem. She concludes that the "brash comic energy of *The Cotillion* is without precedent in Killens's work" (239). However, the unpublished and wildly satirical "The Minister Primarily" was under way years before Killens's work on *Harlem Stirs*, and it provides the precedent that Blair claims was lacking.

34. James Boggs and Grace Boggs to Grace Killens and John Oliver Killens, February 27, 1966.

35. By *Boggsism*, Mullen means a concept of dialectical humanism that has the black experience at the center and that embraces Marxism, though not a vulgar materialism, over an understanding of cultural factors and incorporates Maoism's privileging of political struggle over economic struggle (*Afro-Orientalism*, 115–19).

36. Boggs and Boggs, "City," 40.

37. Grace Killens to John Oliver Killens, February 28, 1966.

CHAPTER SEVENTEEN: Explaining Dissent, 1966–1967

1. Llorens, "Writers Converge," 55.

2. Redding, "Negro Author," 146.

3. Llorens, "Writers Converge," 62.

4. Ibid., 63.

5. "Task of the Negro Writer," 74.

6. Discussion of *'Sippi* is drawn from Gilyard, *Liberation Memories*, 22–26.

7. Killens, *'Sippi*, 399.

8. Ibid., 433.

9. Adam Banks to author, July 26, 2008.

10. John Hunt to Roberta Pryor, March 14, 1966.

11. Killens, "Negroes," 10.

12. J. Hudson to *Saturday Evening Post*, June 17, 1966.

13. John Publius to *Saturday Evening Post*, June 28, 1966.

14. R. W. Pierpont to *Saturday Evening Post*, June 23, 1966.

15. Robert S. Johnson to *Saturday Evening Post*, June 27, 1966.

16. Lorenz Graham to John Oliver Killens, July 31, 1966.

17. Ibid.

18. "Meaning and Measure," 35.

19. John Oliver Killens to Burt Lancaster, August 22, 1966.

20. *The Scalphunters*, scene 3.

21. Buford, *Burt Lancaster*, 249.

22. *Cue*, April 6, 1968.

23. John Oliver Killens and Grace Killens to Haskell Wexler, April 11, 1967.

24. Peeples, "Artist," 11.

25. Ibid.

CHAPTER EIGHTEEN: New Black, 1967–1968

1. Carmichael with Thelwell, *Ready*, 552.

2. Ibid., 554.

3. "On the Conference Beat," 92.

4. Nikki Giovanni Papers, Boston University, Boston.

5. Kalamu ya Salaam, interview by author, April 4, 2008.

6. Gwendolyn Brooks, *Report*, 84.

7. Kent, *Life*, 197.

8. "Task of the Negro Writer," 78.

9. Kent, *Life*, 198–99.

10. Ibid., 199.

11. Ibid., 200–201.

12. Gwendolyn Brooks, *Report*, 85.

13. Sarah Webster Fabio to John Oliver Killens, May 24, 1967.

14. Killens, "Rappin' with Myself," 101.

15. Piri Thomas, interview by Carmen Hernandez, http://www.cheverote.com/reviews/hernandezinterview.html (accessed July 1, 2008).

16. Cleaver, *Target Zero*, 57–58.

17. Killens, "Half," 296; "Killens' Fine, Sensitive New Novel."

18. Alvah Bessie to John Oliver Killens, October 18, 1967.

19. For Baraka's account of his roles in the Newark rebellion and his trial, see *Autobiography*, 366–74, 378–83. Jones refers to Barbara (using the pseudonym *Beverly*) somewhat disparagingly in his memoir.

20. For elaborate accounts of the events at the Algiers Motel, see Hersey, *Algiers Motel Incident*; Sauter and Hines, *Nightmare*, 161–69; Hubert G. Locke, *Detroit Riot*, 45–46, 147–50.

21. Cruse, *Crisis*, 200–201, 500.

22. Mayfield, "Crisis or Crusade?" 23–24.

23. Ronald Milner to John Oliver Killens, January 21, 1968.

24. Nikki Giovanni to John Oliver Killens, June 19, 1968.

25. James Boggs to John Oliver Killens, January 11, 1968.

26. Killens, "Confessions," 34.

27. James L. W. West, *William Styron*, 387. West happens to be my department mate, and I have a high regard for his scholarship overall. However, while no mere apologist for Styron, West could have pushed the political discussion further. West provided an accurate summary of the objections contained in *Ten Black Writers* but failed to weigh any of the arguments in terms of validity, offering instead Eugene Genovese's questionable assertion that the Turner legend had never been known widely among blacks, and Arthur Schlesinger's defense, which is beside the point, that "their Nat Turner is just as much an imagined figure as yours" (388–89). After the initial tempest subsided, literary critic Addison Gayle Jr. wrote a worthy critique in *Way of the New World*. In a discussion of white nationalism, Gayle linked Styron's novel to Norman Mailer's "The White Negro" and Irving Howe's "Black Boys and Native Sons" as inadequate attempts to account for the social psychology of African Americans (234–37).

Mellard, who saw much value in Styron's story, argues, "Black readers of the novel are not wrong to react as many have. There are indeed very troubling aspects to Styron's creation, apart from any apparent or actual distortion of historical facts" ("This Unquiet Dust," 167).

28. John Oliver Killens to Louise Meriwether, March 8, 1968; *Hollywood Reporter*, March 28, 1968.

29. John Oliver Killens to Yakubu Gowon, November 14, 1967; for Soyinka's account of his involvement in the Nigerian civil war and his imprisonment, see *You Must Set Forth*, 99–141.

30. John Oliver Killens to Herbert Biberman, November 20, 1967; Philip Langner to John Oliver Killens, February 7, 1968.

31. John Oliver Killens to Charlie L. Russell, December 9, 1967.

32. *Negro Digest*, January 1968, 13.

33. John Oliver Killens and Grace Killens to Jackie Robinson and Rachel Robinson, March 5, 1968; John Oliver Killens and Grace Killens to Jackie Robinson Jr., March 5, 1968.

34. Jackie Robinson to John Oliver Killens and Grace Killens, March 13, 1968.

CHAPTER NINETEEN: We Must Construct a Monument, 1968–1969

1. Killens, "What Went Wrong?" 25.

2. Killens, "Black Writer," 397.

3. Ibid., 398.

4. Johnston, "Writer."

5. Johnston, "Black Writers." Lee wrote in a 1966 poem, "The New Integrationist," "I / seek / integration / of / negroes / with / black / people" (Madhubuti, "New Integrationist," 21).

6. Killens, "Artist," 63.

7. Killens, "Half," 298.

8. "Game Gets Yeasty," *Negro Digest*, July 1968, 74–78.

9. "Draft Resolution," May 1968.

10. Jeff Donaldson to John Oliver Killens, January 18, 1964; John Oliver Killens to Jeff Donaldson, February 24, 1964.

11. "Game Gets Yeasty," 78.

12. Killens, "Half," 305.

13. Gayle, introduction, 13.

14. James Farmer Flier; for Farmer's full account of his campaign, see *Lay Bare*, 311–14.

15. Askia M. Toure, interview by author, March 26, 2008.

16. Carole Gregory, interview by author, October 21, 2008.

17. Ibid.

18. *New York Times*, March 2, 1969.

19. Jay Martin to John Oliver Killens, December 6, 1968.

20. Ibid., March 20, 1969.

21. Nikki Giovanni Papers, Boston University, Boston.

22. *Publisher's Weekly*, April 14, 1969, 99.

23. Commentary is drawn from Gilyard, *Liberation Memories*, 96–99.

24. Killens, *Slaves*, 11.

25. Ibid., 22, 20–21.

26. Ibid., 40, 47.

27. Ibid., 95.

28. Ibid., 101.

29. Ibid., 7, 46.

30. Lehman, "Development," 161.

31. Ibid.

32. Gayl Jones, *Liberating Voices*, 13.

33. Ibid., 178.

34. Killens, "Rough Diamond," 171.

35. Killens, "Rappin' with Myself," 118.

36. Quoted in Sarah E. Wright, *This Child's Gonna Live*, 277.

37. Killens, "Crisis," 13.

CHAPTER TWENTY: Champeenship of Blackness, 1970–1971

1. *Trinity Tripod*, February 3, 1970.

2. Killens, *Black Man's Burden*, 54.

3. Reed, *Yellow Back Radio*, 36.

4. Paule Marshall to John Oliver Killens, March 6, 1970.

5. Benjamin B. Hickok to John Oliver Killens, March 6, 1970.

6. Shirley Graham Du Bois to John Oliver Killens, March 15, 1970.

7. Sharon Bell Mathis to John Oliver Killens, April 19, 1970.

8. Frederick Cross to John Oliver Killens, April 1, 1970.

9. Shirley Chisholm to John Oliver Killens, May 5, 1970.

10. Killens, *And Then We Heard*, 485.

11. Commentary about *The Cotillion* is drawn from Gilyard, *Liberation Memories*, 80–93.

12. Killens, "Half," 306.

13. Killens, *Cotillion*, 139.

14. Hord, *Reconstructing Memory*, 100.

15. Johnson, *Being and Race*, 91.

16. Travel notes, June–July 1970.

17. Ibid.

18. Ibid.

19. Grace Killens to John Oliver Killens, June 29, 1970.

20. Nathan Hare to John Oliver Killens, July 17, 1970.

21. Killens, "Our Struggle," 8–9.

22. Anonymous to John Oliver Killens, July 1970.

23. Killens, "Rappin' with Myself," 121–22.

24. Killens, "Black Labor."

25. Stuart Sayers to John Oliver Killens, October 27, 1970.

26. Coretta Scott King to Friends, December 1970.

27. Frakes, "Cotillion."

28. Lask, "Daphne Learns."

29. Bond, "Killens' New Novel," 203, 205.

30. Loften Mitchell to John Oliver Killens and Grace Killens, February 18, 1971.

31. Greenlee, "*Cotillion*."

32. Greaves, "Post Book Worm."

33. John A. Williams quoted in press release from Trident Press, ca. 1970.

34. Rob Cohen, "Notes," 3.

35. Killens, "Half," 304.

36. Angus Cameron to John Oliver Killens, March 30, 1971.

37. Herbert Biberman to John Oliver Killens, March 9, 1971.

38. John Oliver Killens to Ewart Guinier, June 29, 1971.

39. John Oliver Killens to Flora Graham, May 30, 1971.

40. Flora Graham to John Oliver Killens, December 1, 1971.

41. John Oliver Killens to Grace Killens, July 1971.

42. Travel notes, July 1971.

43. Killens, "Brutalization or Rehabilitation?"

44. Ewart Guinier to John Oliver Killens, July 2, 1971.

45. John Oliver Killens and Grace Killens to Jackie Robinson and Rachel Robinson, July 3, 1971; John Oliver Killens and Grace Killens to Gale Sondergaard, July 3, 1971.

CHAPTER TWENTY-ONE: Long-Distance Running, 1971–1974

1. John Oliver Killens, "A Eulogy to Mrs. Mabel Ward Jones," February 3, 1972.

2. Dudley Randall to John Oliver Killens, December 29, 1971.

3. Paul Puryear to John Oliver Killens, March 1972.

4. John Oliver Killens to Helen Jackson, February 9, 1972.

5. Killens, "Black Culture," 30.

6. Killens, "Crisis."

7. Newton, "He Won't Bleed Me," 146.

8. Kristen Hunter and John Lattany to John Oliver Killens, July 7, 1972.

9. George Lamming to John Oliver Killens, July 9, 1972.

10. Hoyt Fuller to John Oliver Killens, August 24, 1972.

11. Dudley Randall to John Oliver Killens, August 28, 1972.

12. Ruby Dee to John Oliver Killens, June 9, 1972.

13. Romare Bearden to Grace Killens, June 14, 1972.

14. Amiri Baraka to John Oliver Killens, June 1972.

15. FBI file on John Oliver Killens.

16. John Oliver Killens to Ishmael Reed, October 15, 1972.

17. Ishmael Reed to author, November 17, 2008.

18. John Oliver Killens to Lance Jeffers, November 20, 1972.

19. John Oliver Killens to Nathan Hare, November 20, 1972.

20. Shirley Graham Du Bois to John Oliver Killens, November 12, 1972.

21. John Oliver Killens to Shirley Graham Du Bois, November 28, 1972.

22. The official reason for Robeson's absence was his poor health. However, some attendees grumbled that Paul Robeson Jr. kept his father away for reasons more to do with preserving a political line and controlling an image than with health (Duberman, *Paul Robeson*, 546).

23. Killens, "Wanted," 2, 5.

24. Killens, *Black Man*, 2–4.

25. John Oliver Killens to Nikki Giovanni, July 10, 1973, Nikki Giovanni Papers, Boston University, Boston.

26. Killens, *Black Man*, 10.

27. John Oliver Killens to Grace Killens, July 15, 1973.

28. Killens, *Black Man*, 17.

29. Ibid., 18.

30. Ibid., 19.

31. Trescott, "Debate."

32. Louis Reyes Rivera, interview by author, December 9, 2008.

33. Ibid.

CHAPTER TWENTY-TWO: I Always Said Class and Race, 1974–1977

1. Commentary drawn from Gilyard, *Liberation Memories*, 128–31.

2. John Oliver Killens, "Message from John O. Killens, Director of the National Conference of Afro-American Writers," conference brochure.

3. E. Ethelbert Miller, interview by author, October 9, 2007.

4. Parks, "National Black Writers Convention," 88, 90.

5. Madhubuti, "Latest Purge," 46, 51.

6. For direct criticisms of Madhubuti's article, see S. E. Anderson, "Response"; Alonzo 4X (Cannady), "Response"; Mark Smith, "Response." For broader critiques, see Karenga, "Which Road?"; Baraka, "Some Questions"; Baraka, "Congress." For favorable responses to Madhubuti's article, see Walters, "Response"; ya Salaam, "Response"; Wilcox, "Response."

7. Nathan Hare, "An Open Letter on My Resignation," February 26, 1975.

8. Ibid.

9. Hunter, "Ideology Dispute."

10. Robert Chrisman, Robert Allen, and Glory Bevien, "An Open Letter in Response to Dr. Nathan Hare's Resignation."

11. Hunter, "Ideology Dispute."

12. Hunter, "Black Intellectuals Divided."

13. Quoted in ibid.

14. Ibid.

15. John Oliver Killens to *New York Times*, May 2, 1975.

16. Analysis drawn from Gilyard, *Liberation Memories*, 103–7.

17. Nikola-Lisa, "John Henry," 54.

18. Brett Williams, *John Henry*, 93.

19. John Oliver Killens to Tatiana A. Kudryavtseva, January 9, 1975.

20. Killens, *Man Ain't Nothin'*, 74–76.

21. Ibid., 151.

22. Ibid., 154.

23. Henry Hitz to John Oliver Killens, September 19, 1976.

24. John Oliver Killens, Grace Killens, and Family to Paul Robeson Sr., January 21, 1976.

25. Duberman, *Paul Robeson*, 549.

26. Hollie I. West, "Black Publishing Crisis."

27. Bebe Campbell to John Oliver Killen's, May 7, 1976.

28. Commentary drawn from Gilyard, *Liberation Memories*, 108–11.

29. Killens, *Great Black Russian*, 39, 43, 47, 77.

30. See Peeples, "Artist."

31. Pushkin, *Poems, Prose and Plays*, 14.

32. In terms of concrete political acts, Pushkin is best known as the Bard of the Decembrists. After the death of Czar Alexander in 1825, his brother Nicholas ascended to the throne. A rebellion was planned for December 14 but was crushed by the emperor's Horse Guards. Five members of the group, which became known as the Decembrists, were hanged and several others banished to Siberia. Many were Pushkin's friends and in fact had been inspired by him. The following year, Pushkin was summoned from his exile in Mikhailovskoye by Nicholas for a face-to-face meeting at the conclusion of which Nicholas announced a "new" Pushkin. The next eleven years, the last of his life, were spent in an uneasy relationship with the czar.

33. Killens, "Half," 305–6.

CHAPTER TWENTY-THREE: Pushing Pushkin, 1977–1982

1. Harry Haywood to John Oliver Killens, February 15, 1977.

2. John Oliver Killens to Bonnie Keys, October 1, 1977.

3. Paul Robeson Jr., interview by author, June 19, 2007.

4. Paul Robeson Jr., press release, October 11, 1977.

5. Nikki Giovanni, interview by author, April 24, 2006.

6. Robeson, interview.

7. Welsing quoted in Hollie I. West, "Sexual Politics."

8. Laraine Fergenson to author, January 30, 2008.

9. Quoted in Harvey, "Portrait."

10. Norman Loftis to John Oliver Killens, April 1, 1980.

11. John Oliver Killens to Harry Belafonte, February 20, March 5, 1981.

12. John Oliver Killens to Alice Childress, December 17, 1981, Schomburg Center for Research in Black Culture, New York Public Library, New York.

13. Anne Freedgood to Lawrence Jordan, January 27, 1982.

14. Loften Mitchell to John Oliver Killens, April 7, 1982.

15. Samuel F. Yette to John Oliver Killens, December 11, 1982.

16. Killens, "What Went Wrong?"

17. Ibid., 25.

18. Killens, "What Went Wrong? (A Follow-Up)," 3–4.

19. Ibid., 5.

CHAPTER TWENTY-FOUR: For Freedom, 1982–1986

1. Peeples, "Artist."

2. Killens, "Minister Primarily," 17, 52.

3. Ibid., 173, 396, 224.

4. Ibid., 98, 397.

5. John Oliver Killens to Henry Louis Gates Jr., February 16, 1983.

6. Jerry W. Ward Jr. to author, March 21, 2008.

7. Killens, "Black Tradition," 19–20, 24.

8. John Oliver Killens and Grace Killens to Family and Friends, December 1983.

9. Ibid.

10. Brenda Conner-Bey to John Oliver Killens, January 16, 1984.

11. John Oliver Killens to Samuel F. Yette, January 31, 1984.

12. Flowers, *Mojo Rising*, 44–45.

13. Paule Marshall to John Oliver Killens and Grace Killens, July 19, 1984.

14. George Lamming to John Oliver Killens, July 26, 1984.

15. Killens, "Literary Genius," 131–33.

16. Alice Childress to John Oliver Killens, August 17, 1984.

17. Killens, "Half," 306.

18. Lisa Chapman Jones, "Talking Book," 18.

19. Grace Killens to *Village Voice*, March 15, 1985.

20. John Oliver Killens to Willie Lee Killens, June 14, 1985.

21. Peeples, "Artist," 10.

22. Zizwe Ngafua, B. J. Ashanti, Arthur Flowers, and Louis Reyes Rivera to John Oliver Killens and Elizabeth Nunez, November 5, 1985.

23. Louis Reyes Rivera to John Oliver Killens, ca. 1985.

24. Maya Angelou to John Oliver Killens, August 21, 1985.

25. For further discussion, see Gilyard, *Liberation Memories*, 132–37.

26. Taped conference proceedings, March 22, 1986, Medgar Evers College—CUNY Library, New York.

27. Ibid., March 21, 1986.

28. Ibid., March 22, 1986.

29. Ibid.

30. Ibid.

31. Ibid.

CHAPTER TWENTY-FIVE: Dr. K's Run, 1986–1987

1. Robert Caswell to John Oliver Killens, September 2, 1986.

2. Howard "Stretch" Johnson to John Oliver Killens, January 1987.

3. John Oliver Killens to the Brunson Family, January 20, 1987.

4. John Oliver Killens to Charles Myles Killens Jr. and Helen Killens, 1987.

5. John Oliver Killens and Grace Killens mass mailing, March 20, 1987.

6. Johnetta Cole to Grace Killens and John Oliver Killens, May 14, 1987.

7. Lorenz Graham and Ruth Graham mass mailing, September 1987.

8. John Oliver Killens, interview by author, 1986.

9. Flowers, *Mojo Rising*, 63–64.

10. Carla P. Hoke to John Oliver Killens, October 23, 1987.

11. Norman Loftis, interview by author, June 25, 2007.

12. Major Owens, "In Memory of John Oliver Killens," *Congressional Record*, December 2, 1987.

13. Event brochure.

14. Joseph Kaye, interview by author, June 12, 2007.

15. Paul Robeson Jr., interview by author, June 19, 2007.

16. "Ebony Book Shelf," *Ebony*, October 1989, 22.

Bibliography

Alonzo 4X (Cannady). "A Response to Haki Madhubuti." *Black Scholar*, October
   1974, 52–53.
*The American Negro Writer and His Roots: Selected Papers from the First Conference
   of Negro Writers, March, 1959*. New York: American Society of African Culture,
   1960.
Anderson, Mignon Holland. *The End of Dying*. Baltimore: America House, 2001.
———. *Mostly Menfolk and a Man or Two*. Chicago: Third World, 1976.
Anderson, S. E. "A Response to Haki Madhubuti." *Black Scholar*, October 1974, 50–51.
Anderson, W. T. "Georgia Lynch Law!" *Macon (Georgia) Telegraph*, March 3, 1916.
Angelou, Maya. *The Heart of a Woman*. New York: Bantam, 1981.
———. *I Know Why the Caged Bird Sings*. New York: Random House, 1969.
Ansa, Tina McElroy. *Baby of the Family*. San Diego: Harcourt Brace Jovanovich, 1989.
Aptheker, Herbert. *The Negro People: A Critique of Gunner Myrdal's "An American
   Dilemma."* New York: International, 1946.
Arnold, J., and R. Hargis. *U.S. Commanders of World War II (1): Army and* USAAF.
   Oxford: Osprey, 2002.
Baldwin, James. "Alas, Poor Richard." In *Nobody Knows My Name: More Notes of a
   Native Son*, 181–215. New York: Dial, 1961.
———. *The Fire Next Time*. New York: Dial, 1963.
———. *Go Tell It on the Mountain*. New York: Knopf, 1953.
———. "Many Thousands Gone." *Partisan Review*, November 1951, 665–80.
Baraka, Amiri. *The Autobiography of LeRoi Jones/Amiri Baraka*. Chicago: Hill, 1997.
———. "The Congress of Afrikan People: A Position Paper." *Black Scholar*, January–
   February 1975, 2–15.
———. "Not Just Survival: Revolution." Paper presented at the Black Writers
   Conference at Howard University, April 1976. John Oliver Killens Papers, Emory
   University, Atlanta.

————. "Some Questions about the Sixth Pan-African Congress." *Black Scholar*, October 1974, 42–46.

Bartley, Abel. *Keeping the Faith: Race, Politics, and Social Development in Jacksonville, Florida, 1940–1970*. Westport, Conn.: Greenwood, 2000.

Bergerud, Eric M. *Fire in the Sky: The Air War in the South Pacific*. Boulder, Colo.: Westview, 2001.

Bessie, Alvah. *Inquisition in Eden*. New York: Macmillan, 1965.

————. "Literary Conclave—East of the Wall." *This World*, June 13, 1965.

————. "We Need to Reconstruct So People Take Precedence over Property." *People's World*, January 1, 1966.

Birdoff, Harry. *The World's Greatest Hit: Uncle Tom's Cabin*. New York: Vanni, 1947.

Blair, Sara. *Harlem Crossroads: Black Writers and the Photograph in the Twentieth Century*. Princeton: Princeton University Press, 2007.

Boggs, Grace, and James Boggs. "The City Is the Black Man's Land." *Monthly Review*, April 1966, 35–46.

Bond, Jean Carey. "Killens' New Novel a Satire on Black 'Society.'" Review of *The Cotillion; or, One Good Bull Is Half the Herd*. *Freedomways*, Spring 1971, 203–5.

Branch, Taylor. *Parting the Waters: America in the King Years, 1954–63*. New York: Simon and Schuster, 1988.

————. *Pillar of Fire: America in the King Years, 1963–65*. New York: Simon and Schuster, 1998.

Branch, William. "Marketing the Products of American Negro Writers." In *The American Negro Writer and His Roots: Selected Papers from the First Conference of Negro Writers, March, 1959*, 46–50. New York: American Society of African Culture, 1960.

Breitman, George. *The Last Year of Malcolm X: The Evolution of a Revolutionary*. New York: Pathfinder, 1967.

Brisbane, Robert H. *Black Activism: Racial Revolution in the United States, 1954–1970*. Valley Forge, Pa.: Judson, 1974.

Brooks, Cleanth, and Robert Penn Warren. *Understanding Fiction*. New York: Crofts, 1943.

Brooks, Gwendolyn. *Report from Part One*. Detroit: Broadside, 1972.

Brown, Claude. *Manchild in the Promised Land*. New York: Macmillan, 1965.

Brown, Lloyd L. "The Deep Pit." *Masses and Mainstream*, June 1952, 62–64.

————. "Which Way for the Negro Writer?" *Masses and Mainstream*, March 1951, 53–63.

————. "Which Way for the Negro Writer? II." *Masses and Mainstream*, April 1951, 50–59.

Brown, Sterling A. "Strong Men." 1931. In *The Collected Poems of Sterling A. Brown*, edited by Michael S. Harper, 56–58. Evanston, Ill.: Northwestern University Press, 1980.

Brown, Titus. *Faithful, Firm, and True: African-American Education in the South.* Macon, Ga.: Mercer University Press, 2002.

Buford, Kate. *Burt Lancaster: An American Life.* Cambridge, Mass.: Da Capo, 2001.

Buhle, Mary Jo, Paul Buhle, and Dan Georgakas, eds. *Encyclopedia of the American Left.* New York: Garland, 1990.

Buhle, Paul, and Dave Wagner. *Blacklisted: The Film Lover's Guide to the Hollywood Blacklist.* New York: Palgrave Macmillan, 2003.

———. *A Very Dangerous Citizen: Abraham Lincoln Polonsky and the Hollywood Left.* Berkeley: University of California Press, 2001.

Burnham, Louis. "The Negro Writer in U.S. Is Finding His Way." *National Guardian,* May 4, 1959.

Cameron, Angus. "The Crisis in Books." *California Quarterly,* Spring 1952, 10–19.

Camus, Albert. *The Stranger.* 1942. New York: Knopf, 1993.

Carey, Stephen Anderson. "Black Men's Du Boisian Relationships to Southern Social Institutions in the Novels of John Oliver Killens." Ph.D. diss., University of Texas at Dallas, 1992.

Carmichael, Stokely, with Ekwueme Michael Thelwell. *Ready for Revolution: The Life and Struggles of Stokely Carmichael (Kwame Ture).* New York: Scribner, 2003.

Carson, Clayborne. *In Struggle: SNCC and the Black Awakening of the 1960s.* Cambridge: Harvard University Press, 1981.

———, ed. *The Papers of Martin Luther King, Jr.* Vol. 4, *Symbol of the Movement, January 1957–December 1958.* Berkeley: University of California Press, 2000.

Childress, Alice, Paule Marshall, and Sarah E. Wright. "The Negro Woman in American Literature." In *Freedomways Reader: Prophets in Their Own Country,* edited by Esther Cooper Jackson, 291–98. Boulder, Colo.: Westview, 2000.

Clarke, John Henrik. "The Boy Who Painted Christ Black." 1940. In *Black American Short Stories: A Century of the Best,* edited by John Henrik Clarke, 108–14. New York: Hill and Wang, 1966.

———. "Negro Men at War." Review of *And Then We Heard the Thunder. Freedomways,* Spring 1963, 227–29.

———. *Rebellion in Rhyme: The Early Poetry of John Henrik Clarke.* 1949. Trenton: Africa World, 1991.

———. Review of *Youngblood. Freedom,* August 1954, 7.

———, ed. *William Styron's Nat Turner: Ten Black Writers Respond.* Boston: Beacon, 1968.

Cleaver, Eldridge. *Target Zero: A Life in Writing.* New York: Palgrave Macmillan, 2006.

Clegg, Claude Andrew, III. *An Original Man: The Life and Times of Elijah Muhammad.* New York: St. Martin's, 1997.

Cohen, Rob. "Notes on 'Cotillion.'" John Oliver Killens Papers, Emory University, Atlanta.

Cohen, Robert. *When the Old Left Was Young: Student Radicals and America's First Mass Student Movement, 1929–1941*. New York: Oxford University Press, 1993.

Colburn, David, and Jane Landers, eds. *The African American Heritage of Florida*. Gainesville: University Press of Florida, 1995.

Cone, James. *Martin and Malcolm and America: A Dream or a Nightmare*. Maryknoll, N.Y.: Orbis, 1991.

Cooper, Esther. "Free the Negro People." In *Town Meeting of Youth*, 11–12. New York: American Youth Congress, 1941.

Costello, John. *The Pacific War, 1941–1945*. New York: Quill, 1982.

Cruse, Harold. *The Crisis of the Negro Intellectual: A Historical Analysis of the Failure of Black Leadership*. 1967. New York: Quill, 1984.

———. "Reply on a Black Crisis." *Negro Digest*, November 1968, 19–25, 65–69.

Cutler, Thomas J. *The Battle of Leyte Gulf*. Annapolis, Md.: Naval Institute Press, 1994.

Davidson, Basil. *The Lost Cities of Africa*. Newport Beach, Calif.: Back Bay, 1959.

Davis, Angela. *Angela Davis: An Autobiography*. 1974. New York: International, 1988.

Davis, Arthur P. "Integration and Race Literature." In *The American Negro Writer and His Roots: Selected Papers from the First Conference of Negro Writers, March, 1959*, 34–40. New York: American Society of African Culture, 1960.

Davis, Ossie. "Malcolm X." In *Life Lit by Some Large Vision: Selected Speeches and Writings*, 151–53. New York: Atria, 2006.

Davis, Ossie, and Ruby Dee. *With Ossie and Ruby: In This Life Together*. New York: Morrow, 1998.

D'Emilio, John. *Lost Prophet: The Life and Times of Bayard Rustin*. Chicago: University of Chicago Press, 2003.

De Veaux, Alexis. *Warrior Poet: A Biography of Audre Lorde*. New York: Norton, 2004.

Dietz, Eugene. "Poitier, Belafonte Hit Hard at 'Establishment.'" *Nashville Tennessean*, May 1, 1966.

Dittmer, John. *Black Georgia in the Progressive Era, 1900–1920*. Urbana: University of Illinois Press, 1977.

Douglass, Frederick. "The Significance of Emancipation in the West Indies: An Address Delivered in Canandaigua, New York, on 3 August 1857." In *The Frederick Douglass Papers*, ser. 1, *Speeches, Debates, and Interviews*, vol. 3, *1855–1863*, edited by John Blassingame, 183–208. New Haven: Yale University Press, 1985.

Dowd, Jerome. *The Negro in American Life*. New York: Scribner, 1926.

Duberman, Martin. *Paul Robeson: A Biography*. New York: New Press, 1989.

Du Bois, W. E. B. *Black Reconstruction*. 1935. New York: Atheneum, 1992.

———. "Criteria of Negro Art." *The Crisis*, October 1926, 290–97.

———. "Negro and Socialism." *Horizon*, February 1907, 7–8.

———. "Richard Wright Looks Back." Review of *Black Boy*. *New York Herald Tribune*, March 4, 1945.

———. "Socialist of the Path." *Horizon*, February 1907, 7–8.

———. "Social Planning for the Negro, Past and Present." *Journal of Negro Education*, January 1936, 122–24.

———. *The Souls of Black Folk*. 1903. New York: Penguin, 1989.

———. *The World and Africa: An Inquiry into the Part Which Africa Has Played in World History*. New York: Viking, 1947.

Dunbar, Paul Laurence. "An Ante-Bellum Sermon." 1896. In *The Collected Poetry of Paul Laurence Dunbar*, edited by Joanne M. Braxton, 13–15. Charlottesville: University of Virginia Press, 1993.

———. "The Party." 1896. In *The Collected Poetry of Paul Laurence Dunbar*, edited by Joanne M. Braxton, 83–86. Charlottesville: University of Virginia Press, 1993.

———. "When Malindy Sings." 1896. In *The Collected Poetry of Paul Laurence Dunbar*, edited by Joanne M. Braxton, 82–83. Charlottesville: University of Virginia Press, 1993.

Durham, Earl. "Capturing the Negro Mood." Review of *Black Man's Burden*. *Freedomways*, Spring 1966, 182–84.

Dyson, Michael Eric. *Making Malcolm: The Myth and Meaning of Malcolm X*. New York: Oxford University Press, 1995.

Egri, Lajos. *The Art of Dramatic Writing*. 1946. New York: Touchstone, 1972.

Ellison, Ralph. *Invisible Man*. New York: Random House, 1952.

———. "The World and the Jug." 1963–64. In *The Collected Essays of Ralph Ellison*, edited by John F. Callahan, 155–88. New York: Random House, 1995.

Epstein, Daniel Mark. *Nat King Cole*. New York: Farrar, Straus, and Giroux, 1999.

Evans, Maurice S. *Black and White in the Southern States*. 1915. Columbia: University of South Carolina Press, 2001.

Farmer, James. *Lay Bare the Heart: An Autobiography of the Civil Rights Movement*. New York: Arbor House, 1985.

Farnsworth, Robert. *Melvin B. Tolson, 1898–1966: Plain Talk and Poetic Prophecy*. Columbia: University of Missouri Press, 1994.

Faulkner, William. "A Letter to the North." *Life*, March 5, 1956, 51–52.

Ferguson, Karen. *Black Politics in New Deal Atlanta*. Chapel Hill: University of North Carolina Press, 2002.

Flowers, Arthur. *Mojo Rising: Confessions of a Twenty-first Century Conjureman*. New York: Wanganegresse, 2001.

Ford, Nick Aaron. "A Blueprint for Negro Authors." *Phylon*, Fourth Quarter 1950, 374–77.

Frakes, James R. "The Cotillion." *New York Times Book Review*, January 17, 1971.

Fraser, C. Gerald. "John Oliver Killens, 71, Author and Founder of Writers' Group." *New York Times*, October 30, 1987.

Frazier, E. Franklin. *The Negro Family in the United States*. 1939. Notre Dame, Ind.: University of Notre Dame Press, 2001.

Fuller, Hoyt. "Reverberations from a Writers' Conference." *African Forum* 1, no. 2 (1965): 78–84.

Gallen, David, ed. *A Malcolm X Reader: Perspectives on the Man and the Myths*. New York: Carroll and Graf, 1994.

Gayle, Addison. Introduction to *Great Black Russian*, by John Oliver Killens. Detroit: Wayne State University Press, 1989.

———. *The Way of the New World: The Black Novel in America*. Garden City, N.Y.: Doubleday, 1975.

Geismar, Maxwell. *Writers in Crisis: The American Novel, 1925–1940*. 1947. New York: Dutton, 1971.

Gellermann, William. *Martin Dies*. New York: Da Capo, 1972.

Gilyard, Keith. *Liberation Memories: The Rhetoric and Poetics of John Oliver Killens*. Detroit: Wayne State University Press, 2003.

Glenn, Taylor. "Books and Authors." Review of *Youngblood*. *Bridgeport Sunday Post*, May 30, 1954.

Gloster, Hugh. "Race and the Negro Writer." *Phylon*, Fourth Quarter 1950, 369–71.

Goldman, Peter. "Malcolm." In *A Malcolm X Reader: Perspectives on the Man and the Myths*, edited by David Gallen, 117–35. New York: Carroll and Graf, 1994.

Greaves, Kay. "Post Book Worm." *Sacramento Post*, March 24, 1971.

Greenlee, Sam. "*Cotillion* Is Uneven in Best Sense of the Word." *Chicago Sun-Times*, February 24, 1971.

Greenspun, Roger. "Screen: *Willie Boy Is Here* Opens." *New York Times*, December 19, 1969.

Griffin, John Howard. "Color Line on the Front Lines." Review of *And Then We Heard the Thunder*. *Saturday Review*, January 26, 1963, 46–47.

Guy, Rosa. *Bird at My Window*. Philadelphia: Lippincott, 1966.

Hampton, Henry, and Steve Fayer, eds. *Voices of Freedom: An Oral History of the Civil Rights Movement from the 1950s through the 1980s*. New York: Bantam, 1990.

Handler, M. S. "Negro Novelist Warns Whites on Racial Struggle." *New York Times*, March 29, 1964.

———. "Two Negro Writers Open Talk Series." *New York Times*, April 25, 1965.

Hansberry, Lorraine. "The Negro Writer and His Roots: Toward a New Romanticism." In *Speech and Power: The African-American Essay and Its Cultural Content, from Polemics to Pulpit*, edited by Gerald Earley, 2:129–41. Hopewell, N.J.: Ecco, 1993.

———. Review of *The Outsider*. *Freedom*, April 1953, 7.

Harvey, Harold Michael. "A Portrait of a Southern Writer." *Macon (Georgia) Courier*, January 24, 1979.

Hatcher, John. *From the Auroral Darkness: The Life and Poetry of Robert Hayden*. Oxford: Ronald, 1984.

Hayden, Robert, ed. *Kaleidoscope: Poems by American Negro Poets*. New York: Harcourt, Brace, and World, 1967.

Haygood, Wil. *King of the Cats: The Life and Times of Adam Clayton Powell*. 1993. New York: Amistad, 2006.

Haywood, Harry. *Black Bolshevik: Autobiography of an Afro-American Communist*. Chicago: Liberator, 1978.

———. *Negro Liberation*. New York: International, 1948.

Hepburn, Lawrence R., ed. *Contemporary Georgia*. Athens: Carl Vinson Institute of Government, University of Georgia, 1987.

Herman, Lewis. *A Practical Manual of Screen Playwriting*. New York: New American Library, 1952.

Hersey, John. *The Algiers Motel Incident*. New York: Knopf, 1968.

Hicks, Granville. "Laurie Grows Up." Review of *Youngblood*. *New York Times*, June 6, 1954.

Hill, Herbert. "The Racial Practices of Organized Labor: The Contemporary Record." In *The Negro and the American Labor Movement*, edited by Julius Jacobson, 286–357. Garden City, N.Y.: Anchor, 1968.

Himes, Chester. *If He Hollers Let Him Go*. 1945. New York: Signet, 1971.

———. *The Quality of Hurt: The Autobiography of Chester Himes*. Vol. 1. London: Joseph, 1973.

Hodgart, Matthew. *James Joyce: A Student's Guide*. London: Routledge and Kegan Paul, 1978.

Hoffman, Frederick L. *Race Traits and Tendencies of the American Negro*. Philadelphia: American Economic Association, 1896.

Holloway, Jonathan Scott. *Confronting the Veil: Abram Harris Jr., E. Franklin Frazier, and Ralph Bunche, 1919–1941*. Chapel Hill: University of North Carolina Press, 2002.

Holt, Thomas. "'Knowledge Is Power': The Black Struggle for Literacy." In *The Right to Literacy*, edited by Andrea Lunsford and James Slevin, 91–102. New York: MLA, 1990.

Hope, Richard O. *Racial Strife in the U.S. Military: Toward the Elimination of Discrimination*. New York: Praeger, 1979.

Hord, Fred Lee. *Reconstructing Memory: Black Literary Criticism*. Chicago: Third World, 1991.

Horne, Gerald. "Comrades and Friends: The Personal/Political World of Paul Robeson." In *Paul Robeson: Artist and Citizen*, edited by Jeffrey C. Stewart, 197–215. New Brunswick, N.J.: Rutgers University Press, 1998.

———. *Race Woman: The Lives of Shirley Graham Du Bois*. New York: New York University Press, 2000.

Howe, Irving. "Black Boys and Native Sons." *Dissent*, Autumn 1963, 353–68.

Howe, Russell. "New Civil War If Negro Claims Are Pressed: An Exclusive Interview with William Faulkner." *London Sunday Times*, March 4, 1956.

Hughes, Langston. "A Christian Country." 1931. In *The Collected Poems of Langston Hughes*, edited by Arnold Rampersad, 136. New York: Vintage, 1995.

———. *Famous American Negroes*. New York: Dodd, Mead, 1954.

———. "Goodbye Christ." 1932. In *The Collected Poems of Langston Hughes*, edited by Arnold Rampersad, 166–67. New York: Vintage, 1995.

———. "Notes on Commercial Theater." 1940. *In The Collected Poems of Langston Hughes*, edited by Arnold Rampersad, 215–16. New York: Vintage, 1995.

———. "These Bad New Negroes: A Critique on Critics." *Pittsburgh Courier*, March 22, 1927.

———. "Writers: Black and White." In *The American Negro Writer and His Roots: Selected Papers from the First Conference of Negro Writers, March, 1959*, 41–45. New York: American Society of African Culture, 1960.

Hughes, Langston, and the Editors. "Some Practical Observations: A Colloquy." *Phylon*, Fourth Quarter 1950, 307–11.

Hunter, Charlayne. "Black Intellectuals Divided over Ideological Direction." *New York Times*, April 28, 1975.

———. "Ideology Dispute Shakes Black Journal." *New York Times*, March 11, 1975.

Hunton, Dorothy K. *Alphaeus Hunton: The Unsung Valiant*. Richmond Hill, N.Y.: Hunton, 1986.

Iobst, Richard W. *Civil War Macon: The History of a Confederate City*. Macon, Ga.: Mercer University Press, 1999.

Jackson, Esther Cooper, ed. *Freedomways Reader: Prophets in Their Own Country*. Boulder, Colo.: Westview, 2000.

Jackson, Lawrence. *Ralph Ellison: Emergence of Genius*. New York: Wiley, 2002.

Jacobson, Julius, ed. *The Negro and the American Labor Movement*. Garden City, N.Y.: Anchor, 1968.

Jaffe, Harriet. "John Killens' Powerful Novel Stresses Theme of 'Walk Together, Children.'" Review of *Youngblood*. *Pacific Coast Youth Recorder*, December 1954.

James, Daniel. "The Battle of A. V. C." *The Nation*, June 14, 1947, 706–8.

James, Jennifer C. *A Freedom Bought with Blood: African American War Literature from the Civil War to World War II*. Chapel Hill: University of North Carolina Press, 2007.

Jarrett, Thomas D. "Toward Unfettered Creativity: A Note on the Negro Novelist's Coming of Age." *Phylon*, Fourth Quarter 1950, 313–17.

Johnson, Charles. *Being and Race: Black Writing since 1970*. Bloomington: Indiana University Press, 1988.

Johnston, Rhodes. "Black Writers Told to Unite Own Race." *Nashville Tennessean*, April 21, 1968.

————. "Writer: Negroes' Only Hope Destruction of U.S. System." *Nashville Tennessean*, April 20, 1968.

Jones, Gayl. *Liberating Voices: Oral Tradition in African American Literature*. New York: Penguin, 1991.

Jones, John Henry. "Killens' Fine, Sensitive New Novel." Review of *'Sippi*. *Freedomways*, Fall 1967, 373–75.

Jones, Lisa Chapman. "Talking Book: Oral History of a Movement." *Village Voice*, February 26, 1985, 18–22.

Joyce, James. *Ulysses*. Edited by Hans Walter Gabler. New York: Vintage, 1993.

Kaiser, Ernest. "Racial Dialectics: The Aptheker-Myrdal School Controversy." *Phylon*, Fourth Quarter 1948, 295–302.

————. Review of *The Crisis of the Negro Intellectual*. *Freedomways*, Winter 1969, 24–41.

Karenga, Maulana Ron. "Which Road: Nationalism, Pan-Africanism, Socialism?" *Black Scholar*, October 1974, 21–30.

Keats, Ezra Jack. *John Henry: An American Legend*. New York, Knopf, 1965.

Kent, George. *A Life of Gwendolyn Brooks*. Lexington: University Press of Kentucky, 1999.

Key, V. O. *Southern Politics in State and Nation*. 1949. Knoxville: University of Tennessee Press, 1984.

Khiss, Peter. "Pulitzer Prizes Omitted in Drama, Fiction, Music." *New York Times*, May 5, 1964.

Killens, John Oliver. "25th Session." John Oliver Killens Papers, Emory University, Atlanta.

————. "Address to the Association for the Study of Negro Life and History." John Oliver Killens Papers, Emory University, Atlanta.

————. "Alas My Son." John Oliver Killens Papers, Boston University, Boston.

————. *And Then We Heard the Thunder*. 1962. Washington, D.C.: Howard University Press, 1983.

————. "An Appreciation." In *This Child's Gonna Live*, by Sarah Wright, 277–86. New York: Feminist Press, 1986.

————. "The Armistice." *The Ballardite*, November 13, 1933, Amistad Research Center, Tulane University, New Orleans.

————. "The Artist and the Black University." *Black Scholar*, November 1969, 61–65.

————. "The Black Culture Generation Gap." *Black World*, August 1973, 22–33.

————. "Black Labor and the Liberation Movement." *Black Scholar*, October 1970, 33–39.

————. *Black Man in the New China*. Los Angeles: U.S.-China Peoples Friendship Association, 1975.

————. *Black Man's Burden*. New York: Trident, 1965.

———. "The Black Tradition in American Literature." In *Swords upon This Hill: Preserving the Literary Tradition of Black Colleges and Universities*, edited by Burney J. Hollis, 12–27. Baltimore: Morgan State University Press, 1984.

———. "The Black Writer and the Revolution." *Arts and Society* 5 (1968): 395–99.

———. "Brief in Behalf of Plaintiff Lester Hamilton." John Oliver Killens Papers, Emory University, Atlanta.

———. "Broadway in Black and White." *African Forum* 1, no. 3 (1966): 66–76.

———. "Brutalization or Rehabilitation?" *Amsterdam News*, June 26, 1971, July 3, 1971, July 10, 1971.

———. "The Confessions of Willie Styron." In *William Styron's Nat Turner: Ten Black Writers Respond*, edited by John Henrik Clarke, 34–44. Boston: Beacon, 1968.

———. *The Cotillion; or, One Good Bull Is Half the Herd*. New York: Trident, 1971.

———. "The Crisis in Black Writing." *Sepia*, March 1972, 13–18.

———. "*Darkness at Noon* by Arthur Koestler." John Oliver Killens Papers, Emory University, Atlanta.

———. "Explanation of the 'Black Psyche.'" *New York Times Sunday Magazine*, June 7, 1964.

———. Foreword to *Blood on the Forge*, by William Attaway, 7–13. New York: Monthly Review Press, 1987.

———. "For National Freedom." *New Foundations*, Summer 1949, 245–58.

———. "Frank London Brown." AMSAC *Newsletter*, January 1963, 4–6.

———. "God Bless America." *California Quarterly*, Spring 1952, 37–40.

———. *Great Black Russian: A Novel on the Life and Times of Alexander Pushkin*. Detroit: Wayne State University Press, 1989.

———. *Great Gittin' Up Morning: The Story of Denmark Vesey*. Garden City, N.Y.: Doubleday, 1972.

———. "The Half Ain't Never Been Told." In *Contemporary Authors Autobiography Series*, edited by Adele Sarkissian, 2:279–306. Detroit: Gale, 1985.

———. "He Took His Art More Seriously Than Himself." *Freedomways*, Summer 1980, 192–94.

———. "Hollywood in Black and White." *The Nation*, September 20, 1965, 157–60.

———. "How Long Is a Moment, Mr. Faulkner?: A Letter to William Faulkner and His Middle Grounders." John Oliver Killens Papers, Emory University, Atlanta.

———. "The Image of Black Folk in American Literature." *Black Scholar*, June 1975, 44–52.

———. "The Impact of Richard Wright on Afro-American Literature." John Oliver Killens Papers, Emory University, Atlanta.

———. "Incidents and Experiences of Growing Up in Georgia and Their Impact on My Writing." Paper presented at the University of Cincinnati, November 12, 1985. John Oliver Killens Papers, Emory University, Atlanta.

———. "In the Great Tradition of Black Womanhood." John Oliver Killens Papers, Emory University, Atlanta.

———. Introduction to *ABC of Color*, by W. E. B. Du Bois, 9–13. New York: International, 1969.

———. Introduction to *Black Southern Voices: An Anthology of Fiction, Poetry, Drama, Nonfiction, and Critical Essays*, edited by John Oliver Killens and Jerry Ward Jr., 1–4. New York: Meridian, 1992.

———. Introduction to *The Trial Record of Denmark Vesey*, vii–xxi. Boston: Beacon, 1970.

———. "The Literary Genius of Alice Childress." In *Black Women Writers (1950–1980): A Critical Evaluation*, edited by Mari Evans, 129–33. New York: Anchor, 1984.

———. "Lorraine Hansberry: On Time!" *Freedomways*, Fall 1979, 273–76.

———. *A Man Ain't Nothin' but a Man: The Adventures of John Henry*. Boston: Little, Brown, 1975.

———. "The Minister Primarily." Unpublished manuscript, private collection.

———. "Montgomery Story." John Oliver Killens Papers, Boston University, Boston.

———. "My Turf Is Not a Ghetto." *New York Times*, October 3, 1971.

———. "*The Naked and the Dead* by Norman Mailer." John Oliver Killens Papers, Emory University, Atlanta.

———. "The National Council of Law Students." *The Barrister*, October 1941, 7.

———. "Negroes Have a Right to Fight Back." *Saturday Evening Post*, July 2, 1966, 10, 14.

———. "Novel of Dimensional Reality." John Oliver Killens Papers, Emory University, Atlanta.

———. "Opening Remarks." John Oliver Killens Papers, Emory University, Atlanta.

———. "Opportunities for Development of Negro Talent." In *The American Negro Writer and His Roots: Selected Papers from the First Conference of Negro Writers, March, 1959*, 64–70. New York: American Society of African Culture, 1960.

———. "Our Struggle Is Not to Be White Men in Black Skin." *TV Guide*, July 25, 1970, 7–9.

———. "Paul Robeson: Portrait of a People's Artist." John Oliver Killens Papers, Emory University, Atlanta.

———. "Presentation at the Harlem Writers Guild." John Oliver Killens Papers, Emory University, Atlanta.

———. Prologue to *Harlem Stirs*, by Fred Halstead, Anthony Aviles, and Don Charles, 3–7. New York: Marzani and Munsell, 1966.

———. "Rappin' with Myself." In *Amistad 2: Writings on Black History and Culture*, edited by John A. Williams and Charles F. Harris, 97–136. New York: Vintage, 1971.

———. "The Responsibility of the Black Writer to the Community." Paper presented at the University of Cincinnati, November 12, 1985. John Oliver Killens Papers, Emory University, Atlanta.

———. Review of *Invisible Man. Freedom*, June 1952, 7.

———. Review of *Native Son*. John Oliver Killens Papers, Emory University, Atlanta.

———. "Richard Wright, a Native Son." John Oliver Killens Papers, Emory University, Atlanta.

———. "Rough Diamond." In *Harlem: Voices from the Soul of Black America*, edited by John Henrik Clarke, 169–84. New York: Signet, 1970.

———. "Run Like Hell and Holler Fire!" *Freedomways*, Fall 1983, 244–56, Fall 1984, 260–66.

———. *'Sippi*. 1967. New York: Thunder's Mouth, 1988.

———. *Slaves*. New York: Pyramid, 1969.

———. "The Smoking Sixties." In *Black Short Story Anthology*, edited by Woodie King Jr., xi–xviii. New York: Columbia University Press, 1972.

———. "Stony the Road We Trod." John Oliver Killens Papers, Emory University, Atlanta.

———. "Things Might Have Been." John Oliver Killens Papers, Emory University, Atlanta.

———. "The Trouble with Negroes . . . They Strayed Too Far from Jesus." John Oliver Killens Papers, Emory University, Atlanta.

———. "An Unfair Labor Practice under the Wagner Act." *The Barrister*, October 1941, 1.

———. "Wanted: Some Black Long Distance Runners." *Black Scholar*, November 1973, 2–7.

———. "What Went Wrong?" *National Leader*, August 26, 1982, 23–25.

———. "What Went Wrong? (A Follow-Up)." John Oliver Killens Papers, Emory University, Atlanta.

———. "Wright's Rebels." John Oliver Killens Papers, Emory University, Atlanta.

———. "Write On!: On the Art and Craft of Creative Writing." John Oliver Killens Papers, Emory University, Atlanta.

———. *Youngblood*. 1954. Athens: University of Georgia Press, 1982.

———. "Youngblood Screenplay." John Oliver Killens Papers, Boston University, Boston.

Killens, John Oliver, James Wechsler, and Lorraine Hansberry. "The Black Revolution and the White Backlash." In *Black Protest: History, Documents, and Analyses, 1619 to the Present*, edited by Joanne Grant, 442–48. New York: Fawcett Premier, 1968.

King, Coretta Scott. *My Life with Martin Luther King, Jr.* Rev. ed. New York: Puffin, 1993.

Kitching, Jessie. "Fiction Forecast." *Publishers Weekly*, November 26, 1962, 43–44.

Lask, Thomas. "Daphne Learns the Hard Way." *New York Times*, February 9, 1971.

Latham, Earl. *Communist Controversy in Washington: From the New Deal to McCarthy*. Cambridge: Harvard University Press, 1966.

Lehman, Paul Robert. "The Development of a Black Psyche in the Works of John Oliver Killens." Ph.D. diss., Lehigh University, 1976.

Lenin, V. I. "Preliminary Draft Theses on the National and Colonial Questions." In *Collected Works*, 31:144–51. Moscow: Progress, 1966.

Lewis, David Levering. Introduction to *Black Reconstruction*, by W. E. B. Du Bois, xxv–xlii. New York: Oxford University Press, 2007.

———. *W. E. B. Du Bois: The Fight for Equality and the American Century, 1919–1963*. New York: Holt, 2000.

Lewis, Hylan. "A Focused Memoir, Howard University and Frazier, 1933–1941." In *E. Franklin Frazier and Black Bourgeoisie*, edited by James E. Teele, 21–29. Columbia: University of Missouri Press, 2002.

Llorens, David. "Writers Converge at Fisk University." *Negro Digest*, June 1966, 54–58.

Locke, Alain. "Self-Criticism: The Third Dimension in Culture." *Phylon*, Fourth Quarter 1950, 391–94.

Locke, Hubert G. *The Detroit Riot of 1967*. Detroit: Wayne State University Press, 1969.

Logan, Rayford W. *Howard University, the First Hundred Years, 1867–1967*. New York: New York University Press, 1969.

Long, Susan. "Pleasant Hill's Rich History May Be Recognized." *Macon (Georgia) Telegraph*, July 22, 1984.

Lucas, Molly. "Color Line: Even in War." *Columbia Owl*, May 15, 1963.

Luszki, Walter A. *A Rape of Justice: MacArthur and the New Guinea Hangings*. Lanham, Md.: Madison, 1991.

Macon's Black Heritage: The Untold Story. Macon, Ga.: Tubman African American Museum, 1997.

Madhubuti, Haki. "But He Was Cool; or, He Even Stopped for Green Lights." 1969. In *GroundWork: New and Selected Poems of Don L. Lee/Haki R. Madhubuti from 1966–1996*, 39. Chicago: Third World, 1996.

———. "The Latest Purge: The Attack on Black Nationalism and Pan-Afrikanism by the New Left, the Sons and Daughters of the Old Left." *Black Scholar*, September 1974, 43–56.

———. "The New Integrationist." 1968. In *GroundWork: New and Selected Poems of Don L. Lee/Haki R. Madhubuti from 1966–1996*, 21. Chicago: Third World, 1996.

Malcolm X. "Basic Unity Program, Organization of Afro-American Unity." In *New Black Voices: An Anthology of Contemporary Afro-American Literature*, edited by Abraham Chapman, 564–74. New York: Mentor, 1972.

———. "Statement of Basic Aims and Objectives of the Organization of Afro-American Unity." In *New Black Voices: An Anthology of Contemporary Afro-American Literature*, edited by Abraham Chapman, 558–64. New York: Mentor, 1972.

Manis, Andrew W. *Macon Black and White: An Unutterable Separation in the American Century*. Macon, Ga.: Mercer University Press, 2004.

Marable, Manning. *Living Black History*. New York: Basic *Civitas*, 2006.

Markowitz, Norman. "Progressive Party, 1948." In *Encyclopedia of the American Left*, edited by Mary Jo Buhle, Paul Buhle, and Dan Georgakas, 600–601. New York: Garland, 1990.

Marshall, Ray. *The Negro and Organized Labor*. New York: Wiley, 1965.

Maugham, Somerset. *The Summing Up*. 1938. New York: Penguin, 1963.

Mayfield, Julian. "Crisis or Crusade?" *Negro Digest*, June 1968, 10–24.

———. "Into the Mainstream and Oblivion." In *The American Negro Writer and His Roots: Selected Papers from the First Conference of Negro Writers, March, 1959*, 29–33. New York: American Society of African Culture, 1960.

McGilligan, Patrick, and Ken Mate. "Alvah Bessie." In *Tender Comrades: A Backstory of the Hollywood Blacklist*, edited by Patrick McGilligan and Paul Buhle, 90–111. New York: St. Martin's, 1997.

McGivern, William P. *Odds against Tomorrow*. 1957. New York: Carroll and Graf, 1996.

McKay, Claude. *Banana Bottom*. 1933. New York: Harvest, 1970.

McMichael, Jack. "Youth and the Nation." In *Town Meeting of Youth*, 7–9. New York: American Youth Congress, 1941.

"The Meaning and Measure of Black Power." *Negro Digest*, November 1966, 20–37, 81–96.

Mellard, James M. "This Unquiet Dust: The Problem of History in Styron's *The Confessions of Nat Turner*." In *The Critical Response to William Styron*, edited by Daniel W. Ross, 157–72. Westport, Conn.: Greenwood, 1995.

Meriwether, Louise. "From Cover to Cover." *Los Angeles Sentinel*, February 21, 1963.

Miller, Loren. "Farewell to Liberals." *The Nation*, October 20, 1962, 235–38.

Miller, Warren. *The Cool World*. Greenwich, Conn.: Fawcett, 1959.

Mitchell, Loften. "More about John Oliver Killens." John Oliver Killens Papers, Emory University, Atlanta.

———. "Three Writers and a Dream." *The Crisis*, April 1965, 219–23.

Moon, Henry Lee, ed. *The Emerging Thought of W. E. B. Du Bois*. New York: Simon and Schuster, 1972.

Motley, Willard. *Knock on Any Door*. 1947. New York: Signet, 1950.

Mullen, Bill. *Afro-Orientalism*. Minneapolis: University of Minnesota Press, 2004.

Myrdal, Gunner. *An American Dilemma: The Negro Problem and Modern Democracy*. New York: Harper, 1944.

The Negro Will Defend America. Washington, D.C.: National Negro Congress, 1941.

"The Negro Writer in America: A Symposium." *Negro Digest*, June 1963, 54–65.

Newton, Huey P. "He Won't Bleed Me: A Revolutionary Analysis of Sweet Sweetback's Baadasssss Song." 1972. In *To Die for the People: The Writings of Huey P. Newton*, edited by Toni Morrison, 112–47. New York: Writers and Readers, 1995.

Nichols, Charles. "The Forties: A Decade of Growth." *Phylon*, Fourth Quarter 1950, 377–80.

Nikola-Lisa, W. "John Henry: Then and Now." *African American Review*, Spring 1998, 51–56.

Norford, George. "A Search for Dignity." *The Crisis*, March 1963, 151–54.

Onstott, Kyle. *Mandingo*. Richmond: Delinger, 1957.

"On the Conference Beat." *Negro Digest*, March 1967, 90–93.

Ortiz, Paul. *Emancipation Betrayed: The Hidden History of Black Organizing and White Violence in Florida from Reconstruction to the Bloody Election of 1920*. Berkeley: University of California Press, 2005.

Ottley, Roi. "Negroes Are Saying . . ." 1943. In *Reporting World War II: American Journalism, 1938–1946*, 211–29. New York: Library of America, 2001.

Paine, Thomas. *The Crisis*, no. 1. 1776. In *The Norton Anthology of American Literature*, 6th ed., edited by Nina Baym, A:712–18. New York: Norton, 2003.

Parks, Carole A. "The National Black Writers Convention." *Black World*, January 1975, 86–92.

Peeples, Kenneth, Jr. "The Artist as Liberator: An Interview with John Oliver Killens." *Community Review*, Fall 1984, 6–14.

Perry, Bruce. *Malcolm: The Life of a Man Who Changed Black America*. Barrytown, N.Y.: Station Hill. 1991.

Peterson, Bernard L., Jr., ed. "John Oliver Killens." In *Contemporary Black American Playwrights and Their Plays: A Biographical Directory and Dramatic Index*, 292–93. Westport, Conn.: Greenwood, 1988.

Petry, Ann. "Crossroads, Georgia." A Review of *Youngblood*. *New York Herald Tribune*, July 11, 1954.

Pitts, Raymond, ed. *Reflections from a Cherished Past*. Sacramento: Pitts, 1980.

Platt, Anthony M. *E. Franklin Frazier Reconsidered*. New Brunswick, N.J.: Rutgers University Press, 1991.

———. "Introduction to E. Franklin Frazier." In *The Negro Family in the United States*, vii–xxxii. Notre Dame, Ind.: University of Notre Dame Press, 2001.

Podhoretz, Norman. "My Negro Problem and Ours." *Commentary*, February 1963, 93–101.

Polonsky, Abraham. *Odds against Tomorrow: The Critical Edition*. Edited by John Schultheiss. Northridge, Calif.: Center for Telecommunication Studies, 1999.

Poston, Ted. "A Different Kind of War Novel." A Review of *And Then We Heard the Thunder*. *New York Post*, March 31, 1963.

Pushkin, Alexander. *The Poems, Prose, and Plays of Alexander Pushkin*. Edited by Avrahm Yarmolinsky. 1936. New York: Random House, 1964.

Raine, Kathleen. *Yeats the Initiate: Essays on Certain Themes in the Writings of W. B. Yeats*. Mountrath, Ire.: Dolmen, 1986.

Rampersad, Arnold. *The Life of Langston Hughes*. Vol. 2, *1941–1967: I Dream a World*. New York: Oxford University Press, 1988.

Redding, Saunders. "American Negro Literature." *American Scholar*, Spring 1949, 137–48.

———. "The Negro Author: His Publisher, His Public, and His Purse." In *A Scholar's Conscience: Selected Writings of J. Saunders Redding*, edited by Faith Berry, 140–46. Lexington: University of Kentucky Press, 1992.

———. "The Negro Writer and His Relationship to His Roots." In *The American Negro Writer and His Roots: Selected Papers from the First Conference of Negro Writers, March, 1959*, 1–8. New York: American Society of African Culture, 1960.

———. Review of *Bird at My Window*. *The Crisis*, April 1966, 225, 227.

Reed, Ishmael. *Mumbo Jumbo*. 1972. New York: Avon, 1976.

———. *Reckless Eyeballing*. New York: St Martin's, 1986.

———. *Yellow Back Radio Broke-Down*. Garden City, N.Y.: Doubleday, 1969.

Reinhold, Robert. "Seeks to Recognize People Who Make Notable Impact." *New York Times*, March 28, 1969.

Reuter, Edward Byron. *The American Race Problem: A Study of the Negro*. New York: Cromwell, 1927.

Richmond, Al. "Novel of Negro Family a Literary Milestone." Review of *Youngblood*. *People's World*, August 27, 1954.

Robeson, Paul. *Here I Stand*. 1958. Boston: Beacon, 1988.

Roosevelt, Eleanor. "Keepers of Democracy." *Virginia Quarterly Review*, Winter 1939, 1–5.

Rosen, Sumner M. "The CIO Era, 1935–1955." In *The Negro and the American Labor Movement*, edited by Julius Jacobson, 188–208. Garden City, N.Y.: Anchor, 1968.

Rowley, Hazel. *Richard Wright: The Life and Times*. New York: Holt, 2001.

Sales, William W., Jr. *From Civil Rights to Black Liberation: Malcolm X and the Organization of Afro-American Unity*. Boston: South End, 1994.

Samuel, Maurice. *The Great Hatred*. New York: Knopf, 1940.

Saunders, Kay. "In a Cloud of Lust: Black GIs and Sex in World War II." In *Gender and War: Australians at War in the Twentieth Century*, edited by Joy Damousi and Marilyn Lake, 178–90. Cambridge: Cambridge University Press, 1995.

Sauter, Van Gordon, and Burleigh Hines. *Nightmare in Detroit: A Rebellion and Its Victims*. Chicago: Regnery, 1968.

Sayers, Stuart. "With Color on His Mind." *The Age*, October 24, 1970.

Schickel, Richard. *D. W. Griffith: An American Life*. New York: Simon and Schuster, 1984.

Shinhoster, Yvonne. "Author John Killens Returns to His 'Roots.'" *Macon (Georgia) Telegraph*, January 22, 1979.

Sholokhov, Mikhail. *And Quiet Flows the Don*. 1934. New York: Knopf, 1965.

Silberman, Charles. *Crisis in Black and White*. New York: Random House, 1964.

Smith, Mark. "A Response to Haki Madhubuti." *Black Scholar*, January–February 1975, 44–53.

Smith, William Gardner. "The Negro Writer: Pitfalls and Compensations." *Phylon*, Fourth Quarter 1950, 297–303.

Soyinka, Wole. *You Must Set Forth at Dawn: A Memoir*. New York: Random House, 2006.

Stalin, Joseph. "Marxism and the National Question." In *Works*, 2:300–381. Moscow: Foreign Languages Publishing, 1954.

Stowe, Harriet Beecher. *Uncle Tom's Cabin*. 1852. Columbus, Ohio: Merrill, 1969.

Stull, Bradford T. *Amid the Fall, Dreaming of Eden: Du Bois, King, Malcolm X, and Emancipatory Composition*. Carbondale: Southern Illinois University Press, 1999.

Styron, William. *The Confessions of Nat Turner*. New York: Random House, 1967.

Sugrue, Thomas J. *Sweet Land of Liberty: The Forgotten Struggle for Civil Rights in the North*. New York: Random House, 2008.

Talese, Gay. "Many Words, Mostly Hot, Mark Writers' Parley." *New York Times*, April 26, 1965.

"The Task of the Negro Writer as Artist: A Symposium." *Negro Digest*, April 1965, 54–70, 72–83.

Thurman, Wallace. *Blacker the Berry*. 1929. New York: Collier, 1970.

Tillinghast, Joseph A. *The Negro in Africa and America*. New York: Ayer, 1902.

Town Meeting of Youth. New York: American Youth Congress, 1941.

Trescott, Jacqueline. "Debate on Black Films: Who Has the Integrity?" *Washington Star-News*, February 5, 1974.

Tripp, Janet. *The Importance of Lorraine Hansberry*. San Diego: Lucent, 1998.

Tucker, Samuel J. *Phoenix from the Ashes: EWC's Past, Present, and Future*. Jacksonville, Fla.: Convention, 1976.

Tunney, Gene. "Youth Congress and the Communistic Blight." *Liberty*, August 31, 1940, 14–15.

Tyson, Timothy B. *Radio Free Dixie: Robert F. Williams and the Roots of Black Power*. Chapel Hill: University of North Carolina Press, 1999.

van der Vat, Dan. *The Pacific Campaign: The U.S.-Japanese Naval War, 1941–1945*. New York: Simon and Schuster, 1991.

Voss, Frederick S. *Reporting the War: The Journalistic Coverage of World War II*. Washington, D.C.: Smithsonian Institution Press for the National Portrait Gallery, 1994.

Wald, Alan. *Exiles from a Future Time*. Vol. 2, *Trinity of Passion*. Chapel Hill: University of North Carolina Press, 2007.

Walker, Alice. *The Color Purple*. San Diego: Harcourt Brace Jovanovich, 1982.

———. *Meridian*. 1976. New York: Washington Square, 1977.

Walker, Joseph. "An American Author's Views on Freedom." *Muhammad Speaks*, March 4, 1963.

Walker, Margaret. *How I Wrote Jubilee*. Chicago: Third World, 1972.

Walters, Ronald. "A Response to Haki Madhubuti." *Black Scholar*, October 1974, 47–49.

Ward, W. R. Review of *Black and White in the Southern States*. *Journal of Negro History*, October 1916, 445–46.

Washington, Mary Helen. "Desegregating the 1950s: The Case of Frank London Brown." *Japanese Journal of American Studies* 10 (1999): 15–32.

———. "The Other Black List." Paper presented at the annual convention of the Modern Language Association, 2004.

West, Hollie I. "Black Publishing Crisis." *Washington Post*, April 26, 1976.

———. "Sexual Politics and the Afro-American Writer." *Washington Post*, May 8, 1978.

West, James L. W., III. *William Styron: A Life*. New York: Random House, 1998.

White, Poppy Cannon. "A Thundering Genius." Review of *And Then We Heard the Thunder*. *Amsterdam News*, February 2, 1963.

White, Walter. *Rope and Faggot: A Biography of Judge Lynch*. New York: Knopf, 1929.

Wiggins, William, Jr. "The Structure and Dynamics of Folklore in the Novel Form: The Case of John O. Killens." *Keystone Folklore Quarterly*, Fall 1972, 92–117.

Wilcox, Preston. "A Response by Preston Wilcox." *Black Scholar*, March 1975, 49–51.

Wilder, Larry D. "Author: Black History Should Be Noted All Year." *Macon (Georgia) Telegraph*, February 22, 1982.

Wilkerson, Doxey A. "Negro Culture: Heritage and Weapon." *Masses and Mainstream*, August 1949, 3–24.

Williams, Brett. *John Henry: A Bio-Bibliography*. Westport, Conn.: Greenwood, 1983.

Williams, John A. *The Man Who Cried I Am*. Boston: Little, Brown, 1967.

Wilson, Edmund. *Patriotic Gore: Studies in the Literature of the American Civil War*. New York: Oxford University Press, 1962.

Windham, Revish. "The Long Distance Runner: An Interview with John Oliver Killens." *Black Forum*, Fall–Winter 1978, 4–7, 28–31, 40–43.

Winslow, Henry. "More Film Than Focus." *The Crisis*, October 1954, 511–12, 515.

Wouk, Herman. *War and Remembrance*. 1978. Boston: Little, Brown, 2002.

Wright, Richard. *American Hunger*. New York: Harper and Row, 1977.

———. *Black Boy: A Record of Childhood and Youth*. New York: Harper and Brothers, 1945.

———. "Bright and Morning Star." In *Uncle Tom's Children*, 181–215. 1938. New York: Harper and Row, 1965.

———. "Early Days in Chicago." In *Cross Section 1945: A Collection of New American Writing*, edited by Edwin Seaver, 306–42. New York: Book Find Club, 1946.

———. "Long Black Song." In *Uncle Tom's Children*, 103–28. 1938. New York: Harper and Row, 1965.

———. *Native Son*. 1940. New York: Perennial, 1988.

————. *The Outsider*. New York: Harper and Brothers, 1953.

————. *Uncle Tom's Children*. New York: Harper, 1938.

Wright, Richard, and Edwin Rosskam. *12 Million Black Voices: A Folk History of the Negro in the United States*. 1941. New York: Thunder's Mouth, 1988.

Wright, Sarah E. *This Child's Gonna Live*. 1969. New York: Feminist Press, 1986.

Yago, John W. "Negro Author Speaks Here Today." *Charleston (West Virginia) Gazette*, October 11, 1963.

ya Salaam, Kalamu. "A Response to Haki Madhubuti." *Black Scholar*, January–February 1975, 40–43.

Yette, Samuel F. *The Choice: The Issue of Black Survival in America*. Washington, D.C.: Cottage, 1988.

Zinn, Howard. *A People's History of the United States, 1492–Present*. New York: Perennial, 2001.

————. "Visible Men." *Book Week*, March 27, 1966, 9–10.

Index

Youngblood (*continued*)
　first printing sold out, 120; foreign
　publication/sales, 112, 116, 123–24,
　135; ignored by *Macon Telegraph*, 1;
　informed by Killens's experiences,
　29, 31, 38, 99–100; Pocket Books edi-
　tion, 121; polemical nature of, 100;
　promotional efforts, 111–16; rejected
　by Chicago Central Library, 114–15;
　as rejoinder to *Invisible Man*, 107;
　relationship to *Slaves*, 249; repub-
　lished by University of Georgia Press,
　299–300; reviews of, 110; spiritual
　songs in, 95, 107; whipping scene, 13,
　100, 110, 130, 147

Youngblood, Joe (character, *Young-
　blood*), 107, 110, 146
Youngblood, Robby (character, *Young-
　blood*), 100, 107, 108, 219
Young Communist League, 54, 150,
　336n14
Young People's Socialist League, 54
Youngstein, Max, 160
Yurick Sol, 256

Zinn, Howard: on *Black Man's Burden*,
　213; *The Southern Mystique*, 198
Zu-Bolton, Ahmos, 282, 290

CPSIA information can be obtained at www.ICGtesting.com

228460LV00002B/45/P